I0754480

THE

Jerusalem Delivered

OF

TORQUATO TASSO.

TRANSLATED INTO ENGLISH SPENSERIAN VERSE
WITH LIFE OF THE AUTHOR,

BY

J. H. WIFFEN.

NEW YORK:
HURST & CO., PUBLISHERS,
122 NASSAU STREET.

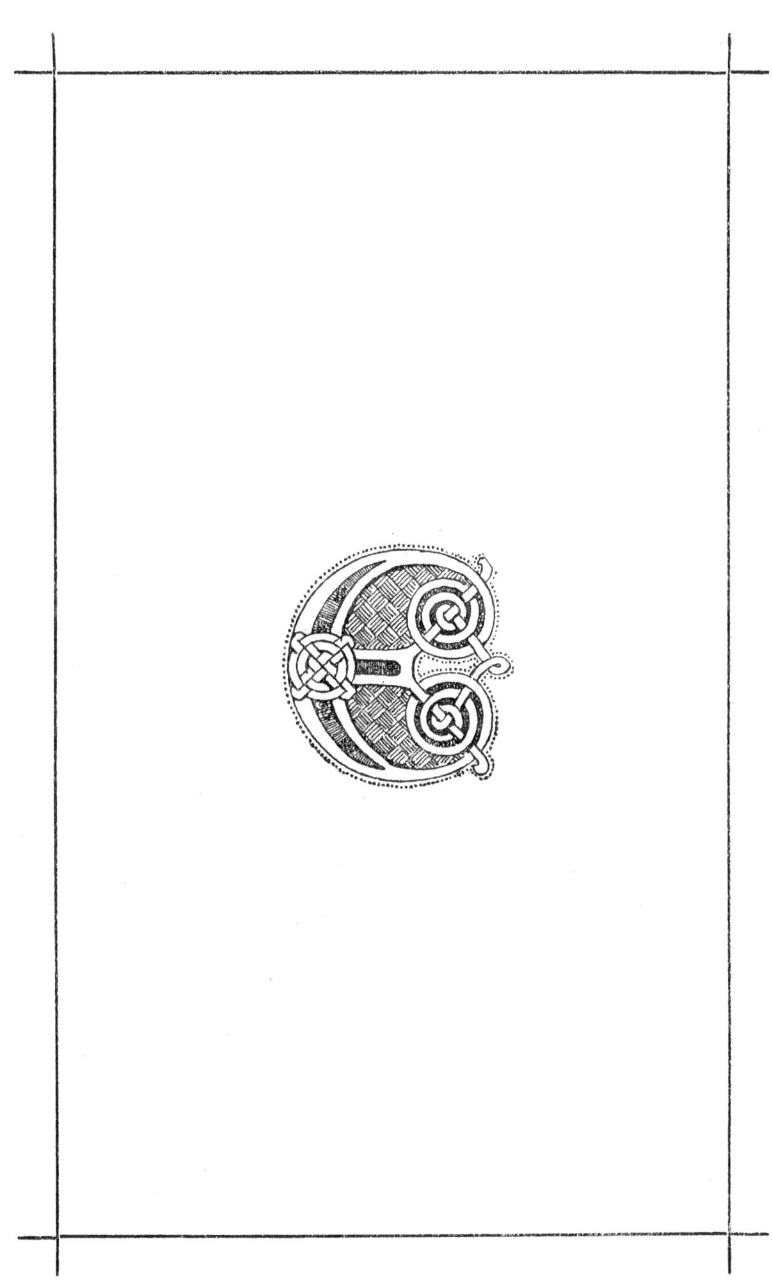

TO

GEORGIANA,

DUCHESS OF BEDFORD.

1. YEARS have flown o'er since first my soul aspired
 In song the sacred Missal to repeat,
Which sainted Tasso writ with pen inspired,—
 Told is my rosary, and the task complete:
And now, 'twixt hope and fear, with toil untired,
 I cast the ambrosial relique at thy feet;
Not without faith that in thy goodness thou
Wilt deign one smile to my acomplish'd vow.

2. Not in dim dungeons to the clank of chains,
 Like sad Torquato's, have the hours been spent
Given to the song, but in bright halls where reigns
 Uncumber'd Freedom,—with a mind unbent
By walks in woods, green dells, and pastoral plains
 To sound, far-off, of village merriment;
Albeit, perchance, some springs whence Tasso drew
His sweetest tones, have touch'd my spirit too.

3. O that, as happier constellations bless
 My studious life, my verses too could boast
Some happier graces, (*should* I wish for less?)
 T' atone for charms unseized and splendors lost!—
No! the rich rainbow mocks the child's caress,
 Who can but sorrow, as his fancy's cross'd,
That e'er so beautiful a thing should rise,
T' elude his grasp, yet so enchant his eyes.

4. On the majestic Sorrentine I gazed
 With a familiar joy—methought he smiled;
But now the vigil's past, I stand amazed
 At the conceit, and sorrow like the child.

What second hand *can* paint the scenes that blazed
  In Tasso's brain, with tints as sweet and wild?
As much the shapes that on his canvass glow,
Their birth to Frenzy as to Genius owe.

5. Yet may I hope o'er generous minds to cast
  A faint reflection of his matchless skill,
For here his own Sophronia, unaghast,
  Flings firm defiance to her tyrant still;—
Clorinda bleeds; lovelorn Erminia fast
  Hies through the forest at her steed's wild will;
And in these pages still Armida's charms
Strike the rapt heart, and wake a world to arms.

6. Thus then, O Lady, with thy name I grace
  The glorious fable; fitly, since to thee
And thine the thanks are due, that in the face
  Of time and toil, the Poet's devotee
Has raised the enchanted structure on its base,
  And to thy hand now yields th' unclosing key,—
Blest, if in one bright intellect like thine,
He wins regard, and builds himself a shrine!

JERUSALEM DELIVERED.

CANTO I.

ARGUMENT.

God to Tortosa sends his Angel down,
Whose mandate Godfrey rev'rently pursues:
A Council call'd—the knights of most renown
Him for their Chief unanimously choose;
He under their blest ensigns first reviews
The number'd troops, then to the plain that leads
To Salem, guides them; troubled by the news,
His wrath Judea's aged tyrant feeds
With cruel schemes, from which he ling'ringly recedes.

CONTENTS.

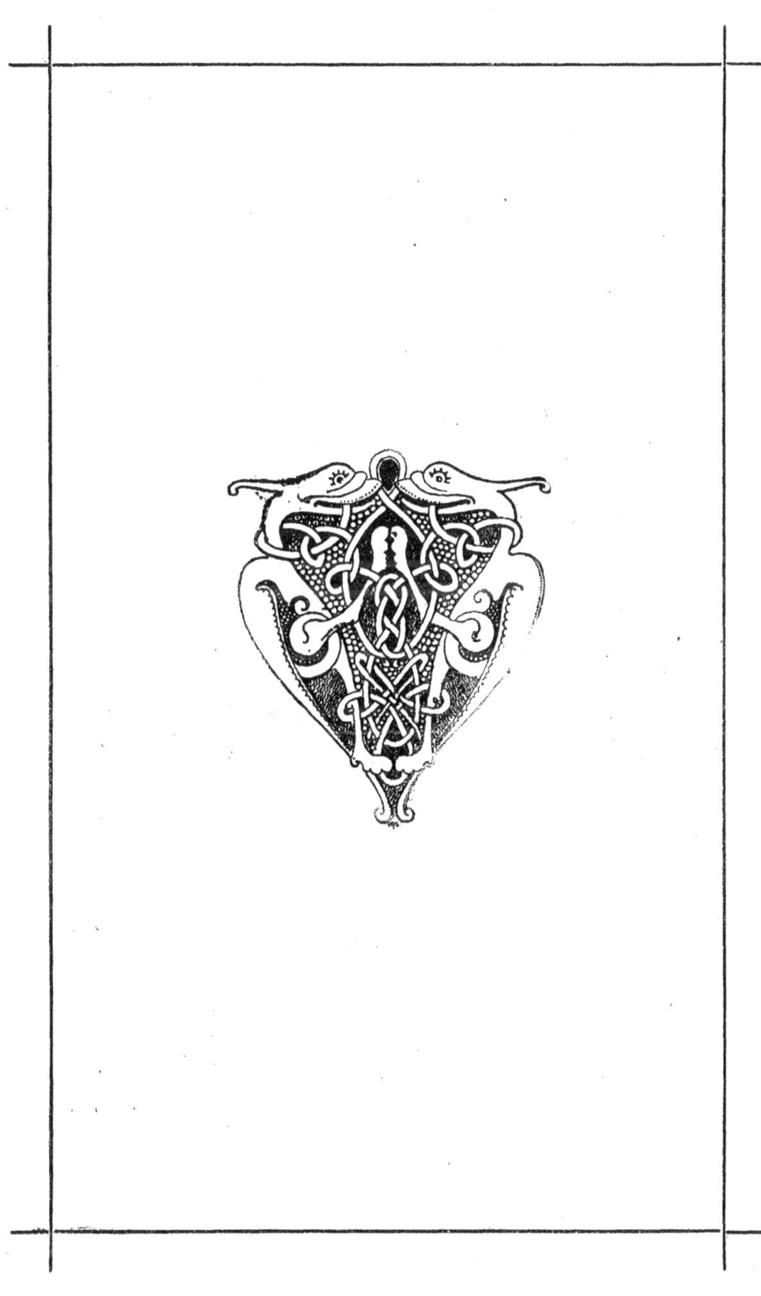

JERUSALEM DELIVERED.

CANTO I.

1. I SING the pious arms and Chief, who freed
The Sepulcher of Christ from thrall profane;
Much did he toil in thought, and much in deed;
Much in the glorious enterprise sustain;
And Hell in vain opposed him; and in vain
Afric and Asia to the rescue pour'd
Their mingled tribes;—Heaven recompensed his pain
And from all fruitless sallies of the sword,
True to the Red-Cross flag his wandering friends restored.

2. O thou, the Muse, that not with fading palms
Circlest thy brows on Pindus, but among
The Angels warbling their celestial psalms,
Hast for thy coronal a golden throng
Of everlasting stars! make thou my song
Lucid and pure; breathe thou the flame divine
Into my bosom; and forgive the wrong,
If with grave truth light fiction I combine,
And sometimes grace my page with other flowers than thine!

3. The world, thou know'st, on tiptoe ever flies
Where warbling most Parnassus' fountain winds,
And that Truth, robed in Song's benign disguise,
Has won the coyest, sooth'd the sternest minds:
So the fond mother her sick infant blinds,
Sprinkling the edges of the cup she gives
With sweets; delighted with the balm it finds
Round the smooth brim, the medicine it receives,
Drinks the delusive draught, and, thus deluded, lives.

4\. And thou, Alphonso, who from fortune's shocks
And from her agitated sea, didst save,
And pilot into port from circling rocks
My wandering bark, nigh swallow'd by the wave!
Accept with gracious smile—'tis all I crave—
These my vow'd tablets, in thy temple hung,
For the fresh life which then thy goodness gave;
Some day, perchance, may my prophetic tongue
Venture of thee to sing what now must rest unsung.

5\. Well would it be (if in harmonious peace
The Christian Powers should e'er again unite,
With steed and ship their ravish'd spoils to seize,
And for his theft the savage Turk requite)
That they to thee should yield, in wisdom's right,
The rule by land, or, if it have more charms,
Of the high seas; meanwhile, let it delight
To hear our verse ring with divine alarms;
Rival of Godfrey, hear, and hearing, grasp thine arms!

6\. Six summers now were pass'd, since in the East
Their high Crusade the Christians had begun;
And Nice by storm, and Antioch had they seized
By secret guile, and gallantly, when won,
Held in defiance of the myriads dun,
Press'd to its conquest by the Persian king;
Tortosa sack'd, when now the sullen sun
Enter'd Aquarius, to breme winter's wing
The quarter'd hosts give place, and wait the coming spring.

7\. And now at length those storms were overblown
That had the trumpet hush'd, and spring was nigh,
When, from his unimaginable throne,
Fix'd in the Empyrean—the pure sky,
Above the highest of the stars more high
Than they from Lucifer's abysmal hall,
Th' Eternal Father downward cast his eye,
And in an instant, at a glance, mark'd all
That pass'd, in light or shade, on earth's terraqueous ball.

8\. All things on earth he views; at length his eyes
Upon the Christian Powers in Syria rest,
And with that clear inspection which descries
The most conceal'd affections of the breast,
He notices how Godfrey burns to wrest
From hand profane the consecrated town,

And, heaven affecting, in what slight request
He holds the meaner joys of earth—renown,
Treasure, and purple power, and glory's meteor crown.

9. Baldwin he sees ambitiously aspire
The height of human grandeur to attain,
And Tancred, victim to a fruitless fire,
Life's choicest blessings gloomily disdain,
While Bohemond in Antioch builds his reign,
And introducing arts and settling laws,
The poise of his new kingdom to sustain,
By power of solemn right and custom, draws
His Turks t' adore aright the one Supernal Cause :—

10. And so absorb'd herein, he seems to lose
All recollection of their first designs ;
An ardent soul, impatient of repose,
The warrior's virtue, in Rinaldo shines,—
Which nor to lust of gold nor power inclines,
But to that quenchless thirst of fame which leads
To generous acts, and for distinction pines ;
On Guelpho's lips he hangs intent, and feeds
On themes of antique worth, and high romantic deeds

11. Of these and other hearts the inmost folds
And motions as th' Omniscient Mind surveys,
Of the angelic splendors him who holds
In the first glorious rank the second place,
Gabriel he calls, the herald of his grace
And faithful messenger, who oft repairs
On blessed errands to the human race,
And, sweetly solacing the virtuous, bears
Back to his mercy-seat the incense of their prayers.

12. To him the Almighty Sire : " To Godfrey go,
And ask what languor has his mind possess'd,—
The war still unrenew'd, unmoved the foe,
And Salem's grievous wrongs yet unredress'd.
A council let him call ; from slothful rest
Rouse the lethargic, and the cold excite ;
Him with the sovereign rule I here invest,
As shall the chieftains upon earth,—each knight
His comrade now no more, but agent in the fight ! "

13. He said, and Gabriel plumed himself to go
Swift on the errand of his Lord ; he roll'd
The air around his viewless essence, so
That mortal eye the vision might behold ;

The aspect human, human was the mold
Assumed, but mix'd with majesty divine;
He wreathes the sunbeams in his locks of gold,
And moves a seraph, whose fair looks define
The age when youth just seems with boyhood to com-
bine.

14. White wings sustain him, edged with golden dyes,
Unwearied, swift, and pliant in their play;
With these he cuts the winds, and clouds, and skies,
And high o'er land and ocean sails away:
Down to Earth's loftier peaks, in this array,
His course the Messenger of Heaven consign'd;
And first on sweet Mount Lebanon to stay,
He, hovering for an instant, seem'd inclined,
And shook his sparkling plumes, self-balanced on the
wind:

15. Then downward, where Tortosa's towers arise,
Urged his precipitate and circling flight;
The sun was rising in the eastern skies,
Part seen, part curtain'd by the waves from sight;
And Godfrey, mindful of the wonted rite,
His matin prayer was offering to the ear
Of the Most High, in lowliness contrite;
When, like the shining sun, but far more clear,
He from the Orient saw the wing'd Archangel steer:—

16. "Godfrey," he said, "the suited time that calls
Beleaguèr'd hosts to arms, at length survey;
Why, while Oppression sits in Salem's halls,
And Fortune beckons, this supine delay?
Call now the Princes of your arm'd array
To solemn council, and if sloth dissuade,
Spur thou them on the city to assay;
Thee God elects to guide their blest crusade,
And, chosen of all, by all thy voice shall be obey'd:

17. "His messenger I am, and thus reveal
To thee his sacred will; of victory rare
What hopes should hence be thine; and O, what zeal
For the brave hosts committed to thy care!"
He spoke; he ceased; and, vanishing in air,
To the serenest, and the loftiest part
Of heaven flew back; long dazzled by the glare
Of the bright vision, and amazed at heart,
Godfrey with upraised eyes remain'd, and lips apart.

18. But when, recovering spirit, he discern'd
Who sent, who came, and what was the command,
If late he glow'd, he now with ardor burn'd
To end the war committed to his hand:
Not that ambition's breath his bosom fann'd
Into vain-glorious pride, from so entire
A preference o'er the rest, but as a brand
Or living coal in a refulgent fire,
In his Lord's will becomes his own desire.

19. Then from their various posts his valiant friends,
Not far dispersed, to council he invites;
Message on message, scroll on scroll, he sends,
And strong entreaty to advice unites;
Whatso might most from indolent delights
Rouse the reluctant, whatso most might reach
And quicken generous natures, he indites;
Meets all men's moods, and with such charms of speech,
That while he all compels, he wins and pleases each.

20. All, except Bohemond, attend; in train
The busy people flock behind; part wait
Without, encamp'd upon the ample plain,
The rest Tortoso holds from gate to gate:
Baron, and prince, and helmed potentate
The Consistory crown, a solemn throng,
When, with an air august, in ducal state
Godfrey arose; majestically strong
His graceful periods flow, and charm the soul along.

21. "Warriors of God, by God himself elected,
Of his true Faith the breaches to restore!
Ye, whom his arm has guided, and protected
From storms by sea and ambuscades on shore!
So that in these few years that have flown o'er,
It has been ours strong monarchies to tame,
Realm after realm, rebellious now no more,
And through the shaken nations spread the fame
Of his triumphant Cross and consecrated name!—

22. "We left not (do I err?) our native land,
Connubial pledges and domestic sweets,
Trusting our fortunes to a faithless strand,
Where battle rages and wild ocean beats,
But to acquire, with its barbaric seats,
A crowd's huzza; if upon this we built,
How poor th' ambition! sense with scorn repeats

The prize, and all the blood our swords have spilt,
Has to our deathless souls been sown in deepest guilt.

23. "But far more glorious were our aims,—we vow'd
The noble walls of Sion to obtain,
And work redemption for the Faithful, bow'd
Beneath subjection's ignominious chain;
Founding in Palestine a purer reign
Where Piety may rest, and Peace recline
In full security, and none restrain
The freeborn pilgrim, passing o'er the brine,
From offering holy vows at meek Messiah's shrine.

24. "Thus then till now we have risk'd much, toil'd more,
Reap'd little good, but for our main intent
None whatsoever, if we here give o'er,
Or turn to other marks the bow we bent:
What will it serve us from the Occident
T' have drawn this splendid force, and to have strown
These fires abroad o'er Asia, if th' event
Of our so mighty movement be alone—
Not glorious kingdoms raised, but ruin'd and o'er-thrown!

25. "He who would here raise empires, must not seek
On worldly policies the base to found,
Where of a fellow-faith his friends are weak
And few, amidst the countless Pagans round,
The land that people,—here, where he no ground
Can have on Grecian succor to presume,
And all too distant from his trumpet's sound
Lies the far West; he builds, but the Simoon
Sweeps round, and instant turns his palace to a tomb.

26. "Turks, Persians, Antioch, (an illustrious prize,
In fame and fact magnificent,) attest
Not our past skill, but the assisting skies;
Victory a wonder was: now, if we wrest
These purposed blessings to an end unblest,
Wronging the Giver who so far has crown'd
The hopes we cherish'd,—Chiefs! I tremble, lest
We vanish to a fable and a sound,—
The brilliant byword pass'd through the wide nations round.

27. "May there be none among us, O my friends,
So to misuse such gifts! your interests see;
With these sublime commencements let the ends,

The filament and woof throughout agree.
Now that the passes of the land are free,
Now that the vernal season clears the plain,
Apt for the enterprise, why rush not we
The crown of all our conquests to attain?
What should prevent the deed? what here our arms detain?

28. "Princes! I vow to you, (and what I vow,
Present and future times alike shall hear;
The very Angels, while I speak it, bow
On their bright thrones, and lend a list'ning ear,)
The period is arrived that we should rear
Our flag aloft; less fortunate will flow
The tide, the longer we delay; things clear
Will set in night, and if our course be slow,
Egypt—assured I speak—will aid the Syrian foe!"

29. He ceased: a hollow hum ensued,—but then,
The primal author of the high crusade,
Peter the Seer, who midst the noblest men
Sat private in the council, rose and said:
"What Godfrey stirs us to, I well have weigh'd,
And second; room for reasoning there is none;
He the true path self-evident has made,
And through the whole clear argument has run;
'Tis yours the plan t' approve,—one word, and I have done.

30. "When I the scorns and discords recollect,
As if on purpose by you borne and given,
Your froward judgments, and proceedings check'd
Just at the moment when they might have thriven,
To a high source, O Princes, am I driven;
I trace the ills, in all their forms and kinds,
To your void powers! our government is even
As a vague pendulum, which each one finds
Struck by as many hands as there are various minds.

31. "Where one alone commands not, upon whom
The cast of parts and offices depend,
The dues of honor and decrees of doom,
There still the helm to some wrong point will tend;
Your separate rights, then, amicably blend
In some one prince, of influence to restrain
The rest,—to one alone dominion lend,
And leave him free, as wisdom will ordain,
A king's prescriptive power and semblance to sustain."

32. Here ceased the Sage: what thoughts, celestial Fire
What hearts, blest Spirit! to thy sweet appeal
Are proof? the Hermit's words didst thou inspire,
And on all hearts imprint them with thy seal.
Ingrafted, e'en innate desires, thy zeal—
The love of honor, liberty and sway,
Check'd in subservience to the public weal;
So that the noblest were the first to say,
"Our Chief let Godfrey be; him swear we to obey!"

33. The rest consent: they marshal on his side,
The power to counsel and command; to give
The vanquish'd laws, and here or there to guide
The war, with uncontroll'd prerogative;
While they, but late his peers, are to receive
His issued mandates with submissive minds,
And aid in ministry executive:
This done, the rumor flies abroad, and finds
Speed in the tongues of men, and spreads on all the winds.

34. He to the soldiers shows himself, and they
Are well content he should the truncheon bear;
The warlike greetings and huzzas they pay,
Calmly he takes, and with a gracious air:
Then, having answer'd courteously and fair
To the frank vows of discipline that stamp
Their love and loyalty, he bids repair
Each to his banner, the collected Camp,
And pass review, when Day next lights its shining lamp.

35. Slow in calm glory from its orient bower
And with unwonted sheen, the Star of day
Rose on the morrow, when from tent and tower,
Issuing in polish'd arms and ranged array,
The squadrons rear their standards and display
Their force, wide wheeling round the vast champaign;
Sole in the center, whence he might survey
Both horse and foot, the Chief observed the chain
Of the whole movement pass, in long revolving train.

36. Sibyl divine, that in thy guardian cell
Treasurest all story! foe to Night and Time!
Aid me with all thine intellect, to tell
What troops and heroes come from every clime;
Their ancient deeds light up and sound sublime,
Now dark and silent grown with years; O bring
From thy rich stores to grace my naked rhyme,

Somewhat with which each list'ning age may ring,
And none have power t' efface—smile on me while I sing!

37. First to the field the gallant Franks advance,
From where, wide sweeping, four bold rivers spread
Beauty and fruitage o'er the Isle of France,—
Flower of her force, and once by Hugo led,
Their good king's brother; but his vital thread
Cut short, the flag in whose field-azure flame
The Golden Lilies, they beneath the dread
Clotharius follow, whom a kingly name
Marks, to perfect his worth and more enhance his fame.

38. A thousand these, completely fenced in mail,
Pace the green turf; a like choice troop succeeds,
In courage, discipline, and massive scale
Of armor like the first,—on generous steeds
Borne to the battle from their Norman meads,
Ten gallant hundreds: and the total ten
A native prince, the bold Duke Robert leads,
From Rollo sprung: two pastor chieftains then,
William and Ademar, bring up their marshal'd men.

39. These held of late authority divine,
The hallow'd priests of piety and pray'r,
Who fearless now in horrid conflict shine,
And press beneath the helm their long black hair:
That from the city and dominions fair
Of ancient Orange to the fierce alarms
Leads full five hundred; this beneath his care,
From whence high Puy the trav'ler's notice charms,
An equal number brings, not less renown'd in arms.

40. Next in the muster Baldwin shows, conjoin'd
With his own Lorrainers, his brother's band,
Which Godfrey to his conduct late resign'd,
When made a captain, captains to command;
Sagacious counsel and a powerful hand
The Count of Chartres grace, who with him leads
Four hundred knights, the bravest of the land;
And thrice that number, arm'd, on prancing steeds,
Baldwin himself conducts:—a noble name succeeds.

41. One whose desert his fortune overweighs,
Though equal with the proudest, Guelpho came;
Who from his sire by sure deduction lays
To Esté's princely house ancestral claim,
But, German by inheritance and name,

Is in the Guelphic stem ingraft ; his sway
Is o'er Carinthia, where barbaric fame
The Sueves and Rhetians reap'd in ancient day,
Where the rough Danube cleaves, the mild Rhine wins
its way.

42. To that maternal heritage his blade
A great and glorious acquisition joins :
And thence a race he brings, who undismay'd
Will march 'gainst Death t' achieve his bold designs,
A race, that when the wintry sun declines,
In warm abodes the sullen hours revive
With gay carousals and the flow of wines ;
Five thousand left their homes,—a third survive
Sole from the Persian spear, in battle still to strive.

43. Next comes the fair-hair'd race whose lands incline
Betwixt the Frank and German to the main,
Bathed by the swelling Meuse and fruitful Rhine,—
A pastoral people, rich in herds and grain ;
Th' industrious Islanders augment their train,
Whose rampired banks, though fenced with all the
powers
Of art, th' insulting Ocean scarce sustain,—
The wild voracious Ocean, which devours
Not fleets alone, but realms with all their towns and
tow'rs.

44. Two thousand these the hopes of honor bring
Beneath a second Robert ; somewhat more,
William, the young son of the English king,
Conducts in arms from Britain's chalky shore ;
Long bows the English at their shoulders bore,
With those whom Ireland, nearer to the pole,
Sends from wild woods resounding to the roar
Of wintry winds,—the limit of the whole
Well-peopled earth, round which its last drear oceans
roll.

45. Then Tancred follows to the war, than whom,
Save young Rinaldo, is no nobler knight,
More mild in manners, fair in manly bloom,
Or more sublimely daring in the fight !
If any shade of error makes less bright
His rich endowments and heroic charms,
It is the foil of Love, which at first sight
Born of surprise, amid the shock of arms,
Grows with increase of tears and sorrow's fond alarms.

46. In noon of that auspicious day which wrought
The Persian's overthrow, faint with the chase
Of fugitives, 'tis rumor'd that he sought
For his o'erwearied limbs and glowing face,
Repose and cool refreshment; with slow pace
He reach'd at length, with green seats compass'd round,
And summer woods, which shaded all the place,
A living spring, that with melodious sound
Flowed from a hollow rock, in many a fall profound.

47. To the same warbling of fresh waters drew,
Arm'd, but unhelm'd and unforeseen, a maid;
She was a Pagan, and came thither too,
To quench her thirst beneath the pleasant shade;
Her beautiful fair aspect, thus display'd,
He sees; admires; and, touch'd to transport, glows
With passion rushing to its fountain head,
The heart; 'tis strange how quick the feeling grows;
Scarce born, its power in him no cool calm medium knows.

48. She reassumed her helm, and threat'ning stood
To strike the chief, but others drawing nigh,
Within the mazes of the leafy wood,
Compell'd by numbers, not by fear to fly,
The haughty Lady rush'd; but still her high
And warlike image with a faith so true
He fosters in his heart, it ne'er can die;
The act, the scene where first she charm'd his view,
Forever haunt his thoughts, and fan the fire anew.

49. And in his aspect legibly is traced
The hopeless flame that frets his life away;
He comes with sighings, and his eyes, abased,
A melancholy languishment betray:
Eight hundred horse have left beneath his sway
Campania's paradise, a pomp of scene
The noblest sure that Nature in her play
Of power e'er shaped—plains, woods, and hills between,
Woo'd by the Tyrrhene sea, mild, fertile, smooth and green.

50. Two hundred follow, from Greek heroes sprung,
Who nearly void of all defense are found;
Sole at their side short crooked swords are hung,
And bows and quivers at their backs resound:

Lean coursers have they, in the race renown'd,
Proof to fatigue, of diet spare and slight;
Mounted on these, they seem to wing the ground;
Nimble alike in onslaught and in flight,—
Wide and dispersed they act, and e'en while flying, fight.

51. Tatine commands the troop, the only Greek
Who join'd the Latin arms; oh Greece, let shame
Forever sit upon thy passive cheek!
The wars are near thee now, yet, meanly tame,
Thou sitt'st a calm spectator of the game,
Thy shield scarce lifted, and thy sword in rust;
If now (complain not) destitute of fame,
Thou art a vassal humbled to the dust,
Thy doom no outrage is, but retribution just.

52. Lo now, the last in order of command,
But first for honor, skill, and glorious scars,
The Adventurers come, a brave, unconquer'd band,
The dread of Asia, thunderbolts of Mars!
Cease, Argo, thy renown'd Adventurers,
Thy errant Peers, prince Arthur, cease to cite,
Filling our books with fable! fame instars
All antique story with a beam less bright
Than theirs;—now what fit chief may lead them to the fight?

53. Dudon of Consa! for, as hard it was
Their birth and bravery to decide between,
All had agreed to rank beneath his laws,
As one who most had both achieved and seen.
In the last stage of mellowing manhood, keen
Shines his gray eye, and with his silver hairs
He shows a strength still juvenile and green;
While, as in noble proof of what he dares,
He many a seam and scar in front imprinted bears.

54. There Eustace ranks, whom much his brother's worth
Much native merit for applause marks down;
There vaunts Gernando his illustrious birth,
His titles, stars, and hoped Norwegian crown.
Roger, of Barneville surnamed, Renown
And ancient Story with the noblest class;[2]
Gentorio, Engerlan, Rambaldo own
As fair a fame; distinguish'd from the mass,
Brave above many brave the two young Gerards pass.

55. Nor Ubald, nor Rosmondo, the rich heir
Of English Lancaster, nor must the pride
Of Tuscan bravery, Obitzo, e'er
Sink unredeem'd to Lethe's greedy tide;
Nor to the Lombard brothers, side by side,
Achilles, Sforza, Palamed the mild,
Nor to strong Otho be the verse denied,—
Otho, who conquer'd from the Paynim vilde
That shield whereon the snake devours a naked child.[3]

56. Nor yet shall Guasco nor Ridolpho grieve,
Nor the two Guidos, whom the famed admire,
Nor Everard, nor Gernier will I leave
In mute inglorious silence to expire;
My hand falls weary on the numb'ring wire;
Where force ye me, as though your love I slighted.
Edward and sweet Gildippe? all my lyre
Is yours,—oh twins, in battle firmly plighted,
You, e'en when dead, in song shall not be disunited!

57. What learn we not within the school of love?
There she became a heroine of a bride;
Nor toil, nor deepest danger can remove
The fair fond lady from her husband's side;
To the same fortune are their lives allied;
The blow falls not that hurts but one,—their pains
Are mutual as their joys; for if the tide
Of her dear blood bedews the hostile plains,
What she in person bears, in spirit he sustains.

58. But these, and all, the boy Rinaldo far,
Oh far excels! supremacy is thrown
Upon his forehead like a shining star,
And every eye is fix'd on him alone;
Hope, and his years he far outstrips; scarce blown
Appear his blossoms, than the fruit's reveal'd;
So sweetly fierce, that when his face is shown
You deem him Love, but Mars, when helm'd and steel'd,
He mounts his fiery barb, and fulmines through the field.

59. Him fair Sophia to Bertoldo bore,
Where the clear Adige's swift waters wind,
The lovely to the potent; and before
He well was wean'd, the infant she consign'd
To queen Matilda, who, sincerely kind,
Foster'd, and taught him, as in years he grew,
All princely arts; her care his docile mind

Requited well, and thus his calm hours flew,
Till in the radiant East the martial trumpet blew.

60. Then, ere his youth could three short lusters boast,
Alone he fled by unknown tracks,—he pass'd
Th' Egæan billows, the Ionian coast,
And reach'd in climes remote the camp at last;
A flight well fit some young enthusiast
In after days should follow, who would win
The like renown;[4] three years their fruits had cast,
Since with the warring armies he had been,
Yet still the tender down scarce feather'd o'er his chin.

61. The horsemen now have pass'd, and Godfrey views,
The foot advance with Raymond at their head,
Duke of Narbonne, who ruled in fair Toulouse,
And his well-disciplined four thousand led,
Between the Ocean and the Garonne bred,
And misty Pyrenees; a people free,
Firm in fatigue, incapable of dread,
At all points arm'd; and led they could not be
By one of greater skill or hardihood than he.

62. But Stephen of Amboise leads from Blois and Tours
Troops full five thousand, register'd aright,
A nerveless race unable to endure
Fatigue, though wholly sheath'd in armor bright;
The land luxurious, delicate, and light,
With a rich soil and a delicious air,
Produces like inhabitants; in fight,
The first assaults impetuously they dare,
But quickly tire with strife, and languish through the war.

63. Third comes Alcasto, cradled on the crag,
Threat'ning and stern as Capaneus of old
Before the Theban town; beneath his flag,
From each Helvetian tower and Alpine hold,
Six thousand fierce plebeians are enroll'd,
Sharp'ning the ploughshare to the sword they rise;
And he who turn'd the furrow, watch'd the fold,
Now fearlessly the war's grim ridges eyes,
And with the mightiest match'd, the strength of kings defies.

64. The lofty banner next is seen dispread,
Which bears Saint Peter's keys and mitred crown,
Seven thousand foot, by good Camillus led,

In massive armor sheath'd, beneath its frown:
Glad that Heav'n calls him to the sacred town
In so divine a cause, he marches on,
There to renew his sires' antique renown,
Or prove at least, that if in aught outshone
By Latin worth, 'twill be in discipline alone.

65. But now the whole gay pageant had pass'd by
In regular review; when Godfrey sent,
And to the noblest chiefs assembled nigh,
In brief discourse imparted his intent:
"My pleasure is, when next the firmament
Yields its first light, that you the hosts array,
And ere the foe anticipates th' event,
Or vaward scouts our quick descent betray,
March to the hallow'd town, as swiftly as we may.

66. "Thus, then, prepare you for the march required,
And for the strife, and for the victory near!"
This daring speech from one so wise, inspired
In each, fresh courage, confidence, and cheer.
All ready stand for the sublime career,
And, unindulgent of the night's repose,
Wait with impatience till the morn appear;
In Godfrey's breast, albeit, from foresight rose
Fears which his cautious mind to no one would disclose.

67. For he by certain tidings understood
That Egypt's king was now upon his way
To Gaza's towers, a fortress strong and good,
Which seaward on the Syrian frontiers lay;
Nor could he think a prince so swift to prey
On whatso'er his enterprising mind
Was fix'd to win, would trifle time away;
In him expecting a sharp foe to find,
He to his envoy's zeal this secret charge consign'd.

68. "In a light brigandine compact and fleet,
Go thou to Greece; where the Propontic sea
Washes the seven-hill'd City, thou wilt meet,
(As I have word from one who ne'er to me
Errs in advice,) of regal dignity,
A dauntless youth whose fix'd intentions are
Forthwith to bear us martial company;
Prince of the Danes, he marches to the war
A numerous host from realms beneath the Arctic Star.

69\. "But since perchance the faithless Byzantine
Will practice on him each accustom'd art
To turn him back, or on some new design
Alien from ours, persuade the youth to start,—
Counsel him earnestly, my friend, apart,
To shun th' advice of that insidious king;
Both for his good and ours dispose his heart
With all convenient speed his aids to bring;
Say, that all stay were now an ignominious thing.

70\. "Come not thyself with him; but in the train,
And at the court of the Greek prince abide,
Those ofttimes-talk'd-of succors to obtain,
By treaty promised, due, but still denied."
To speak, instruct, and to his care confide
Letter of credence and of greeting fair,
Short time sufficed; the herald then applied,
His busiest thoughts to expedite th' affair,
And Godfrey sought his tent, and gave a truce to care.

71\. When now the Orient open'd to the Sun
Its shining gates, the mingled voice profound
Of trumpet, tambour, horn, and cymbalon,
Cheer'd to the march the stirring troops around;
Not half so grateful is the thunder's sound
In the hot dog-days to the world forlorn,
Presaging freshness to the thirsty ground,
As to these warlike tribes the music drawn
From marshal tubes that treat of battles to be born.

72\. Straitway, spurr'd on by strong desire, they dress'd
Their limbs in wonted armor; straight, in sheen
Of perfect panoply, the soldiers press'd
Beneath their several regencies convene;
Ranged, the hosts join; and to the winds serene
Straight the borne banners all at once are given;
And in th' imperial gonfalon is seen
The Cross, triumphantly outspread, and driven
Abroad in waving folds voluminous to heaven.

73\. Meanwhile the Sun in the celestial fields
Perpetually advancing, rose in height,
And struck from pointed helms and bossy shields,
Clear, trembling lusters that torment the sight;
The broad air burns with glory, like a bright
And boundless conflagration; neighings shrill,
From fierce steeds ramping in their wild delight,
Mix with the sound of smitten steel, and fill
The deafen'd country round, hill answering loud to hill.

74. The prudent Chief, to guard from ambuscade
His marching army, sent a troop before,
Of light-arm'd horse, with orders to invade
The hollow woods, and each strange place explore;
And first the pioneers advancing, bore
Their instruments, whereby the rugged way
Gives easy access; rivers are bridged o'er,
Dells fill'd, mounts level'd; shaggy woods display
Their tracks, and each close pass admits the lively day.

75. There are no moated towers, no massy woods,
No levies gather'd by their Pagan foes,
Nor bursting streams, nor Alpine solitudes,
To countervail their course, or interpose
Cause of delay: thus in his grandeur flows
The King of Floods, when proudly he disdains
His limitary shores,—the torrent grows,
Swells o'er its ruin'd banks, and to the plains
Roaring sweeps down, nor aught its headlong wrath restrains.

76. The king of Tripoli alone might hope
In his munition'd fortress, with success,
Powerful in forces, arms, and coin, to cope
With the Frank army, or their march distress;
But fearful to oppose them or repress,
Their jealous doubts he studies to appease
With entertainments and with gifts, nor less
To Godfrey's keep submits the kingdom's keys,
And from his hand accepts the articles of peace.

77. There from Mount Seir, which rises on the east
Of the nigh city, crowds on crowds descend
Of the true Faith,—prince, worshiper, and priest
Virgins, and youths, and matron-age attend;
Beneath refreshments for the host they bend,
Inly rejoiced; and using, side by side,
Familiar talk, their wonder knows no end.
The pilgrims' arms admiring;—they with pride
Furnish, at Godfrey's wish, a sure and friendly guide.

78. Ever in sight of the blue sea his host
By unobstructed ways direct he leads,
Well knowing that along th' adjacent coast
The friendly navy in its course proceeds;
Whence whatsoe'er so large an army needs
May be supplied, since each Greek island reaps
Corn but for him, since but for him Crete feeds

The thousand flocks that range her tangled steeps,
And Scio's rocky isle her wine celestial weeps.

79. The bordering ocean groans beneath the prores
Of the swift vessels and their wealthy freight,
So that no longer the Levantine shores
To the false Turk give access as of late;
Beside the argosies of noblest rate
Arm'd by Saint Mark and by Saint George, which there
Cruise from rich Venice and the Genoese state
Others from fruitful Sicily repair,
And England, Belgium, France, alike equip their share.

80. And these, which now in firmest bonds combined
With the sublime crusade confederate stand,
From various shores are fraught with every kind
Of stores that Godfrey may at need demand;
Who, finding free the passes of the land,
And that the frontiers of the realm present
No force, his onward progress to withstand
Or question, thither makes his swift descent,
Where Christ the pangs of death and darkness under-
went.

81. Yet not so swift, but that light Fame, the post
Of falsehood as of truth, flies far before,
And paints the fortunate, triumphant host,
United, moving, indolent no more;
What and how strong the squadrons, o'er and o'er
Recounts, with all whose deeds of valor grace
The herald's scrolls, from each romantic shore;
Narrates their vaunts, and with determined face,
The high usurping powers from Salem threats to chase.

82. And look'd-for evil is a greater ill
Than the wing'd mischief when it comes; each ear
Hangs on each whisper in suspense, and still
The face shows sadness, and the eye its tear.
A melancholy hum, confused and drear,
On wing within, on wing without the gates,
The fields and doleful city fills with fear;
But the old king, in these momentous straits,
Close in his dubious heart ferocious schemes debates.

83. This prince, named Aladine, by recent crime
Raised to the throne, perpetual cares pursued;
He had been cruel once, but mellowing time
His native fierceness somewhat had subdued.

He, having now but too well understood
That the Franks seek in battle to inclose
The town, much muses in his restless mood!
On former terror new suspicion grows;
Much he his subjects fears, and much he fears his foe.

84. For in his city a mix'd people lived,
Of adverse Faiths: the weaker few retain'd
The laws of Christ,—in Mahomet believed
The stronger many, and his rule maintain'd;
But when the king the crown of Sion gain'd,
And sought to 'stablish there his Court in state,
He on his loving Mussulmans ordain'd
Taxes and levies of a lighter rate,
But on the hapless Franks imposed a tenfold weight.

85. This thought now fretting into gall, awoke
Within him all that cruelty which Time
Had lull'd asleep, and giantlike he broke
From slumber, thirsting but the more for crime.
So the snake slumbers out the winter rime;
So fiercely wakes when summer warms the plain;
So the tamed lion from his burning clime
Torn, if provoked, assumes his fire again,
Rolls the red eye in rage, and shakes the bristling mane.

86. "I see," said he, "in this perfidious brood
Undoubted signs of new-conceived delight;
The public evil is their private good,
Our common sorrows but their smiles excite:
And now, e'en now perchance, in fraudful spite,
Each busy traitor with himself debates
How he may kill me, or at least by night
To my stern foe and his consorted mates,
May with most sure address unbar the guarded gates.

87. "But no! the fangs of the assaulted snake
Have one preventative—I'll wreak my will;
Destroy them all; a sharp example make;
Safe in the mothers' arms the infants kill,
Their temples fire, and to the lowest sill
Burn their abodes; these sacrificial cares
I owe to those whose blood th' invaders spill;
And first on yon scorn'd Sepulcher of theirs,
Shall the cowl'd priests be slain, midst all their vows
and pray'rs."

88. Thus he soliloquized ; his acting hand
With his dire scheme, 'tis true, but ill concurs ;
But if he issues not the fierce command,
Baseness it is, not pity, that deters ;
For while one fear to barbarous fury spurs
His earnest will, a stronger still in show
Keeps it in check, and moves his just demurs ;
He dreads the means of treaty to forego,
Or raise too high the rage of the victorious foe.

89. Yet, though thus temper'd was his wolfish wrath,
Elsewhere he gives his violence the rein ;
The rustic's home he levels, and with scath
Of fire lays waste the cultivated plain ;
He leaves no valley green with rising grain,
Where the Frank host may pleasantly repose,
Or reap subsistence ; then with busy brain
In every fountain noxious drugs he throws,
And the polluted stream with secret poison flows ;—

90. Crafty in cruelty ! meantime no means
To reinforce the city he neglects,
Strong on three sides ; but northward intervenes
A rampart less secure,—he there erects
Walls on the first alarm, and its defects
Repairs with battlements that brave the skies,
And scorn subjection ; lastly, he collects
His subject troops and subsidized allies,
And from his lofty towers the coming storm defies.

END OF CANTO I.

JERUSALEM DELIVERED.

CANTO II.

ARGUMENT.

New charms Ismeno tries, which proving vain,
The King a slaughter of the Franks decrees;
Bashful Sophronia and Olindo fain
Would die, his fatal anger to appease;
Clorinda, hearing their sad story, frees
From ruffian hands th' incomparable pair;
Argantes and Alethes treat of peace;
Which Godfrey not accepting, they forbear
No longer, mortal war against him to declare.

JERUSALEM DELIVERED.

CANTO II.

1. WHILE the vex'd Tyrant thus prepared to arm,
Alone to him one day Ismeno drew;
Ismeno, who from the closed tomb can charm
The dead, and make them feel and breathe anew;
Ismeno, who oft, as tales devoutly true
Affirm, by whisper'd rhyme and murmur'd spell
Unbinds the demons of the deep to do
Deeds without name, or chains them in his cell,
And makes e'en Pluto pale upon the throne of hell.

2. A Christian once, he now adores Mahound,
Yet former rites not wholly can forego,
But oft to foulest use will he confound
The laws of both, though well he neither know;
And now from caves where fern and nightshade grow,
Far from the vulgar, where in glooms immersed,
He his black arts is wont to practice, slow
Glides he to front the storm about to burst,—
To an accursed king a counselor more accursed.

3. "Oh king! the dreaded armies come," he cries,
"Unlingering, conquering; yet be not dismay'd;
Let us but worthy of ourselves arise,
Both heaven and earth will give the valiant aid;
Well as the scepter canst thou wield the blade,
And quick to furnish, skillful to foresee,
The duties of a king hast thou display'd
To admiration; if all act like thee,
For thy advancing foe this land a tomb shall be.

4. "For me, I come my succor to impart,
Thy friend alike in peril and in pain;
The utmost efforts of my magic art,

And the deep counsels of my aged brain,
Are at thy service ; yea, I will constrain
The Angel hosts from blessedness that fell,
Part of th' impending labor to sustain ;
But where I purpose to commence the spell,
And by what simple means, give audience while I tell.

5. "Low in the Christian temple, under earth,
Stands in a secret grotto the rich shrine
Of her who gave their buried God to birth,
The Virgin Mother and the Saint divine ;
Before the veil that screens her Image shine
Undying lamps, that to the mummery lend
Bright pomp ; and round, with many a senseless sign,
The sapient devotees their gifts suspend,
There in long vigils kneel, in dumb devotions bend.

6. "Now this their image I would have convey'd,
With thine own hand from their invaded fane,
To the chief Mosque, and on it shall be laid
Spells of such pow'r, that long as we retain
The new Palladium in our keep, a train
Of mighty spirits shall protect thy states ;
While steel attacks and fire assaults in vain,
Unrent the wall, impregnable the gates,
We shall the war roll back, and disappoint the fates !"

7. He said : the king approved ; and all in haste
Sped to the Christian sanctuary, and tore
Down from its shrine the Image of the Chaste,
And with irreverence to the temple bore,
Where oft his impious Mussulmans adore,
High Heav'n incensing ; there in dreadful style
His spells the black Magician mumbles o'er
The holy image in th' unholy pile,—
Hymns which insult the skies, and praises which revile.

8. But when in heav'n the morning light appear'd,
The startled guardian of the mosque profane
Saw not the image where it had been rear'd
The previous night, and sought for it in vain
Through every part of the extensive fane ;
Straight to the king the tidings he convey'd,
Who fancying now in his mistrustful brain
That the illustrious prize had been betray'd
Back to some Christian Priest, unbounded rage display'd.

9. Whether it were that Christian hands by guile
Did bear off secretly the ravish'd prize,
Or that Heav'n, angry that a place so vile
Should shroud her form who walks the glorious skies,
Put forth its power from these indignities
Its Goddess-queen to save, is vainly sought
In erring fame ; but piety supplies
The heav'nly luster that irradiates thought,
Nor doubts that Heav'n itself the glorious wonder wrought.

10. In every temple, hermitage, and hall,
A long and eager search the monarch made,
And tortures or rewards decreed to all
Who screen'd the guilty, or the guilt betray'd ;
Nor ceased the Sorcerer to employ in aid
Of the inquiry all his arts, but still
Without success ; for whether Heav'n convey'd
The prize away, or power of human will,
Heav'n close the secret kept, and shamed his vaunted skill.

11. But when the king found all expedients vain
To trace th' offender, then, beyond disguise,
Flamed forth his hatred to the Christians ; then,
Fed by wild jealousies and sharp surmise,
Immoderate fury sparkled in his eyes ;
Follow what may, he will revenge the deed,
And wreak his rage : "Our wrath shall not," he cries,
"Fall void, but root up all th' accursed seed ;
Thus in the general doom the guilty yet shall bleed !

12. "So that he 'scapes not, let the guiltless die.
But wherefore thus of guiltlessness debate?
Each guilty is, nor 'mongst them all know I
One, well-affected to the faith and state ;
And what if some be unparticipate
In this new crime, new punishment shall pay
For old misdeeds ; why longer do ye wait,
My faithful Mussulmans ? up ! up ! away !
Hence with the torch and sword—seize, fire, lay waste, and slay !"

13. Thus to the crowd he spake : the mandate flew,
And in the bosoms of the Faithful shed
Astonishment and stupor ; stupor threw
On every face the paleness of the dead ;
None dared, none sought to make defense, none fled,

None used entreaty, none excuse ; but there
They stood, like marble monuments of dread,
Irresolute,—but Heav'n conceived their prayer,
And whence they least had hope, brought hope to their despair.

14. Of generous thoughts and principles sublime,
Among them in the city lived a maid,
The flower of virgins, in her ripest prime,
Supremely beautiful ! but that she made
Never her care, or beauty only weigh'd
In worth with virtue ; and her worth acquired
A deeper charm from blooming in the shade ;
Lovers she shunn'd, nor loved to be admired,
But from their praises turn'd, and lived a life retired.

15. Yet could not this coy secrecy prevent
Th' admiring gaze and warm desires of one
Tutor'd by Love, nor yet would Love consent
To hide such lustrous beauty from the sun ;
Love ! that through every change delight'st to run,
The Proteus of the heart ! who now dost blind,
Now roll the Argus eyes that naught can shun !
Thou through a thousand guards unseen dost wind,
And to the chastest maids familiar access find.

16. Sophronia hers, Olindo was his name ;
Born in one town, by one pure faith illumed ;
Modest—as she was beautiful, his flame
Fear'd much, hoped little, and in naught presumed ;
He could not, or he durst not speak, but doom'd
To voiceless thought his passion ; him she slighted,
Saw not, or would not see ; thus he consumed
Beneath the vivid fire her beauty lighted ;
Either not seen, ill known, or, known, but ill requited.

17. And thus it was, when like an omen drear
That summon'd all her kindred to the grave,
The cruel mandate reach'd Sophronia's ear,
Who, brave as bashful, yet discreet as brave,
Mused how her people she from death might save:
Courage inspired, but virginal alarm
Repress'd the thought, till maiden shyness gave
Place to resolve, or join'd to share the harm ;
Boldness awoke her shame, shame made her boldness charm.

18. Alone amidst the crowd the maid proceeds,
Nor seeks to hide her beauty, nor display ;
Downcast her eyes, close veil'd in simple weeds,
With coy and graceful steps she wins her way :
So negligently neat, one scarce can say
If she her charms disdains, or would improve,—
If chance or taste disposes her array ;
Neglects like hers, if artifices, prove
Arts of the friendly Heavens, of Nature, and of Love.

19. All, as she pass'd unheeding all, admire
The noble maid ; before the king she stood ;
Not for his angry frown did she retire,
But his indignant aspect coolly view'd :
"To give,"—she said, "but calm thy wrathful mood,
And check the tide of slaughter in its spring,—
To give account of that thou hast pursued
So long in vain, seek I thy face, O king !
The urged offense I own, the doom'd offender bring !"

20. The modest warmth, the unexpected light
Of high and holy beauty, for a space
O'erpower'd him—conquer'd of his fell despite,
He stood, and of all fierceness lost the trace.
Were his a spirit, or were hers a face
Of less severity, the sweet surprise
Had melted him to love ; but stubborn grace
Subdues not stubborn pride ; Love's potent ties
Are flatt'ring fond regards, kind looks, and smiling eyes.

21. If 'twere not love that touch'd his flinty soul,
Desire it was, 'twas wonder, 'twas delight :
"Safe be thy race !" he said, "reveal the whole,
And not a sword shall on thy people light."
Then she : "The guilty is before thy sight,—
The pious robbery was my deed ; these hands
Bore the bless'd Image from its cell by night ;
The criminal thou seek'st before thee stands,—
Justice from none but me her penalty demands."

22. Thus she prepares a public death to meet,
A people's ransom at a tyrant's shrine :
O glorious falsehood ! beautiful deceit !
Can Truth's own light thy loveliness outshine ?
To her bold speech misdoubting Aladine
With unaccustom'd temper calm replied :
"If so it were, who plann'd the rash design,
Advised thee to it, or became thy guide ?
Say, with thyself who else his ill-timed zeal allied ?"

23. "Of this my glory not the slightest part
Would I," said she, "with one confederate share;
I needed no adviser; my full heart
Alone sufficed to counsel, guide, and dare."
"If so," he cried, "then none but thou must bear
The weight of my resentment, and atone
For the misdeed." "Since it has been my care,"
She said, "the glory to enjoy alone,
'Tis just none share the pain; it should be all mine own."

24. To this the tyrant, now incensed, return'd,
"Where rests the Image?" and his face became
Dark with resentment: she replied, "I burn'd
The holy image in the holy flame,
And deem'd it glory; thus at least no shame
Can e'er again profane it—it is free
From further violation; dost thou claim
The spoil or spoiler? this behold in me;
But that, while time rolls round, thou never more shalt see.

25. "Albeit no spoiler I; it was no wrong
To repossess what was by force obtain'd:"
At this the tyrant loosed his threatening tongue,
Long-stifled passion raging unrestrain'd:
No longer hope that pardon may be gain'd,
Beautiful face, high spirit, bashful heart!
Vainly would Love, since mercy is disdain'd,
And Anger flings his most envenom'd dart,
In aid of you his else protecting shield impart!

26 Doom'd in tormenting fire to die, they lay
Hands on the maid; her arms with rough cords twining,
Rudely her mantle chaste they tear away,
And the white veil that o'er her droop'd declining:
This she endured in silence unrepining,
Yet her firm breast some virgin tremors shook;
And her warm cheek, Aurora's late outshining,
Waned into whiteness, and a color took,
Like that of the pale rose, or lily of the brook.

27. The crowd collect; the sentence is divulged;
With them Olindo comes, by pity sway'd;
It might be that the youth the thought indulged,
What if his own Sophronia were the maid:
There stand the busy officers array'd
For the last act, here swift the flames arise;

But when the pinion'd beauty stands display'd
To the full gaze of his inquiring eyes,—
Tis she ! he bursts through all, the crowd before him flies.

28. Aloud he cries : " To her, O not to her
The crime belongs, though phrensy may misplead !
She plann'd not, dared not, could not, king, incur
Sole and unskill'd the guilt of such a deed !
How lull the guards, or by what process speed
The sacred Image from its vaulted cell ?
The theft was mine ! and 'tis my right to bleed ! "
Alas for him ! how wildly and how well
He loved th' unloving maid, let this avowal tell.

29. " I mark'd where your high Mosque receives the air
And light of heaven ; I climb'd the dizzy steep ;
I reach'd a narrow opening ; enter'd there,
And stole the Saint, while all were hush'd in sleep :
Mine was the crime, and shall another reap
The pain and glory ? grant not her desire !
The chains are mine : for me the guards may heap
Around the ready stake the penal fire ;
For me the flames ascend ; 'tis mine, that funeral pyre ! "

30. Sophronia raised to him her face,—her eye
Was fill'd with pity and a starting tear ;
She spoke—the soul of sad humanity
Was in her voice, " What phrensy brings thee here,
Unhappy innocent ! is death so dear,
Or am I so ill able to sustain
A mortal's wrath, that thou must needs appear ?
I have a heart, too, that can death disdain,
Nor ask for life's last hour companionship in pain."

31. Thus she appeals to him ; but scorning life,
His settled soul refuses to retreat :
O glorious scene, where in sublimest strife
High-minded Virtue and Affection meet !
Where death 's the prize of conquest, and defeat
Seals its own safety, yet remains unblest !
But indignation at their fond deceit,
And rage, the more inflames the tyrant's breast,
The more this constant pair the palm of guilt contest

32. He deems his power despised, and that in scorn
Of him they spurn the punishment assign'd :
" Let," he exclaim'd, " the fitting palm adorn

The brows of both! both pleas acceptance find!"
Beckoning he bids the prompt tormentors bind
Their galling chains around the youth—'tis done;
Both to one stake are, back to back, consign'd,
Like sunflowers twisted from their worship'd sun,
Compell'd the last fond looks of sympathy to shun.

33. Around them now the unctuous pyre was piled,
And the fann'd flame was rising in the wind,
When, full of mournful thoughts, in accents wild,
The lover to his mate in death repined:
"Is this the bond then which I hoped should bind
Our lives in blissful marriage? this the fire
Of bridal faith, commingling mind with mind,
Which, I believed, should in our hearts inspire
Like warmth of sacred zeal and delicate desire?

34. "Far other flames Love promised to impart,
Than those our envious planets here prepare;
Too, ah too long they kept our hands apart,
But harshly now they join them in despair!
Yet does it sooth, since by a mode so rare
Condemn'd to die, thy torments to partake,
Forbid by fate thy sweetnesses to share;
If tears I shed, 'tis but for thy dear sake,
Not mine,—with thee beside, I bless the burning stake.

35. "And oh! this doom would be indeed most bless'd,
My sharpest sufferings blandishments divine,
Might I but be permitted, breast to breast,
On thy sweet lips my spirit to resign;
If thou too, panting toward one common shrine,
Wouldst the next happy instant parting spend
Thy latest sighs in sympathy on mine!"
Sorrowing he spake; she when his plaints had end
Did thus his fond discourse most sweetly reprehend.

36. "Far other aspirations, other plaints
Than these, dear friend, the solemn hour should claim.
Think what reward God offers to his saints;
Let meek repentance raise a loftier aim;
These torturing fires, if suffer'd in his name,
Will, bland as zephyrs, waft us to the blest;
Regard the sun, how beautiful his flame!
How fine a sky invites him to the west!
These seem to soothe our pangs, and summon us to rest."

37. The Pagans lifting up their voices wept;
In stifled sorrow wept the Faithful too;
E'en the stern king was touch'd,—a softness crept
O'er his fierce heart, ennobling, pure, and new;
He felt, he scorn'd it, struggled to subdue,
And lest his wavering firmness should relent,
His eyes averted, and his steps withdrew:
Sophronia's spirit only was unbent;
She yet lamented not, for whom all else lament.

38. In midst of their distress, a knight behold,
(So would it seem) of princely port! whose vest,
And arms of curious fashion, grain'd with gold,
Bespeak some foreign and distinguish'd guest;
The silver tigress on the helm impress'd,
Which for a badge is borne, attracts all eyes,—
A noted cognizance, th' accustom'd crest
Used by Clorinda, whence conjectures rise,
Herself the stranger is—nor false is their surmise.

39. All feminine attractions, aims, and parts,
She from her childhood cared not to assume;
Her haughty hand disdain'd all servile arts,
The needle, distaff, and Arachne's loom;
Yet, though she left the gay and gilded room
For the free camp, kept spotless as the light
Her virgin fame, and proud of glory's plume,
With pride her aspect arm'd; she took delight
Stern to appear, and stern, she charm'd the gazer's sight.

40. While yet a girl, she with her little hand
Lash'd and rein'd in the rapid steed she raced,
Toss'd the huge javelin, wrestled on the sand,
And by gymnastic toils her sinews braced;
Then through the devious wood and mountain-waste
Track'd the struck lion to his enter'd den,
Or in fierce wars a nobler quarry chased;
And thus in fighting field and forest glen,
A man to savage beasts, a savage seem'd to men.

41. From Persia now she comes, with all her skill
The Christians to resist, though oft has she
Strew'd with their blood the field, till scarce a rill
Remain'd, that ran not purple to the sea.
Here now arrived, the dreadful pageantry
Of death presents itself,—the crowd—the pyre—
And the bound pair; solicitous to see,
And know what crime condemns them to the fire,
Forward she spurs her steed, and hastens to inquire.

42. The throng falls back, and she awhile remains,
The fetter'd pair more closely to survey ;
One she sees silent, one she sees complains,
The stronger spirit nerves the weaker prey :
She sees him mourn like one whom the sad sway
Of powerful pity doth to tears chastise,
Not grief, or grief not for himself ; but aye
Mute kneels the maid, her blue beseeching eyes
So fix'd on heaven, she seems in heaven ere yet she dies.

43. Clorinda melts, and with them both condoles ;
Some tears she sheds, but greater tenderness
Feels for her grief who most her grief controls,—
The silence moves her much, the weeping less ;
No longer now does she delay to press
For information ; turning towards one
Of reverend years, she said with eagerness,
"Who are they ? speak ! and Oh, what crime has won
This death? in Mercy's name, declare the deed they've done ! "

44. Thus she entreats ; a brief reply he gives,
But such as well explains the whole event :
Amazed she hears it, and as soon conceives
That they are both sincerely innocent ;
Her heart is for them, she is wholly bent
T' avert their fate, if either arms can aid,
Or earnest prayers secure the king's consent ;
The fire she nears, commands it to be stay'd,
That now approach'd them fast, and to th' attendants said :

45. " Let none of you presume to prosecute
Your barbarous office, till the king I see ;
My word I pledge, that at Clorinda's suit
Your fault he will forgive, if fault it be : "
Moved by her speech and queenlike dignity,
The guards obey, and she departs in quest
Of the stern monarch, urgent of her plea :
Midway they met ; the monarch she address'd ;
And in this skillful mode her gen'rous purpose press'd :

46. "I am Clorinda ; thou wilt know perchance
The name, from vague remembrance or renown ;
And here I come to save with sword and lance
Our common Faith, and thine endanger'd crown ;
Impose the labor, lay th' adventure down,
Sublime I fear it not, nor low despise ,

Thus she entreats; a brief reply he gives,
But such as well explains the whole event:
Amazed she heard it, and as soon conceives
That they are both sincerely innocent;
Her heart is for them, she is wholly bent
To' avert their fate, if either arms can aid,
Or earnest prayers secure the king's consent;
The fire she nears, commands it to be stayed,
That now approached them fast, and to the' attendants said:

STANZA XLIV; CANTO II.

In open'd field or in the straiten'd town,
Prepared I stand for every enterprise,
Where'er the danger calls, where'er the labor lies!"

47. "What region so remote," replied the king,
"From the sun's track or Asia's golden zone,
To which, heroic maid, on wonder's wing
Thy fame has not arrived, thy glory flown?
Now that with mine thou deign'st to join thine own
Unconquer'd sword, I shake away all sense
Of fear, and hope for my assaulted throne;
No—I could have no surer confidence,
If e'en united hosts were arm'd in my defense!

48. "Now then the mighty Godfrey comes too late
To my desire; exploits are thy demand,
But only worthy thy sublime estate
I hold the daring, difficult, and grand;
The rule of all our warriors to thy hand
Do I concede; thy standard be their guide
In battle, and a law thy least command!"—
She nor assumed his praises, nor denied,
But bow'd her grateful thanks, and courteously replied:

49. "'Twould be assuredly a thing most rare,
If the reward the service should precede;
But of thy bounty confident, I dare
For future toils solicit, as my meed,
Yon lovers' pardon; since the charge indeed
Rests on no evidence, 'twas hard to press
The point at all, but this I waive, nor plead
On those sure signs which, urged, thou must confess
Their hands quite free from crime, or own their guilt far less.

50. "Yet will I say, though here the common mind
Condemns the Christians of the theft, for me,
Sufficient reasons in mine own I find
To doubt, dispute, disparage the decree;
To set their idols in our sanctuary
Was an irreverence to our laws, howe'er
Urged by the sorcerer; should the Prophet see
E'en idols of our own establish'd there?
Much less then those of men whose lips his faith forswear!

51. "The Christian statue ravish'd from your sight
To Allah, therefore, rather I impute,

In sign that he will let no foreign rite
Of superstition his pure place pollute :
Spells and enchantments may Ismeno suit,
Leave him to use such weapons at his will ;
But shall we warriors by a wand dispute ?
Now no ! our talisman, our hope, our skill,
Lie in our swords alone, and they shall serve us still ! "

52. She ceased ; and he, though mercy could with pain
Subdue a heart so full of rage and pride,
Relents, her reasons move, her prayers constrain,—
Such intercessor must not be denied ;
Thus, though reluctant, he at length complied :
" The plea for the fair pleader I receive ;
I can refuse thee nothing ; this," he cried,
" May justice be or mercy,—let them live ;
Guiltless—I set them free, or guilty I forgive ! "

53. Restored to life and liberty, how blest,
How truly blest was young Olindo's fate !
For sweet Sophronia's blushes might attest,
That love at length has touch'd her delicate
And generous bosom ; from the stake in state
They to the altar pass ; severely tried,
In doom and love already made his mate,
She now objects not to become his bride,
And grateful live with him who for her would have died.

54. But as the tyrant deem'd it insecure
That such rare virtues should so near combine,
Their pleasant home he forced them to abjure,
And banished both the bounds of Palestine ;
Nor wholly yet renouncing his design
Against the rest, he follows up the blow ;
Some does he exile, some does he confine ;
O with what sorrow, yea, with what deep woe,
Their babes, their ancient sires, and dwellings they forego !

55. For those alone his jealousy exiled,
Of vigorous manhood and sagacious wit :—
The softer sex, the grandsire, and the child,
For daring deeds and fearful aims unfit,
As pledges he retains ; the many quit
Their homes as wanderers, many brave his hate,
And, brooding in rebellion, but submit
To his scorn'd power his fall t' accelerate ;—
These join the Christian host now entering Emmaus gate.

56. Emmaus, a city at so short a space
From regal Salem, that a youth in June,
Walking for pleasure at a careless pace,
From dewy morn, may reach the town by noon;
So near, what joys the soldiers' hearts attune!
O with what deep desire they burn, to tread
The glorious City they shall see so soon!
But the sun hastens to his seagreen bed,
And Godfrey gives command the evening tents to spread.

57. They were already pitch'd and twilight gloom
Was gath'ring fast round eve's declining light,
When lo! two Barons in a strange costume,
And pomp of foreign bearing, came in sight;
Their state seem'd fashion'd to a peaceful plight,
And every desultory movement told
A friendly purpose; tendant on each knight
Rode many a page and armor-bearer bold;
From Egypt's king they come, high argument to hold.

58. The one, Alethes, of vile lineage sprung,
Who in obscurest shade his course began,
Rose, by smooth flatt'ries and a fluent tongue,
To the first honors of the grave Divan;
A supple, crafty, various-witted man,—
Prompt at deceit, perfidious in his phrase,
He with a smile of sweetness could trepan;
And wove his webs in such ingenious ways,
That each calumnious charge had all the air of praise.

59. Argantes the Circassian, his compeer,
Came to the Court a stranger, but endow'd
With valor equal to the loftiest sphere,
Was soon a Satrap of the realm avow'd;
Impatient, fierce, implacable and proud,
In arms unwearied and unmatch'd, he trod:
A scorner of all faiths, with vaunts aloud
He braved the world; his argument his nod,
He made his will his law, and his good sword his God.

60. They ask'd an audience, and on equal feet
Enter'd the tent of Godfrey: him they found
In simple vesture on a simple seat,
Calmly conversing with his chieftains round;
But genuine worth, though negligent, is crown'd
With a sufficient ornament, array'd
In its own excellence; no mark profound
Of his respect the frank Argantes paid,
But with unstudied ease just bow'd his haughty head.

61. But on his heart Alethes laid his hand,
And bow'd his head to earth, and every sign
Of honor show'd, that glory could demand,
Or the smooth flattery of the East combine.
He spake, and from his lips than golden wine
More sweet, the floods of eloquence distill'd ;
And as the Franks the speech of Palestine
Now comprehended, and at need could build,
'Twas thus his rich-toned voice the mute assembly fill'd.

62. "O Thou, th' alone deserving to preside
O'er these illustrious heroes, who have known
Through thy wise councils, hitherto, the pride
Of conquest—laurels won, and states o'erthrown !
Thy name, which brooks not in the narrow zone
Of brave Alcides' bounds to be confined,
E'en to the land of Egypt has been blown ;—
Through all our realms does Fame her clarion wind
Sounding thy glorious deeds from Nile to utmost Ind.

63. "Nor midst so many Princes is there one
Whose deepest wonder these do not excite ;
But mine indeed receives them, not alone
With admiration, but supreme delight ;
He joys to show them in each shifting light,
And loves in thee what with the rest but cause
Envy and fear ; admiring thus thy might,
And to thy valor yielding meet applause,
With thee he seeks to join, in love if not in laws.

64. "Urged then by this benign desire, he sends,
The branch of peace to ask and to bestow,
And since not Faith can mediate to our ends,
Let mutual Virtue wreathe the sacred bough ;
But since the rumor meets his ear, that thou
Art arm'd to drive from Salem his ally,
His princely mind he wills that we avow,
Ere the full tempest overcasts the sky,
So may succeeding ills thy borders come not nigh.

65. "He begs thy generous spirit to forbear,
And rest content with what thy sword has won ;
Nor vex Judea, but all regions spare
That lie beneath the favor of his sun
He, on his part, no sacrifice will shun
To fix thy infant power upon a rock ·
Whence, should the Turks and Persians seek to o'er-
run

The land once more, united you shall mock
Their overweening hopes, and smile away the shock.

66. "Thy mighty deeds in this brief period wrought,
Years of oblivion shall corrode in vain!
Armies and cities conquer'd, perils sought,
Fatigues surmounted, unknown wilds made plain!
So that the nations far and near remain
Dumb with amazement, stupid with dismay:
Yet other empires thou perhaps might'st gain,
But Glory is thy bankrupt, nor would they,
Void of renown, the toil of victory repay.

67. "Now is thy noon of honor, but the night
Succeeds to noon: and wise it surely were
To shun the dubious accidents of fight,—
If conqueror, conquest proves a fruitless care;
But—once beguiled in Fate's malignant snare,
Empire, past spoils, and victories, all are cross'd!
He is the fool of fortune who should dare
To stake a sure against a doubtful cost,
Where slight the gain must prove, but great th' advantage lost!

68. "Yet the advice of some one whom it grieves
That others long should keep what they acquire,
The having gather'd victory's laurel leaves
In every contest, and th' innate desire
Which glows, and always lights its fiercest fire
In greatest hearts, to see thy harness'd car
Drawn by dependent kings,—these will inspire
Thy mind, perchance, to banish peace afar,
With a more eager zeal than others angry war.

69. "Such will exhort thee to pursue the path
Which Fate expands to thy dilating eye,
And not to sheathe the famous sword whose wrath
Calls down obsequious conquest from the sky,
Till Mahomet's tall fanes in ruin lie,
And Asia has become one wilderness
Resounding only to the dragon's cry:
Things sweet to hear, deceits in brilliant dress,
But full of dangerous ills, and pregnant with distress.

70. "But if thine eye no keen resentment veils,
If it strikes not the light of reason blind,
With fear, not hope, must thou regard the scales
Of war, and tremble as the beam's inclined;

For Fortune's favor is a varying wind,
Wafting now ill, now good,—now joy, now woe!
She least rewards us when she seems most kind;
Oft serpents lurk where freshest roses blow,
And for the loftiest flight a gulf yawns deep below

71. "Say, if Cassano's son with his allies,
Persian and Turk, the struggle should renew;
If to thy cost all Egypt should arise,
In gold, arms, wisdom, mighty to subdue;
Whence, as more near the gathering tempests drew,
Wouldst thou thine armaments command, or where
Escape the peril? wouldst thou seek, anew,
From the Greek prince professions yet more fair,
And, of his aid assured, the frightful contest dare?

72. "Who knows not to what end the Grecian swears,
Yet from a single treason gather all,—
From thousands rather, for a thousand snares
Has he disposed, thy warriors to enthrall;
Think of his avarice, his mistrust recall!
Will he who own'd your mission, yet withstood,
Now risk his life at your beseeching call?
He who forbade the route by all pursued,
Yield to a tottering cause his own luxurious blood?

73. "But, it may be, that all thy hopes repose
On these brave hearts that gird thee as a zone;
Perhaps thou think'st to crush united foes
Lightly as one by one they were o'erthrown;
Although thy squadrons, as thyself must own,
Are much reduced by hardships and by fight;
Though fresh antagonists surround thy throne;
And, numerous as our locusts to the sight,
With Turk and Persian both th' Egyptians may unite.

74. "But granting Heaven's almightiness decree
That War's devouring minister, the sword,
Which fatal proves to others, harm not thee,
Famine will bow thee still! when, unrestored,
Life's rosy currents from the heart are pour'd,
Where wilt thou turn? what refuge will remain?
Quails in the desert will thy God afford?
Wave thy bright sword, thy javelin shake!—'tis vain;
Victory will nothing be but mockery of thy pain.

75. "The prudent people, politic in need,
Have fired their cultured fields, despoil'd their bowers,

And ere thy coming stored the golden seed
In stubborn walls and high protecting towers;
Thou, whose hot zeal spurr'd on the lazy hours
To speed thee here, how wilt thou banquet these,
Thy horse and foot? Thou wilt reply, 'My Powers
Are safe, my rich Armada sweeps the seas:'
Does then your life depend upon the shifting breeze?

76. "Perhaps thy Genius rules the winds to be
Stormy or calm, as it may suit thy will!
Though proof to prayers and wailings, the deaf sea,
Like a lull'd child, will hear thy voice, and still
Its stormy waves! but have we then no skill
With the brave Turks and Persians to combine,
Man the joint navy, to the breezes shrill
Spread out its sails, and rushing through the brine,
Boldly confront those vast leviathans of thine?

77. "A double victory must thou win, to gain
In this emprise the merit of success;
One battle lost makes all thine efforts vain,
Makes glory shame, and luxury nakedness;
For if our winged fleets thy fleet oppress
At sea, the distant host with hunger dies,
And if the host in battle we distress,
Thy naval spoils are vain indemnities,—
Thy watery empire gain'd, an unsubstantial prize!

78. "Now, in this aspect of affairs, if thou
The peace and friendship of our king decline,
Let truth but license have, she will avow,
Thy other virtues far thy sense outshine;
But ah, may Heaven, if such be thy design,
From the enthralling charm thy mind release!
That so at length afflicted Palestine—
That Asia so may from her sorrows cease,
And thou thy victor's fruits enjoy in perfect peace!

79. "And you, who in deep troubles, perils dark,
And fancied glory, are with him combined!
Let not kind Fortune tempt you to embark
In other wars; but dread the woes behind!
The pilot who, from the capricious wind,
O'er seas where quicksands lurk and breakers roar
Has steer'd his vessel to the port assign'd,
Should gather in his canvas, heave ashore,
Nor trust the traitor winds nor cruel Ocean more!"

80. Alethes ceased, and the brave Lords return'd
A murmur like the sound of fire, that told
How angrily his overtures they spurn'd ;
Fierce were their gestures, and their action bold ;
Godfrey his eyes thrice round the circle roll'd ;
Thrice the knights' faces scann'd with conscious pride ;
Then, as in act his purpose to unfold,
The fluent Copt significantly eyed,
And with determined tone thus placidly replied :

81. "Bravely, Ambassador, hast thou set forth,
Now mild, now stern, the terms on which you treat :
If thy king love me, and applaud our worth,
The love is grateful, as the praise is sweet ;
The after portion of thy speech, replete
With threats of war from Heathendom combined,
And like denunciations, I will meet,
And in the native frankness of my mind
Answer in simple words, sincere, if less refined.

82. "Know, then, that we have borne all this distress
By land and sea,—war, want, reverses—all !
To the sole end that we might gain access
To sacred Salem's venerable wall ;
That we might free the Faithful from their thrall,
And win from God his blessing and reward :
From this no threats our spirit can appall,
For this no terms be esteem'd too hard—
Life, honors, kingdoms lost, or dignity debarr'd.

83. "For not the lusts of power or gold affect
The hearts of those who rank beneath the Cross ·
Heaven's gracious Father chasten and correct
The deadly sins, if such our souls engross!
Nor let th' insidious plague, the pleasing gloss
Of honey'd guilt infect us, or delude !
But may his holy fires purge off our dross,
Through stony hearts infuse a milder mood,
Bind the rebellious will, and teach us to be good !

84. "This has impell'd us, guided, guides us now
Through every peril, obstacle, and snare ;
This makes the vales aspire, the mountains bow ;
Tempers the summer-heat, the winter air ;
This makes the loud seas still, the rivers bare,
Chains the wild tempest in its secret cave,
Sends the four seasons mild, the blue skies fair,
Beats down high bulwarks and unnerves the brave ;
Scatters our foes in flight, or dooms to the dark grave.

85. "Hence zeal and hope, hence strength, hence safety springs
Not from our own force, wasted, worn and frail;
Not from the rich Armada's outspread wings;
Not from the succors that from Greece may sail!
Power, hosts, and fleets, were else of small avail:
But since high Heaven our banner thus befriends,
We little reck what other aids may fail;
Who knows both how it strikes, and how defends,
Will ask none other shield when peril swift descends.

86. "But should our sins, or secret judgment doom
Us, of his aid deprived, to pass away,
Which of us would not yearn to have his tomb,
Where once the limbs of the Celestial lay?
Yes, we shall die, nor envy them the play
Of being who survive! yes, we shall fall,
But fall not unrevenged, in meek array;
Asia shall smile not at our funeral;
We shall not grieve to die, but furnish grief for all.

87. "As others fear and shun the battle-field,
Think not the happy arts of peace we fly;
That union with thy king no joy would yield,
Or that we should not rate his friendship high;
But Palestine does not subjected lie
To him; thou know'st it; whence then all this care
On its account? would he to us deny
Conquest of others' states? let him forbear;
And rule in peace his own, rich, flourishing, and fair!"

88. Thus answer'd Godfrey, and his calm reply
Stung to the quick Argantes' heart of pride,
He did not veil it, but approaching nigh,
With quivering lips in proud assumption cried:
"Who wills not peace the battle can abide!
Ne'er was there penury of risk or woe
To those whose rashness dared to be defied,
Too well a warlike spirit will thou show,
If the fair gifts we bring thou carest to forego!"

89. He took his mantle by the skirt; he curved
As to an urn the implicated fold,
And holding it on high, his language nerved
With angrier eye and malice uncontroll'd:
"Ho, thou contemner of strong Fate, behold!
I bring thee in this urn both war and peace;
Make now thy choice, and quickly be it told—

War, peace or war; whichever most may please—
What more thou wouldst demand, thine own right hand
must seize!"

90. At his fierce gesture and disdainful voice,
Inflamed, from all their seats the Barons sprung;
They waited not to hear their Leader's choice,
"War! war!" they cried, with simultaneous tongue.
He far abroad the fatal mantle flung,
And shook it in their teeth: "Then evermore
Take mortal war!" he cried: so wildly rung
The words, it seem'd the adamantine door
Which awful Janus keeps, flew open to the roar.

91. It seem'd that from the shaking of the fold
Gigantic Discord and mad Fury flew;
That in his frightful eyes they might behold
Megara and Alecto rise to view;
So stood, perchance, the Giant, when he drew
To Shinaär's plain his nations, to defy
The God of Heaven, and as the huge Tower grew
Upward from earth, perchance with such an eye
He watch'd it pass the clouds, and threat the starry sky

92. Then Godfrey spake: "Our answer ye have heard;
Back to your monarch, and our choice relate:
Here let him haste, or, on a Prince's word,
Nile shall behold us at Alcairo's gate."
Then in mild accents ending high debate,
He honors them with gifts of noble price;
A splendid helmet, temper'd to rebate
The keenest falchion, and of rare device,
He to Alethes gave, a spoil from conquer'd Nice.

93. Argantes has a sword of princely cost,
Whose hilt and pommel, gay with jewels flame,
Set in bright gold so curiously emboss'd,
That the rare workmanship might almost shame
The rich material; he its temper'd frame
Shrewdly examined, the keen edge assay'd,
Found the fine steel th' adornments well became,
And said to Godfrey, as he sheath'd the blade;
"Soon shalt thou see the use that of thy gift is made!"

94. No more he deign'd, but took his leave: "And now,
My brave Alethes, let us both begone;
I to Jerusalem, to Egypt thou,—
Thou when morn's roses o'er the skies are strown,

With our attendant pages, I alone
By the nocturnal stars. You need not us,
Nor our advices to instruct the throne;
Bear thou the answer,—I'll no longer thus
Stand trifling here, since arms the subject must discuss."

95. Thus parts the foe who came ambassador:
Whether his well or ill-timed haste offend
The law of realms and usages of war
He thinks not, cares not, so he gains his end;
Nor waits to hear the answer which his friend
Has on his lips, but through the twilight-shade
His steps to high Jerusalem ascend,
Impatient of delay; and those who stay'd,
Did with no less disdain the slow-paced hours upbraid.

96. 'Tis eve; 'tis night; a holy quiet broods
O'er the mute world—winds, waters are at peace;
The beasts lie couch'd amid unstirring woods,
The fishes slumber in the sounds and seas;
No twitt'ring bird sings farewell from the trees.
Hush'd is the dragon's cry, the lion's roar;
Beneath her glooms a glad oblivion frees
The heart from care, its weary labors o'er,
Carrying divine repose and sweetness to its core.

97. But not the midnight hush, nor starlight balm,
Nor sweet oblivion of all things in sleep,
Can to the Chief or army bring the calm
Of blest repose, such eager watch they keep,
In their desire to see the morning peep,
And give that long-sought City to their sight,
Where they the fruits of battle hope to reap;
Oft looking out to mark if yet the light,
Breaking the dappled East, clears up the shades of night.

END OF CANTO II.

JERUSALEM DELIVERED.

CANTO III.

ARGUMENT.

CLORINDA bravely meets the Franks in fight,
When at Jerusalem the host arrives;
Erminia's love awakens at the sight
Of Tancred in the field; his own revives,
When a strange knight, with whom in war he strives,
Appears unmask'd; Argantes at a blow
The brave Adventurers of their Chief deprives:
Dudon interr'd, for timbers to lay low
The town, to antique groves the Latin soldiers go.

JERUSALEM DELIVERED.

CANTO III.

1. THE odorous air, morn's messenger, now spread
Its wings to herald, in serenest skies,
Aurora issuing forth, her radiant head
Adorn'd with roses pluck'd in Paradise ;
When in full panoply the hosts arise,
And loud and spreading murmurs upward fly,
Ere yet the trumpet sings : its melodies
They miss not long, the trumpet's tuneful cry
Gives the command to march, shrill sounding to the sky.

2. The skillful Captain, with a gentle rein
Guides their desires, and animates their force ;
And though 'twould seem more easy to restrain
Charybdis in its mad volubil course,
Or bridle Boreas in, when gruffly hoarse
He tempests Apenninus and the gray
Ship-shaking Ocean to its deepest source,—
He ranks them, urges, rules them on the way ;
Swiftly they march, yet still with swiftness under sway.

3. Wing'd is each heart, and winged every heel ;
They fly, yet notice not how fast they fly ;
But by the time the dewless meads reveal
The fervent sun's ascension in the sky,
Lo, tower'd Jerusalem salutes the eye !
A thousand pointing fingers tell the tale ;
"Jerusalem !" a thousand voices cry,
"All hail, Jerusalem !" hill, down, and dale,
Catch the glad sounds, and shout, "Jerusalem, all hail !"

4. Thus, when a crew of fearless voyagers,
Seeking new lands, spread their audacious sails
In the hoar Arctic, under unknown stars,

Sport of the faithless waves and treach'rous gales ;
If, as their little bark the billow scales,
One views the long-wish'd headland from the mast,
With merry shouts the far-off coast he hails,
Each points it out to each, until at last
They close in present joy the troubles of the past.

5. To the pure pleasure which that first far view
In their reviving spirits sweetly shed,
Succeeds a deep contrition, feelings new,—
Grief touch'd with awe, affection mix'd with dread ;
Scarce dare they now upraise the abject head,
Or turn to Zion their desiring eyes,
The chosen city ! where Messias bled,
Defrauded Death of his long tyrannies,
New clothed his limbs with life, and reassumed the skies!

6. Low accents, plaintive whispers, groans profound,
Sighs of a people that in gladness grieves,
And melancholy murmurs float around,
Till the sad air a thrilling sound receives,
Like that which sobs amidst the dying leaves,
When with autumnal winds the forest waves ;
Or dash of an insurgent sea that heaves
On lonely rocks, or lock'd in winding caves,
Hoarse through their hollow aisles in wild low cadence raves.

7. Each, at his Chief's example, lays aside
His scarf and feather'd casque, with every gay
And glitt'ring ornament of knightly pride,
And barefoot treads the consecrated way.
Their thoughts, too, suited to their changed array,
Warm tears devout their eyes in showers diffuse,—
Tears, that the haughtiest temper might allay ;
And yet, as though to weep they did refuse,
Thus to themselves their hearts of hardness they accuse:

8. "Here, Lord, where currents from thy wounded side
Stain'd the besprinkled ground with sanguine red,
Should not these two quick springs at least, their tide
In bitter memory of thy passion shed !
And melt'st thou not, my icy heart, where bled
Thy dear Redeemer? still must pity sleep?
My flinty bosom, why so cold and dead ?
Break, and with tears the hallow'd region steep :
If that thou weep'st not now, forever shouldst thou weep !"

9\. Meanwhile the Guard that from a lofty tower
In the far city cast abroad his view,
Mark'd the dust rise, and like a thunder-shower
Printed in air, turn dark th' ethereal blue ;
The gloomy cloud seem'd pregnant as it flew
With fire,—anon, bright metals flash'd between
Its shaken wreaths, and as it nearer drew,
Dim through the storm were apparitions seen—
Spearmen, and issuing steeds, and chiefs of godlike mein

10\. He saw, and raised his terrible alarm ;
"O rise, all citizens below, arise ;
Mount to the walls ; haste ! arm ! this instant arm !
Lo, what a dust upon the whirlwind flies,
And lo, the lightning of their arms !" he cries,—
"The foeman is at hand !" then, yet more loud,
He calls, "Shall the swift foe the town surprise ?
Quick, seize your weapons ; mark the dusty cloud
That hither rolls ! it wraps all heaven within its shroud !"

11\. The simple infant and the aged sire,
Matrons and trembling maids, to whom belong
Nor strength, nor skill to make defense, retire,
A pale, disconsolate, and suppliant throng,
In sad procession to the mosques : the strong
In spirit as in limbs, obey the call ;
Seizing their arms in haste, they speed along,
Part flock to guard the gates, part man the wall :
The king to all parts flies, sees, cares, provides for all.

12\. His orders given, for every need prepared,
He from the thick'ning tumult has withdrawn,
And scales a tower that 'twixt two portals rear'd,
O'erlooks the plain, and holds the hills in scorn.
His steps Erminia, lovely as the morn,
At call attends ; with all respect received,
His royal Court her winning charms adorn,
Since Antioch by the Christians was achieved,
And o'er her kingly sire the orphan-princess grieved.

13\. Meantime Clorinda hastes against the Franks,
First of her band, with many a gallant knight,
While in a secret porch Argantes ranks
His troops, prepared for rescue or for fight.
Her words, intrepid as her mein, excite
Fire in all hearts, as thus the heroine spoke :
"Well it becomes us, arm'd in Asia's right,

To found the loosening of her hated yoke
On the auspicious base of some determined stroke !

14. Lo, Fortune, as she speaks, th' occasion yields !
A band of Franks sent onward to forecast
The army's wants, from foraging the fields,
Near them, with flocks and herds returning, pass'd
She towards them, and to her rush'd as fast
Their Chief, when he beheld her silver crest ,—
Guardo his name, a man of puissance vast,
But weak with her the laurel to contest ;—
Onward abrupt they drove, their lances laid in rest.

15. Breathless to earth the hapless Frank was strook
By the fierce shock, in either army's sight ;
From his mischance the shouting Pagans took
Their joyous augury of the future fight :
Onward she flew upon the rest, the might
Of numbers flashing in her single blade ;
Fast in their serried ranks she pour'd the light ;
Her warriors follow'd through the gap she made,
Where her assault had been, where yet her falchion play'd.

16. Soon from the spoiler they the spoil obtain ;
The Franks give way, yet to their standard keep,
Till slow the summit of a hill they gain,
And stand assisted by the rising steep :
When as a tempest, which the whirlwinds sweep
Abroad, breaks loose, and in aërial dance
Warm from its skirts the vivid lightnings leap,
Tancred at Godfrey's beck made swift advance
With his Italian troop, and couch'd his quivering lance.

17. The kind beheld him from his tower, and deem'd
Him of all men the choicest cavalier,
So young, so resolute, so brave he seem'd,
And bore with such a grace his beamy spear :
Whence he bespake the fair Erminia near,
Whose palpitating heart in secret thrill'd
As at the sight of something deeply dear ;
"Well shouldst thou know, in many a fighting field
Mark'd out, each Christian knight, howe'er in arms conceal'd."

18. "Who then is this, that in fierce grace outstrips
All other knights ?" In room of a reply,
The quick breath flutter'd round her lovely lips,

The big tear trembled in her full blue eye:
These she reclaim'd, yet not so carelessly
As to escape regard,—a conscious red
Tinged her averted cheek, the sudden sigh,
Choked to a groan, spoke plain of feeling fled,
And o'er her tearful eyes a radiant circlet spread.

19. In these delusive words her answer ran
Veiling her love beneath the mask of hate;
"Too well I know th' inexorable man,
And should, amidst a thousand! but of late,
His savage soul I saw him satiate
With slaughter,—saw him flesh his angry steel
Upon the best of our Assyrian state:
Cruel are all his strokes! the wounds they deal,
No magic charm can stanch, no breathing balsam heal!

20. "He is Prince Tancred; oh that he, some day,
Might be my slave! I would not wish him dead;
Glad that he lives, so might I thus repay
In sweet revenge my wrongs upon his head!
That would indeed be some small joy," she said.
And the king fail'd not, as she wish'd, to wrest
The meaning of her words, ascribed, instead
Of love, to hate: she ceased, but from her breast
Stole forth a mournful sigh that would not be repress'd.

21. Meanwhile Clorinda rushes to assail
The Prince, and level lays her spear renown'd:
Both lances strike, and on the barr'd ventayle
In shivers fly, and she remains discrown'd;
For, burst its silver rivets, to the ground
Her helmet leap'd, (incomparable blow!)
And by the rudeness of the shock unbound,
Her sex to all the field emblazoning so,
Loose to the charmed winds her golden tresses flow.

22. Then blazed her eyes, then flash'd her angry glance,
Sweet e'en in wrath; in laughter then what grace
Would not be theirs!—but why that thoughtful trance?
And, Tancred, why that scrutinizing gaze?
Know'st not thine idol? lo, the same dear face,
Whence sprang the flame that on thy heart has prey'd
The sculptured image in its shine retrace,
And in thy foe behold the noble maid,
Who to the sylvan spring for cool refreshment stray'd.

23. He, who her painted shield and silver crest
Mark'd not at first, stood spell-bound at the sight;
She, guarding as she could her head, still press'd
Th' assault, and struck, but he forbore the fight,
And to the rest transferring his despite,
Plied fast his whirling sword; yet not the less
Ceased she to follow and upbraid his flight,
With taunt and menace heightening his distress;
And, "Turn, false knight!" she cried, loud shouting through the press.

24. Struck, he not once returns the stroke, nor seeks
So much to ward the meditated blow,
As in those eyes and on those charming cheeks
To gaze, whence Passion's fond emotions flow:
"Void," to himself he says, "too cruel foe,
Void fall the strokes which that beloved arm
Distributes in its wrath! no fatal throe
Is that thy cimeter creates; the harm
Is in thy angry looks, that wound me while they charm!"

25. Resolved at length not unconfess'd to fall,
Though hopeless quite her pity to obtain,
That she might know she struck her willing thrall,
Defenseless, suppliant, crouching to her chain;
"O thou," said he, "that followest o'er the plain
Me as thine only foe, of all this wide
Presented people! yet thy wrath restrain;
The press let us forsake, so may aside
Thy force with mine be proved, my skill with thine be tried.

26. "Then shalt thou measure in the face of day
Thy strength with mine, nor own my valor less."
Pleased she assents, and boldly leads the way,
Unhelm'd,—he follows in his mute distress.
Already stood th' impatient Warrioress
Prepared, already had she struck, when he
Exclaim'd: "Hold! hold! ere we ourselves address
To the stern fight, 'tis fit we should agree
Upon the terms of strife; fix first what these shall be!"

27. Her arm she stay'd; strong love and wild despair
A reckless courage to his mind impart;
"These be the terms," said he, "since you forswear
All peace with me, pluck out my panting heart,
Mine own no more! I willingly shall part
With life, if farther life thy pride offend;

Long have I pined with love's tormenting smart;
'Tis fit the fond and feverish strife should end;
Take then the worthless life which I will ne'er defend.

28. "Behold! my arms are offer'd,—I present
My breast without defense,—spare not to smite!
Or shall I speed the task? I am content
To strip my cuirass off, and thus invite
Thy cruel steel!"—in harsher self-despite,
The mournful youth would have proclaim'd his woes;
But suddenly, in craft or panic fright,
The Pagans yield to their pursuing foes,
And his brave troops rush by, and numbers interpose.

29. Like driven deer before th' Italian band
They yield, they fly in swiftness unconfined;
One base pursuer saw Clorinda stand,
Her rich locks spread like sunbeams on the wind,
And raised his arm in passing, from behind,
To stab secure the undefended maid;
But Tancred, conscious of the blow design'd,
Shriek'd out, "Beware!" to warn th' unconscious maid,
And with his own good sword bore off the hostile blade.

30. Still the stroke fell, and near the graceful head
Her snowy neck received the point, which drew
Some rosy drops, that crimson'd, as they shed,
Her yellow curls with their bespangling dew,
E'en thus gold beams with the blush-rose's hue,
Wher round it rubies sparkle from the hand
Of some rare artist; trembling at the view,
His wrath the Prince no longer may command,
But on the caitiff falls, and shakes his threatening brand.

31. The villain flies, and full of rage the knight
Pursues,—as arrows swift, they scour the plains:
Perplex'd she stands, and keeps them both in sight
To a great distance, nor to follow deigns,
But quickly her retreating band regains;—
Sometimes she fronts in hostile attitude
Th' arrested Franks, now flies, and now disdains
To fly,—fights, flies again, as suits her mood,
Nor can she well be term'd pursuer or pursued.

32. So in the Circus the fierce bull turns back
To gore the baying mastiffs that pursue;
They pause—but still as he resumes his track,

Their ruffian clamors savagely renew.
She, as she fled, above her shoulders threw
Her guardian buckler, like an orbed sun;
So at their sports gymnastic may we view
The fugitive Morescos shielded run,
Dext'rous the darted balls on nimble feet to shun.[5]

33. While these give chase, and those assaulted fly,
To the town-walls they now approaching drew,
When on the sudden, with a frightful cry,
Back on the Christians came the Pagan crew;
First wheeling far aloof, and then anew
Returning nigh, with circumventing skill
They on the wings and rear tempestuous flew;
While undisguised Argantes down the hill
Moved to assail the front, and shouted wild and shrill.

34. Before his troops the fierce Avenger pass'd,
All eager first to pounce upon the prey;
Over and over, at one charge he cast
The horse and rider that first cross'd his way;
And ere to shivers flew his lance, there lay
Whole heaps of such in his encumber'd track;
Then from its scabbard leaps his sword, and aye
Whom it but fully reaches to attack,
It either kills, or wounds, or beats affrighted back.

35. In rivalry of him Clorinda slew
Ardelio brave, of years now most mature,
But though by age untamed, and fenced by two
Bold sons, he was not from her sword secure:
For a sharp wound which he could ill endure,
First from the sire removed his eldest pride,
Unblest Alcander; and his trust, the sure
Young Polypherne, assistant at his side,
For his own menaced life but barely could provide.

36. But Tancred, finding that he vainly chased
The ruffian, who a swifter steed display'd,
Look'd back and saw how far intemperate haste
Hurried the valor of his bold brigade;
Hemm'd in he saw it, to the sword betray'd,
And spurring back, to the corrected rein,
His gallant steed, came quickly to their aid;
Nor he alone, but that adventurous train,
Who every risk of war unshrinkingly sustain.

37. Dudon's choice phalanx to the rescue throng,
The flower of heroes, dragons of the fight;
And noblest, bravest, foremost rush'd along,
The gay and versatile Rinaldo, light
As the wild wind; Erminia knew the knight
By his bold port and azure-tinted shield,
Where the bird argent spreads its plumes for flight,[6]
And to the king, who watch'd him through the field,
Exclaim'd, "Lo there the youth to whom all knights must yield!

38. "But few or none in tournament can vie
With him, though yet but into boyhood grown;
Could Europe six such paragons supply,
Salem were not, and Syria were o'erthrown;
The South her strong supremacy would own,
Kingdoms that lie beneath the morning star
Stoop to her rule, and in the burning zone,
Vainly perhaps would Nilus seek afar,
Amid his secret springs a refuge from the war!

39. "Rinaldo is his name; his angry sword
More threats your walls than the most huge machine;
But turn to where I point; yon noble lord,
Glitt'ring in armature of gold and green,
Is gallant Dudon, to whose call convene
The band to which I see your eyes advert,
Advent'rers chivalrous,—a warrior keen,
Who high-born, active, and in arms expert,
Greatly transcends in years, nor yields in true desert.

40. "That towering figure, sheath'd in brown, has birth
From Norway's king, Gernando is his name:
No prouder creature breathes, throughout the earth
A single foible sullying all his fame.
But lo, urged on forever by one aim,
Where Edward and his dear Gildippe move!
Their mantles, arms, and ornaments the same,
Argent! in bridal harmony they rove,
Famed both for deeds of arms, and loyalty of love."

41. While thus Erminia communes with the king,
Below, yet deeper carnage dyes the fields;
There Tancred and Rinaldo break the ring,
Dense with conflicting men and serried shields;
Then pour th' Adventurers in, and bravely wields
Each knight the weapon of his sharp disdain;
Argantes' self, the proud Argantes yields;

Beat by Rinaldo backward on the plain
In sudden shock, he scarce his footing can regain :—

42. Nor e'er had he renew'd the stern debate,
But the same instant fell Rinaldo's steed,
And from the pressure of its cumbrous weight
The noble youth not easily was freed.
Meanwhile, diffused in flight, with headlong speed,
On to the barbican the Pagans hied ;
Argantes and Clorinda sole impede—
Mounds to its wrath—th' irruptions of the tide
That on them bursts behind with such insulting pride.

43. Last they retire, and the pursuing force
Of battle hold in check, and so restrain,
That those who flee before, screen'd in their course,
With less of ruin gored the city gain.
Still Dudon, flush'd with conquest, gave the rein
To his curveting horse, that with a bound
Bore down the fierce Tigranes ; not in vain
The sharp sword struck ; he headless fell to ground,
And, savage e'en in death, superb defiance frown'd.

44. Naught his fine hauberk Algazel avails,
Naught his strong helmet Corbano defends ;
Them through the nape and back he so assails,
That through the face and breast the steel protends.
With fell Almanzor next two valiant friends,
Mahmoud and Amurath, his trenchant brand
From pleasant life to Lethe quickly sends ;
'The valor flashing from his armed hand,
Not e'en Circassia's Duke could unannoy'd withstand.

45. He frets within himself, with rage he burns,
Oft stops, wheels round, yet still the field forsakes ;
At last so sudden on his foe he turns,
And with a spring like the uncoiling snake's,
At Dudon's side so fierce a thrust he makes,
That deep within, it bathes the griding blade,
And from the Chief all power of motion takes ;
He falls ; and his shut eyes, with pain o'erweigh'd,
An adamantine sleep and quietude invade.

46. Thrice he unclosed them, and the sun's sweet light
Sought to enjoy ; thrice on his arm arose,
And thrice fell back ; then dark the veil of night
Involved his eyes, which, tired, forever close.
His limbs relax ; from all his members flows

A dead cold sweat; the pulses cease their play,
And sensibly an icy stiffness grows:
Upon the knight now dead, no idle stay
The fierce Argantes makes, but instant hies his way.

47. Yet turning, as he speeds, his cruel eye
On his antagonists, he cries aloud:
"This falchion, streaming with so bright a dye,
Is that which yesterday your prince bestow'd!
Quick! be its quittance to his ear avow'd;
Tell him what havoc it has done to-day;
Glad will he be to find a gift so proud,
Brought to its trial, stand the sharp assay;
How I must prize it, think,—how I have used it, say!

48. "Tell him, that soon he may expect to see
In his own bowels proof of it more sure;
That if he hastes not to the battle, we
Will drag him from his tented coverture!"
The irritated Franks but ill endure
The brutal message and insulting call;
All press'd to charge him; but he pass'd secure
Beneath the favor of the guarded wall,
And reach'd the rest that fled, unhurt, unharm'd of all.

49. Then from the battlements of either tower,
A storm of stones obscured the sleety air,
And arrows, an immitigable shower,
Innumerable archers fulmine there
From the tough bow; the Christians pause,—they dare
No further press, but shrinking from the storm,
Perforce the relics of the Pagans spare;
'Twas then Rinaldo show'd his martial form,
Freed from his fallen horse, as Jove's red lightnings warm.

50. He came, on the barbaric homicide
Slain Dudon's debt with usury to repay,
And to his pausing troops sublimely cried,
"What wait you for! what means this base delay?
Slain is the gallant lord, your Chieftain,—say,
What is it stays you? what is it appalls?
Forward this instant, and the town essay!
What! when so great a cause for vengeance calls,
Shall we be held in check by these weak mold'ring walls?

51. "No! though with adamant each charmed tower
Were flank'd or triply fenced with stubborn steel,
Safe in its pale th' assassin should not cower,
But the full measure of your vengeance feel;
On! on!" and seconding the high appeal
By instant action, to the walls, before
All else he rushes; in his ardent zeal
Scorning with guarded head the shower and roar
Of stones and shafts, and darts, that from the engines
pour.

52. He shakes his sable plumes, he lifts his face,
So full of fierce resolve, that it enchains
The energies of all who guard the place,—
An icy fear runs thrilling through their veins
While thus the seized advantage he maintains,
And those to menace seeks, and these to cheer,
In rushes one who his desire restrains;
Godfrey has sent to them the good Sigièr,
Of his discreet command th' executor severe;

53. Who in his reverenced name commands them back,
And chides a step so rash and so absurd:
"This is no time," he cries, "for the attack;
Godfrey recalls you from the risk incurr'd.
Back! back!" Rinaldo, who the rest had spurr'd
To the near danger, thus compell'd to yield,
Slowly receded, utt'ring not a word,
But inly chafed, and outwardly reveal'd
More than one pregnant sign of anger, ill conceal'd.

54. Unharrass'd of the foe, by due degrees,
The Franks bore off, and full of sorrow paid
The last sad rites, and solemn offices
Due to the person of the noble dead;
Borne in their pious arms, his friends convey'd
The sacred weight along,—while on the height
Of fair Mount Olivet, the Duke survey'd
The city's strength, appliances, and site;
Rampire, and battled crag, and fastness shaped for fight.

55. On two bold hills Jerusalem is seen,
Of size unequal, face to face opposed;
A wide and pleasant valley lies between,
Dividing hill from hill; three sides, the coast
Lies craggy, difficult, and high, disposed
In steep acclivities; the fourth is cast
In gentlest undulations, and inclosed

By walls of height insuperable and vast,
That seem to brave the sky, and face the Arctic blast.

56. Cisterns for rain, canals, and living fountains
Make glad the thirsty city ; but around,
Barren, and bare, and naked are the mountains,
And scarce one solitary flower is found
To blosom near : no sylvans, sun-embrown'd,
Shut out the fervid noon ; no valley shines
With lapse of lakes, nor falling waters sound ;
One forest yet the blue horizon lines,
Black with the baleful shades of cypresses and pines.

57. Here, tow'rd the regions of the orient day,
The stately Jordan leads its happy wave ;
There, where the solemn sunset fades away,
A sandy shore Levantine billows lave ;
North, with Samaria Bethel stands, which gave
Fires to the Golden Calf, of hell beguiled ;
And last, where Auster from his southern cave
Let loose the showery winds and tempest wild,
Bethlehem, whose matron lap received the Heaven-born Child.

58. Now as the Chief the city's walls espied—
Its strength, its site—and in his wisdom weigh'd
Where best he could encamp, and on which side
The hostile towers might safest be essay'd,
To Aladine divine Erminia said,
Her eager finger pointing to the place ;
"That Godfrey is, in purple robes array'd !
Observe, with what a military grace
He moves ! august his port, and dignified his pace !

59. "He of a truth was born for empire : yes !
So well he knows to govern and command ;
Great as a general, as a knight no less,
Scepter and sword were fashion'd to his hand !
I know not one of all that countless band,
More warlike, or more wise ; Raymond the sage,
Perhaps in counsel by his side might stand,
Rinaldo, Tancred equal warfare wage,
These from their sprightlier youth, and Raymond from his age."

60. "Him," the king answer'd, "I remember well :
I saw him at the splendid Court of France,
When envoy there from Egypt, and could tell

How gallantly in joust he bore his lance ;
And though his years, which then did scarce advance
Beyond gay boyhood, had begun to grave
No manly lines on his smooth cheek, his glance
Bold deeds, reflective mind, and semblance brave,
Of loftiest hopes e'en then a certain presage gave.

61. "Too sure, alas !" and here his troubled eyes
He cast to earth, till gath'ring voice, he said :
"But who is he that as an equal vies
With him, in mantle of resplendent red ?
How like in form and visage ! e'en his tread
Betrays a strange similitude, though less
I deem his stature : " "That," rejoin'd the maid,
"Is Baldwin, like in aspect and address.
But brother most in soul and princely nobleness.

62. "Now mark the man near Godfrey, in the guise
Of an adviser ; he deserves all praise !
That is Earl Raymond, prudent, close, and wise,
Of rev'rend tresses white with length of days ;
Such politic maneuvers none displays—
Latin or Frank—in battle to o'erwhelm
Or to deceive ; but he that blinds our gaze,
The sunshine playing on his gilded helm,
Is William, the young hope of Britain's distant realm.

63. "With him is Guelph, in rich estates, high blood,
And thirst for honor equal with the best ;
I know him well by his firm attitude,
By his broad shoulders and dilated chest :
But my chief foe, for whom in eager quest
I have so long look'd round, I nowhere see,
Fell Bohemond, th' assassin ! he oppres'd
My subjects, slew my sire, and left to me
No joy but that of tears, no friends but Heaven and thee !"

64. Thus commune they ; while, having well survey'd
The City, Bouillon join'd his hosted train,
And as he judged that battery and scalade
On all sides else would be essay'd in vain,—
Against the Northern Gate, on the near plain
Fixing his standard, he encamps ; and thence
His quarter'd troops extending, till they gain
The Corner Tower, the whole vast field presents
One long continuous scene of equipage and tents.

65. By this extensive circuit the third part
Of the devoted City was embraced;
And though it baffled all his power and art,
(Such was its range) the whole to circumvest,
Yet what he could to obviate and arrest
All partial aids that to the town might flow,
His active genius compass'd; he possess'd
The heights around, the valley-paths below,
And each strong pass that gave admittance to and fro.

66. And fortified his camp, and fenced it well
With bristling palisade and yawning fosse,
Strong to oppose the sallying Infidel,
And all eruptions of a foreign force.
That task accomplish'd, he would see the corse
Of his slain friend; he reach'd the fatal tent,
Where, grieving at th' irreparable loss,
The soldiers o'er their lifeless Chieftain bent,
And one wild sob ran round of anguish and lament.

67. His bosom friends the high bier had adorn'd
With ceremonial pomp, a solemn show;
And when the Chief appear'd amidst them, mourn'd
In louder accents, with a tenderer woe;
But pious Godfrey gave no tear to flow,
Not all serene, nor clouded was his look;
Dumb for awhile, his fix'd eyes seem'd to grow
To the loved form they contemplate:—he broke
Silence at length, and thus in calm dejection spoke:

68. "Tears are not now thy due! from the world's toil,
Gone to assume in heaven the brighter birth;
A winged Angel, from thy mortal coil
Escaped, thy glory lingers yet round earth!
Christ's hallow'd warrior living thou went'st forth,
Christ's champion didst thou die; and now, blest Shade,
The crown and palm of righteousness and worth
Thou wear'st, with joys unspeakable repaid,
Feeding thine eyes on things to fancy unportray'd!

69. "Yes! thou liv'st happy; and if yet we keep
Vigils of grief, and echo groan for groan,
'Tis not for thee, but for ourselves we weep,
Whose noblest pillar lies in thee o'erthrown;
But though pale Death (a title we disown)
Of earthly aid has stripp'd and render'd vain
Our arms, bright legions stand before the throne,

And raised thyself to that selected train,
Still may thy suit for us celestial aids obtain.

70. "And as we saw thee, while a mortal, shield
With mortal arms our cause, let us descry
Thy conqu'ring hand for our advantage wield
Heaven's fatal arms, a spirit of the sky!
Hear now the vows we offer up; be nigh,
And in the hour of ultimate distress
Send down immortal succors from on high;
So will we raise to thee for wrought success,
Hymns of triumphal praise, and in our temples bless!"

71. He ceased: the last bright beams of day were spent,
And eve ascending in the starless air,
Imposed a sweet oblivion on lament,
Rest to each toil, a truce to every care;
But Godfrey still watch'd, anxious to prepare
The mighty engines, without which he knew
The toil of war would be a brave despair;
Then how to frame their shape, and whence to hew
Materials for the work, perplex'd his mind anew.

72. But when the morn look'd forth on Jordan's flood,
The fun'ral pageant he lamenting led;
An odoriferous ark of cypress wood,
Near a green hill, became Lord Dudon's bed;
The hill adjoin'd the Camp, and overhead
A loftly palm its verdant foliage flung;
Last, white-robed Priests their anthem o'er the dead,
Slow-moving, hymn'd, and many a tuneful tongue
Sweet at the solemn close his requiescat sung.

73. And here and there the tree's proud branches bore
Ensigns and arms, the banner and the bow,—
Spoils, which in fight more fortunate he tore
Or from the Syrian or the Persian foe;
In midst, his own pierced cuirass they bestow,
His hollow helmet, his inverted spear—
And grave this legend on the trunk below:
"*Pilgrim, a champion of the Cross revere;*
And pass this tomb with awe—brave Dudon slumbers here."

74. The Duke, when thus his piety had paid
The fun'ral rites, and shed his duteous tears,
Sent all his skill'd mechanics to invade
The forest, guarded by a thousand spears;

Veil'd by low hills it stood, the growth of years,—
A Syrian shepherd pointed out the vale,
And thither brought the Camp artificers
To fabricate the engines doom'd to scale
The City's sacred towers, and turn her people pale.

75. Each cheers on each, and to the gen'ral call
Unwonted ravage rends the woods around;
Hew'd by the iron's piercing edge, down fall,
And with their leafy honors heap the ground,
Pines, savage ashes, beeches, palms renown'd,
Funereal cypresses, the fir-tree high,
Maple, and holm with greens eternal crown'd,
And wedded elm to which the vines apply
Their virgin arms, and curl, and shoot into the sky.

76. Some fell the yews, some fell the warrior-oaks,
Whose trunks have budded to a thousand springs,
And braved immovable the thousand shocks
Of Boreas rushing on his wintry wings;
And here the alder nods, the cedar swings
On creaking wheels; some bark the trees, some square;
With shouts and clang of arms the valley rings,—
Sick with the sound, the Nymphs their haunts forswear,
The stork her nest forsakes, the lioness her lair.

END OF CANTO III.

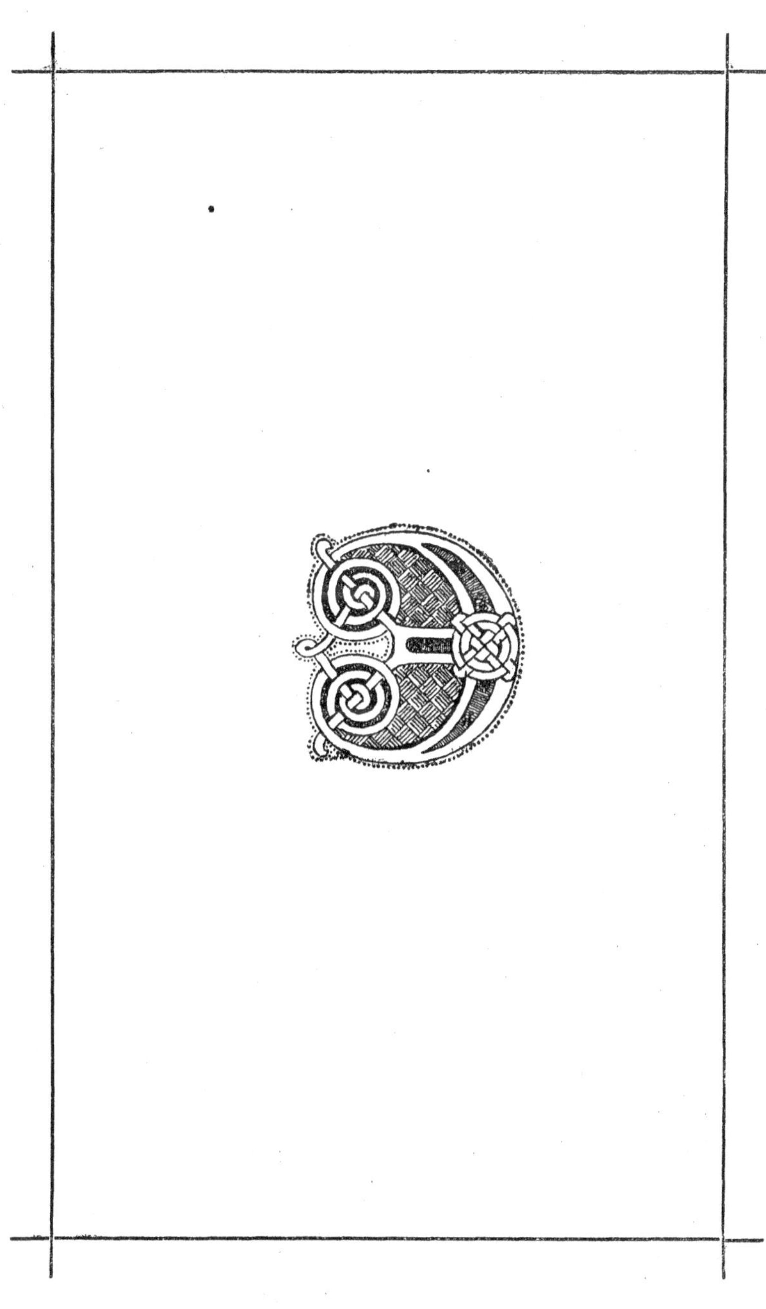

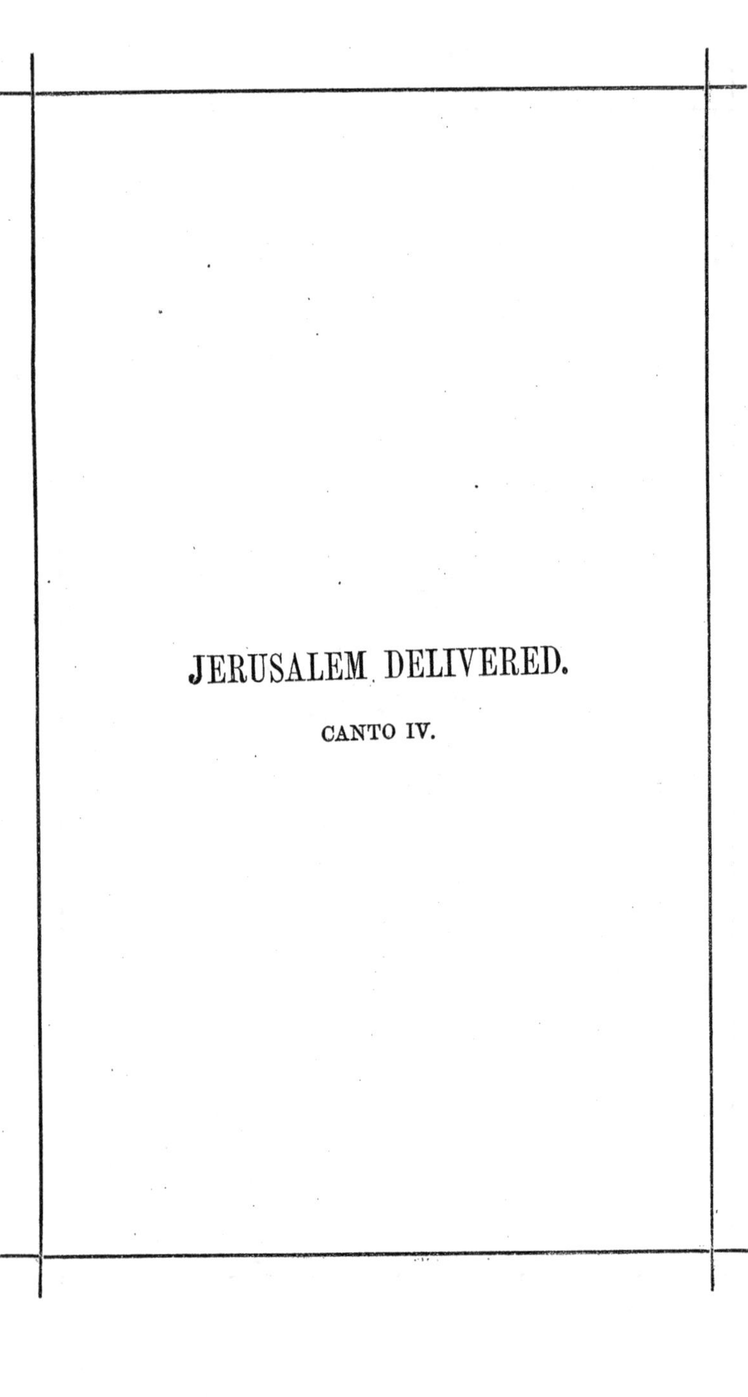

JERUSALEM DELIVERED.

CANTO IV.

ARGUMENT.

The Prince of Darkness in the realms below
His powers assembles, and in grief and rage
From Orcus lets them loose, a war of woe,
With all their art against the Franks to wage.
By them incited, Idraote the Sage
Burns with ambition, and in flatt'ring style
Studies Armida's influence to engage;
Urged, she proceeds to smooth by her sweet smile
His way—her only arms, wit, beauty, youth, and guile

JERUSALEM DELIVERED.

CANTO IV.

1. While thus in fervent toil the artisan
His warlike engines framed, of largest size,
To storm the city, the grand foe of man
Against the Christians turned his livid eyes;
And seeing them in glad societies,
On the new works successfully engaged,
Bit both his lips for fury, and in sighs
And bellowings, like a wounded bull enraged,
Roar'd forth his inward grief, and envy unassuaged.

2. Then, having run through every mode of thought
To work them sharpest ills, he gave command
That all his angels should make swift resort
To his imperial court, a horrid band!
As though it were a trivial thing to stand
(O fool!) th' antagonist of God, and spite
His will divine! unmindful of the hand
That, thund'ring through all space, from heaven's blest height
Hurl'd him of yore down—down to Tartarus and Night.

3. Its hoarse alarm the Stygian trumpet sounded
Through the dark dwellings of the damn'd; the vast
Tartarean caverns tremblingly rebounded,
Blind air rebellowing to the dreary blast:
Hell quaked with all its millions: never cast
Th' ethereal skies a discord so profound,
When the red lightning's vivid flash was past
Nor ever with such tremors rock'd the ground,;
When in its pregnant womb conflicting fires were bound.

4. The Gods of the Abyss in various swarms
From all sides to the yawning portals throng,

Obedient to the signal—frightful forms,
Strange to the sight, unspeakable in song!
Death glares in all their eyes; some prance along
On horny hoofs,—some, formidably fair,
Whose human faces have the viper's tongue,
And hissing snakes for ornamental hair,
Ride forth on dragon folds that lash the lurid air.

5. There might you hear the Harpy's clang'rous brood,
The Python's hiss, the Hydra's wailing yell,
Mad Scylla barking in her greedy mood,
And roaring Polypheme, the pride of hell;
Pale Gorgons, savage Sphinxes, Centaurs fell,
Geryons, Chimeras breathing flakes of fire,
Figures conceptionless, innumerable,
Multiform shapes conjoin'd in monsters dire,
To the vast halls of Dis in hideous troops aspire.

6. They took their station right and left around
The grisly king; he, cruel of command,
Sate in the midst of them, and sourly frown'd,
The huge, rough scepter waving in his hand.
No Alpine crag, terrifically grand,
No rock at sea in size with him could vie;
Calpe, and Atlas soaring from the sand,
Seem'd to his stature little hills, so high
Rear'd he his horned front in that Tartarean sky.

7. A horrid majesty in his fierce face
Struck deeper terror, and increased his pride;
His bloodshot eyeballs were instinct with rays
That like a baleful comet, far and wide,
Their fatal splendor shed on every side;
In rough barbaric grandeur his hoar beard
Flow'd to his breast, and like the gaping tide
Of a deep whirlpool his grim mouth appear'd,
When he unclosed his jaws, with foaming gore be-
smear'd.

8. His breath was like those sulph'rous vapors born
In thunder, stench, and the live meteor's light,
When red Vesuvius showers, by earthquakes torn,
O'er sleeping Naples in the dead of night
Funereal ashes! while he spoke, affright
Hush'd howling Cerberus, the Hydra's shriek;
Cocytus paused in its lamenting flight;
Th' abysses trembled; horror chill'd each cheek;
And these the words they heard the fall'n Archangel
speak:

9. "PRINCES OF HELL! but worthier far to fill
In Heaven, whence each one sprang, his diamond throne;
Ye, who with me were hurl'd from the blest hill,
Where brighter than the morning-star we shone,
To range these frightful dungeons! ye have known
The ancient jealousies and fierce disdains
That goaded us to battle; overthrown,
We are judged rebels, and besieged with pains,
While o'er his radiant hosts the happy victor reigns.

10. "And for th' ethereal air, serene and pure,
The golden sun, the starry spheres, his hate
Has lock'd us in this bottomless obscure,
Forbidding bold ambition to translate
Our spirits to their first divine estate;
Then, ah the bitter thought! 'tis this which aye
Stings me to madness,—then did he create
The vile worm man, that thing of reptile clay,
To fill our vacant seats in those blue fields of day.

11. "Nor this sufficed: to spite us more, he gave
His only Son, his darling to the dead;
He came, he burst hell's gates, and from the grave,
Compass'd our kingdoms with audacious tread;
The souls in torment doom'd to us, he led
Back to the skies—his richly-ransom'd throng;
And, in our teeth, hell's conquer'd ensigns spread,
Abroad on heaven's bright battlements uphung,
The while ten thousand saints their halleluiahs sung.

12. "But why renew afflictions so severe,
By numb'ring up our wrongs, already known!
When, or on what occasion did ye hear
He paused in wrath, and left his works undone?
No more o'er past indignities I run,
But present injuries and future shame—
Shall we pass these? Alas! we cannot shun
The consciousness, that now his envious aim
Is the wide nations round from darkness to reclaim.

13. What! shall we pass in sloth the days and hours,
Cherish no wrath-born lightnings in our veins,
But leave his principalities and powers
To reap fresh laurels on the Asian plains?
To lead Judea in their servile chains,
And spread his worship'd name from clime to clime?
Sound it in other tongues, in other strains,

And on fresh columns sculpture it sublime,
To teach the future age, and mock almighty Time?

14. "Must then our glorious idols be o'erthrown?
Our altars change to his? our temples nod?
Gold, incense, vows, be paid to him alone,
And Baäl bow before the shrine of God?
In the high Groves where erst we made abode
Must priest, nor charm, nor oracle remain?
And shall the myriad spirits who bestow'd
Tribute on us, that tribute now disdain,
And o'er dispeopled realms abandon'd Pluto reign?

15. "No! for our essences are yet the same,
The same our pride, our prowess, and our power,
As when with sharp steel and engirding flame,
In godlike battle we withstood the flower
Of heaven's archangels: we in evil hour
Were foil'd, I grant; but partial chance, not skill,
Gave them the victory,—still we scorn'd to cower;
Victory was theirs, but an unconquer'd will
Nobly remain'd to us—it fires our spirits still!

16. "Why longer then delay! arise, take wing,
My hope, my strength, my trusty cohorts, fly;
Plagues and swift ruin on these Christians bring,
Ere reinforced by any fresh ally;
Haste! quench the spreading flame of chivalry,
Ere in its blaze Judea all unites;
Your arts exert, your strong temptations ply;
Enter at will among their armed knights,
Now practice open force, and now use secret sleights.

17. "Let what I will, be fate! give some to rove
In exile, some in battle to be slain;
Let some, abandon'd to a lawless love,
Make woman's smiles and frowns their joy and pain,
And brilliant eyes their idols; let some stain
Their swords in civil strife; let some engage
In crimes against their Chief; let murder reign
With treason, rage with murder, hate with rage;
So perish all—priest, king, prince, noble, serf, and sage!"

18. Ere yet the Anarch closed his fierce harangue,
His rebel angels on swift wings were flown,
Glad to revisit the pure light;—a clang
Of pinions pass'd, and he was left alone.

As in their deep Eolian grottoes moan
The Spirits of the storm—as forth they sweep,
Or ere the signal of the winds is blown,
With howling sound, high carnival to keep,
And in wild uproar all embroil both land and deep;—

19. So the loosed Fiends o'er valley, wave, and hill,
Spreading their nimble wings, themselves dispersed;
Solicitous to frame, with demon-skill,
New-fancied snares, and urge their arts accursed:
But say, sweet Muse! of various ills, what first
Their malice wrought, and by what agents, say;
Thou know'st it; Fame the tidings has rehearsed,
But in the gloom remote of times grown gray,
Long ere it reach our ear, her weak voice melts away.

20. A mighty wizard in Damascus reign'd,
Prince Idraotes; who from childhood pored
O'er dark divining volumes, till he gain'd
The potent knowledge which his soul adored:
But what avail'd his whole collected hoard
Of signs and charms, if he could not foretell
The war's uncertain issues? his search soar'd
To heaven—no star, no planet own'd the spell,
Nor would one parleying ghost divulge the truth from hell.

21. And yet he thought (blind human wit, how vain
And crooked are thy thoughts!) that Heaven had bless'd
The Paynim arms, and surely would ordain
Death to th' unconquer'd armies of the West;
He judged that Egypt from their grasp would wrest
The palm of war, and from the dazzling game
Depart a winning victor, and impress'd
With this delusive hope, resolved to claim
Part in the grand award of conquest, wealth, and fame.

22. But as their prowess drew his high esteem,
The war's vague chances he forbore to dare,
And long revolved how by some deep-laid scheme
The Christian princes he might best ensnare,
And by diminishing their strength, prepare
The path for Egypt; when, with ruin rife,
Her hosts the conquering sword abroad should bear;
His evil angel mark'd the mental strife,
Made quick the embryo thought, and push'd it into life.

23. He framed the fraud, the counsel he inspired,
And made his purpose easy to pursue ;
He had a niece, whose beauty was admired
Of the whole Orient, parallel'd by few,
And to the echo vaunted ; one who knew
Each fine discretion, each beguiling art
Of virgin and enchantress ; her he drew
To his saloon, and thus to her apart,
In nectarous words made known the wishes of his heart:

24. "Dear niece ! that underneath these locks of gold,
And that fair face, so young yet so divine,
Dost hide a heart, wise, masculine, and bold,
And magic skill transcendent over mine,—
I nurse a mighty project : the design
But needs thy gentle guidance to command
My hopes to sure success ; the thread I twine,
Weave thou the web, the lively colors blend ;
What cautious Age begins let dauntless Beauty end.

25. "Go to the hostile camp ; weep, tremble, sigh,
Each female charm that lures to love employ ;
Let the lips aid the witchcraft of the eye,
Smiles flash through tears, and grief despond in joy :
Now shrink from notice, now with prayers annoy ;
In weeping beauty o'er the wise prevail ;
Go ! storm th' obdurate bosom, win the coy,
In seeming truth clothe fiction's specious tale,
And with deep maiden shame thy bold advances veil.

26. "First, if thou can'st, take Godfrey in the thrall
Of thy sweet looks and amiable address,
Till his soul sickens at the trumpet's call,
And the world's war dissolves in a caress ;
But if this feat surpass thy skill, possess
His bravest nobles, and in friendship's guise
Transport them to some boundless wilderness,
Ne'er to return : "—he opens his device,
And adds—" All means our faith—our country sanctifies !"

27. Armida, in her youth and beauty's pride,
Assumed th' adventure, and at close of day,
Eve's vesper star her solitary guide,
Alone, untended, took her secret way.
In clustering locks and feminine array,
Arm'd but with loveliness and frolic youth,
She trusts to conquer mighty kings, and slay

Embattled hosts ; meanwhile false rumors soothe
The light censorious crowd, sagacious of the truth.

28. Few days elapsed, ere to her wishful view
The white pavilions of the Latins rise ;
The camp she reach'd—her wondrous beauty drew
The gaze and admiration of all eyes ;
Not less than if some strange star in the skies,
Or blazing comet's more resplendent tire
Appear'd ; a murmur far before her flies,
And crowds press round, to listen or inquire
Who the fair pilgrim is, and soothe their eyes' desire.

29. Never did Greece or Italy behold
A form to fancy and to taste so dear !
At times, the white veil dims her locks of gold,
At times, in bright relief they reappear :
So, when the stormy skies begin to clear,
Now through transparent clouds the sunshine gleams;
Now, issuing from its shrine, the gorgeous Sphere
Lights up the leaves, flowers, mountains, vales and streams,
With a diviner day—the spirit of bright beams.

30. New ringlets form the flowing winds amid
The native curls of her resplendent hair ;
Her eye is fix'd in self-reserve, and hid
Are all Love's treasures with a miser's care ;
The Rival Roses upon cheeks more fair
Than morning light, their mingling tints dispose ;
But on her lips, from which the amorous air
Of paradise exhales, the crimson rose
Its sole and simple bloom in modest beauty throws.

31. Crude as the grape unmellow'd yet to wine,
Her bosom swells to sight ; its virgin breasts,
Smooth, soft, and sweet, like alabaster shine,
Part bare, part hid by her invidious vests ;
Their jealous fringe the greedy eye arrests,
But leaves its fond imaginations free,
To sport, like doves, in those delicious nests,
And their most shadow'd secrecies to see ;
Peopling with blissful dreams the lively fantasy.

32. As through pure water or translucent glass
The sunbeam darts, yet leaves the crystal sound,
So through her folded robes unruffling pass
The thoughts, to wander on forbidden ground :

There daring Fancy takes her fairy round,
Such wondrous beauties singly to admire ;
Which, in a pleasing fit of transport bound,
She after paints and whispers to Desire,
And with her charming tale foments th' excited fire.

33. Praised and admired Armida pass'd amid
The wishful multitudes, nor seem'd to spy,
Though well she saw, the int'rest raised, but hid
In her deep heart the smile that to her eye
Darted in prescience of the conquests nigh :
While in the mute suspense of troubled pride
She sought with look solicitous, yet shy,
For her uncertain feet an ushering guide
To the fam'd Captain's tent, young Eustace press'd her side.

34. As the wing'd insect to the lamp, so he
Flew to the splendor of her angel face,
Too much indulgent of his wish to see
Those eyes which shame and modesty abase ;
And, drawn within the fascinating blaze,
Gath'ring, like kindled flax, pernicious fire
From its resplendence, stupid for a space
He stood—till the bold blood of blithe desire
Did to his faltering tongue these few wild words inspire:

35. "Oh Lady ! if thy rank the name allow,
If shapes celestial answer to the call,—
For never thus did partial Heaven endow
With its own light a daughter of the Fall,—
Say on what errand, from what happy hall,
Seek'st thou our camp ! and if indeed we greet
In thee one of the tribes angelical,
Cause us to know—that we, as were most meet,
May bend to thee unblamed and kiss thy saintly feet."

36. "Nay," she replied, "thy praises shame a worth
Too poor to warrant such a bold belief ;
Thou seest before thee one of mortal birth,
Dead to all joy, and but alive to grief ;
My harsh misfortunes urge me to your Chief ;
A foreign virgin in a timeless flight ;
To him I speed for safety and relief,
Trusting that he will reassert my right ;
So far resounds his fame, for mercy and for might.

37. "But, if indulgent courtesy be thine,
To pious Godfrey give me strait access!"
"Yes, lovely pilgrim," he replied, "be mine
The task to guide thee in thy young distress:
Nor is my interest with our Chieftain less
Than what a brother may presume to vaunt;
Thy suit shall not be wanting in success;
Whate'er his scepter or my sword can grant;
Shall in thy power be placed, to punish or supplant."

38. He ceased, and brought her where, from the rude crowd
Apart, with captains and heroic peers,
Duke Godfrey sate; she reverently bow'd,
A sweet shame mantling o'er her cheek, and tears
Stifling her speech: he reassured her fears,
Chid back the blush so beautifully bright,
Till, sweeter than the music of the spheres,
Their captive senses chaining in delight,
Her siren voice broke forth, and all were mute as Night.

39. "Unconquer'd Prince!" she said, "whose name supreme
Flies through the world on such a radiant plume,
That kings and nations conquer'd by thee deem
Their deed of vassalage a glorious doom,—
Well known thy valor shines, thy virtues bloom;
And while thy foes revere them and admire,
They, on their part, invite us to assume
The confidence we need, and to desire
Aid at thy hands, and aid requested to acquire.

40. "Thus I, though nurtured in the faith you hate,
And strive to cancel from the world's wide page,
Hope to regain by thee my lost estate,
My scepter, and ancestral heritage:
Others, oppress'd by foreign force, engage
The succors of their kindred; I, alas,
Defrauded of their pity at an age
Which claims it most, against my kindred, pass
And hostile arms invoke—the ghost of what I was!

41. "To thee I call, on thee depend, for thou
Alone canst conquer back mine ancient crown;
Nor shouldst thou be less prompt to raise the low,
Than on the proud to call destruction down;
Lovelier is Mercy's smile than Valor's frown,
A suppliant cherish'd than a foe undone:

And 'twere less glorious to thy just renown,
Whatever hazards in the task were run,
To lay whole realms in dust, than thus relumine one.

42. "But if our varying faiths—my Gentile creed—
Move thee to disregard my humble prayer,
Let my sure faith in thine indulgence plead
My cause, nor prove an illusory snare :
Lo ! before universal Jove I swear,—
God over all, from whom all empire flows,—
A juster quarrel never claim'd thy care ;
But listen ! frauds, conspiracies, and foes,
Of these my story treats,—a tale of many woes.

43. "The daughter I, of Arbilan who reign'd
In fair Damascus—less by birth made great,
Than merit ; Queen Cariclea he obtain'd
In marriage, and with her possess'd the state ;
Her death, alas, did almost antedate
My worthless life ! I issued from the womb
As she expired ; the self-same hour of fate,
(Oh birth too dearly bought ! oh ill-starr'd doom !)
Me to the cradle gave, my mother to the tomb.

44. "Five summer-suns had scarcely spent their fire,
Since Death's pale Angel call'd her to the skies,
Than, yielding to the lot of all, my sire
Rejoin'd her sainted shade in Paradise ;
He left his brother, by his last devise,
Sole regent of the kingdom and of me ;
Thinking that if the natural pieties
In mortal breast had mansion, they must be
Lock'd in his kindred heart with virtue's strictest key

45. "Thus then he play'd the tutor to my youth,
And with such show of kindness, that each wind
Voiced far and near his uncorrupted truth,
Paternal love, and bounty unconfined :
Whether the guilty movements of his mind
Beneath a flatt'ring face he thought to hide,
Or that he then sincerely was inclined
To make me happy, as the destined bride
Of his ungracious son—'twere idle to decide.—

46. "I grew in years and with me grew his son ;
But to no brave accomplishments, no store
Of sciences or arts could he be won,
He hated knightly deeds and princely lore :

Beneath a hideous countenance he bore
A baser soul, while pride and avarice
His heart pervaded to its inmost core;
Savage in manners, slave to drink and dice,
None but himself could be his paragon in vice.

47. "And now it was that my kind guardian strove
To wed me with this ill-assorted thing,
A goodly gallant for a lady's love,
To charm as bridegroom, and to reign as king!
Rhetoric he used—he used address to bring
The ardent hopes with which his fancy swell'd,
To their vow'd end, but never could he wring
From me the fatal promise,—I rebell'd,
And all his golden lures disdainfully repell'd.

48. "At last he left me with a gloomy face,
His elvish heart transpicuous in his look;
Too well my future story could I trace
In the dire leaves of that prophetic book!
Thenceforth each night alarming visions shook
My slumbers,—in my ears strange outcries shrill'd,
And phantoms frown'd on me; my spirit took
The ghastly impress of their forms, and thrill'd
With dread forbodings, since—how fatally fulfill'd!

49. "And oft my mother's piteous ghost appear'd;
'Ah! how unlike her smiling face portray'd
In picture, loving, lovely, and endear'd,
Now all illusion, and a pallid shade!
'Fly! O my child, fly! fly!' the figure said,
'Instant death threatens thee, and swift as light
Will the stroke fall;—the traitor's toils are laid;—
The poison in its gay glass sparkles bright.'
This said, it glided by, and melted into night.

50. "But what, alas, avail'd it that my heart
Received this presage of the perils near,
When, unresolved to act the counsel'd part,
My sex and tender age gave way to fear!
To rove through deserts, woods, and mountains drear,
In willing exile,—undefensed to go
From my paternal realm, seem'd more severe
Than to yield up the struggle to my foe,
And the reto close mine eyes where first they woke in woe.

51. "I dreaded death; yet, (will it be believed?)
With death at hand, I durst not flee away;

I fear'd e'en lest my fear should be perceived,
And thus accelerate the fatal day:
Thus restless, thus disturb'd, without one ray
Of comfort, I dragg'd on my wretched life,
In a perpetual fever of dismay;
Like the doom'd victim, who, in thought's last strife,
Feels, ere th' assassin stabs, th' anticipated knife.

52. "But, whether my good Genius ruled, or Fate
Preserved me yet for days of deeper gloom,
One of the noblest ministers of state,
Whose youth my sire had foster'd, sought my room;
In brief disclosing, that the hour of doom
Fix'd by the fiend, was now upon the wing;
That he himself had promised to assume
The murd'rous office, and the poison wring,
That night, in the sherbet my page was wont to bring.

53. "Flight, he assured me, was my sole resource
In this my crisis of despair, and pray'd
That since bereft of every other force,
I would accept his own effective aid:
His counsels, full of comfort, soon persuade
My undetermined spirit; to the wind
I gave my fears, and only now delay'd
Till eve's gray veil the tell-tale light should blind,
To leave all that I loved and hated, far behind.

54. "Night fell; an ebon darkness, more obscure
Than usual, its kind shadows round us spread,
When with two fav'rite maids I pass'd secure
The guarded palace, join'd my guide, and fled:
But through the trembling tears I ceaseless shed,
Long look'd I back on the receding towers,
Insatiate with the sight; all objects fed
My sorrow; each one spoke of happier hours,
The hills, the lamp-lit mosques, and hallow'd cypress-bowers.

55. "To them my looks, my thoughts, my sighs were given,
As on I speeded, malcontent though free;
I fared like an unanchor'd pinnace driven
From its loved port by whirlwinds far to sea:
All the long night and following day we flee,
By paths no human foot had ever press'd;
Till on the confines of my realm we see
Its last baronial seat,—there, tired, we rest,
Just as the sun's slow orb forsook the fulgent west.

56\. "It was the castle of the gen'rous knight,
Arontes, who had made my life his care;
But when the baffled traitor by our flight
Perceived I had escaped the mortal snare,
His rage flamed forth against us both; and ere
I could arraign him, intricate in ill,
Gathering a fresh presumption from despair,
He charged on us his own all-evil will,—
The selfsame crime which he was studious to fulfill.

57\. "He said I had the false Arontes bribed
To mix destroying poisons in his bowl,
Impatient of the maxims he prescribed
To curb my lust, that free from all control,
I might pursue the bias of my soul,
And with voluptuous blandishments commend
My beauty to a thousand youths:—Skies! roll
Your thunders, let avenging fires descend,
Ere I thy sacred laws, blest Chastity, offend!

58\. "That avarice and ambition, pride and pique
Urge him to shed my guiltless blood, must claim
Grief and alarm; but that the wretch should seek
To fix dishonor on my spotless name,
Goes to my heart: he, fearing now the flame
Of pop'lar rage, with smooth-tongued eloquence,
Forges a thousand falsehoods to my shame;
So that the city fluctuates in suspense,
Betwixt the guilt of both, nor arms in my defense.

59\. "Yea, though he sits on mine authentic throne,
Though my tiara sparkles on his brow,
Dominion spurs him but more keenly on,
To work me farther injury, shame, and woe:
With fire and sword he threatens to o'erthrow
Arontes in his fortress, if in chains
He yield not, and on me denounces now
Not merely war, but stripes and fearful pains,
While flows one drop of blood in my rebellious veins.

60\. "This—under color of a lively zeal
To purge away the stains of my disgrace,
And to its ancient purity anneal
The golden scepter which my crimes debase!
But the true motive is a wish to place
His claims beyond dispute: while I remain
Heir to the crown, he fears no plea can grace
His kingly usurpation, so is fain
To build upon my death the basis of his reign.

61. "And e'en such end awaits his fell desire;
He must enjoy what he is fix'd to gain,
And in my heart's blood quench the boundless ire
Which all my tears were powerless to restrain
If thou, alas, my suppliant prayer disdain!
To thee—a wretched girl, weak, innocent,
Orphan'd—I fly; must my sad tears in vain
Fall on thy holy robes? relent! relent!
Oh, by the knees I grasp, forbid his fierce intent.

62. "By these thy feet, that on the proud and strong
Triumphantly have trod; by thy right hand;
By thy past victories, a choral throng!
And by the temples of this sacred land,
Freed by the sword, or to be freed,—withstand,
Thou only canst, his merciless decree;
My crown, my life preserve, secure, command,
Merciful Sire! but vain is mercy's plea,
If first religious right and justice move not thee.

63. "Beloved of Heaven! thou destined to desire
That which is just, and thy desires achieve,
Save me! my kingdom thou wilt thus acquire
Which I in fief shall thankfully receive;
Let ten of these heroic champions leave
The camp beneath my conduct; their renown,
Spread through the city, will my cause retrieve,
Will win my faithful people to strike down
With ease the man of crime, and repossess my crown.

64. "Yea, more: a Noble to whose keeping falls
A secret gate, has promised me access,
At dead of night, to my paternal halls;
But some small aid he counsel'd me to press:
The least, the least thou grantest to redress
The grievances I suffer, will inflame
His hopes with surer prospects of success,
Than if from other kings whole squadrons came.
So high he ranks thy flag, so high thy simple name!

65. She ceased; but still her mute imploring eye
Spoke eloquence beyond the reach of prayer:
Doubtful alike to grant as to deny,
A thousand various thoughts, absorb'd in care,
Godfrey revolved; he fear'd some Gentile snare
Couch'd in her tears, some ambuscade of art;
He knew who kept not faith with God, would dare
Break league with man; still pity pleads her part
Pity—which never sleeps within a noble heart.

66. His native ruth inspires the wish that she
Deserved the grace ; and policy on ruth
Succeeding, whispers it were wise to free,
And fix in rich Damascus one whose truth,
Enforced by the dependency of youth,
May much avail him, with her feudal arms,
The course of his sublime designs to smooth,—
To minister supplies against th' alarms
Of Egypt's muster'd tribes and tributary swarms.

67. While thus from wav'ring thought to thought he flies,
Revolves, and re-revolves, the eager maid
Fix'd on his downcast face her pleading eyes,
And its least workings breathlessly survey'd :
And when his answer longer was delay'd
Than she had hoped, she trembled, droop'd, and sigh'd
Her quiv'ring lips the heart's alarm betray'd ;
Pale grew her face : at length the Prince replied,
And in these courteous words mildly her suit denied.

68. "If God's own quarrel had not claim'd these swords,
Now oath-bound to his cause, thy hopes might rest
Thereon in perfect trust,—not pitying words,
But valid actions had thy wrongs redress'd ;
But while His heritage is thus oppress'd
Beneath the harsh rod of a tyrant king,
How can we grant, fair Lady, thy request ?
Divided hosts declining fortunes bring,
And check the flowing tide of vic'try in its spring.

69. "But this I promise,—firmly may'st thou trust
The word I pledge, and live secure from fear,—
If e'er we conquer from a yoke unjust
These towers, to Heaven and piety so dear,
To pity's voice I will incline mine ear,
Thee on thy lost throne to exalt ; but now,
No pitying sympathies must interfere
To cancel what to the Most High we owe,
And for a mortal's sake dissolve our solemn vow."

70. At this the mournful Princess droop'd her head,
And stirless stood, as Niobe of yore ;
Then raised her eyes, impearl'd, to heaven, and said
While all the woman at their founts ran o'er,—
"Lost ! lost ! O skies ! O stars ! what evils more
Do ye prescribe ? did ever one fulfill
A doom so harsh, so merciless before !
Woe's me! all nature's change; the world grows chill;
I only vary not, immutable in ill !

71\. "Now farewell hope! now welcome misery!
All prayer in human breasts has lost its force;
Am I to hope the tears that touch'd not thee,
Will move the barb'rous tyrant with remorse?—
Yet, though denied this pitiful resource,
With no reproach thy rigor shall be paid;
It is my Genius I accuse—the source
Of all my ills,—my Genius, who has made
Godfrey's a ruthless heart,—'tis him that I upbraid.

72\. "Not to thee, gracious Chieftain? not to thee
Lay I this crime, but to imperious Fate;
Oh, that her active tyranny would free
My weary spirit from a world I hate!
Was't not enough, stern Power, to dedicate
Mother and sire e'en in their morn of life
To the dark grave, that from my high estate
Thou hast now toss'd me on the sea of strife,
And giv'n thy victim bound and blinded to the knife!

73\. "Now holy sanctitude and maiden shame
Urge me to go, but whither shall I fly?
There is no refuge for a blighted name;
Earth holds no spot beneath the boundless sky
So secret, but the tyrant's active eye
Will find it, and transpierce me; but—I go;
The Angel of Death approaching I descry;
Naught now is left but to forestall his blow;
None but Armida's arm shall lay Armida low!"

74\. She ceased: a gen'rous and majestic scorn
Fired all her features to a rose-like red,
And then she made as she would have withdrawn,
With grief and anger in her farewell tread:
Her eyes, 'twixt sorrow and resentment, shed
Tears thick as summer's heat drops—tears, that shine
With the sun's golden rays athwart them spread,
Like falling pearls, like crystals argentine,
Or sparkling opal-drops from some far Indian mine.

75\. Her fresh cheeks, sprinkled with those living showers,
Which to her vesture's hem, down gliding, cling,
Appear like snowy and vermilion flowers
Humid with May dews, when romantic Spring,
In shadow of the green leaves whispering,
Spreads their closed bosoms to the amorous air;—
Flowers, to which sweet Aurora oft takes wing,
Which with gay hand she culls with such fond care
In morn's melodious prime, to bind her vagrant hair.

76. But the clear drops that, thick as stars of night,
On those fair cheeks and on that heaving breast
So shine, have all th' effect of fire, and light
A secret flame in each beholder's breast :
Oh Love ! the marv'lous rod by thee possess'd,
Forever poweful over Nature, draws
Lightning from tears, and gives to grief a zest
Beyond the bliss of smiles ; but Nature's laws
Its magic far transcends, in this thy darling's cause.

77. Her feign'd laments from roughest warriors call
Sincerest tears ;—their hearts to her incline ;
Each is afflicted at her grief, and all
At Godfrey's speech thus whisp'ringly repine :
"Surely he made the vex'd sea-roaring brine
His nursing cradle, and wild wolves that rave
On the chill crags of some rude Apennine,
Gave his youth suck : O, cruel as the grave,
Who could view charm like hers, and not consent to save !"

78. But Eustace, in whose young and gen'rous blood
Pity and love flow'd strongest, while the rest
But murmur'd and were silent, forward stood,
And dauntlessly his brother thus address'd :
"My Lord ! far too inflexibly thy breast
Keeps to the firmness of its first design,
If to the common voice which would obtest
Thy clemency, thou dost not now incline ;
Reverent of mercy's claims and quality divine.

79. "Think not I urge the princedoms and the powers
Who rank dependent tribes beneath their care,
To turn their arms from these assieged towers,
And the first duties of the camp forswear ;
But, warriors of adventure, we, who bear
Nor feudal flag nor delegated trust,
Who act without restriction, well may spare
At thy wise choice, and in a cause most just,
Ten guardian knights to one so helpless, so august.

80. "Know, he assists the cause of God, who toils
The rights of outraged virgins to maintain ;
And precious in his sight must be the spoils
Which freemen hang on Freedom's holy fane,
The glorious trophies of a tyrant slain :
Though then no interest counsel'd to the deed,
Duty would urge, and Knighthood would constrain

Me to assist the damsel in her need,
And without scruple go, where'er her voice may lead.

81. "Oh, by yon bright sun, tell it not in France!
Publish it not where courtesy is dear!
That of our nobles none would break a lance
In Beauty's quarrel, let not Europe hear!
Henceforth, my lords, sword, corslet, helm and spear
I toss aside, and bid farewell to fame;
No gen'rous steed shall bear me in career
With swordless chiefs, where Chivalry weds Shame,—
I will no longer bear the knight's degraded name!"

82. Thus spoke the youth, and all his Order there,
Applausive murmur'd in loud unison;
Praised his good counsel, and with urgent prayer
Closed round their Captain on his ducal throne.
"I yield," at length he said, "but yield alone
To the desire of numbers, since the plea
Is one my private judgment would disown;
Grant we her boon, if such your pleasure be;
But know th' advice as yours, it not proceeds from me.

83. "And, far as Godfrey's counsel can persuade,
Temper your sympathies, be closely wise:"
He said no more, it was enough,—they paid
The kind concession with delighted cries.
What cannot Beauty, when her pleading eyes
From their deep fountains shower down tears of pain,
And to her armorous tongue sweet speeches rise?
From her divine lips glides a golden chain,
That wins to her dear will who most those tears disdain.

84. Eustace recall'd her, took her passive hand,
And said, "Now cease, dear Lady, to repine;
The utmost succors that thy fears demand,
(Weep not) shall all, and speedily be thine:"
Then the dark aspect of her face grew fine,—
With her white veil she wiped the tears away,
And gave a smile so brilliant and benign,
You would have thought th' enamor'd God of Day
In sunshine kiss'd the lips whose luster shamed his ray.

85. And in her sweet voice and pathetic tone,
She gave them thanks for their exceeding grace;
Saying it should to the wide world be known,
And ever and forever have a place
Within her grateful heart: her working face,

And gestures with impassion'd meanings fraught,
Told what the tongue was powerless to express;
Thus masking in false smiles the end she sought,
Her varied web of guile she unsuspected wrought.

86. Who but Armida now exults to see
How fortune and kind fate the fraud befriend?
Who o'er each dark suggestion broods, but she,
To bring the plot to a successful end?
With beauty and sweet flat'ries to transcend
Whate'er Medea's witchcraft e'er design'd,
Or Circe's incantations wrought,—to blend
Mischief with mirth, and the most watchful mind
As in Elysian sleep with siren songs to bind?

87. All arts th' enchantress practiced to beguile
Some new admirer in her well-spread snare;
Nor used with all, nor always the same wile,
But shaped to every taste her grace and air:
Here cloister'd is her eye's dark pupil, there
In full voluptuous languishment is roll'd;
Now these her kindness, those her anger bear,
Spurr'd on or check'd by bearing frank or cold,
As she perceived her slave was scrupulous or bold.

88. If she mark'd some too bashful to advance,
Sick if unnoticed, diffident if seen,
Forth flew her radiant smile, her thrilling glance,
Sunny as summer and as eve serene:
Thus reassured, their dying hopes grow keen;
The faint belief, the languishing desire
Reviving brighten in their eager mien;
Those looks a thousand am'rous thoughts inspire.
And Fear's pale frost-work melts in Fancy's lively fire.

89. If some make bold to press her virgin palm,
Too rashly building on her former cheer,
She grows a miser of her eye's mild charm;
Spares her fond smile, and frowns them into fear;
But through the wrath that fires her front austere,
And ruffles her sweet cheek, they may discern
Rays of forgiving pity reappear;
Thus do they droop, but not despair, and yearn
Tow'rds her in deepest love when she appears most stern.

90. Sometimes in lonely places she dissembled
Deep grief—the voice, the action, and the tread;

And oft when in her eye the loose tear trembled,
Crush'd, or reclaim'd it to the fountain-head.
Soon as those tragic gestures were aread,
A thousand striplings, vanquish'd by her art,
Would come and weep around her : Envy fed
Their frenzy, and Love, temp'ring his keen dart
In Pity's scalding tears, shot torture through the heart.

91. Anon she starts from her abstraction, wakes
With hope's fresh whispers to her spirit : seeks
Her many lovers, talks to them, and shakes
The bright locks on her brow for joy, that speaks
Life to her lips, and to her glowing cheeks
New smiles ; her eyes then sparkle as in scorn
Of their late griefs,—as when Apollo streaks
With fire the op'ning eyelids of the morn,
And every dark'ning cloud to distance has withdrawn.

92. But while she sweetly speaks and sweetly smiles,
And with this twofold sweetness lulls the sense,
She from its blissful cage well-nigh exiles
The soul, unused to rapture so intense ;
Ah cruel Love ! whether thy hand dispense,
Wreath'd with the cypress or the lotos-leaf,
Thy gall or nectar-cup, its quintessence
Maddens with ecstasy, or blights with grief ;
Fatal thy sickness is, and fatal thy relief !

93. Through all these shifting tempers, while each knight
Fluctuates disturb'd, uncertain of her choice,
Through fire and frost, smiles, tears, fear, hope, delight,
The beauteous witch his agony enjoys :
If any e'er presumes with trembling voice
To tell his secret pain, her guilefulness
The glorious vision of his soul destroys ;
She nor perceives his meaning, nor can guess,—
The very fool of Love and frank unconsciousness.

94. Or, casting down to ground her bashful eyes,
The blush of honor o'er her face she throws,
So that the alabaster white, which lies
In sweet confusion underneath the rose
That her celestial cheek irradiates, glows
Like the rich crimson on Aurora's face,
When from the Orient first her form she shows ;
And the red flush of anger keeping pace
With shame, combines to shed round shame a sweeter grace.

95. But if she one perceives resolved t' avow
His warm desire, she stops her charmed ears ;
Now shuns his converse, grants an audience now,
Then flies, returns, smiles, frowns, and disappears:
Thus in a war of wishes, sighs, and tears,
In vain pursuit he wastes his life away ;
And with deluding hopes, afflicting fears,
Fares like the hunter who at dying day
Has lost in pathless woods all traces of his prey.—

96. These were the arts by which Armida took
A thousand spirits captive to her sleight,
Or rather, these the arms, with which she strook,
And made them bondslaves in their own despite.
What marvel elder Love subdued the might
Of Theseus fierce, and Hercules the strong ;
When those who drew the sword in Jesu's right,
Sooth'd by a siren's smile,—a siren's song,
Wore his enfeebling chains, and gloried in the wrong!

END OF CANTO IV.

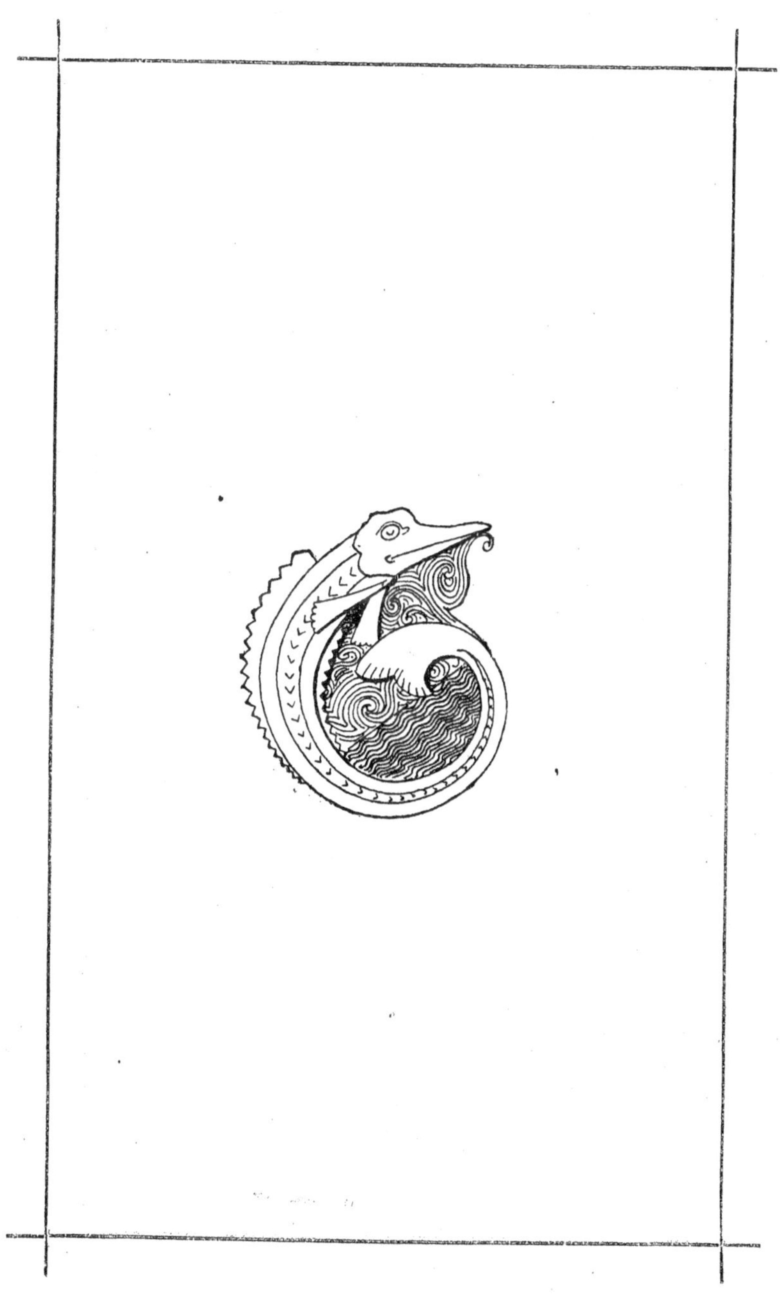

JERUSALEM DELIVERED.

CANTO V.

ARGUMENT.

GERNANDO scorns Rinaldo should aspire
To the command which he himself would fain
Receive ; and, urged by jealousy and ire,
Insults the youth, and is in duel slain ;
The slayer lingers not till gyve or chain
Binds his free limbs, but into exile flees
Content, Armida with a splendid train
Departs, while Godfrey from the navied seas
Hears news of sharp concern, that leaves him ill at ease.

JERUSALEM DELIVERED.

CANTO V.

1. WHILE thus th' insidious Beauty, day by day,
 Lured to her love the Nobles, and beside
 The promised number, thought to charm away,
 At stealth, fresh vassals to her power and pride,
 Godfrey revolved to whom he should confide
 Her dubious restoration, through the host
 Casting his thoughts ; nor could at first decide,—
 As all th' Adventurers wish'd the pleasing post,
And each had bravery, rank, or excellence to boast.

2. But he at last adopts the wise resolve,
 To urge them first a Leader to elect
 In Dudon's room, and after to devolve
 On him the charge to single or reject
 Those who aspire the Damsel to protect ;
 Thus, none, aggrieved, his partial choice could blame ;
 While he himself would show supreme respect—
 A tribute their achievements justly claim—
To that illustrious band, the glorified of fame.

3. To him he call'd them then, and thus address'd :
 "Knights ! you have heard our sentiments, which were
 Not to refuse the Syrian maid's request,
 But our intended succors to defer
 To a maturer season ; I recur
 To the same charge,—your judgment yet is free
 To follow my proposal ; in the stir
 Of this unstable world, how oft we see
That 'tis true wisdom's part to change her own decree.

4. "But yet, if still you deem it base to shun
 The risk, if still your gen'rous hearts disdain

My wary counsels as the fears of one
Too coldly scrupulous,—your own retain ;
Go ! ne'er shall it be said that I constrain
Reluctant minds, revoke a gift once given,
Or bind your wishes with a forceful chain ;
No ! gentle be my rule, and gracious, even
As the mild starlight dews and influences of heaven.

5. "Proceed or stay then at your own free will ;
To your discretion I the choice confide ;
But first by suffrage fix on one to fill
Slain Dudon's post, your arm'd array to guide ;
He on your high pretensions shall decide,
But choose not more than ten : to me you gave
Powers paramount, to royalty allied ;
This my prerogative I cannot waive ;
No ! for a powerless Chief is but a glorious slave."

6. Thus Godfrey spake ; and to his word of grace
By joint consent young Eustace made reply :
"As that deliberate judgment is thy praise
Which looks far into futurity,
So strength of heart and hand, a courage high,
Prompt the first risks of enterprise to face,
Are ask'd of us, the Lights of Chivalry ;
And that ripe tardiness, which in the case
Of some would prudent be, in us would prove most base.

7. "Then, since the hazard is so far outweigh'd
By the advantage, let them straight proceed,
The chosen ten, in wrong'd Armida's aid,
And boldly dare the meritorious deed."
With this adorn'd pretense he strives to lead
Opinion blinded to his fervent flame,
By show of knightly zeal ; the others read
His secret passion and dissembled aim,
Favor the fond deceit, and counterfeit the same.

8. But am'rous Eustace whenso'er he eyed
Rinaldo's excellences, as mental grace
More winningly attracts when beautified
By a brave figure and a handsome face,
Wish'd him away ; and shrewdness, keeping pace
With anxious jealousy's increasing smart,
Urged him at length his rival to displace,
By deep address ; whence, drawing him apart,
He thus his proem tuned with all the flatterer's art :

9. "O, of great father greater son ! O thou,
The young Achilles of this glorious land !
What Chevalier shall lead to conquest now
The gallant warriors of our matchless band ?
I, who to noble Dudon's mild command
Could scarcely stoop, who only bent the knee
In rev'rence of his silver locks, who stand
So near our Chief in kindred and degree,
To whom should I submit ? to none, if not to thee.

10. "Thee ! who art equal to the best in birth,
Whose splendid merits cast a shade on mine ;
Not e'en would Godfrey scorn to own his worth
In the stern proof of battle, less than thine !
Thee for our Chief I claim then, if to shine
The bold assertor of this lady's right
Be not thy wish ; and ne'er canst thou design
To challenge praise achieved by secret sleight,
Or round thy brows to bind the laurels reap'd by night.

11. "Here may'st thou feats accomplish, that will hand
Thy name, embalm'd by some celestial Muse,
To long posterity ; the chief command
Will I procure (away with vain excuse !)
From the assenting Knights who cannot choose
But sanction what my praise shall recommend,
If, when elected, thou wilt not refuse
The favor to thine undecided friend,
At will to war with thee, or with Armida wend."

12. He spake not this without a blush that sped
Its deep confusion to the guilty eyes ;
His glowing secret well Rinaldo read,
And archly smiled at the ill-dress'd disguise :
But he was studious of a loftier prize,
And if a chance-shaft from Armida's bow
Grazed him, its challenge he could half despise ;
He neither in a rival fear'd a foe,
Nor cared for love the chase of glory to forego.

13. But deeply sculptured in his thoughts sublime
Memory of Dudon's bitter death he kept,
And deem'd it a disparagement and crime
That yet Argantes lived, and vengeance slept ;
Then to hear Eustace urge him to accept
The proffer'd honor, made his heart rejoice ;
And while into his ear the music crept

Of praise, his spirit echo'd the sweet voice,
Whisp'ring, his early worth deserved the flatt'ring choice.

14. Whence frankly he replied : "The first degree
I wish to merit rather than acquire,
And if by worth sublimed, the dignity
Of rule I need not envy, nor desire ;
But since to this invited to aspire,
Since worthy of the noble trust I seem,
I'll not decline th' acceptance you require ;
And of this perfect proof of pure esteem,
Dear to a warrior's pride most gratefully I deem.

15. "Amidst the elected champions, thou, besure,
Shalt rank, if I obtain the vacant post :"
Eustace, this heard, departed to secure,
Apt to his wish, the homage of the host
But prince Gernando to himself proposed
The prize ; for though Armida had not fail'd
T' engage his thoughts, an innate pride opposed
Her power, and lady-love with him prevail'd
Less than the lust of rule, which most his heart assail'd.

16. He from the blood of royal Norway springs,
To whom unnumber'd thanes in homage crowd ;
A long succession of ancestral kings,
Of coronets and scepters, made him proud :
To grander Gods Rinaldo's spirit bow'd,—
Of his own actions haughtier than the bright,
Blue scutcheon of his fathers,—self endow'd ;
Yet full five hundred years, as heralds write,
Had these stood famed in peace, and unsubdued in fight.

17. But the barbaric Peer, who all things weigh'd
By gold, and rank, and amplitude of state,
Whose fancy cast all excellence in shade
That crowns and stars did not illuminate,
Could not endure that any should debate—
Much less Rinaldo—the command with him ;
To such excess did anger, scorn and hate
Transport him, reason's guiding light grew dim,
And Passion's mustering storm distended ev'ry limb.

18. So that of Hell's foul sprites the most malign,
Who saw unwatch'd the op'ning avenue,
Crept to his heart with still coils serpentine,
And at the helm of thought reclining, blew

To flame the sparks of hatred, till they grew
Hot for revenge; yet still he piqued, still stung
His angry soul to agony anew;
The while, as warbled by a siren's tongue,
Clear through his haughty heart this flatt'ring prelude rung.

19. "What! were his antique chiefs lords paramount
Of earth, that thus with thee Rinaldo vies?
Since he will mate with thee, let him recount
His govern'd millions and subdued allies,
Let him bring forth his crowns, and equalize
His scepter'd ghosts with thy live kings; can one,
The owner of a few poor seignories,
Born beneath Italy's inglorious sun,
Dare to aspire so high?—what frenzy goads him on?

20. "But, win or lose, he reap'd a victor's bays
When first he thought thy title to transcend:
The world will say, (to him the highest praise),
'Lo, with Gernando this man dared contend!'
The station fill'd by thy departed friend
Glory and splendor round thy path may shower,
But not less honor thou to that wilt lend,—
The prize lost half its value from the hour
When he desired it too, and sought to mate thy power.

21. "And if the soul, when left this breathing frame
To our affairs its conscious thoughts apply,
Think with how brave a wrath th' ambitious aim
Fires good old Dudon in the radiant sky,
When on this forward Page he casts his eye,
And sees his pride so far the dues subvert
Of rev'rend age, as with himself to vie;
And, while but yet a child and unexpert,
Stand for a public post of such sublime desert.

22. "Yea, this he hopes, this he attempts, and bears
Honor and praise, not chastisement abroad:
And some there are who second what he dares,
(O common shame!) and what he dares, applaud:
But if Duke Godfrey, seeing him defraud
Thee of thy dues, should countenance the plan,
Endure it not; but openly, unawed
By power or threats, confront the mighty man,
And show both who thou art, and what thy valor can!"

23. At the shrill music of these words, disdain
Glow'd like a torch when shaken in the wind;
It fired his heart, swell'd in each pregnant vein,
Flash'd in his eye, and in his tongue repined;
Whatever fancied foible he could find
In young Rinaldo, he exposed to shame;
He paints him vain and arrogant of mind,
And styles his valor rashness; each fond aim
Of his ingenuous mind industrious to defame.

24. All that in him was glorious, graceful, pure,
Gen'rous, or great, or beautiful, or wise,
While his invidious arts the truth obscure,
He boldly censures as the height of vice:
This vital scorn, these wide-wing'd calumnies
His rival gathers in the public breath;
Yet still with no less rancor he decries
The noble Child, nor less he scorns to sheath
In silence the keen tongue that tempts him to his death.

25. For the vile fiend whose motions ruled his tongue
In lieu of judgment, influenced him to frame,
Hour after hour, fresh outrages and wrong,
Still adding fuel to the bosom'd flame;—
Wide space was there in camp, where daily came
A band of gallant youths with spear and shield;
Where in gay tournay and gymnastic game
They perfected their skill, their courage steel'd,
And nerved their strenuous limbs to bide a ruder field.

26. There, at an hour when thickest was the crowd,
Urged by the whisp'rings of the inward snake,
His tongue its customary scorn avow'd,
Infused with venom of th' Avernian lake;
The knight, in hearing of the words he spake,
To irrepressible resentment stirr'd,
Fix'd the long dues of vengeance now to take,
Shouted, "Thou liest!" and sudden as the word,
Cross'd the traducer's path, and drew his poignant sword.

27. His voice the thunder seem'd, his sword the flash
Which of its coming warns the world; too late
Repenting fears the criminal abash,—
He saw no refuge from impending fate;
Yet in this last, irreparable strait,
As all the Camp were witnesses, he made
Proud show of courage, with a look elate
Awaited the stern foe, his distance weigh'd,
And in the guarding act unsheath'd the battle-blade.

28. Instant a thousand lifted swords were seen
All sparkling to one center, and a swarm
Of warriors from all sides rushed to the scene
Of strife, to stay each warrior's angry arm.
All was vague clamor and confused alarm:
And such a sudden whirl of voices tore
The startled air, as in the gath'ring storm,
Among the pendent cliffs of the wild shore,
Sound the shrill murm'ring winds to the loud sea-wave's roar.

29. But not the prayers of thousands can allay
Th' offended hero's agony of ire;
The shout, the press, the concourse of the way,
He scorns, and dares to vengeance still aspire;
Through men and arms in many a giddy gyre
His fulminating sword darts, and demands
A vacant space; the daunted crowd retire,—
And to the shame of all his guardian bands,
Free to his fierce affronts, Gernando singly stands.

30. His hand, unmaster'd by his rage, at will
A thousand stabs delivers, and divides
With the head, heart, and bosom, as his skill
Instructs, or the unguarded part provides;
Impetuous, rapid as the foam that rides
The whirlpool, his all-present steel appears,
The eye bewilders, and its art derides;
Where least expected, there it most careers;
There most it strikes and wounds, where least his rival fears.

31. Nor did it cease, until its point had found
Twice the pure life-blood of his bosom gored;
The hapless Prince sank grov'ling on his wound,
His vital spirits from the fount were pour'd,
And through the twofold pass his spirit soar'd
The knight stay'd not; his steel, incarnadined
As it had been, he to the sheath restored;
Then stalk'd away, and with the scene resign'd
His own inflamed desires and ruthlessness of mind.

32. To the loud uproar Godfrey drawn meanwhile
Saw dismal cause of unexpected pain,—
Gernando, his loose locks and mantle vile
Reeking with blood, with visage where, too plain,
Death spread the pallid banners of his reign;
And there were tears on many a soldier's lid,

Outcries, and shrieks, and wailings for the slain :
Amazed he asks, there where 'twas most forbid,
Whose so audacious hand the deed of horror did.

33. Arnaldo, dearest to the Prince bewail'd,
In terms that sought the guilt to aggravate,
Tells how Rinaldo had his friend assail'd
In the blind fury of intemp'rate hate,
Built on a slight and frivolous debate ;
Thus, the sword vow'd to Christ's blest service, he
Had turn'd against Christ's hallow'd delegate :
Scorning not less his rule, than the decree
Long since promulged, whereof he ignorant could not be.

34. And that the law had thus already sign'd
The warrant of his death ;—'twas clear, the case ;
First, as the fact was of a heinous kind,
Next, as committed in a sacred place :
For such a crime were he to meet with grace,
Fresh criminals would rise, both bold and strong,
In his escape to beard you to your face,
And execute revenge for ev'ry wrong,
Which to the Judge alone for judgment should belong.

35. Thus discord, thus dispute, thus civil ire,
Would raven all, as with a tiger's tooth ;
All that disdain and pity could inspire,
He pleads in merit of the murder'd youth :
But Tancred with the jealousy of truth
His tale impugns, and paints in colors clear
The actual cause of strife ; to which in sooth
The just Judge listens, but his brow severe
Seems less t' encourage hope than countenance his fear

36. "My Lord," he adds, "in wisdom weigh both who
And what Rinaldo is—his deeds recount ;
Judge what regard to his deserts is due ;
From princely sire to sire illustrious mount,—
Trace his long flow of glory to the fount,—
Think on his uncle Guelpho's high estate ;
All equal crimes are not of like account,
Nor should the self-same punishment await
Vassal and highborn lord, the lowly and the great."

37. Godfrey replied, "'Tis for the great to give
Proof of obedience to the lowly ; ill
Are these thy counsels, Tancred, which would leave
The Mighty to their own unbridled will.

Think what our empire were, did we fulfill
Its functions only to the vile and base,—
A powerless scepter, or, more shameful still,
An execrated rod, derided mace!
If with such laws 'twas given, I spurn your gift of grace.

38. "But frank and awful was it given, unsought,
Nor shall its virtue be abridged by me;
And well I know both where and when I ought
To punish and reward, and now to be
The prompt reverser of my own decree,
Yet still between the lowly and the high
Hold even Law's just balance." Thus spoke he;
Nor aught could Tancred venture to reply,
Awed by his righteous words and his majestic eye.

39. Stern pupil of austere Antiquity,
Raymond commended his discourse, and said:
"These are the arts by which true sov'reignty
Becomes revered,—for discipline is dead,
Or at the least defective, where, instead
Of pain, Guilt looks for pardon; to be mild,
Power should be based in fear; when rulers spread
Too wide their mercy, Liberty runs wild,
And States decay." He ceased, and like a Spartan smiled.

40. Tancred of his advice took silent heed;
Longer he linger'd not, but leap'd astride
His manageable horse, whose hoofs for speed
Seem'd fledged with wings, and to Rinaldo hied
He, soon as he had quell'd the boist'rous pride
Of fierce Gernando, to his private tent
Retired, the issues calmly to abide;
Here Tancred found him, and with discontent
Detail'd in every point the late sharp argument.

41. "And though," he adds, "I deem the visnomy
But a fallacious index of the heart,
Since oft the thoughts of mortals secret lie,
In depths that mock th' observer's nicest art;
Yet, from what Godfrey's face betray'd in part
To my perusing eye, with what his mind
Clearly avow'd, I fear not to assert,
That as a common culprit he would bind
With gyves thy warrior limbs, to Law's strict power resign'd."

42. Rinaldo smiled ; but breaking through his smile
A flash of high defiance might you see :
"Let him defend his cause in fetters vile
Who vassal is, or vassal deigns to be !
Free was I born ; free have I lived ; and free
Will I expire, ere one base fetter weighs
My hands down in its cank'ring tyranny,—
They have been used to no such slave-essays,
But to consult the sword, and reap victorious bays.

43. "If Godfrey thus reward our worth, if thus
As a base slave he would incarcerate,
And fix his foul plebeian bonds on us,
Here let him come in all his pomp of state ;
I place my proud foot on the ground, and wait
His unfear'd presence and his scorn'd decree ;
Sharp arms shall be our only jurors, Fate
Sole arbitress, and foemen flock to see
The sportful Drama play'd,—a deep, deep tragedy !"

44. He shouted for his armor, robed his form
In helm and brigandine of steel, applied
The shield enormous to his active arm,
And hung the dancing falchion at his side :
Magnificent, august, and fiery-eyed,
He sparkled in his arms like flashing levin,
And look'd the God of Battle when in pride
Descending from the fifth red sphere of heaven,
In rattling iron girt, by Fright and Fury driven.

45. Tancred this while used every art to soothe
His wounded pride and his intemp'rate rage ;
"I know," said he, "that thou, unconquer'd youth,
Wouldst in the hardiest enterprise engage ;
That ever amid arms and on the edge
Of doom, thy valor is secure from harm ;
But Heaven forbid that e'er on such a stage
Thou shouldst let loose the gladiator's arm,
To work our army woe, and break the magic charm.

46. "Say, what is thine intent? wilt thou imbrue
Thy hands in kindred blood? with frantic aim
Wounding thy friends, transpiercing Christ anew,
Whose members they, and part of whom I am?
Shall the vain lust of transitory fame,
That like a summer sea-wave swells and dies
As the wind lists, enforce a stronger claim
Than that which faithborn piety supplies,
Of bliss all bliss beyond, eternal in the skies?

47. "No! be the victor of thyself, and still
This raging gust, this whirlwind of the mind;
Yield! from no fear, but from a virtuous will;
With worthier palms compliancy will bind
Thy brows, than ever were to pride assign'd:
And if mine unripe years, though young and few,
May yield th' example, I by acts unkind
Was also once provoked, yet never drew
My sword in civil strife, but did my wrath subdue.

48. "I took Cilicia, and on Tarsus' towers
Planted the Cross before all people's eyes,
But Baldwin came, and with his peaceful Powers
Admitted, basely robb'd me of my prize;
Such friendship he profess'd, so fair a guise
Mask'd his ambitious purpose from my sight,
That ere I was aware, his avarice
Had sprung the mine: yet would not I by fight
The spoils regain, although e'en yet perhaps I might.

49. "But if indeed those ignominious bands
As a base weight thy spirit would refuse,
Following the nice opinions and demands,
The subtile laws which men of honor use,
Leave it to me thy anger to excuse;
To Antioch fly,—with Bohemond, thy friend,
Seek an asylum secret and recluse;
To wrath's first gust I deem it best to bend;
A cause by Power prejudged 'twere fruitless to defend.

50. "But rest assured, if vig'rously assail'd,
If round us Egypt or the Arabs swarm,
Deeply indeed thy flight will be bewail'd;
While, at a distance from the vast alarm,
Thy valor will acquire a tenfold charm;
Without thy sword, the nerveless camp must prove
A trunk deprived of its protecting arm:"
Here Guelph arrives, his lips the speech approve,
Urging him straight from Camp discreetly to remove.

51. To their grave counsels the disdainful heart
Of the bold youth at length inclining, bends,
And he no longer scruples to depart
In willing exile: of his faithful friends
Meanwhile a num'rous crowd his course attends;
To share his flight and fortunes each aspires,
And earnestly solicits; he commends
Their zeal with thanks, but takes alone two squires;
Vaults on his sprightly steed, and from the camp retires.

52. He rides—the thirst of pure and endless glory
Inflames his spirit to the inmost core ;
Exploits he plans shall shame the vaunts of story,
Ten thousand glorious deeds undream'd before,—
To rush, in favor of the Cross he bore,
Midst hostile millions, gath'ring in his course
Cypress or noble palms, scour Egypt o'er
As on the Samiel's wing, and passage force
E'en to the awful depths of Nile's mysterious source !

53. But Guelpho, when the fervent boy at last,
Press'd to depart, had bade his last adieu,
No longer there delay'd, but forward pass'd
Where likeliest Godfrey might arrest his view ;—
Who, seeing him, exclaim'd, "Hail, Guelph ! for you
I have long sought, and but this moment sent
Some of my fleetfoot heralds to pursue
The search throughout the camp, from tent to tent,
Well does thy coming now their diligence prevent !"

54. He bade all else withdraw, and in a tone
Of graver utt'rance his discourse renew'd ;
"Deeply, my lord ! do I regret to own
The lengths to which thy nephew has pursued
The rage admitted in his hasty mood :
He ill, methinks, can justify the brawl,
Much less the frightful issue of the feud ;
Glad shall I be, if so it should befall,
But Godfrey still must act impartially to all.

55. "The sacred claims of lawful and of just
Defend I will, on all and each occasion,
Preserving ever, in my sov'reign trust,
A heart unsway'd by prejudice or passion.
Now if, as some say in extenuation,
Rinaldo was compell'd his wrongs to quit,
'Gainst the known edict, and in violation
Of martial rule, why let him, as is fit,
Come, and his proofs at once to our award submit.

56. "And let him come unmortified by chains,
The grace I can, I to his worth allow ;
If this his high rebellious heart disdains
(And well his fiery temperament I know
To be rebellious), be it thine to show
His pride the path of duty, ere he draws
A man by nature merciful, and slow
To cherish wrath, but stern should he give cause,
T' avenge his power defied and violated laws."

57. He ceased, and Guelph made answer : " Where's the soul
Free from all infamy, that if it heard
The voice of insult, haughty, false, and foul,
Would not with scorn resent th' injurious word !
And if the sland'rer fall beneath the sword,
Who can place bounds to a just wrath ? who suit
Exact acquittance to the guilt incurr'd,
Or weigh revenge out in a scale minute,
While in full fury glows th' unscrupulous dispute ?

58. " But that the youth, as you require, should yield
To your just judgment, which he ought, of right,
Cannot, it grieves me, be ; since far from field
He has withdrawn in no imprudent flight ;
But here I offer with my sword to write
Liar on his false forehead who again
Impugns his act,—on whatsoever knight
Wounds his good name ; and fearlessly maintain,
The Prince was justly served for his unjust disdain.

59. " With reason, I aver, he shore the crest
Of arrogant Gernando ; if in aught
He err'd, 'twas this, that thy supreme behest
He for an instant in his wrath forgot ;
This I lament, and this extenuate not : "
" 'Tis well," the other answer'd, " let him wend,
And brawl elsewhere ; nor foster in thy thought
The seeds of fresh dispute, but here, my friend,
Let all dissensions cease, and discord have an end ! "

60. Thus they ; meanwhile the smiling Traitress never
Ceased importuning for the promised aid ;
Throughout the livelong day each strong endeavor
Of genius, art, and beauty she essay'd ;
But when pale Eve, in twilight stole array'd,
Far in the west the dying Day inurn'd,
Betwixt two knights and matron dames convey'd
Back to her rich pavilion she return'd,
Till o'er blue orient hills resurgent morning burn'd.

61. But though Persuasion seem'd her spell-bound slave,
Spite of her bland words, her refined address,
And beauty such as nature never gave,
Before or since, dear woman to possess ;
Though in the trammels of her golden tresse
A deep o'ermast'ring transport had enchain'd
The noblest heroes, not with all her stress

Of artifice, could Godfrey's heart be gain'd ;
Unmoved, her charming smiles and flatt'ries he sustain'd.

62. In vain she studied to inflame his eye
With sweet temptations to a life of love,
For as the gorged falcon scorns to fly
When the pleased hawker points the passing dove,—
So he his wishes fix'd on joys above,
Sick of the world, with mortal pleasures cloy'd,
Despised the lure ; her beauty fail'd to move,
And all th' enchanting dalliance she employ'd,
Tutor'd by faithless love, his virtue render'd void.

63. No obstacle can turn his pious steps
From Duty's circumscribing walk ; she tries
A thousand arts, in thousand changeful shapes
Appears before him, and with Proteus vies
In ev'ry form of magical disguise ;
She has fond looks, lithe motions, bland alarms,
T' attract his gaze, and melt away the ice
From his cold heart, but heavenly grace disarms
Of power her visor'd trains, and shames her blandish'd charms.

64. She, who had thought one blink of her bright eyes
Would kindle passion in the purest mind,
How was she mortified ! with what surprise,
Yea, with what scorn and anger she repined ;
Frowning, her purpose she at length resign'd,
And muster'd for an enterprise more fair
Her charming force ; so chieftains, when they find
Impregnable the tower they gird, forbear
To press th' unprosp'rous siege, and turn their arms elsewhere.

65. Nor less was Tancred proof to the control
Of her seducing beauty ; he could share
With no new face th' affections of his soul ;
Clorinda only held dominion there :
For, as used poisons oft to poisons bear
Strong counter charms, e'en so 'twixt dame and dame,
Love neutralizes love ; Armida's snare
These shunn'd,—all others idolized her name,
And sported more or less around th' enchanting flame.

66. She, though she mourn'd that her designs should prove
But half successful, somewhat was consoled,

When she review'd the multitudes, which Love
Beneath her conqu'ring colors had enroll'd ;
And thus, ere chance to any should unfold
Her schemes, or ere her false mask should slip by,
Resolved to lead them to a stronger hold,
And forge them fetters of a stricter tie,
Than those same flow'ry bands in which e'en yet they lie.

67. When therefore the declining day was flown,
By Godfrey fix'd to grant the promised aid,
Before him she appear'd, and bending down
In humble rev'rence at his footstool, said :
"The period, gracious Sire, prefix'd is fled ;
And if the barb'rous tyrant from his spies
Shall learn that I for succors here have fled,
He will prepare his powers against surprise,
And much more dang'rous then will be the bold emprise.

68. "Ere then his couriers or discursive fame
Th' important tidings to his ear betray,
Let thy Compassion mine avengers name,
And send us forth, preventing all delay :
When, if the eye of Heaven with grace survey
Th' affairs of mortals, if the innocent's plea
Be in its sacred scrine recorded, they
Will throne me in my realm, which thus shall be
Ever, in peace and war, subsidiary to thee."

69. She said ; the Chief, unable to recede
From his engagement, bow'd to her request ;
And as she seem'd so urgent to proceed,
Saw well th' election with himself must rest:
But of her vow'd idolaters all press'd
To be admitted of the guardian band ;
While Jealousy, infix'd in every breast,
Kept dragon watch his rivals to withstand,
And deepen'd with his cry th' importunate demand.

70. She, who the sparkling secret clearly read,
Made it at once subserve her ill intent,
Using the spur of envy and of dread,
Their ling'ring course to quicken and torment,
For well she knew without some impulse lent
To stir the long dejection of the mind,
The flow of love in stagnancy is spent ;
Slow runs the steed that can outstrip the wind,
If one speeds not before, or follows fast behind.

71. The glance that flatter'd and the smile that woo'd,
She shared with words so seemingly sincere,
That each grew envious of the other's good,
And hope stood trembling on the brink of fear;
Her lovers, sanction'd by her gracious cheer,
And the false charter of her loving look,
Rush'd headlong on in folly's wild career,
By principle uncurb'd, of shame forsook,
Reckless of Godfrey's frown, keen scorn, or sharp rebuke.

72. He, who made justice his supreme delight,
Partial to none, to gladden all aspired;
And though the follies of each am'rous knight
With anger and deep shame his bosom fired;
Yet, seeing that which blindly they desired
Determinedly persisted in, he tried
Another mode to grant the boon desired:
"Each separate warrior write his name," he cried;
"A vase shall hold the lots, and chance the cause decide."

73. Their names the Chiefs with acclamations write,
Collect, and shake within an urn of gold;
At hazard drawn, the first that leaps to light,
Is Pembroke's Earl, Artemidore the bold:
The next whose title the blind Fates unfold,
On its white leaf the name of Gerard bears;
A third the fears of Vincilas consoled,
Who, late so grave and wise in all affairs,
Now plays the lovesick youth, and shames his hoary hairs.

74. Oh, what delight these three first chosen show
At their extreme good fortune! their fond eyes
With tears that from the full heart overflow,
Grow big, and sparkle o'er the happy prize;
The rest, whose doom still undetermined lies
In the dark urn, show signs of secret hate,
Sore jealousy, and panting, pale surmise;
Mute on the herald's lips they hang, and wait,
Breathless, the brief decree that seals their future fate.

75. To Guasco fourth, succeeds Ridolpho's name;
The sixth the fates to Olderic accord;
With Count Roussillon next, two peers of fame,
Henry the Frank, Bavarian Everard,
And, last, Rambaldo closed the blind award;—

Rambaldo, who for love of that false maid
(Has Love indeed such power?) renounced his Lord,
A traitor knight, a perjured renegade,—
The rest, shut out from hope, their fortune loud upbraid.

76. Inflamed with envy, jealousy, and rage,
They call her partial, wicked, and unkind;
They e'en accuse thee, Love, that thou shouldst gage
Thy judgment to an arbitress so blind:
But, as instinctively the human mind
More ardently desires what Heaven denies,
Many, in spite of fortune, have design'd
To follow yet their Lady in disguise,
Soon as night's falling shades obscure the lucid skies.

77. Follow they will, in sunshine and in shade,
And venture life in battling for her right:
She her last thanks to all saluting paid,
With broken hints and sighings, that incite
The Chiefs yet more to their intended flight;
With this, with that she grieved, or seem'd to grieve,
That she must part without the dear delight
Of his desired society;—'tis eve;
Th' elected Champions arm, and throng to take their leave.

78. Each after each the Chief advised apart
That Pagan faith was but a hollow reed,
As light and insecure; and with what art
They should from snares and adverse ills recede:
His words are utter'd to the winds,—none heed
His wise advise, for when did Wisdom sway
The ear of Love? permitted to proceed
At length they part; Armida leads the way,
All too impatient she to wait the dawn of day.

79. Conqueress she parts, and in a sumptuous train,
Triumphal, leads along her rival foes;
While still behind a countless throng remain,
Lovelorn, abandon'd to a thousand woes.
But when the Night on silent wings arose,
By Peace consorted in her gentle mood,
And Dreams, the erring pupils of Repose,—
With Love's divine intelligence endued,
Their Lady's printless path they secretly pursued.

80. First Eustace follow'd: scarcely could he wait
The ling'ring hours of ebbing eve,—he hied

Swiftly away, with heart and hope elate,
Through the blind darkness, led by his blind guide;
All the moist night serene he wander'd wide;
But when the sky's proud Sultan had possess'd
The ruby gates of Morning, he descried
With all her guards the Lady of his quest,
In a small village near, her last night's bower of rest.

81. Him by his arms at once Rambaldo knew,
As on fleet foot he moved to join the maid,
And cried aloud: "What seek'st thou? with what view
Com'st thou to us, in helm and mail array'd?"
"I come," said Eustace, "in Armida's aid;
Nor shall she have, if she my zeal approve,
A trustier friend:" "And who," Rambaldo said,
"On this high task commission'd thee to move?
Who authorized thy flight?" "Love," Eustace answer'd, "Love!

82. "Venus was my Electress, Fortune thine;
Advise which has the most authentic grant!"
To whom Rambaldo: "Off! the claim resign;
False is thy title, and impugn'd thy vaunt;
With us, legitimately call'd to plant
This virgin lily, ne'er shalt thou ally
Thy lawless aid!" Indignant at the taunt,
The youth rejoin'd, "And who will dare deny
My claims at proof of sword!" Rambaldo answer'd, "I!

83. "That which I dare avow, I dare maintain
At my sword's point!" he said, and saying, drew:
Not with less ardor, not with less disdain,
Insulted Eustace to the quarrel flew:
But here their Mistress rush'd betwixt the two;
Staying their swords, she sooth'd their angry vein:
To that she utter'd, "What is it you do;
If you a comrade, I a champion gain,
Why should you take offense? of what can I complain?

84. "Seek you my safety? why would you deprive
My straighten'd cause of so renown'd a knight?"
To Eustace then, "Most welcome! you arrive
In happy hour, protector of my right:
What shade of reason can I have to slight
So grateful an ally, the prince of Franks!
Fortune forbid I should the zeal requite

With rude neglect!" while yet she paid her thanks,
From ev'ry quarter round, fresh champions join'd her ranks.

85. Unknown to each they came, and frown'd askance
With hatred at their rivals; she received
All with the like smooth smiling countenance,
And whisper'd them what comfort she conceived
From their arrival; now when Light relieved
The dusky watch of morning, Godfrey knew
Of their defection and his loss; he grieved,
Deeply he grieved o'er the prophetic view
Seal'd on his sight, of ills that hence must needs ensue.

86. While musing thus, a messenger appears,
Swift, dusty, out of breath, a shape of woe;
Like one who news of bitter import bears,
With grief engraven on his gloomy brow:
"Signior," he said, "th' Egyptian fleets e'en now
Put out to sea, and crowd all sails in air;
Gray ocean whitens with the moving show:
William the Admiral, beneath whose care
The Genoese navy ranks, this message bids me bear.

87. "Nay, more; our convoy from the navied seas,
Well victuall'd for the camp, its fate has found;
One night, encamp'd among palmetto trees,
The steeds and burden'd camels grazing round,
A horde of Arabs in the glen profound
Ambush'd, sprang forth, the slumberers to assail
In front or flank; they slew them, or they bound
As slaves of war; nor from the fatal vale
Did one escape, but he who bore th' afflicting tale.

88. "Th' audacity of these marauding bands
Is now grown so licentious, that they spread
Like an o'erwhelming torrent from the sands,
Without control, and to a desert tread
The fruitful fields they traverse; to strike dread
Into their hearts, 'tis fit that thou ordain
A troop of horse their coverts to invade;
And from the sea of Palestine, the plain
That to the army leads, inviolate maintain."

89. These tidings, magnified from tongue to tongue,
Known in a moment, palsied ev'ry ear;
On ev'ry rumor the light vulgar hung,
In all th' uncertainty of anxious fear;

For fancied Famine was already near,
And the grim skeleton of Death : the Chief,
Who saw their courage droop, essay'd to cheer
Their dying hopes, and to disperse their grief,
With lively looks and words persuasive of relief.

90. "Ye, who through thousand perils, long flown o'er,
Have pass'd secure with me, in war and peace !
Champions of God, elected to restore
His frustrate faith ! who over hills and seas,
The arms of Persia, the designs of Greece,
Thirst's burning torment, hunger's keen distress.
Frost, whirlwind, storm, the billow and the breeze,
Have triumph'd gloriously, O say, for less
Alarms shall daunting fear your spirits now possess?

91. "In the good care of God, whose Spirit gave
Your mind its impulse, can ye not confide?
Is his arm shorten'd, that it cannot save?
That arm so oft in deeper perils tried !
A time will come not distantly descried,
When to remember ev'ry past dismay
Will be no less a pleasure than a pride ;
Hold then courageous on, and keep, I pray,
Your noble hearts in cheer for that victorious day."

92. These words of Godfrey, and his lively air,
Exiled their terror, and revived their pride ;
But many a preying thought and anxious care,
Deeply secreted, in his breast abide ;
How for such various nations to provide
In the prevailing scarceness : how afford
Help to his navy on the ocean wide,
Against th' Egyptian fleet ! and how his sword
May fitly reach and quell the Arabs' plund'ring horde.

END OF CANTO V.

JERUSALEM DELIVERED

CANTO VI.

ARGUMENT.

ARGANTES dares the Franks to single fight;
His prowess first undaunted Otho shows,
Too rashly; tumbled from his steed, by right
Of martial law he into thraldom goes.
Tancred, whom Godfrey for his champion choose,
Renews the conflict, and his falchion plies
Till twilight's gathering glooms a truce impose;
To cure her wounded lord, Erminia hies
From the well-guarded town, at dew-fall in disguise.

JERUSALEM DELIVERED.

CANTO VI.

1. But better hopes inspirit and make blithe
The hearts of the besieged: beside the grain
Stored from the reaping sickle and the scythe,
Beneath night's fav'ring darkness they obtain
Fresh stores; and flank, and fortify amain
With engines and grim frieze the Northern wall,
Which, grown to giant height, seems to disdain
The shock of brazen rams, as idle all,
Nor dreads what man can do to work its purposed fall.

2. Yet still at morn, at eve, at radiant noon,
The Monarch higher gives his towers to soar;
Nor quits his labor when the stars and moon
Silver the dusk of night; and evermore,
New arms for battle forging to the roar
Of swelt'ring fires, armorer and artisan
Toil with strong limbs, till vigor be no more
As thus th' intolerable moments ran,
To him Argantes came, and boastful thus began:

3. "How long in these vile walls must we be bound,
Rebellious pris'ners, tamed by slow blockade?
I hear the clang of anvils; the shrill sound
From hauberk, helm, and shield, my ears invade;
But to what purpose is the proud parade?
These robbers at their license don the crest;
Scour all our fields; our palaces invade;
Yet none of us their progress dare molest,
Or one clear trumpet sound, to scare their golden rest.'

4. "Them the gay lute and bounding dance employ
Unbroken banquets and secure delights:
Their day is one long carnival of joy,

And ease and quiet crown their blissful nights:
But thou at length, when fiercely famine bites,
Conquer'd must fall, and with submission buy
The victor's insults and the foe's despites;
Or die without a blow, as cowards die,
If Cairo send not soon our ling'ring, late ally.

5. "Ne'er o'er the dial of my life shall run
The oblivious darkness of a death it hates;
Not e'en the luster of another sun
Shall see me shut within these cursed gates:
With this, my life's poor fragment, let the Fates
Do what is fix'd for it in heaven or hell;
None e'er shall say in these inglorious straits,
That with his sword in sheath Argantes fell;
He will revenge disgrace, and earn his tomb too well.

6. "But if one spark of thy first chivalry
Still in thy bosom shed its fervent charm,
I should not hope in noble strife to die,
But live, enrich'd with honor's proudest palm;
With one accord let us resolve to arm,
Confront the Christians, and the field contest;
How oft in deepest peril and alarm,
The most audacious strokes have proved the best;
And ills which Care increased, Distraction has redress'd.

7. "But if thou dread'st to play so bold a game;
If to stake all thy forces to decide
The war at once, be judged a frantic aim,—
At least in duel let the strife be tried:
And that with livelier willingness and pride
The Captain of the Franks may entertain
Our challenge, and th' arbitrament abide,
Let him choose arms, take vantage of the plain,
And fix the terms of fight as he himself may deign

8. "Then, if no hundred-handed Briareus
Arm on his side, how fierce soe'er he be,
Dread not that evil chance thy cause will lose,
Upheld by justice, and secured by me;
In place of fate and fortune's blind decree,
My strong right hand shall from the stars pluck down
Consummate conquest for thy realms and thee:
Grasp it in pledge; now, by my old renown,
Trust me, they shall not shake one jewel from thy crown!"

9. He ceased, and Aladine replied: "In truth,
Though Age my pristine vigor has defaced,
Think not this scrupulous hand, too fervent youth,
A traitor to the sword it once embraced;
Think not my spirit slothful or debased;
Sooner with honor by the sword or spear
Would I expire, than die a death disgraced;
If I could entertain misdoubt or fear
That the distressful ills, announced, were really near.

10. "Allah such shame avert! What deep my art
From others hides, to thee shall now be shown:
The mighty Solyman, who burns in part
T' avenge the loss of his Nicean throne,
Has roused Arabia from her utmost zone
Of sand to Alcaïro, and relies
On all her tribes, when once his trumpet's blown,
In the black night the foeman to surprise,
And pour into the town fresh succor and supplies.

11. "Soon will he join us; if meanwhile they reign
In our spoil'd castles, blinded by conceit
And careless ease, fret not, while I retain
My purple mantle and imperial seat;
But that rash courage and intemp'rate heat
Which hurries thee to such excess, abate;
And for a dignified occasion, meet
For thy renown and my deep vengeance, wait;
Soon the black storm will burst, and lightnings seal their fate."

12. The haughty Pagan frown'd at this: high pride
And bitter spite boil'd in his breast, to hear
How on this Nicene prince the king relied,
His ancient rival and most fierce compeer:
"Sir," he replied, in icy tone austere,
"'Tis thy undoubted right to wage or end
War at thy pleasure; I have done; wait here
The shiver'd sword of Solyman thy friend;
Let him who lost his own thy kingdoms safe defend.

13. "Proud as a patron God let him advance
To free thy people from their yoke abhorr'd;
Myself am my palladium 'gainst mischance,
Nor freedom ask but from this single sword.
But while the rest repose, the grace accord,
That I at least may my own wrongs requite;
That from the town descending to the sward,

Not as thy champion but a private knight,
I may at least engage the Franks in single fight."

14. The king replied, "Although thou shouldst reserve
Thy sword and anger for a nobler use,
That thou defy some knight, if that will serve
Thy purpose, Aladine will not refuse."
His herald then without a moment's truce
Argantes spake, and with the daring boast
Dilating, said: "Give all thy swiftness loose;
And let this not mean challenge be proposed
To the Frank Duke below, in hearing of his host.

15. "Say, that a knight who longer scorns to crouch
Within the marble ramparts of the town,
Burns in the eye of angels to avouch,
By fact of arms, his prowess and renown;
That he to duel hastens to come down
Upon the plain midway 'twixt tent and tower;
To prove his valor on the golden crown
Of whatsoever Frank, of Franks the flower,
Dares to accept the gage, and try his martial power.

16. "And that not only is he girt to wage
Victorious battle with a single foe,
But with the third, fourth, fifth he will engage,
Villain or lord, with high-born or with low;
The vanquish'd shall the victor serve, for so
The rules of war ordain:" his message done,
The silver-scepter'd herald turn'd to go,
And lightly threw his purple surcoat on,
Emblazed with golden arms that glitter'd in the sun.

17. When reach'd the tent of Godfrey the divine,
In presence of his Barons, "Prince," he said,
"May perfect liberty of speech be mine
To tell a daring message without dread?"
He in assent inclined a haughty head,
And answer'd, "Ay! without the thought of fear,
Before us be the mighty venture spread:"
Then thus the herald, "Now will it appear
If the great news sound sweet or frightful to your ear."

18. The knight's defiance he at large exposed,
In glorying terms, magnificent and high;—
Loud murmur'd the fierce Lords, and round him closed,
Scorn on each lip, and pride in ev'ry eye:

Quickly their Lion-leader gave reply :
"A modest task methinks the knight has mused ;
What think ye, Peers ? dare we the battle try ?
Much I misdoubt when he his sword has used
On the fourth knight. the fifth will wish to stand excused !

19. "But let him put it to the proof ; I grant
Safe field and lib'ral ; we have some shall dare
Advance, to lessen his presumptuous vaunt,—
They shall no vantage use, nor fact unfair,
I lift my scepter to the stars, and swear !"
This heard, the sov'reign of the silver mace
Turn'd back by the same path he trod whilere :
Nor till he saw Argantes face to face,
Slack'd, for a moment slack'd, the swiftness of his pace.

20. "Arm !" he exclaim'd, "why hesitate to arm ?
The challenge they accept with glad surprise ;
Like sov'reign heroes there the meanest swarm
To front you,—visors close, and lances rise ;
I saw rage lighten in a thousand eyes ;
I saw a thousand hands caress the sword
In passion for the fight ; hark, how the skies
Sound to their shout, as though a river roar'd !—
Safe guard and ample field their Captain will afford !"

21. He heard, he call'd his Squire, and hurriedly
Braced on his mail, impatient for the plain ;
While to the fair Clorinda standing by,
The king exclaim'd : "Brave Lady ! to abstain
From arms, and in the city to remain,
While free Argantes issues out to fight,
Suit not thy rank ; take then an armed train
For surer safety, and attend the knight ;
At distance range their spears, but keep the lists in sight."

22. He ceased, and soon under the open sky
The troop rode forth in beautiful array,
And mark'd far on before how gallantly
The knight, in wonted arms and trappings gay,
Cheer'd to the frequent spur his ardent bay :—
A plain there was, seem'd, form'd by art, between
The camp and town ; of wide extent it lay,
As though the Campus Martius it had been
Before another Rome, unswelling, smooth, and green.

23. There singly he descended ; there, in sight
Of the collected camp his station took ;
By his brave heart, great bulk, and brawny might
Magnificent, and menacing in look
As huge Goliath by the vale's clear brook,
Or grim Enceladus, before whose stride
Th' aërial pines, and fields of Phlegra shook ;
But many without fear the giant eyed,
For none his utmost strength in battle yet had tried.

24. Though Godfrey yet no champion had selected,
Whose brav'ry best the Camp might represent,
It was no secret whom they most affected—
All eyes, hopes, wishes were on Tancred bent ;
To him the favor of all faces lent,
Spoke him th' ascendant genius of the crowd ;
And first a whisper round the circle went,
Which, faint awhile, grew momently more loud ;
Nor less the General's looks his own desire avow'd.

25. To him the rest give place, nor silent then
Remain'd the Duke ; "The tilt be thine," he cried ;
"Tancred, meet thou the ruffian Saracen,
Repress his fury, and abase his pride :"
In Tancred's face I would you had descried
What exultation shone, what boldness glow'd ;
Proud to be named th' antagonist defied,
He call'd for helm and steed ; his steed bestrode ;
And straight with num'rous friends from forth the intrenchments rode.

26. Within a bowshot of the ample field
Wherein Argantes for his champion stay'd,
On the near hill, upgazing, he beheld
The warlike figure of his Persian maid :
White were the vests that o'er her armor stray'd,
As snows on Alpine glaciers, and her face
(For she her visor had thrown up) display'd
Grandeur sublime so sweet'ning into grace,—
The region seem'd to him some heavenly-haunted place.

27. He noted not where the Circassian rear'd
His frightful face to the affronted skies,
But to the hill-top where his Love appear'd,
Turn'd, slack'ning his quick pace, his am'rous eyes,
Till he stood steadfast as a rock, all ice
Without, all glowing heat within ;—the sight
To him was as the gates of Paradise ;

And from his mind the mem'ry of the fight
Pass'd like a summer cloud, or dream at morning light.

28. Th' impatient Pagan, seeing none appear
In act preparative for battle, cried :
" Desire of gallant conflict brought me here,
Come forward one, and let the tilt be tried."
Still Tancred stood as he were stupified ;
The hero's shout broke not his thoughtful trance ;
But Otho, striking in his courser's side
His shining rowels, bravely made advance
First in the vacant lists, and couch'd his eager lance.

29. He was of those whose ardent hope and aim
It was, with fierce Argantes to have fought ;
To Tancred he indeed resign'd his claim,
And with the rest that Prince to battle brought ;
But noticing him now, absorb'd in thought,
Fail the desired advantage to employ,—
Seeing the tournay he before had sought
Free to his lance, the bold impatient boy
Seized on the offer'd chance with rash and greedy joy.

30. Swift as the tiger or voracious pard
Springs through the crashing forest, Otho press'd
To the stout Mussulman, who, on good guard,
Laid his tremendous spear in sudden rest :
Then Tancred first awoke ; then from the zest
Of am'rous thoughts as from a sweet dream started ;
And cried, " The fight is mine ! his course arrest ! "
But the young champion now too far had darted
Within the lists, to be from his opponent parted.

31. Therewith he stay'd, while wrath and crimson shame
Glow'd on his cheek, and in his bosom boil'd,
Deeming it worse than falsehood to his fame,
Thus of the field's first risks to be beguiled :
Meantime in mid career the hardy Childe
Struck the Circassian's burganet, and tore
The feathers from its crown ; but he, half wild,
With naked spear implacable for gore,
Quite clove his Redcross shield, and through the breast
plate bore !

32. Push'd from his seat by rudeness of the blow,
The Christian fell, half senseless from the shock ;
But his more vig'rous and athletic foe
Bore it unbow'd, impassive as a rock ;

And thus began the prostrate knight to mock,—
Fierce was his gesture, insolent his tone,—
"Yield thee my slave! where proudest nobles flock,
'Twill be enough for thy renown, to own
That thou hast fought with me and thus been overthrown!"

33. "No!" said the youth, "not quite so soon we use
To yield our arms and ardor on command;
Let others as they list my fall excuse,
I will revenge it, or die sword in hand!"
Fierce as Alecto, pitilessly grand,
With all the Gorgon raging in his face,
And breath like that of Ate's flaming brand,
Argantes said, "And scorn'st thou my good grace?
Learn then my power!" he spoke, and speaking spurn'd the place.

34. His rampant steed he drove at him, nor heeded
What to his chivalry was due; the Frank
From the rude onset, quick as thought, receded,
And dealt, in passing, at his dexter flank
A stroke so strong, that through his armor sank
The sword, incarnadine with blood;—the ground
Some rosy drops of the libation drank;
But what avail'd it to inflict a wound
That raised the conqu'ror's rage, and left his vigor sound?

35. He curb'd his courser, whirl'd him round, bore back,
And almost in the twinkling of an eye,
Ere his charged foe could guard against th' attack,
Trampled him down in grim ferocity:
Short drew his breath; quiver'd in agony
His legs, and with a faint, lamenting shriek
He swoon'd away; now low behold him lie,—
On the hard earth thrown panting, bruised, and weak;
Half closed the languid eye, and pale the suff'ring cheek.

36. Argantes, drunk with rage, enforced his way
With high curvetings o'er his victim's chest;
And cried, "Let all proud knights obedience pay,
Like him whom thus my horse's hoofs have press'd;"
Undaunted Tancred in his manly breast
At this barbaric action could restrain
His wrath no longer; shaking his black crest,

He forward spurr'd, ambitious to regain
His wonted fame eclipsed, and clear its recent stain.

37. "And O," he cried, advancing, "spirit base!
E'en in thy conquests, infamous! what meed,
What title to esteem, what claim to praise
Hop'st thou, accursed, from such a villain's deed!
With Arab robbers or the like fierce breed
Of ruffians, surely thou wert bred;—away!
Back to thy loathed den of darkness speed;
Midst hills and woods go raven for thy prey
With other wolves by night, more savage far than they!"

38. The Pagan Lord, to such affronts unused,
Bit both his lips, wrath's strangled orators;
He would have spoke, but only sounds confused
Broke forth, such sounds as when a lion roars;
Or, as when lightning cleaves the stormy doors
Of heaven, to rouse from its reluctant rest
The thunder growling as the tempest pours;
For ev'ry word which he with pain express'd,
Escaped in tones as gruff, from his infuriate breast.

39. When by ferocious threats they each had fired
His rival's pride, and fortified his own,
Some paces back they rapidly retired,
And met, like two black clouds together blown.
Queen of the Lyre! down from thy Delphic throne
Descend with all thy talismans and charms;
Breathe in my ringing shell thy hoarsest tone,
That to their rage attemper'd, its alarms
May with the shock, repeat the clangor of their arms!

40. Both placed in rest, and level'd at the face
Their knotty lances;—ne'er did tiger's spring,
Nor ardent charger in the rushing race,
Match their swift course, nor bird of swiftest wing;
Here Tancred, there Argantes came!—to sing
The force with which they met, would ask the cry
Of angels,—sudden the shock'd helmets ring;
Their spears are broke; and up to the blue sky
A thousand lucid sparks, a thousand shivers fly.

41. That shrill blow shook Earth's firm volubil ball;
The mountains, sounding as the metals clash'd,
Pass'd the dire music to the towers, till all
The City trembled; but the shock, which dash'd

Both steeds to earth, as each for anguish gnash'd
Its teeth, and shriek'd its noble life away,
Scarce bow'd their haughty heads ; they, unabash'd,
Sprang lightly up, war's perfect masters they,
Drew their gold-hilted swords, and stood at desp'rate bay.

42. Warily deals each warrior's arm its thrust,
His foot its motion, its live glance his eye ;
To various guards and attitudes they trust ;
They foin, they dally, now aloof, now nigh,
Recede, advance, wheel, traverse, and pass by,
Threat where they strike not, where they threat not dart
The desp'rate pass ; or, with perception sly,
Free to the foe leave some unguarded part,
Then his foil'd stroke revenge, with art deriding art.

43. Prince Tancred's thigh the Pagan knight perceives
But ill defended, or by shield or sword ;
He hastes to strike, and inconsid'rate leaves
His side unshielded as he strides abroad ;
Tancred fail'd not instinctively to ward
The stroke, beat back the weapon, and, inspired
With eager hope, the guardless body gored ;
Which done, of either gazing host admired,
He nimbly back recoil'd, and to his ward retired.

44. The fierce Argantes, when he now beheld
Himself in his own gushing blood baptized,
In unaccustom'd horror sigh'd and yell'd,
With shame discount'nanced, and with pain surprised ;
And, both by rage and suff'ring agonized,
Raised with his voice his sword aloft, to quit
The sharp rebuke ; but Tancred, well advised
Of his intent, afresh th' assailant smit,
Where to the nervous arm the shoulder-blade was knit.

45. As in its Alpine forest the grim bear,
Stung by the hunter's arrow, from its haunts
Flies in the face of all his shafts, to dare
Death for the wild revenge, no peril daunts ;
Just so the mad Circassian fares, so pants
For blood, as thus the foe his soul besets,
When shame on shame, and wound on wound he plants ;
And his revenge his wrath so keenly whets,
That he all danger scorns, and all defense forgets.

46. Joining with courage keen a valor rash,
And untired strength with unexampled might.
He showers his strokes so fast, that the skies flash,
And earth e'en trembles in her wild affright:
No time has the alarm'd Italian knight
To deal a single blow; from such a shower
Scarce can he shield himself, scarce breathe; no sleight
Of arms is there t' assure his life an hour
From the man's headstrong haste and brute gigantic power.

47. Collected in himself, he waits in vain
Till the first fury of the storm be past;
Now lifts his moony targe; now round the plain
Fetches his skillful circles, far and fast;
But when he sees the Pagan's fierceness last
Through all delay, his own proud blood takes fire,
And, staking all his fortunes on the cast,
He whirls his sword in many a giddy gyre,
Requiting strength with strength, and answ'ring ire with ire.

48. Judgment and skill are lost in rage; rage gives
Resentment life; fresh force resentment lends;
Where falls the steel, it either bores or cleaves
Chainplate or mail; plumes shiver, metal bends,
Helms crack, and not a stroke in vain descends;
The ground is strew'd with armor hewn asunder,
Armor with blood, with ruby blood sweat blends;
Each smiting sword appears a whirling wonder,
Its flash the lightning's fire, its sullen clang far thunder.

49. Both gazing nations anxious hung suspended
Upon a spectacle so wild and new;
With fear, with hope, the issue they attended,
Some good or ill perpetually in view;
Not the least beck or slightest whisper flew
Mid the two hosts so lately in commotion;
All nerve alone, all eye, all ear, they grew
Fix'd mute, and soundless as an eve-lull'd ocean,
Save what the beating heart struck in its awful motion.

50. Now tired were both; and both their spirits spent,
Had surely perish'd on the field of fight,
Had not dim eve her length'ning shadows sent,
And e'en of nearest things obscured the sight;

And now on either side in apposite
Array, a rev'rend herald rose, and sought
From the keen strife to sep'rate each his knight;
This Aridos, Pindoro that, who brought
Of late th' insulter's boast, and terms on which they fought.

51. Safe in the sacred laws of nations kept
Religiously from hallowing age to age,
The swords of both they dare to intercept
With their pacific scepters, and the sage
Pindoro spoke: "Suspend, my sons, your rage;
Equal your glory, equal is your might;
No longer then th' invet'rate warfare wage,
Nor with rude sounds unamiable affright
Rashly the holy ear of quiet-keeping Night!

52. "Lull'd in soft rest by night each creature lies;
Man should but toil while shines the daily sun,
And noble bosoms will but lightly prize
E'en noble deeds in silent darkness done."
Argantes then: "To quit the strife begun
Pleases me ill, though darkness ride the air;
Yet worthier far will be my conquest won
Beneath the eye of day; then let him swear,
Here for fresh proof of arms again to make repair."

53. To whom the high Italian: "Thou too plight
Thy promise to return, and bring with thee
Thy captive to the lists, or ne'er, proud knight,
Look thou for other time than this from me."
Thus swear they both by what may holiest be;
And the choice heralds meditate what time
May best subserve the combat; they decree
(Consid'rate of their wounds) the hour of prime,
When the sixth morning's breeze sheds coolness through the clime.

54. This dreadful battle left in every heart
Deep horror, mighty wonder, and chill fear,
Which cannot be forgot, nor soon depart,
And open gloom and counterfeited cheer.
The force and valor shown by either peer
Alone the talk of all employ'd—how well,
And stubbornly they fought; but which with clear
Pre-eminence of power did most excel,
Perplex'd the vulgar thought; in sooth no tongue could tell.

55. All wait in deep anxiety to see
What fate will crown the strife; if rage shall quail
To the calm virtue of pure chivalry,
Or giant strength o'er hardihood prevail:
But deepest cares and doubts distract the pale
And sensitive Erminia; her fond heart
A thousand agonies and fears assail;
Since, on the cast of war's uncertain dart,
Hangs the sweet life she loves, her soul's far dearer part.

56. She, daughter to Cassano, who the crown
Wore of imperial Antioch, in the hour
When the flush'd Christians won the stubborn town,
With other booty fell in Tancred's power:
But he received her as some sacred flower,
Nor harmed her shrinking leaves; midst outrage keen,
Pure and inviolate was her virgin-bower;
And her he caused to be attended, e'en
Amidst her ruin'd realms, as an unquestion'd queen.

57. The gen'rous knight in ev'ry act and word
Honor'd her, served her, sooth'd her deep distress,
Gave her her freedom, to her charge restored
Her gems, her gold, and bade her still possess
Her ornaments of price: the sweet Princess,
Seeing what kingliness of spirit shined
In his engaging form and frank address,
Was touch'd with love; and never did Love bind
With his most charming chain a more devoted mind.

58. Thus, though in person free, her spirit ever
Remain'd his willing thrall; and many a tear,
Many a last look, many a vain endeavor,
It cost her to depart from one so dear,
And quit her blissful cage; but shame austere,
And princely chastity, whose least command
The high-soul'd lady ever must revere,
Forced her to take her aged mother's hand,
And an asylum seek in some far friendly land.

59. To tower'd Jerusalem she came, and there
Was richly entertain'd; but 'twas her doom
Too soon the sable vests of woe to wear,
And plant the cypress round her mother's tomb;
But not the grief, the sickness, and the gloom,
Not all that bitter exile could inspire,

From her delicious cheek might brush the bloom,
The rosy bloom of amorous desire,
Or quench in her soft heart pure Passion's ling'ring fire.

60. She loved, she glow'd, poor girl! and yet was far
From happy, for her love hoped no return;
Indeed, she turn'd far oftener to the star
Of Mem'ry, than of Hope; as in an urn
Hiding within her breast the thoughts that burn
Fiercest in secret: to foment the flame,
Vain as it was, was long her sole concern;
Till with the war to Salem, Tancred came,
And Hope again flash'd forth like lightning through her frame.

61. Others beheld with gloom and pale dismay
Such tameless numbers to the plain advance:
But her dark looks at once grew bright, and gay
She mark'd the banners float, the white plumes dance,
And roll'd throughout the host an eager glance,
The gen'rous hero of her heart to see;
Oft the vain search her sadness would enhance;
Yet oft she recognized him, in fond glee
Shook her rich locks, and said: "That, that indeed is he!"

62. Near to the walls, within the palace, soar'd
A lofty tower antique, from whose steep height
The eye at its own pleasant will explored
The camp, the mountains, and the field of fight;
There would she sit from the first hour that light
Bathed the gray battlements, till seas and skies
Grew dark with the impurpling hues of night;—
There would she sit, fond dreamer! with her eyes
Turn'd to the Christian camp, and spend her soul in sighs.

63. 'Twas thence she view'd the battle, whose least blow
Made her heart tremble in its dainty cell,
And send its strong pulsations to and fro,
As if in solemn tone it toll'd the knell
Of hope, and sounded to her soul—"Farewell
To Tancred!" troubled thus, with fear profound
She watch'd each fortune that her knight befell;
And ever as the Pagan's sword flew round
Felt in her own fond heart and brain th' inflicted wound.

64. But when the fatal tidings reach'd her ear
That the fierce conflict must afresh be tried,
Her sick blood curdled in its flow; blank fear
Appall'd her, and her heart within her died ;
Now she pour'd forth wild tears ; now sorely sigh'd ;
And now to unseen glooms stole, seeking there
The strong convulsions of her soul to hide ;
Grief in her gaze, distraction in her air,
She seem'd the passive slave and picture of Despair.

65. And frightful shapes and images possess'd
The organs of her fancy ; types and themes
More drear than death, if e'er she sank to rest,
Throng'd to her sleep, and shook her midnight dreams.
Now to her sight her loved Crusader seems
Mangled and bleeding, or assaulted rears
To her his fond beseeching arms, and screams
For her vain help ; till, leaping with her fears,
She wakes, and finds her eyes and bosom bathed with tears.

66. But dread of future ills was not the worst
Of her solicitudes ; rude visitings
Of fancy thoughtful of his wounds unnursed,
Ruffled her soul, and loosed its silver springs ;
Nor less each fresh report that Rumor brings
In her fallacious circuit, magnifies
Her pict'rings of unknown and distant things,
Till she at length admits the wild surmise,
That at the point of death her languid warrior lies.

67. And as her mother taught her in her youth
The virtues of all herbs by saint or sage
For medicine cull'd, with all the charms that soothe
The thrilling wound, and calm the fever's rage,—
An art which from the Patriarchal Age
The East's prescriptive usages accord
To virgins e'en of princely parentage,—
With her own hand would she, of risk unaw'd,
Tend, and to health restore the bruises of her lord.

68. To heal her love was her desire, to cure
His foe her bitter task : she thought to seek
Sometimes for pois'nous herbs that might ensure
His death ; but such malignant arts her meek
And pious hands recoil'd from—she could speak,
Not execute the scheme : but she might nurse
At least the wish, her piety to pique,

That some kind power the blessings would reverse
Of all her balms and spells, and change them to a curse.

69. She had no fear to go midst adverse nations,
Who was so much a pilgrim ; she had seen
The anarchy of battle, desolations,
Adversities, and slaughters ; and had been
So toss'd by Fate through each tumultuous scene,
That now her gentle mind a strength display'd
That was not in its nature,—fix'd, serene ;
No more to shake with ev'ry wind that play'd
Amongst the midnight woods, nor shriek at ev'ry shade.

70. But more than all, Love, headstrong Love, removed
From her all sense of fear : she would have faced,
Devoid of terror, for the man she loved,
The snakes and lions of the Lybian waste,
And deem'd her passage sure ; but though in haste
To please her will existence she disdain'd,
She trembled lest her name should be disgraced ;
Two potent rivals, Love and Honor, reign'd
Within her maiden breast, and dubious strife maintain'd.

71. "Beloved young Virgin," Honor whisper'd, "well
Hast thou preserved my statutes to this hour !
Think how I kept, by mine immortal spell,
Chaste thy fair limbs when in the spoiler's power ;
And wilt thou, now that thou art free, the flower
Of holy Chastity unwoo'd resign,
So closely treasured then ? beshrew thy bower ?
How canst thou once indulge the dread design !
What thoughts, alas, what hopes, dear maid, are these of thine !

72. "Hold'st thou thy glory at a price so slight,
The priceless glory of a maiden's fame,
That thou must go, Love's paranymph, by night
Mid adverse hosts to court unquestion'd shame?
'No,' the proud victor coolly will exclaim,
'Thou with thy throne thy dignity of mind
Hast lost,—a prize so worthless I disclaim ;'—
Say, canst thou brook to be by one so kind
To some more vulgar feere contemptuously resign'd !"

73. Next Love, the flatt'ring sophist, with a tongue
Sweet as the nightingale's, her soul beguiled :
"Thou wert not, gentle maid, from rude rocks sprung,
Or nursed by wild wolves in the fruitless wild,
That thou shouldst scorn soft Cytherea's child,

His admirable bow and dulcet dart,
Foreswearing bliss; then blush not to be styled
His votaress, young and charming as thou art,—
Heaven ne'er has cursed that form with an unyielding heart.

74. "Go then where mild Desire thy steps invites!
Canst thou conceive thy victor harsh or vain,
Who know'st how much thy grief his grief incites,
How thy complaints e'en move him to complain?
'Tis not his harshness then, but thy disdain
That thou shouldst deprecate, who with so slow
An inclination mov'st to ease his pain;
Thy virtuous Tancred dies, stern girl, and lo—
Thou must be sitting here to aid his worthless foe!

75. "Yes, cure Argantes, that his sword may smite
Thy benefactor to the dead! what then,
Wouldst thou thus cancel, wouldst thou thus requite
Th' unmeasured kindness of the best of men?
Canst thou once doubt, that the vile Saracen
Will fail on Tancred and on thee to bring
Yet sharper pangs, restored to arms again?
Let the mere dread and horror of the thing
Suffice to speed thee hence as on the turtle's wing.

76. "It would be some humanity to stand
His dutiful physician! what delight
Would it not be to lay thy healing hand
Upon the brave man's breast! how exquisite
To watch, as at thy call, the roseate light
Of health descend with freshness to displace
The pallid hues which now his beauty blight,
And on the coloring roses of his face,
As on thine own rich gifts, admiringly to gaze!

77. "So shouldst thou share in all the after-fame
Of his romantic exploits; so should sweet
And unreproved caresses crown thy flame;
And prosp'rous nuptials make thy joy complete:
Then into beauteous Italy, the seat
Of high-born worth, thou go'st, a glorious bride;
While Latin girls and mothers at thy feet
Scatter young flowers, and point at thee with pride,
Seated in Tancred's car, like Love by Valor's side."

73. With these light hopes, sweet simple girl, upbuoy'd,
She fondly deem'd all Paradise her own;

Yet still a thousand doubts her mind annoy'd—
How could she pass out through the gates, unknown ?
For trumpets at the least alarm were blown,
And station'd guards paraded without pause,
The court, the streets, and ramparts of the town ;
Nor might the gates, by Aladine's wise laws,
Be night or day unbarr'd, but on some urgent cause

79. It was Erminia's wont, long hours, to hold
Converse with brave Clorinda : them the sun
Together view'd, as down the skies he roll'd—
Them, when his orient progress was begun ;
And when his circuit through the heavens was run,
On the same couch together they reposed ;
And all her thoughts and feelings, save the one
Her glowing spirit loved and mused on most,
Were to the Persian maid familiarly disclosed.

80. This only secret to herself alone
She kept ; and if she did but once complain,
Or unawares let fall a sigh or groan,
Straight she disguised it on pretence of pain
For her remember'd home : so strict the chain
Of their connection now was grown, that ne'er
Did mute or maiden offer to restrain
Erminia's access to her, whatsoe'er
Might be th' immediate theme that claim'd their Lady s care.

81. She came one eve—Clorinda was away,—
Yet pensive she sat down, and inly weigh'd
Each mode of art by which she might essay
The so-much-wished departure, unbetray'd ;
There while a thousand thoughts her mind, unstay'd
In its designs, revolved, nor could decide
Which to adopt, by the mild light that play'd
On the white walls, suspended she descried
Clorinda's arms and vest : she saw them and she sigh'd :

82. And sighing, thus exclaim'd : " Heroic dame,
How envy I thy fortune ! not that thou
Art lovely in thy might,—not for the fame
And vaunt of thy wild beauty, Dearest, no !
But thee no envious cell restrains ; no flow
Of cumbrous garments curbs thy steps,—thy weeds
Are of the beaten silver ; thou canst go

By night or day where'er thy humor leads ;
No fear thy course controls, no bashfulness thy deeds.

83. "Ah, wherefore did not Heaven to me accord
A strength like hers ! then might I change the veil
For the plumed helm, the quiver for the sword,
And pall of purple for the shirt of mail :
Then neither thunder, heat, nor hoary hail
Should mew my love within these towers of stone :
But or in open day, or by the pale
Pure planet of the night, would I begone,
Arm'd, to the Christian camp, attended or alone.

84. "Then thou, accursed Argantes, hadst not fought
First with my lord : I would have sought the plain,
And struck, perhaps a noble conquest wrought,
And hither brought my vassal to sustain,
Forged by revengeful Love, a red-rose chain
Gay as the light, and playful as the air ;
Charm'd with that fond beguilement of my pain,
I should have felt the bonds he makes me wear,
Sweet for my servant's sake, and passing light to bear.

85. "Or else his hand the passage had explored
To my poor heart, and piercing through my breast,
His kindly-cruel and unhinder'd sword
Had cured the wound his image there impress'd :
Then would my weary spirit be at rest ;
Perchance the victor, piteous of my doom,
With one kind tear my obsequies had graced;
Raised the lone urn, and o'er my early tomb
Bade the green cypress wave, th' unwith'ring laurel bloom.

86. "Alas, I dream wild things ! what have I said ?
My thoughts are in a maze of follies lost ;
Shall I then stay, lamenting, yet afraid
To act, like a weak slave or shiv'ring ghost ?
I will not ! no ! mount, spirits, to your post !
My bold heart, fortify my tim'rous cheek !
Can I not use these arms for once ? at most,
It is but a brief hardship that I seek ;
Can I not bear their weight, though tender, faint, and weak ?

87. "I can ; I will ! true Love will make me strong,—
Love gives the weakest strength : e'en the tame deer,
Prick'd by his kindly heat, to battle throng

In antler'd vigor, without care or fear :
I have no wish indeed with helm or spear
To war, like them ; but only, by their rape,
Like my beloved Clorinda to appear ;
If I of her but take the armed shape,
Beneath the pleasant fraud I make my sure escape.

88. "The warders will not dare but ope for her
The portal-gates, and a free pass allow ;
I think again . . . . no other means occur ;
This method only can avail my vow.
O, gentle Love ! in this sharp need, do thou
Favor my flight, as thou inspir'st my wit ;
And Fortune, stand benignant ! even now
Prove I your power,—this is the time most fit,
While yet Clorinda's cares the mask'd attempt permit!"

89. Thus, fix'd was her resolve ; delay was none ;
By the rash fervor of her passion sway'd,
From her friend's near apartment to her own,
Clorinda's arms she secretly convey'd,—
For at her entrance each attendant maid
Retired, and she remain'd alone ; while Night,
Blind patroness of thefts and frolics play'd
By gentle lovers, fav'rer of her flight,
Rose o'er the silent world, and hid the spoils from sight.

90. She, when she saw the bloom of sunset fade,
And Love's pale star put forth its sparkling fire,
No moment of her precious time delay'd,
But sent a secret summons for her squire,
And for her fav'rite maid, in whose entire
Devotion to her person she reposed
Implicit trust : to them her strong desire
To quit th' invested city she disclosed ;
But feign'd that other cause the timeless step imposed.

91. Quick was the Squire, and active to provide
What for the journey he conceived was meet ;
While young Erminia laid her vests aside,
That hung for pomp below her graceful feet ;
And to her flower'd cymar disrobed complete.
Never did virgin bride a shape display
So elegantly slender ; charms so sweet
Surpass the power of fancy to portray :
Prompt stands the fav'rite maid her Lady to array.

92. The hard cold steel oppresses and offends
Her delicate smooth neck and golden hair;
Her arm, unequal to the burden, bends
Beneath the huge shield she aspires to bear:
Arm'd, the bright Virgin cast a dazzling glare,
And fashion'd her nice step and aspect mild
To a proud stride and military air;
Love near her clapp'd his little wings, and smiled,
As when in female weeds Alcides he beguiled.

93. Oh, how fatiguing every moment grew
Th' unequal weight! how slow her falt'ring pace!
Faint to her handmaid for support she drew,
And by her help moved onward a short space;
But Love renews her spirits, bright hopes brace
Her sinews strength'ning as her fear abates;
So that at length they reach the chosen place,
Where the mute Squire for their arrival waits,
Vault on their steeds, and seek at once the guarded gates.

94. Disguised they went, the least-frequented ways
Selecting well; yet pass'd they many a band
Of soldiers under arms, and saw the blaze
Of bick'ring armor flash on ev'ry hand;
But none of those they met with durst withstand
Their uncommission'd progress, nor presume
E'en to require the signal of command;
Awed they pass'd on, for through the evening gloom
All knew the silver arms and dreaded tigress plume.

95. Erminia, though this homage had dispersed
The strongest of her doubts, was ill at ease;
Still for her bold design she fear'd the worst;
And heard discov'ry sound in ev'ry breeze.
But now the portals of the town she sees;
Checks her alarm, and in commanding state
Boldly confronts the keeper of the keys:
"For Aladine!" she cries, "unbar the gate!
Heave the portcullis up! the hour is waxing late."

96. Her female tone and form give added power
To the masked fraud; (for who would think to see
Arm'd and in saddle, at so dusk an hour,
A gentle lady of her high degree?)
So that the guard obeys at once, and she,
With the two press'd attendants that partake
Her flight, proceeds; for full security

Resolved to thread the vales, by bush and brake
Gliding in noiseless stealth, long winding tracks they take.

97. But when Erminia saw herself at last
Deep in the lonely vales, she curb'd her steed;
For her first peril she accounted past,—
And well aware that she had now no need
For apprehension, gave attentive heed
To the still voice of prudence, which, she grieved,
Had been in her desire's impetuous speed
Pass'd by unheard: her access she perceived
Would prove more hard to win than she at first believed.

98. She now perceived the folly of a flight
In borrow'd arms amid her angry foes;
Nor, on the other hand, till to the knight
She came, would she her rank or name disclose;
But, secret and reserved as the moss-rose
In its infolding leaves, would first acquire
Pledge of deserved reception; whence she goes
More gently o'er the grass, and her desire,
Lower'd to cool caution's key, thus trusts to her sure squire.

99. "My faithful servant; thee have I design'd
For my precursor; but be swift and wise:
Haste to the camp, and some auxiliar find
To introduce thee where Prince Tancred lies;
Him of my coming tranquilly apprize:
Say, 'That a pitying lady comes to pour
Oil in his wounds, and on his grace relies
For peace, whom warring Love has wounded sore;
So may our mutual gifts our mutual ease restore!

100. "'One, who on him does such full trust repose,
That in his hands she fears nor wrong nor scorn:'
This only—to his private ear disclose,
And if he wishes aught beside to learn,
Tell nothing, nothing know, but straight return;
I (for the spot a sense of safety brings)
Will maenwhile in the valley make sojourn:"
This said, her faithful herald forward springs;
And scours the vale as though endued with actual wings.

101. With such a dext'rous skill his aim he wrought,
He won the jealous sentries, pass'd them clear,
And to the warrior on his couch was brought,

Who heard the message with delighted ear.
Left to himself, th' astonished cavalier
Lay full of thought, and in his fancy weigh'd
A thousand doubtful things, by hope and fear
At once possess'd: the answer which he made
Was, that she safe might come, and secret as the shade.

102. But she meanwhile impatient, in whose eyes
Each moment seem'd an age, to care a prey,
Counts to herself each sep'rate step, and cries,
"Now he arrives, now speaks, now hastes away;"
Next she upbraids his indolent delay;
Chides his unusual want of diligence;
And, weary grown of his eternal stay,
Spurs till she gains the nearest eminence,
Whence her dilating eye discerns the distant tents.

103. On high were the clear stars; the gentle Hours
Walk'd cloudless through the galaxy of space,
And the calm moon rose, lighting up the flowers
With frost of living pearl: like her in grace,
Th' enamor'd maid from her illumined face
Reflected light where'er she chanced to rove;
And made the silent Spirit of the place,
The hills, the melancholy moon above,
And the dumb valleys round, familiars of her love.

104. Seeing the Camp, she whisper'd: "O ye fair
Italian tents! how amiable ye show!
The breathing winds that such refreshment bear,
Ravish my soul, for 'tis from you they blow!
So may relenting Heaven on me bestow,—
On me, by froward Fate so long distress'd,—
A chaste repose from weariness and woe,
As in your compass only lies my quest;
As 'tis your arms alone can give my spirit rest.

105. "Receive me then, and in you let me find
Love's gentle voice, which spoke of pity, true;
And that delightful music of the mind,
Which in my bless'd captivity I drew
From my lord's mercy; patronized by you,
I have no wish to reobtain and wear
My regal crown,—adieu, vain pomps, adieu!
Enough for me if Tancred grants my prayer;
More bless'd in you to serve, than reign a queen elsewhere."

106. Ah, little does she think, while thus she dreams,
What is prepared for her by Fortune's spite !
She is so placed, that the moon's placid beams
In line direct upon her armor light :
So far remote into the shades of night
The silver splendor is convey'd, and she
Surrounded is, with brilliancy so bright,
That whosoe'er might chance her crest to see,
Would of a truth conclude it must Clorinda be.

107. And, as Fate will'd, close couch'd in the high fern,
In stations due of distance interposed,
Two brave Italian brothers, Polypherne,
And, paramount, Alcander, had disposed
Full fifty youths, the flower of Tancred's host,
To intercept the Saracens' supply
Of flocks and herds from the Arabian coast ;
Erminia's servant but escaped their eye
By his long winding track, and speed in gliding by.

108. Watchful young Polypherne, whose aged sire
Before his eyes Clorinda lately slew,
Saw the white arms, the feminine attire,
And the charged helmet for Clorinda's knew ;
Rash and unguarded in his wrath, he drew
His urged attendants from the covert near ;
And, as on fire for vengeance forth he flew,
Shouted aloud, " 'Tis well ; death waits thee here ! "
And lanced, but lanced in vain, his formidable spear.

109. As when a hind, inflamed with fervid thirst,
Seeking the cool refreshing fountains, sees
A clear spring gushing from a crag, or burst
Of some cascade o'erbower'd with leafy trees,—
If, while she thinks to taste the shade at ease,
And quaff the waves up that so sweetly roar,
The hunter's horn sounds shrilly in the breeze,
Back, back she rushes, nor remembers more
The faintness, thirst, and heat, that fired her limbs before,

110. So she, who thought in Tancred's pure embrace
To quench the love which she began to find
Inflame her heart, and, anchor'd on his grace,
To woo repose to her so weary mind,
Hearing the clang of weapons on the wind,
And the loud menace of the hunters arm'd
To thwart her pleasures, tremblingly resign'd

Thought of the joy that woo'd, the wish that warm'd,
And spurr'd her courser back, distracted and alarm'd.

111. Away the Princess flies, her snorting steed
Trampling with swift intelligential feet
The echoing soil ; with imitative speed
Flies too her handmaid, while with steps less fleet
The troop pursue ; and now the squire discreet,
With his untimely tidings comes in sight
Of the pale maid, perceives her in retreat,
And, press'd, participates her dubious flight ;
Wide o'er the plains they speed, diversely driven by fright.

112. But the more wise Alcander, though he too
Had the same counterfeit Clorinda seen,
Would not th' already challenged maid pursue,
But kept still close within his leafy screen ;
And sent to say, that through the valleys green
Nor fleecy sheep had pass'd, nor lowing steer ;
And that no foe had intercepted been,
But strong Clorinda, who in panic fear
Fled from his brother's call and close-pursuing spear.

113. And that he could not reas'nably conceive
That she, the Lady Chieftain of the land,
Not a mere warrioress, would choose to leave
The town at such an hour, but on some grand
And hardy enterprise, for mischief plann'd
Against the camp ; yet, ere he shifted thence,
He look'd for Godfrey's counsel or command :
The scout that brought the news of these events,
Passing, divulged it first amid th' Italian tents.

114. Tancred, who yet had scarce the doubts allay'd
Raised by the message which the Syrian bore,
Thinks, what if for my sake the courteous maid
Risks her dear life ! ah ! what if all be o'er !
He leaps from off his couch, assumes no more
Than half his arms, in still and secret haste
Climbs to his steed, the strange event t' explore,
And, following the clear footmarks freshly traced,
Glides like a shooting star across the moonbright waste.

END OF CANTO VI.

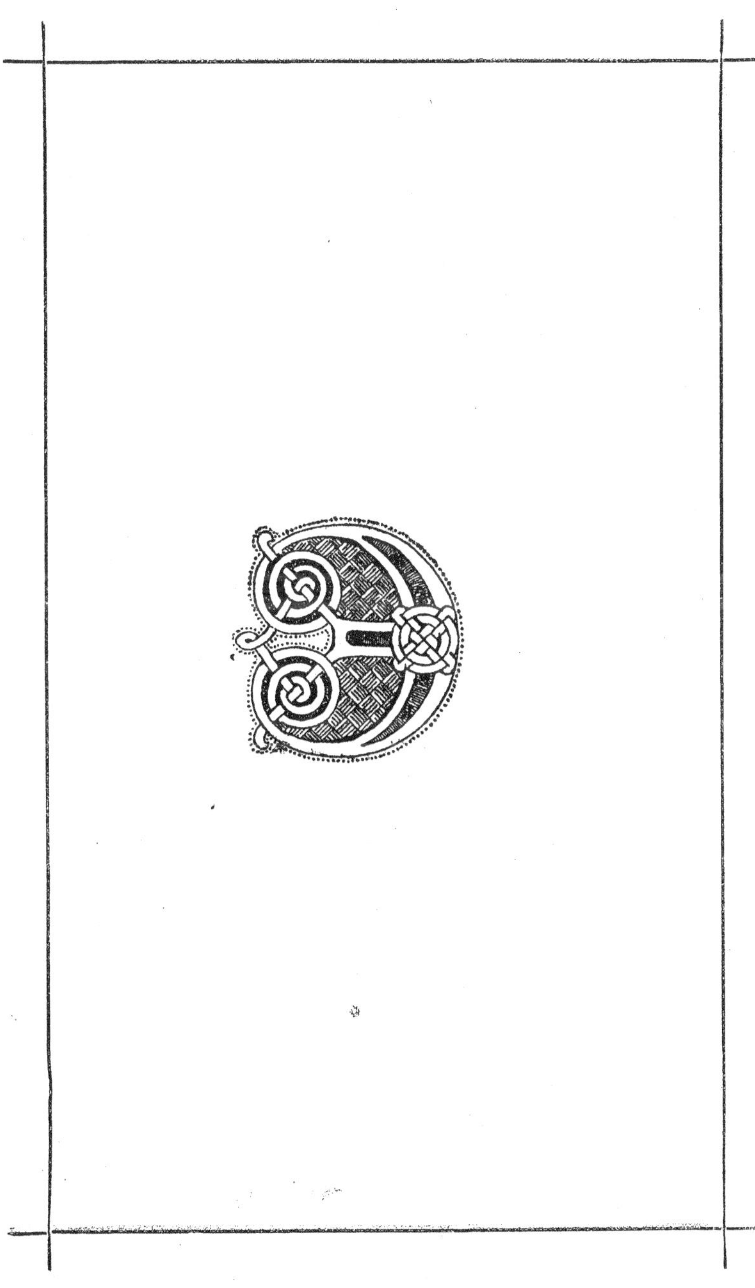

JERUSALEM DELIVERED.

CANTO VII.

ARGUMENT.

A HOSPITABLE shepherd entertains
Forlorn Erminia; her undaunted knight,
Seeking the frighted Damsel, in the trains
Of false Armida, is entrapp'd by sleight.
Raymond with proud Argantes dares the fight
And gains an Angel for his guard; betray'd
By rage to deepest risk, in helpless plight
The Pagan stands, till Belzebub, in aid,
Blends the two gazing hosts in uproar, storm, and shade.

JERUSALEM DELIVERED.

CANTO VII.

1. THROUGH the brown shade of forests ivied o'er
With age, meanwhile, divine Erminia fled ;
Her trembling hand the bridle ruled no more ;
And she appear'd betwixt alive and dead.
The steed that bore her with th' instinctive dread
Of danger, at its own wild mercy, through
Such winding paths and bosky mazes sped,
That it at length quite rapt her from the view ;
Baffling the eager hopes of those that would pursue.

2. As when, after some long and toilsome chase,
The hounds return, a sad and panting train,
Leaving the prey it mocks their skill to trace,
Lodged in some thicket from the open plain ;
So, full of shame, resentment, and disdain,
Their far pursuit the weary knights resigned;
Yet still the timid Virgin fled amain
Through the drear woods, disconsolate of mind,
Nor once look'd back to mark if yet they press'd behind.

3. All night she fled ; and all the day succeeding,
Still without guidance or reflection, flies
O'er dale and hill, naught list'ning to, or heeding,
But her own tears, but her own mournful cries ;
Till now, what time the sun, descending, dyes
The clouds with crimson, leaving earth in shade,
Fair Jordan's lucid current she descries ;
There first her steed's bewilder'd step she stay'd ;
Her bed the chill green bank, her bower the wild woods made.

4. Repast she yet had none ; her only diet
The food that sorrow from remembrance brings ;
But Sleep at length, pain's balm, and care's sweet quiet,
O'er her closed eyes displays his brooding wings ;
Seals with his opiate rod the many springs
Of thought, and in serene oblivion steeps
Her sense of grief ; but forms of vision'd things
Disturb her flutt'ring spirit while she sleeps,—
Still Fancy's pictured porch unsilenced Passion keeps.

5. She slept, till in her dreaming ear the bowers
Whisper'd, the gay birds warbled of the dawn ;
The river roar'd ; the winds to the young flowers
Made love ; the blithe bee wound its dulcet horn :
Roused by the mirth and melodies of morn,
Her languid eyes she opens, and perceives
The huts of shepherds on the lonely lawn ;
While seeming voices, 'twixt the waves and leaves,
Call back her scatter'd thoughts,—again she sighs and grieves.

6. Her plaints were silenced by soft music, sent
As from a rural pipe, such sounds as cheer
The Syrian shepherd in his summer tent,
And mix'd with past'ral accents, rude but clear.
She rose ; and gently, guided by her ear,
Came where an old man on a rising ground
In the fresh shade, his white flocks feeding near,
Twig-baskets wove, and listen'd to the sound
Trill'd by three blooming boys, who sate disporting round.

7. They at the shining of her silver arms
Were seized at once with wonder and despair ;
But sweet Erminia sooth'd their vain alarms,
Discov'ring her dove's eyes, and golden hair.
"Follow," she said, "dear innocents, the care
Of fav'ring Heaven, your fanciful employ !
For the so formidable arms I bear,
No cruel warfare bring, nor harsh annoy,
To your engaging tasks, to your sweet songs of joy !

8. "But, Father, say, while the destructive fire
Of war lays waste the country wide and far,
How live you free from military ire,
Beneath the charm of what benignant star ?"
"My son," said he, "from the rude wrongs of war

My family and flocks in this lone nook
Were ever safe; no fears my quiet mar;
These groves to the hoarse trumpet never shook;
Calm rolls yon stately stream, calm flows yon woodland brook.

9. "Whether it be that Heaven protects in love
The chaste humility of shepherd swains,
Or, as its lightnings strike the crag's tall grove,
But leave untouch'd the roses of the plains,—
That so the wrath of foreign swords disdains
To harm the meek heads of the lowly poor,
Aiming alone at lofty kings,—our gains
Tempt not the greedy soldier to our door;
Safe stands our simple shed, despised our little store.

10. "Despised by others, but so dear to me,
That gems and crowns I hold in less esteem;
From pride, from avarice is my spirit free,
And mad ambition's visionary dream.
My thirst I quench in the pellucid stream,
Nor fear lest poison the pure wave pollutes;
With flocks my fields, my fields with herbage teem;
My garden-plot supplies nutritious roots;
And my brown orchard bends with Autumn's wealthiest fruits.

11. "Few are our wishes, few our wants; Man needs
But little to preserve the vital spark:
These are my sons; they keep the flock that feeds,
And rise in the gray morning with the lark.
Thus in my hermitage I live; now mark
The goats disport amid the budding brooms;
Now the slim stags bound through the forest dark;
The fish glide by; the bees hum round the blooms;
And the birds spread to heaven the splendor of their plumes.

12. "Time was (these gray hairs then were golden locks)
When other wishes wanton'd in my veins;
I scorn'd the simple charge of tending flocks,
And fled disgusted from my native plains.
Awhile in Memphis I abode, where reigns
The mighty Caliph; he admired my port,
And made me keeper of his flower-domains;
And though to town I rarely made resort,
Much have I seen and known of the intrigues of court.

13. "Long by presumptuous hopes was I beguiled,
And many, many a disappointment bore;
But when with youth false hope no longer smiled,
And the scene pall'd that charm'd so much before,—
I sigh'd for my lost peace, and brooded o'er
Th' abandon'd quiet of this humble shed;
Then, farewell State's proud palaces! once more
To these delightful solitudes I fled;
And in their peaceful shades harmonious days have led."

14. This his discourse so sweetly did subdue
The secret sorrows of the list'ning maid,
Each word, descending to her heart, like dew,
The fev'rish passion of her soul allay'd:
That, when the measure she had inly weigh'd—
Her present peace, and her so late dismay,—
She stood resolved within the silent shade
Of these sweet solitudes, at least to stay,
Till for her safe return kind Heaven might smooth the way;

15. And thus replied: "O fortunate and wise!
Who hast thyself experienced, nor forgot
The ills of cruel fortune! if the skies
Be nothing jealous of thy blissful lot,
Pity my woes, and to this pleasant spot
Deign to receive me, stung with sorrow's smart;
In the safe shelter of thy welcome cot
And these still shades, I may perhaps in part
Lose the oppressive weight that hangs around my heart.

16. "And if what crowds fall down to and adore
As idols, gold and jewels, thou shouldst prize,
Rich e'en in ruin, I have here a store
That well thine utmost wishes may suffice."
Then, show'ring from her bright benignant eyes
Tears like those dropp'd from heaven's resplendent bow,
Part of her story she told: with sighs
And tears, in concord with her own that flow,
The pitying shepherd heard the narrative of woe;

17. And straight, with all a father's love and zeal,
He took her to his heart, sooth'd her distress,
And to his wife, whose heart alike could feel
For others' sorrows, led the fair Princess.
Her arms she changes for a pastoral dress,
And with rude ribbon binds her dainty hair;

Yet still, her graceful manner of address,
Movement of eyes and steps the truth declare,—
Was never woodland girl so delicately fair !

18. Those rustic weeds hid not the princely fire
And grandeur so instinctively her own ;
In every action through her quaint attire,
The latent spirit of the Lady shone ;
Whether she drove her flocks to range alone
The thymy down, or penn'd them in the fold ;
Or, to wild ditties sung in mournful tone,
The dulcet cream in churns revolving roll'd,
Till firm the fluid fix'd, and took the tinge of gold

19. Oft when her flocks, from summer's noontide rays,
Lay in cool shades o'erarch'd by gadding vines,
She carved on beeches and immortal bays
Her Tancred's name, and left the mossy pines
With sad inscriptions flourish'd, silent signs
Of the unhappy flame her fancy fed ;
And when again she saw her own fond lines,
As she the melancholy fragments read,
Fresh tears of grief uncheck'd her lovely eyes would shed :

20. And weeping she would say : "Forever be,
O ye dear trees, historians of my woe !
That when two faithful lovers rest, like me,
In the cool shade your verdant boughs bestow,
Their hearts with gen'rous sympathy may glow :
And, as this volume of my griefs they view,
Say to themselves, 'Ah, never may we know
Her pangs, poor maid ! 'tis hard a love so true
Should be so ill repaid by Love and Fortune too.'

21. "Perhaps, if Heaven benignly hears the vow
And prayer affectionate of girls unblest,
He who cares nothing for Erminia now
May wander to these woods, where buried rest
Her virgin relics, early dispossess'd
Of life's pure fire,—may, glancing on my grave,
White with spring's violets, beat his manly breast,
And to my griefs—the first he ever gave—
Yield a few gracious tears, too late, alas, to save !

22. "Thus, though in life most miserable, in death
Bliss to my spirit shall at least arise ;
And my cold ashes, quicken'd by his breath,

Enjoy what now my evil star denies."
While thus, the tears fast streaming from her eyes,
To the deaf trees she talk'd in fondest phrase,
Th' unconscious object of her plaintive cries,
As chance or froward fortune guides him, strays
In search of her, far-off, through dark and dreary ways.

23. Following the impress of her horse's hoof,
He reach'd the neighb'ring wood; there brier and fern
So choked the way, and from its leafy roof
The checker'd shade grew momently so stern,
That he no more could 'mid the trees discern
The recent prints, but through the gloom profound
Wander'd perplex'd; at almost every turn
List'ning if, chance, from the deep glens around,
Of arms or trampling steeds his ear might catch the sound.

24. And if but the night breeze in beech or oak
Shook the still leaves, if but a timid bird
Sped through the rustling boughs, from slumber woke,
Or fiercer creature in the thicket stirr'd,
To the vague murmur instantly he spurr'd;
At length he issued from the wood's blind maze,
And to a noise mysterious, which he heard
Remote,—beneath the yellow moon's bright rays,
Rode, till he held the cause subjected to his gaze.

25. A steep he reach'd, where from the living stone
Fell in full streams a beautiful cascade;
Which, curb'd into a flood, went roaring on,
And the whole valley like a garden made.
Here he his fruitless steps dejected stay'd;
He call'd—but Echo of his eager cries
Made mock'ry, vocal from the greenwood shade,—
None else; meanwhile he saw—with tranquil eyes,
Blooming with white and red the new Aurora rise.

26. He sigh'd, he storm'd, he angrily repined,
And of his disappointment Heaven accused;
But deepest vengeance vow'd, if he should find
That the dear maid had been at all abused.
Back to the Camp at length, when he had mused
What step to take, his course he fix'd to steer,
Although the way was dubious and confused;
For well he knew the stated time drew near,
When he again should fight th' Egyptian cavalier.

27. Through many a winding path as he advanced,
He heard the sound of hoofs ; nor was it long,
Ere up the narrow vale in prospect, pranced
One, courier-like, who shook a waving thong ;
Gay at his side by chains of silver hung
An ivory horn, in our Italian mode
Across his shoulders negligently slung ;
Tancred of him inquired the nearest road
To Godfrey's camp, which straight the ready stranger show'd.

28. Adding in Tuscan : "Thither am I bent,
By Bohemond's command ;" the knight, this heard,
Deem'd him his uncle's post, and with him went,
In full reliance on his guileful word.
They came at length to where, alike unstirr'd
By breeze or storm, a stagnant lake embay'd
A castle ; huge the pile its waters gird ;
On the dark towers the sun one moment play'd,
Then sudden sank to sea, and left the world in shade.

29. Arrived, the courier blew his signal horn,
Instant a drawbridge fell athwart the fosse ;
"Sir Knight," he said, "thou here canst rest till morn,
If Frank thou art, or follower of the Cross ;
These towers Cosenza's Earl, with little loss,
Three days since wrested from the Turk :" the knight
Gazed on the antique structure,—gray with moss,
Gloomy, yet grand it show'd, of giant height,
Nobly defensed by art, impregnable in site.

30. A pile so strong, conceal'd, he was afraid,
Some secret treason or malignant charm ;
But, to all risks accustom'd, he betray'd
Neither by sound nor sign the least alarm ;
For well he trusted in his own right arm,
Where'er by choice or Fortune led, to make
Terms of complete security from harm ;
But, pledged already, and his fame at stake,
No fresh adventure now he cared to undertake.

31. Before the Castle, where in the green lea
The drawbridge ceased to span the sullen tide,
He therefore paused ; nor would persuaded be
To follow o'er the flood his wily guide.
But now an armed warrior he descried

On the pontoon, of fierce and scornful mien ;
Sublime his statue, haughty was his stride ;
In his right hand a naked sword was seen,
And thus he spake in terms decisive, stern, and keen.

32. "O thou whom choice conducts, or fortune charms
To tread, beguiled, Armida's fatal lands !
Think not of flight ; strip off those idle arms,
And to her chains submit thine abject hands.
Free to thy feet her guarded palace stands,
The bliss to taste, the fealty to swear,
Which she to others offers, and commands ;
Look not to see heaven's sunshine more, whate'er
May be thy youth of years, or hoariness of hair :—

33. "Unless thou swear her edicts to enforce,
And with her other slaves to death pursue
All Christ's detested sons ;" at this discourse
The knight regarded him, on closer view,
The arms and accents recognized, and knew
Rambaldo for his foe,—the Gascon base,
Who with Armida from the camp withdrew,
Pagan became, and here, to his disgrace,
Maintain'd the evil rules and customs of the place.

34. The pious warrior blush'd with holy scorn,
And answer'd : "Cursed apostate ! know that I
That Tancred am, who aye for Christ have borne
The warrior's weapon on my martial thigh.
Strong in his strength, his rebels I defy,
And tame ; as thou, if thou but enterprise
Thy sword with mine, shalt surely testify ;
For the just anger of th' insulted skies
Has chosen this strong right hand thy treason to chastise.

35. Aghast at mention of his glorious name
Stood the false knight, but cloak'd his fear, and said :
"Ill-starr'd the hour when to these shores you came,
In Eblis' halls to join the silent dead !
Here shall thy crest be shorn, thy spirits shed ;
To the last drop thy heart's blood will I spill,
And to your Captain send that haughty head,
In gift of grace, if but my prowess still
Be, what it ever was, consistent with my will."

36. While thus the Pagan spoke, the shades of night
Shut up their view ; when swift, around, on high,

Cressets, and lamps, and urns of golden light
Fill'd the dusk element with brilliancy ;
Gay shone the Castle to th' enchanted eye,
As in a theater the shifted scene,
When gorgeous Tragedy sweeps scepter'd by ;
And in her lofty latticed bower, the Queen
Unmark'd spectatress sate, and smiled behind her screen.

37. Meanwhile the Christian Chief begins to fit
His arms and courage to the coming fight,
Nor on his feeble courser will he sit,
His foe on foot, bnt gen'rously alight.
The foe comes cover'd with his buckler ; bright
The helmet glitters on his head, and bare
Shines his raised cimeter in act to smite ;
'Gainst him the Prince too flies, his worst to dare,
Like thunder sounds his voice, his eyes like lightnings glare.

38. That, in wide circles wheels averse, in strict
Defence of art, feigns, motions, falsifies ;
This though late wounds and faintness sore afflict
With bold impatience the near conflict plies ;
And when his foe draws back, in quick surprise
Springs with the utmost speed he can command,
To intercept, or smite him as he flies ;
While ever and anon his active hand
To the unguarded face directs its flashing brand.

39. With yet more eagerness the Prince assails
The vital parts, and every stroke he deals
Quits with high threats ; the Gascon's courage fails,
His ears ring inward, and his blood congeals ;
Now here, now there in panic fear he wheels,
Lithe and alert as an assaulted snake ;
With live eye circumspect his blows he steals ;
And now with sword, now shield, essays to make
The knight's impetuous steel a slant direction take.

40. But he to ward off harm is not so swift
As that fierce foe is active to assail ;
Batter'd his helm, his shield's already cleft,
And bored and bloody is his plated mail.
Of Tancred's meditated blows, none fail
Of their effect, not one descends in vain ;—
Each keenly wounds ; the renegade turns pale,
And his heart writhes at once beneath the pain
Of anger, pride, remorse, love, conscience, and disdain.

41. On one last effort of despairing pride
Resolved at length his dying hopes to set,
He casts the fragment of his shield aside,
Grasps with both hands his sword, uncrimson'd yet,
And, closing nimbly with his foe, to get
The full command and vantage of the ground,
Quits with so sharp a stroke his heavy debt,
That through both plate and mail the flesh it found
And in the warrior's side impress'd a grisly wound.

42. Next on his spacious brows he struck,—the steel
Like an alarm-bell rang; a stroke so dire
And unexpected made the warrior reel
Some paces back, yet left the helm entire.
Red grew the prince's cheeks for very ire;
In agony of shame his teeth he gnash'd;
His eyes were like two coals of living fire,
And ev'ry glance that through his visor flash'd,
Blasted the Gascon's pride, both blasted and abash'd.

43. He heard the hissing of th' Avenger's steel,
Brandish'd aloft; its shining he descried;
Already in his breast he seem'd to feel
Th' accelerated sword his heart divide,
And tremblingly recoil'd; the blow fell wide
On an antique pilaster that emboss'd
The marble bridge,—sparks flash'd on ev'ry side:
Fragments sprang forth and in the skies were lost;
While to the traitor's heart fear shot its arrowy frost.

44. Back to the bridge he rush'd, in speed reposing
His hopes of life,—behind, th' Avenger hung
On his fleet steps, now near, now nearer closing,
One hand already to his shoulder clung;
When lo! from trembling air the lights are wrung;
The cressets disappear; the tapers die;—
Gone was each star that in blue ether hung;
The yellow moon drew in her horns on high;
And all grew hideous shade beneath the vacant sky.

45. Through the thick glooms of witchcraft and of night
Naught could the Prince distinguish to pursue;
Still he press'd on, though ignorant if aright,
His steps confused and dubious as his view:
Bewilder'd thus, he to the portals drew,
By evil chance the threshold he pass'd o'er,
And of his fatal entrance nothing knew,
Till hoarse behind, with repercussive roar,
The sullen hinge flew back, and lock'd the closing door.

46. As from our seas to the Comacchian bay,
Urged by the fury of the driving tide,
The vex'd fish joys to cleave its wanton way
Where calm and smooth the silent waters glide,
And locks itself unconsciously inside
The marshy jail; nor finds, till it would dart
Back to the ocean, all escape denied;
For the strange estuary, with curious art,
To all free access yields, but lets not one depart.

47. So Tancred there (such artful springs involved
The wizard work of that mysterious den)
Enter'd with ease, but found, on flight resolved,
No human foot might pass its walls again.
He shook the massy gate with might and main;
The lock essay'd; the brazen hinges tried;
But found the effort void, the project vain ·
"In vain," a loud voice in the distance cried,
"Seek'st thou to flee from hence, lorn thrall of queen Armide!

48. "Here thou, thus livingly entomb'd, shalt waste
(Fear not for death) thy days and years alone;"
The hardy knight replied not, but compress'd
Within his heart affliction's rising groan.
Love inly he accused,—love, fate, his own
Small wit, and his false guide's deceptions fell;
"'Tis not," he murmur'd in desponding tone,
"'Tis not to bid the cheerful sun farewell
Can make my heart with grief or proud resentment swell.

49. "That were small suff'ring; but I lose, alas,
Of a diviner sun the lovelier grace!
Ignorant if e'er these gates I shall repass,
Or e'er again the blissful sight embrace
Of my love's stately form and radiant face;"
Therewith the image of Argantes came,
And deepen'd his distress; "O dire disgrace!"
He cried; "with too just cause will he defame
My truth; alas th' affront! the fix'd eternal shame!'

50. While love, while honor thus his spirit stings,
Nor peace, nor rest the fierce Argantes knows
On his soft pillow; from the couch he springs,
And such his scorn of indolent repose,
Such lust for glory in his bosom glows,
That though his former wounds are yet unsealed,

And twinge him still with intermittent throes,
He burns to see the sixth day-dawn revealed,
And hear the trumpet sing his summons to the field.

51. Scarce could the Paynim rest the previous night,
Scarce close an eyelid ; restless with desire,
He rose while heaven was starry, long ere light
Had touch'd the mountain-peaks with ruddy fire ;
And "Bring my arms !" he shouted to his squire,—
His ready arms the active servant brought ;
Not those he wont to wear, but bright attire
Of plate, which Aladine had late besought
The man t' accept, with skill and wondrous labor wrought.

52. He takes them, little curious of their pride,
Not ill his limbs the weighty burden bear ;
And last, his wonted saber to his side
He girds, of purest steel, antique and rare.
As with its bloody locks let loose in air,
Horribly bright, the Comet shows whose shine,
Plagues the parch'd world, whose looks the nations scare,
Before whose face states change, and powers decline,
To purple Tyrants all an inauspicious sign,—

53. So in his arms he sparkled, and askance
His eyes, with blood and rage inebriate, roll'd
A mortal menace shone in ev'ry glance,
Nor of his vassals was there one so bold,
As trembled not sincerely, to behold
His face of horror, and the scorn display'd
In fierce gesticulations ; in his hold
He strain'd, he raised, he shook his naked blade
Wounding the empty air and unessential shade.

54. "Right soon," he cried, "shall the vain-glorious wretch
That in close fight with me presumed to stand,
Faint at my feet his bleeding carcass stretch,
And soil his flowing tresses in the sand.
Yet shall he live to see my conqu'ring hand
Despite his baffled God, triumphant tear
His arms away, shall with entreaties bland
Beg me, but vainly beg, his limbs to spare,
Vow'd to the growling dogs, and griffins of the air!"

55. E'en as a bull, that, stung with hot desire,
Horribly roars, and with his roaring shakes
The nodding groves, thus cherishing his ire,
Till anger burns, and all the brute awakes:
He whets his horns against the oaks, and makes
As he to battle would the winds invite,
With empty strokes; then from the thicket breaks,
And spurns the yellow sands with hoofs that cite
The rival of his love, far-off, to mortal fight.

56. With such blind fury moved, Argantes sent
To call the herald, and abruptly cried:
"Go to the Camp, and bid, in Godfrey's tent,
The Christian champion fiercely be defied!"
For none he waits, but with impatient pride
Vaults to his saddle, and commands to lead
The conquer'd Otho fetter'd at his side;
Then, issuing from the town, his snorting steed
Spurs down the vales in rash and unrelaxing speed.

57. He blew his hollow horn,—the startling sound
Roll'd o'er the hills in echoes far away,
And like the thunder the dark storm flings round,
Fill'd both the ear and spirit with dismay.
Soon within Godfrey's tent in fair array
The Christian knights were met; his haughty claim
The herald made,—with all his challenge lay,
But Tancred he distinguish'd first by name,
Then on insulting heel turn'd back to whence he came.

58. In deep suspense, with slow and serious glance,
Godfrey contemplated each chief and knight;
Long grew his gaze, yet would not one advance
To undertake the formidable fight.
His bravest Chiefs were wanting to his sight,—
Tidings were none of Tancred, since the hour
Of his alarm and surreptitious flight,
Bohemond far, and self-exiled the flower
Of all his force, the knight who quell'd Gernando's power.

59. While yet, beside the chance-elected ten,
His most experienced, most renown'd in wars
Following had join'd Armida's subject train,
Beneath the favor of the midnight stars;
The rest, coy fav'rites of a feebler Mars,
Though blushing for the fault, stood mute and tame;
None cared at such a risk to purchase scars,

Though with sure promise of a glorious fame,
So much their sense of fear o'erpower'd their sense of shame.

60. In their long silence, in their looks, too plain
In ev'ry sign he traced the thoughts that scare
Their timid souls ; and with sublime disdain
Upstarting sudden from his ducal chair,
Said : "Most unworthy should I be to bear
Life, O my Peers, if, raised to this high post,
That life to hazard I should now forbear,
Leaving it in a Pagan's power to boast
He under-foot had trod the honor of our host.

61. "Sit still, my knights, and safe from all alarms
View at your perfect ease the risk I run ;
Bring me my arms, Sigero, bring my arms !"
Decisively he spoke, and it was done.
But Raymond, who from ripe old age had won
Like ripe discretion and consistent thought,
Whose strength, still verdant, was surpass'd by none
In that assembly, better counsels brought,
Stood forth, turn'd to his Chief, and turning, thus besought :

62. "Ah no, my Prince ! stake not the lives of all
Upon the hazard of thine own ! look round ;
No simple soldier art thou ; shouldst thou fall,
The grief were public, public were the wound :
On thee our Faith and empire rest, renown'd
By thy wise rule ; on thee it is we build
Our hopes to raze this Babel to the ground :
To others leave the use of sword and shield ;
Fight thou by mind alone, alone the scepter wield.

63. "I, though bow'd down by age, will not refuse
The fight,—let others shrink when Battle rears
His frightful voice,—gray hairs shall not excuse
My spirit, joyful in the strife of spears :
O that I were but in my youth of years,
Like you, my gallants, who with downcast eyes
Stand spell-bound thus, enslaved by empty fears,
Whom wrath nor shame can influence to chastise
The man who to your teeth all Christendom defies !

64. "Such as I was, when, gazed by all the peers
Of Germany, at Conrad's court I drew
My maiden sword on Leopold the fierce,

Reach'd his mail'd bosom, and at odds o'erthrew!
To spoil a warrior brave as him I slew,
Was sure a deed that claims superior praise
Than here, unarm'd, unaided, to subdue,
Put to foul flight, and singly hold in chase,
Whole herds of foes like these, superlatively base.

65. "If still that vigor braced my limbs austere,
I had by this time quell'd that haughty foe;
Old as I am, I am too young to fear,
Nor is my blood all frozen in its flow;
And, if it be my fate to be laid low,
While my soul burns in brightness to the last,
Home with content my Victor shall not go!
Arm them I will; this brilliant day shall cast
Light over all my track, and shame the luster past."

66. Thus spoke the sage: his words like spurs awake
Their slumb'ring worth, that they who late were dumb
And timid, now brave show of courage make,
And loudly clamor for the fight to come:
Not only terror does not now benumb
Their hearts to shun the quarrel, but the prize
Is sought by all, contended for by some;
Baldwin demands it, Guelph, the two bold Guys,
And with Rogero Stephen, with Stephen Gernier vies:

67. And Pyrrhus, whose praised stratagem betray'd
To Bohemond proud Antioch, forward press'd;
The battle too, for battle well array'd,
Rosmond, Fitz-raphe, and Everard request,—
All from the sister-kingdoms of the West,
Albion, Ierne, and blue Scotia—lands
Barr'd from our world by seas that never rest;
With Edward last, divine Gildippe stands,
And each with equal warmth the challenged fight demands.

68. But in the good old Count Tolouse is shown
The liveliest ardor and most keen desire;
Arm'd cap-a-pie he stands, or wants alone
His lucid helm to make the suit entire:
To whom the Chief: "O venerable Sire!
Mirror of ancient zeal, in whom we see,
And seeing learn the virtues we admire;
Art, honor, discipline, and worth in thee,
Shining with knightly grace, harmoniously agree."

69. "If but ten more, thine equals in desert,
Of vig'rous years, were in my aid combined,
This haughty Babel soon would I subvert,
And spread the Cross from Thulé e'en to Ind:
But be this needless enterprise resign'd
To younger champions; for a nobler fight
Reserve thy vig'rous arm and ardent mind;
And leave these candidates their names to write,
And in a helmet cast,—let chance select the right;—

70. "Or rather, Providence on high, whose will
Fortune and Chance, his ministers, unfold;"
But Raymond in his claim persisted still,
And with the other knights his name enroll'd.
In his own helmet rimm'd with shining gold,
Godfrey received, and carelessly anew
Mingled the shaken papers; when, behold,
The first chance scroll which thence at ease he drew
The name of Count Toulouse exhibited to view!—

71. Loud acclamations follow; none presume
To blame the lot; and Raymond's visage clears,
His hoar trunk seems rebursting into bloom,
Renew'd no less in vigour than in years:
Thus the blithe snake when renovated rears
High the gay crest, and proudly in the sun
Blazons its golden coils: the rival Peers,
But Godfrey most, extoll'd him as he shone,
Promised him sure success, and cheer'd with praises on.

72. Then from his side his poignant sword he took,
And giving it to Raymond, said: "This blade
Is that which once the mighty rebel Duke,
Rodolph of Saxony, in battle sway'd;
From him by force I took it, and repaid
At the same moment, by a death condign,
A life by thousand crimes notorious made:
In my caress, 'tis Victory's surest sign;
Take it, and may it prove as fortunate in thine!"

73. Meanwhile, impatient of their long delay,
In fierce derision the Circassian cries:
"Ho, men unmatch'd! ho, Europe's brave array
Of chiefs! 'tis but one man your host defies:
Since on his prowess he so much relies,
Send now your late stern Tancred to the fight;
Or on soft down does he prefer with wise

Consistency to wait, until the night,
Which saved him once before, again shall blind my sight?

74. "Send others, if he fears me; band on band,
Horsemen, foot, all, come all, it recks not me,
Since none dares singly meet me hand to hand,
Of all your Barons, thousands though there be.
On to the tott'ring Town! look up, and see
The Sepulcher where lies the Son adored
Of sweet saint Mary! lo, the path is free!
Why pay ye not your vows, thereto restored?
For what more sapient use reserve you now the sword?"

75. With such like taunts the savage Pagan lash'd
The minds of all; but most his words inflame
The Count Toulouse,—his eyes defiance flash'd,
And ill could he endure th' imputed shame:
His courage, stigmatized, more fierce became,
Ground on the whetstone of his wrath; that, freed
From all prévention, a delay so tame
He breaks, and leaps to Aquiline his steed,
Named from the Northern Wind, and like that wind in speed.

76. Upon the banks of Tagus was he bred,
Where oft the mothers of those martial steeds,
When with her warmth inspiring Spring has fed
The eager heat which genial instinct breeds,
Mad o'er the mountains, o'er the spacious meads,
Run open-mouth'd against the winds of May,
And greedily receive their fruitful seeds;
Whence growing quick, they (singular to say)
Give, when ripe time rolls round, their issue to the day.

77. And, to see Aquiline, you would say
None but the sprightly Wind could be his sire,
So instantly his feet cut short the way;
Swift to rush forward, nimble to retire,
And wheel to right and left in narrowest gyre,
Yet leave no print upon the sands he trode,—
Playful, yet proud; though gentle, full of fire;
Such the Count's steed: he, as to war he rode,
Thus with uplifted eyes preferr'd his prayers to God.

78. "O Thou, that to Goliath's brow didst guide,
By Terebinth's sad vale and sanguine spring,
Untutor'd arms, so that the Scorner died

By the first pebble from a stripling sling !
Like aid, O Lord ! to-day vouchsafe to bring ;
That, struck by me, this ruffian with like shame
May vanquish'd fall to earth ; with vigor string
My feeble Age his arrogance to tame,
As feeble Youth of yore th' uncircumcised o'ercame !"

79. Thus pray'd the noble veteran ; and his prayer,
Wing'd by firm faith and piety sincere,
Soar'd, naturally as fire ascends in air,
Swifter than thought to the celestial sphere :
Th' Eternal Father bent a gracious ear
To the request, and from th' angelic band
That round in glorious sanhedrim appear,
Appointed one in his defence to stand,
And thus restore him safe from foil'd Argantes' hand.

80. The destined Angel to whose charge was given
The guardianship of Raymond, from his prime,
When new and naked to the light of heaven
He first began to run the race of time,—
Soon as the king of the celestial clime
This welcome duty had afresh imposed,
Flew to a crystal rock that soars sublime
Above all height, where of Heaven's total host
The fine refulgent arms from battle are disposed.

81. Here does the lance that pierced th' old Serpent lie,
With the pernicious shafts that smite the earth,—
Those shafts, invisible to mortal eye,
That give the horrid plague and fever birth;
And here, suspended with the darts of dearth,
Are hung the writhen bolts, midst pennons furl'd,
Which turn to deepest dread all human mirth,
When, through the steadfast empyrean hurl'd,
Cities are ground to dust, and Earthquake rocks the world

82. Here too with chariots, harnessries, and helms,
A dazzling shield of brightest diamond blazed,
Whose sphere might cover half the lands and realms
That lie 'twixt Atlas and the Scythian waste :
Herewith are holy kings and cities chaste
In ev'ry age defensed and fortified ;
This on his arm the plumed Seraph braced,
Shot down to earth in secret, undescried,
And took his station'd watch by good Count Raymond's side.

83. And now the turban'd Moslem, young and old,
Swarm to the walls ; and, such the tyrant's will,
Clorinda with her band moved on to hold,
Firmly conjoin'd, the midway of the hill.
In order ranged of military skill,
Arm'd, on the other hand, a Christian force
Like space at ceremonial distance fill ;
And to the champions leave a spacious course,
Betwixt both gazing hosts, for ev'ry chance resource.

84. Argantes look'd—no Tancred could he see,
But the strange figure of an unknown knight,
Who now came up, and "Thank thy stars," said he,
"Absent's the chief for whom thou strain'st thy sight;
Yet vapor not, while I the loss requite ;
For here I stand, prepared to prove again
The utmost rage and malice of thy might ;
As Tancred's substitute I seek the plain,
Or on mine own account th' engagement good maintain."

85. At this the Pagan proudly smiled, and said :
"What then does Tancred? where does he abide?
Of late he braved all heaven, and now is fled ;
In dancing heels alone can he confide !
But to earth's center let him flee, or hide
In the deep main ; no place shall bar from me
The flying wretch !" "Thou liest," the knight replied,
"To say that he, th' unmatch'd in fight, that he
Flies from thy arms : his worth outvalues ten like thee !"

86. Wrathful, the piqued Circassian cut him short :
"Take then his place, the favor I accord ;
We shall see shortly how thou wilt support
The rash bravade of that injurious word."
Thus to the tilt they moved ; their chargers spurr'd
And their long lances to the helm address'd ;
Raymond, whose practiced arm but rarely err'd,
Struck where he aim'd, the visor he impress'd,
But shook his rival not, scarce bow'd his haughty crest

87. But fierce Argantes less successful fared,
The lance struck not which rarely fail'd to wound,
Driv'n far aslant by the Celestial guard,
Whose shield the good old Earl encompass'd round.
Grimly the disappointed Pagan frown'd,
And bit his lips, and forth wild curses threw ;
His faithless spear he snapp'd against the ground,
And with drawn sword upon his rival flew,
Burning with tenfold rage to try the course anew.

88. His coal-black steed he urged with all his might,
As butting rams their horned foreheads bow;
But Raymond shunn'd th' encounter, to the right
Wheel'd, and in passing, struck his scowling brow:
Back rush'd the Egyptian Cavalier, and now
Back wheel'd the Earl with swiftness uncontroll'd,
And on his helmet dealt a nobler blow;
But still in vain; the helmet's massy mold
Had all the temper'd strength of adamant or gold.

89. The Pagan, weary of such futile play,
To gripe his foe next tries each strong resource;
But he, lest the colossal bulk should weigh
To earth both steed and rider, shuns his force;
Now strikes; now yields; and in his circling course,
As though endued with viewless wings, maintains
The rotatory war; his matchless horse
Obeys each mandate of the flutt'ring reins:
Nor one false footstep e'er its nimbleness restrains.

90. And as the Chief who some strong tower essays
Amid cloud-kissing hills or marshy vales,
Seeks access by a thousand wiles and ways,
So the Earl scans the giant he assails;
And, as no power of his can cleave the scales
That shield his breast, nor all his thousand arts
Shiver the glist'ning burganet that veils
His brows, he long explores the quilted parts,
And there 'twixt joint and joint his active falchion darts.

91. Those arms, in many points already bored,
Are red with streaming blood, while his remain
Untouch'd, nor from his helmet has the sword
Struck one gay plume, or cut one sparkling chain;
In vain Argantes rages, strikes in vain,
Yet stubbornly toils on, with careless skill;
He fails not, faints not, flags not in his pain,
But doubles ev'ry pass,—from erring skill
Deriving fiercer strength, a more impetuous will.

92. After a thousand blows, the Saracine
At last struck one when Raymond was so nigh,
That 'twas believed his nimble Aquiline
Could scarcely from its sweeping fury fly;
But not the watchful Seraph of the sky,
In the pure sunshine at his side conceal'd,
Fail'd him at need; his arm he stretch'd on high,
And on his heavenly adamantine shield
Took the pernicious sword, and all its rage repeal'd.

93. The saber broke ; for, not with all the charms
Of art, can metals forged by earthly hand,
The unalloy'd imperishable arms
Temper'd by heaven's own alchemy, withstand :
In million sparks, minuter than the sand,
Its fragments fell,—the Emir saw them shine—
Naught but the golden hilt was in his hand ;
Yet doubted he the fact, nor could divine
What arms his rival bore, so magically fine.

94. Amazed he stood, and thought the brittle blade
Shiver'd on Raymond's shield,—so deem'd the knight
Who nothing knew of the celestial aid,
Sent to protect him from the Pagan's might :
And when he saw th' informidable plight
Of the disarm'd Circassian, he remain'd
In doubt if longer he should press the fight ;
A vile inglorious laurel he disdain'd,
Nor could the vict'ry prize by pure advantage gain'd.

95. "Go, seek," he would have said, "another brand,"
But a new thought within his breast arose—
The public cause was trusted to his hand,
And should he fall, he would dishonor those
For whom he fought ; thus neither could he close
In shameful fight to win inglorious bays,
Nor Godfrey's honor to vain risks expose ;
While thus he stood debating on the case,
Argantes hurl'd the hilt and pommel in his face,—

96. And forward spurr'd, by grappling to o'erwhelm
His gaunt antagonist ; the darted blow
Struck fiercely on his bright Tolosan helm,
And bent the batter'd visor to this brow.
But he, undiscomposed, wheel'd round, and so
Shunning th' encounter, gash'd the hand he saw
Stretch'd out in muscular disdain, as though
To grasp its prey, unsparing as the paw
Of the voracious wolf, or vulture's horny claw.

97. Now there, now here, the circled sands he spurn'd ;
Then back again wheel'd round, now here, now there;
Nor when he spurr'd abroad, nor when return'd,
Did his eye pity, or his falchion spare.
Whate'er he can of strength ; of art whate'er ;
Whate'er of old disdain or present ire
The knight can muster, he now brings to bear
Against the foe : and with his strong desire
To end the conflict, Heaven and Fortune both conspire.

98. Fenced in fine arms and in himself, the foe
Yet braves his mighty strokes, from all fears free;
Like a vast ship with shatter'd sails, whose prow
At random drives upon a stormy sea;
Which, though she bears all Neptune on her lee,
Ribb'd round with heart of oak, firm, stubborn, stout,
Starts not a plank, but in proud majesty
Endures the rushing waves, with not a doubt
That her well-timber'd frame will ride the tempest out.

99. Such was thy risk, Argantes! when to aid
Thy cause, the Prince of Air himself address'd;
Straight of a painted cloud the empty shade
He to the figure of a man compress'd;
And on the visionary shape impress'd
Clorinda's likeness,—the same lively grace,
Rich shining armor, and embroider'd vest;
Gave it organic breath, and in the place
Of mind, her well-known voice, demeanor, port and pace.

100. To Oradine, a man of matchless skill
In archery, the beauteous Image came,
And whisper'd: "Prince of shooters! who at will
Canst strike all marks at which thou takest aim,—
Judge what would be our loss, and what our shame,
Should Syria's brave protector thus expire,
And, supercilious in the victor's claim,
By law of arms yon Christian should acquire
His ornamental spoils, and safe to Camp retire!

101. "Now prove thy cunning; give thine arrows wing;
And quick and sure let the Frank villain bleed;
Beside th' eternal glory of the thing,
Expect rewards proportion'd to the deed."
Charm'd with the promise of the future meed,
Th' unhesitating Traitor smiled assent;
Then from his weighty quiver snatch'd a reed,
Its notch adapted to the bowstring, bent
With ease the tough yew bow, and prophesied th' event.

102. Twangs the tense cord, and with a whistling sound
The feather'd arrow flies its mark to win;
Aim'd where the decorated belt clasps round
The hero's waist, it strikes, and enters in:
Cleaves the rich buckles; cleaves the armor thin,
And dyes its point with blood; there, short of fate,
It stays, just piercing through the tender skin;

For the prompt Angel did its force abate,
Nor let the eager steel too deeply pierce the plate.

103. The blood spun largely from the wounded vein,
Soon as the Count essay'd the shaft to draw ;
And, fill'd with gen'rous anger and disdain,
He chid the Pagan for the breach of law :
Godfrey, who could not his charm'd eyes withdraw
A single instant from his much-loved knight,
Moved with the liveliest indignation, saw
The flying shaft, and knowing not how slight
Th' inflicted puncture was, grew pale with sore affright.

104. With hand and tongue at once alarum sounding,
He urged his knights to see the wrongs redress'd ;
Then were seen visors closing, war-barbs bounding,
Tight bridles slacked, and lances laid in rest.
So instantly both hosts to battle press'd,
Their course was finish'd as it seem'd begun ;
Sands, stamped to dust, the vanish'd space confess'd,
Which, whirl'd in breezy billows, dense and dun,
Soar'd to the steep of heaven, and veil'd the shining sun.

105. Of helms, and clashing shields, and lances brast
In the first shock, loud rumor roars around ;
Here rolls a steed, and there, his rider cast,
One gallops, madd'ning at the trumpet's sound.
Here lies a warrior lifeless on the ground ;
And here another, compass'd by his foes,
Groans in the anguish of his mortal wound ;
Dire is the fight, and still, the more they close,
And mix, more bloody, sharp, and obstinate it grows.

106. Light leap'd Argantes in the midmost throng,
And from a soldier wrung his iron mace ;
Bursting the dense crowd as he rode along,
He whirl'd it round, and soon made ample space :
Raymond alone he looks for ; holds in chase ;
With Raymond only struggles to engage ;
Pressing against him with a giant's pace,
He like a wolf seem'd burning to assuage,
With his quaff'd blood, the thirst and hunger of his rage.

107. But many a harsh impediment he met ;
Still fierce encounters his rash course controll'd ;
Him the two Gerards, with Ormane beset,
Guido and Barneville, the brave and bold :

Yet not e'en these his progress can withhold ;
Foaming he toils, he struggles to the last ;
As cavern'd streams, or fires in prison roll'd,
Wage fiercer war when loose outbursts the blast,
So raged his power opposed, so forth in splendor pass'd.

108. He slew Ormano, wounded Guido, fell'd
Barneville, stunn'd and stretch'd amidst the slain ;
But fast the gath'ring crowd against him swell'd,
And circling lock'd him in a tenfold chain
Of men and arms that pinion and restrain
His giant powers ;—while by his single hand
The scales of war an equal poise maintain,
To Baldwin, Godfrey issues his command :
"Now to the conflict move thy gallant Frison band ;

109. "And on the left, where most the battle raves,
Charge them in flank !" he heard, and he obeyed :
Swift as the roll of ocean's mountain waves
Before the wind, was the encounter made :
An energy so mountainous o'erweighed
The Asian troops, too languid to sustain
The Frank's fresh shock,—in ruin retrograde
They bend—their lines are broke—and on the plain
Roll horsemen, horses, flags, and pennons snapp'd in twain.

110. From the same charge the right wing turn'd and fled ;
None, save Argantes, made defense or stay ;
With gory rowels and loose reins they sped
In haste, urged headlong by supreme dismay ;
Alone the bold Argantes stood at bay ;
He faced the driven storm ; the rushing bands ;
Nor made less havoc on that signal day,
Than if Earth's Titan with his hundred hands,
Had brandish'd fifty shields, and fifty flashing brands.

111. The thrust of swords, the shock of lances thrown,
The clang of maces and career of steeds
He braves, to all sufficient, though alone,
And dares on ev'ry side stupendous deeds.
His limbs all bruised, his marr'd arms cleft, he bleeds,
And sweat rolls down with blood, yet, fenced with phlegm,
He heeds it not ; but crowd to crowd succeeds ;
Press'd, overborne, he fails the tide to stem ;
Onward abrupt they drive, and he perforce with them.

112. To the wild fury of the tide he bends,
That like a cataract hurries him along:
Not like a man that flies, his heart commends
Fresh acts of slaughter to a hand still strong:
His eyes yet keep the terrors that belong
To their grim balls; he still in high disdain
Hurls forth defiance, and his flying throng
Seeks by all modes in battle to retain,—
But no! his earnest toils their stupor renders vain.

113. His noble spirit neither can restrain,
Nor regulate their flight; for hasty fear
Casts off all conduct, foams against the rein,
And like the adder closes its deaf ear
To prayers though mild, and threats howe'er severe;
But the wise Chief, to whose reflective eye
Fortune and beck'ning Victory appear
To crown his hopes, sends forth fresh troops to ply
The glad pursuit, and cast the day's decisive die.

114. And, but the special day prefix'd by God,
Was not yet given to run its golden round,
The Christians then in Salem's courts had trod,
And a blest period to their labors found:
But Hell's black Angels, from the Deep unbound,
Who saw how fast their tyranny declined
In the tremendous conflict, swarm around
(Of heaven permitted) in an instant bind
The air in billowy clouds, and raise th' ungovern'd wind.

115. From mortal eyes dark vapors snatch the sun;
Fires flash; the kindred elements rebel;
All heaven burns black, and, smold'ring, shows more dun
E'en than the horrible obscure of hell:
Mid showers of hail the long, loud thunders yell;
Fields float; the leas are drown'd; not boughs alone
Crash in the rushing blast's sonorous swell,
But oaks, rocks, hills to their foundation-stone,
Quake to the roaring storm, or in the whirlwind groan.

116. At once the hail, the lightning, and the wind
Full in the Christians' eyes with fury play'd;
Forced, they recede! blank sadness fills each mind,
And sudden terrors their stout hearts invade.
Few, few (as little through the hideous shade
Could be discern'd) around their flags abide;
Which when Clorinda distantly survey'd,

She seized the sign, and with inspiring pride
Shaking aloft her sword, thus to her soldiers cried :

117. "Lo, friends, Heaven fights for us ! the hours are number'd,
And Fate and Justice to our aid arise ;
Our faces are untouch'd, our hands uncumber'd,
The storm beats only in the Christians' eyes ;
On them alone the irritated skies
Pour doubt and death, pour ruin and dismay ;
And Heaven strikes down their lances, and denies
To their bewilder'd view the light of day ;
On ! where God's finger points, 'tis Vict'ry leads the way !"

118. Thus cheer'd the Amazon her drooping ranks,
And, bearing on her back the horrid rain
Of hell, in furious charge assail'd the Franks,
And scorn'd the idle thrusts they gave again.
Then too Argantes turn'd his bridle rein,
And dreadful slaughter of the victors made ;
Who the fierce brunt ill able to sustain,
Yielded the point, and but their backs display'd
To bide the infuriate storm, and sharp vindictive blade.

119. The rage immortal and the mortal sword
Upon their shoulders smote them as they fled,
Whose blood, in union with the rain that pour'd,
Fell in fast showers, and dyed th' arena red.
Here midst the heap of dying and of dead,
Pyrrhus and good Ridolpho slumber'd calm ;
Death on their eyes his purple finger laid :
This sigh'd out life beneath Argantes' Arm,—
Of that, Clorinda boasts th' imperishable palm.

120. Thus fled the Franks; nor meanwhile ceased all hell,
Nor ceased the Syrians still to give them chase ;
Sole against arms, threats, hailstones, the dire swell
Of whirlwind, thunder, and the arrowy blaze
Of momentary lightnings, his bold face
Godfrey advanced ; and with supreme disdain
Chiding his Barons for a flight so base,
Spurr'd forth, the Camp-Gate sternly to maintain,
And in the trenches saved his scared and scatter'd train.

121. And twice, despite the hurricane that roar'd,
Against Argantes furiously he flew ;
Twice beat him back ; as oft, his naked sword

Pierced the thick phalanx, bathed in lightnings blue.
At last within the ramparts he withdrew
In the lorn rear of his disorder'd ranks,
And conquest yielded to th' infernal crew;
The foe returns, and the dishearten'd Franks
Rest, like a flood retired within its reed-crown'd banks.

122. Nor can they wholly yet the furies shun
Of the black storm, which lightens, rains, and hails;
Quench'd are their lights and torches one by one,
And the flood deepens, and the wind prevails;
Breaks the strong cordage; splits the beams and rails,
Plucks up whole tents, which far, far off are whirl'd;
The rains beat time to the loud-roaring gales;
And in the tune from Heaven's dread organ hurl'd,
Hell's bellowing thunders join, and stun th' affrighted world.

END OF CANTO VII.

JERUSALEM DELIVERED.

CANTO VIII.

ARGUMENT.

A KNIGHT, to Godfrey sent, relates with tears
The valiant deeds and downfall of the Dane;
Th' Italians, trusting to vague signs and fears
Of treach'ry, deem their loved Rinaldo slain.
Her torch Alecto whirls, and with disdain
And lust of vengence sets their souls ablaze;
They menace Godfrey with their threats insane;
But he, unawed, to Heaven for succor prays,
And with his voice alone th' infuriate storm allays.

JERUSALEM DELIVERED.

CANTO VIII.

1. THE roar of the loud tempest now was ceased ;
Whist were the winds ; the bellowing thunders mute ;
And the calm morn, in the cerulean east,
With cheek of rose and golden-sandal'd foot,
Left her divine pavilion to salute
With smiles the world : but they whose wrath awoke
The storm, yet ceased not their malign dispute
And damned charms ; first Ashtaroth silence broke,
And to Alecto thus, her snaky sister, spoke :

2. "Alecto ! mark, where, posting o'er the sands
Fleet as an angry ghost, careers yon knight,
Who living has escaped the Soldan's hands,
Nor is it in our power to stay his flight !
Grave deeds he very soon will bring to light ;
Deeds sore upon the Frank,—his comrades' fall,
Thousands left stark upon the field of fight
With their hot Chief,—from which, I doubt not, all
The Christian host will urge Rinaldo's quick recall.

3. " How fatal this were, judge ; we must oppose
Our force and craft to the consulting Peers ;
Arouse thee, then ; descend amidst our foes,
And what this herald to insatiate ears
Tells with good purpose, turn to blood and tears ;
Up ! up ! breathe fire, breathe poison in the veins
Of the mix'd nations ; stir up tumults fierce ;
Move wrath, revenge ; move discord, and disdains,
Till through the total Camp unbounded uproar reigns !

4. "This work becomes thee and the noble vaunt
Made to our Prince ;"—the monster naught replied,—
It was enough—the words her soul enchant,

The project charms,—she spreads her hoarse wings
wide,
And downward hurries with the morning tide.
The Knight, meanwhile, who thus their notice took,
The Camp approach'd, and to the warders cried,
With haste and deep emotion in his look,
'Warriors, I claim your grace ; conduct me to your
Duke !"

5. Numbers were ready of the curious crowd
Eager to hear the news he had to name,
To guide him to their Chief ; he lowly bow'd,
And kiss'd the honor'd hand that made the frame
Of empires tremble : " Sire," he said, " whose fame
Is bounded only by th' Atlantic beach
And starry roof of heaven ! would that I came
Knowledge of happier incidents to teach !"—
Awhile his face he veil'd, then thus resumed his speech:

6. "Sweno, the Thane of Denmark's only son,
The stay and glory of his failing years,
Burn'd to be rank'd with those thy gonfalon
Conducts, the valiant troop of chevaliers
Who wield the sword for Jesus ; not the fears
Of toil and peril, not the hope t' acquire
Soon the void throne, not e'en th' appealing tears
Shower'd from the fond eyes of his aged sire,
Could in his gen'rous heart control the high desire.

7. " He glow'd to learn the military art—
Perils to dare and hardships to endure,
Of thee, their noble Chief ; he felt, in part,
Shame and resentment for his name obscure,
Hearing on every hand what praise mature
In his green youth Rinaldo had acquired ;
But that which most his spirit did allure,
Was less the wish of man to be admired,
Than zeal for God's renown, by lively faith inspired.

8. " The shrewd delays his father's fears contrived
He baffled, form'd an army bold and brave,
And, marching straight for Thrace, at length arrived
Where throned Byzantium towers above the wave.
Here the Greek Cæsar in his palace gave
The Prince warm welcome ; here an envoy came
From thee, who, prompt the onward path to pave
Of our adventure, told at large the fame
Of Antioch won, and held to Persia's lasting shame ;—

9. "Held in despite of Persia, who at once
Moved to invest it, with the boast rebuoy'd
Of powers so vast, it seem'd that all her sons
Swarm'd to her war and left her kingdoms void ;
First upon thee, on others next he joy'd
To touch—on Raymond's prudence, Tancred's might,
Till to Rinaldo passing, he employ'd
A world of words to paint his first bold flight,
And each fair wreath which since his sword has reap'd
in fight.

10. "He told, in fine, how that your hosts around
These towers already in strict siege were cast ;
And woo'd him, yet unlaurel'd, to be found
In this proud field, the noblest and the last :
His words roused Sweno's spirit like a blast
Of trumpets, and in his young bosom bred
A wish so strong, that ev'ry hour he pass'd
Appear'd an age, till he himself should tread
The hallow'd soil, and turn his unflesh'd falchion red.

11. "Your glory prey'd on him ; the world's applause
Seem'd to upbraid his spiritless career ;
Those who or begg'd or counsel'd him to pause,
Alike he heard not, or disdain'd to hear ;
No fear of peril knew he but the fear
Lest he too late should be in thine to share,—
This only hazard seem'd to him severe ;
Those with which others peopled their despair
He either not perceived, or stood resolved to dare.

12. "His own brave zeal precipitates his fate,
Fate—his woo'd guide, and our enforced ally,
Since scarce for his departure would he wait
Till the first rays of morning streak'd the sky :
Of various routes, he counted the most nigh
The best,—enough ! it was our Chief that chose ;
No pass so close, no mountain shows so high,
Too deep no forest waves, no torrent flows,
For us to scale or stem, though held by furious foes.

13. "Now round our steps the arm'd barbarians press,
Mow spring from ambush : hunger, toil, and pain
In turn we bore ; but over all distress
We triumph'd,—scatter'd were our foes, or slain ;
Success assured us, vict'ry made us vain,
And, day by day, more confident we grew ;
Till one fair eve we camp'd upon the plain,

With Palestine's green hills almost in view,
Blind to th' events, alas, that did so soon ensue!

14. "Sudden our scouts return'd; they had beheld
The Turkish Crescent in our van appear,
Had caught the sullen clang of sword and shield,
And deem'd, by various signals to the ear
And eye, some vast embattled army near:
On many a soldier's face these tidings spread
The pallid whiteness of despairing fear;
Sweno alone, of all the host he led,
Changed not in thought or look, in gesture, voice, or tread.

15. "'Brothers, he cried, 'O now, how near we clasp
The victor's laurel, or the martyr's crown!
The first I hope, nor less desire to grasp
The greater merit with the like renown:
This very field, let fate or smile or frown,
Shall Memory vest with an immortal bloom,
And as a hallow'd spot deliver down
To future times, which, glorying in our doom,
Shall either point our spoils, or flower-intwine our tomb!'

16. "This said,—our posts mark'd out, the watch disposed,
He bade us all upon our shields to rest;
Nor, while in needful slumber he reposed,
Would he of helm or mail himself divest.
'Twas midnight: Sleep on every eye had press'd
Th' oblivious sweetness of her tranquil spell,
And the tired soldier was in visions blest,
When instantaneously a barb'rous yell
Rose to the silent stars, and shook th' abyss of hell.

17. "'To arms!' we shout, 'to arms!' and, cased in arms,
See Sweno first before all else aspire;
While, gath'ring grandeur from the loud alarms,
His eyes and cheeks are flush'd with gen'rous fire.
Lo, we are charged! a circle deep and dire
Fronts and assails us, wheresoe'er we move:
And thick'ning, deep'ning, drawing nigh and nigher,
Round us of swords and spears a twilight grove
Frowns, and an arrowy cloud falls hissing from above.

18. "Uneven the fight! against a single Dane
Full twenty Arabs laid their weapons bare;
Many of these were wounded, many slain
By darts toss'd blindly through the gloom of air;
But of the numbers struck or slaughter'd there,
And by what hands, the dusky shades amid,
No mortal eye could mark, nor tongue declare;
The Night our loss beneath her mantle hid,
And, with the loss we bore, the valiant deeds we did.

19. "But through the thick press of the fighting crowd,
And through the dark concealment of the hour,
Prince Sweno shone; his valor was avow'd
By a sublime ubiquity of power,
Surpassing all belief; of blood a shower,
And heaps of slaughter'd form'd around the slayer
A crimson moat—a rampart and a tower;
And, wheresoe'er he rush d, he seem'd to bear
Death in his red right-hand, and in his eyes despair.

20. "Thus fought we, till the Virgin of the Morn
Arising touch'd the heavens with rosy red;
But when the night's dusk horrors were withdrawn
That hid from view the horror of the dead,
The so long-wish'd-for light before us spread
A scene, oh God! the stoutest to appal,
Of grief, of pity, agony, and dread;
The Camp was piled with corpses, as though all
Were of our army swathed in Death's purpureal pall.

21. "Of full two thousand, ninety scarce remain;
When Sweno saw the multitudes that slept
Pale in their gore, if aught of grief or pain,
If aught of sadness o'er his brave heart crept,
He showed it not,—his eye its luster kept,
His voice its tone: 'Come, follow,' was his cry,
'These brave companions who have far o'erstepp'd
The streams of Tartarus, and with footsteps high
Printed in glorious blood our pathway to the sky!'

22. "He said: and glad, I think, of hasting fate
No less in spirit than in aspect, bore
With breast intrepid and with brow elate
Against the ruinous assault and roar
Of the barbarians; not the plate they wore,
Although 'twere thrice refined, nor cap of steel,
Though into diamond charm'd by wizard lore,
Might stand the strokes his fire and fury deal,
Into one total wound till gash'd from head to heel.

23. "It was not life, but valor's subtle fire
Sustain'd the living corse no strength could tame;
Struck, he re-strikes, nor yet his members tire,
The more they maim him, more he them doth maim;
When lo! loose-raging from the bloody game,
A Turk arrived, who all the rest surpass'd
In savage aspect and gigantic frame;—
Long time they obstinately fought; at last,
By numbers press'd, to ground the dauntless youth was cast.

24. "He fell—ah, bitter fate!—nor left behind
One that could yield revenge: oh, blood well-pour'd,
Oh bones, abandon'd to the bleaching wind,
Poor mangled relics of my Prince adored!
I summon you; speak! if I sought to hoard
My hated life, if then I did deny,
My breast to spear, mace, saber, shaft, or sword.
No! had it pleased our Arbiter on high,
Death had I dared enough, to be allow'd to die.

25. "Senseless amid my slaugter'd friends I fell,
And there was left for dead; nor what our foes
Since or sustain'd or acted can I tell,—
An icy torpor all my senses froze;
But when at length my faint eyes did unclose
From blank unconsciousness, the wings of Night
Seem'd o'er the shadowy landscape to repose;
Feebly I oped them, and a glimm'ring light
Far-off appear'd by fits to swim before my sight.

26. "Albeit, no strength had I to recognize
E'en nearest objects through the void opaque,
But saw as one whose overwearied eyes,
Nor all asleep, nor openly awake,
Close and unclose without the power to take
Regard or cognizance of things most nigh;
And now my cruel wounds began to ache,
Bit by the keen night air, doom'd thus to lie,
Faint, on the naked earth, beneath a freezing sky.

27. "Meanwhile the light drew momently more near
Till it arrived and rested at my side;
Then gentle whisp'rings murmur'd in my ear,—
I raised with pain my eyelids, and descried
Two tall commanding figures near me glide,
Clothed in long robes, and shaking in the air
Two torches: 'Son,' I heard them say, 'confide

In Him who oft consents the good to spare,
And with his grace forestalls the sacrifice of prayer.

28. " And speaking thus, the awful two their palms
O'er me in holy benediction spread,
And in low accents murm'ring mystic psalms,
Then little heard and less conceived, they said:
'Arise!' all lightly from my grass-green bed
I rose; new light flow'd to my eye-balls dim;
My wounds were healed; my thrilling pains were fled;
O marv'lous grace! I seem'd in bliss to swim,
And felt new life and strength uplifting ev'ry limb.

26. " Awe-struck I view'd them, and could scarce believe
The truths that struck my dazzled sprite, till one
Of the cowl'd sages said: 'What doubts affright?
On what illusions do thy fancies run,
O thou of little faith? in us, my son,
Men of like flesh and blood thy wonder meets;
Servants of Jesu, we have wish'd to shun
The flatt'ring world, its fables and false sweets,
And here as hermits live in rocks and lone retreats.

30. "'Me to this service did that God ordain,
Whose throne is builded in ubiquity;
Who by ignoblest means does not disdain
To work his will, the wonderful and high:
He would not that the form, which to his eye
Inclosed of late so beautiful a sprite,
Should on these lonely wilds neglected lie,—
The which, when made immortal, robed in light,
Yet with its radiant twin shall one day reunite;—

31. "'No! Sweno's sanctified remains must have
A tomb befitting valor so sublime,
To which alike the beautiful and brave,
Virgins and chevaliers from every clime,
Shall point the finger through all future time;
But lift thine eyes now to the stars, and mark
The one that to the crown of heaven doth climb
As on its golden car! that sunlike spark
Shall to his noble corse direct us through the dark.'

32. "I look'd; and as the brilliant meteor roll'd
(Or rather midnight sun) a ray descended,
Which, like a glorious line of liquid gold
Ruled by some pencil, to the earth extended;
And o'er the body, when its flight was ended,

Shook from its skirts so beautiful a flood
Of color'd light, that all its wounds shone splendid,
Each like a ruby ring or golden stud,
And straight the face I knew, in its grim mask of blood.

33. "He lay not prone, but as his high desire
Was ever turn'd toward the stars, his face,
E'en as the martyr's from his couch of fire,
Look'd upward still to heaven's blue fields of space :
Closed was his red right-hand in strict embrace
Grasping that sword, in act to strike, whose blade
Such ravage wrought ; his left, with careless grace
In meek devotion on his breast was laid,
As though for peace to God the parting spirit pray'd.

34. "While I his wounds bedew'd with tears, that eased
None of my anguish for his fall deplored,
The ancient sage drew forward, and released
From his reluctant hand th' inviolate sword ;
And said to me : 'This crimson glave which pour'd
Such streams of blood from bosoms of the foe,
Observe ! perhaps the world cannot afford—
(Its strength none better than thyself can know)—
One or of finer mold or more superb in show.

35. "'Hence, Heaven wills not, although a timeless doom
Has from its lord divorced the glorious brand,
That here with sordid rust it should consume
But pass admired from martial hand to hand ;—
To one who, with a spirit no less grand,
Shall with like force and skill its lightnings sway
For longer time, a happier fate command,
And with it wreak,—his ghost awaits the day—
Full vengeance wreak on him, who did Lord Sweno slay.

36. "''Twas Solyman slew Sweno ; Solyman
Must therefore by the sword of Sweno fall !
Take it, and bear it then where breezes fan
The Christian banners round high Salem wall ;
Nor let a single fear thy mind appal,
That in these regions, or by night or day,
Fresh obstacles shall rise, or ills befall ;
For He who sends thee forth, shall, when astray,
Guide thee, and smooth with flowers the roughness of thy way.

37. "'There 'tis his will that thou declare at length,
For to this end art thou to health restored,
The zeal, the piety, and valiant strength
Which thou hast witness'd in thy darling lord;
That others on their mantles bright and broad
May stamp the purple Cross, with holy aim
Caught from this tale,—a tale for Time to laud
Through long futurity, the while his name
In like illustrious minds lights up young Glory's flame.

38. "'What Christian hero may deserve the meed
Of this bequest, remains to be made known;
It is Rinaldo, to whom all concede
The palm of prowess, yet, a branch scarce blown.
Bear it to him, and say, to him alone
The eyes alike of men and angels look
T' avenge his death, and for his loss atone;'
While on his lips I hang, in wonder's book
A new portentous page my charm'd attention took.

39. "For sudden, where the warrior's corse reposed,
A rich sarcophagus was seen to rise,
Which in its heart his relics had inclosed,
I know not how, nor by what rare device;
And, briefly blazon'd with heraldic dyes,
Shone forth the name and virtues of the dead;
From the strange sight my fascinated eyes
I could not lift; each glance fresh marvel bred;
Now I the porphyry scann'd, and now th' inscription read.

40. "'Here,' said the ancient, 'near his friends shall lie
Thy prince's corse, safe shrined from vulgar sight
While their pure spirits, pass'd into the sky,
From the full fountain of divine delight
Quaff endless joy; but thou the last sad rite
Of tears—the all that piety can pay,
Hast paid, and nature claims repose; this night
I claim thee for my guest, until the ray
Of the new morning rise, to light thee on thy way.'

41. "O'er hill and dale we walk'd, a devious track;
Scarce could my weary steps with theirs keep pace;
Till high, midst toppling crags and cedars black,
A hollow cave received us, round whose face
Green ivies cluster'd,—his lone dwelling-place
Romantic; here amongst the wolves and bears
With his disciple safe he spends his days;

Clear Innocence his shield, his breastplate prayers,
Armor of trustier proof than aught the warrior wears!

42. "My food was roots,—moss, leaves, and dulcet thyme
The couch whereon I slept fatigue away;
But soon as zephyr rang his earliest chime
Among the pines, and morn's arising ray
Tinted the eastern cliffs with gold and gray,
The watchful Hermits rose to matin prayer,
And I with them; I next inquired my way
Through the strange region; of the holy pair
Grateful my farewell took; and here my tale declare."

43. He ceased, and Godfrey answer'd: "Tears, Sir Knight,
Tears for thy tale, 'tis all we can, receive;
Things strange and doleful hast thou brought to light,
Whence we with reason veil our face, and grieve;
Alas th' injustice of that cruel eve!
That friends so full of zeal, so brave in fight,
Fate should from pleasant life so soon bereave!
Thy valiant Lord was, like a flash of light,
One glitt'ring instant shown, then sudden snatch'd from sight.

44. "But wherefore grieve? the prize of realms and gold
Shows mean, compared with this their blissful doom;
Never were bays so glorious, e'en of old,
Giv'n in the car-climed Capitol of Rome!
Throned in Heaven's star-lit temple, they assume
Scepters of palm, and crowns of flowers that grow
In Eden, odorous with immortal bloom;
There, to the radiant wounds received below,
Each joyous martyr points, and glories in the show.

45. "But thou, who for fresh toils and dangers new
With the church militant art left behind,
Shouldst in their blissful triumphs triumph too,
And, to the wise decrees of Heaven resign'd,
Give now to joy thy melancholy mind;
And, for Bertoldo's son,—know that he strays
Far from the camp,—the wand'rer who may find?
But tempt not thou the desert's doubtful ways
In search, till certain news iustructs us where he strays."

46. This their discourse in others' breasts renew'd
Their latent love for fair Sophia's son;

And some exclaim'd, "Through what wild desert
rude
Does not the youth now rove? what risks not run
From the marauding hordes?" nor was there one
That had not some brave story in his praise
To tell the Dane, of laurels nobly won;
The long bright tissue of his deeds they blaze;
Which he with transport hears, and undisguised amaze.

47. When now remembrance of the absent youth
Had touch'd all hearts, and melted many an eye
To tears of tenderness, and anxious ruth,
Behold, the troops, commission'd to supply
The camp, from nightly forage far and nigh
Return! vast flocks and herds with them they lead,
That fill the region with their welcome cry;
Corn, though not much, and fragrant hay to feed,
With the fat beeves they bring, each knight his hungry
steed.

48. And last, not least, a too decisive sign
Of tragic chance, severely to be rued,—
The good Rinaldo's vests and armors fine,
Those rent and bloody, these all hack'd and hew'd!
Quick through the host, in sad incertitude,
And keen alarm, the sudden rumor flew;
For who such things could hide? the multitude,
Sore grieving at the tidings, thronged to view
The brave young hero's arms,—they saw them, and
they knew.

49. Too well they knew his hauberk's pond'rous plates
And moony shield, far-flashing, on whose face
Is seen emblazed the bird which educates
Her unquill'd infants on the sun to gaze,
With eyes undazzled by its ardent rays;
Or first, or all alone, it used to strain
Its proud wings fearless, giving glory chase;
Now, not without deep pity, wrath, and pain,
They see it cleft, and streak'd with many a sanguine
stain.

50. While the crowd whisper, and the dark event
In various wise account for each to each,
The virtuous Duke for Aliprando sent,
Chief of the troop, a man sincere of speech,
And whose ingenuous words might none impeach,
Stamp'd as they were with truth's inviolate seal;

Then thus : "The meaning of this mystery teach ;
Both how and whence these arms were had, reveal,
Nor, whether good or bad, the slightest fact conceal."

51. "For as an active trav'ler may attain
In two days' journey hence," the knight replied,
"In hollow of high hills, a little plain
Lies from the road to Gaza somewhat wide ;
To which a brook's slow waters gurgling glide
'Twixt brier and bough, from tangled steep to steep ;
Low down, o'erarching oaks on every side
Fling their brown shadows o'er a dingle deep ;
Fit screen for ambush'd men their watch unseen to keep.

52. "And as we sought in this sequester'd nook,
For herds or flocks that to its grass-green bed
Might come to graze, we saw beside the brook,
Stretch'd on the purpled herbs, a knight lie dead ;
Crimson his vests, his arms were dropp'd with red ;
Through every heart instinctive horror shot,
For well we knew them, though with blood o'erspread.
To view his face, I, hast'ning to the spot,
Found but a headless trunk—the sever'd head was not !

53. "The right hand too was gone, and many a wound
His noble body bore, from back to breast ;
Hard by, the argent Eagle on the ground
Lay with his vacant helm and batter'd crest :
While round the greenwood shade we gazed, in quest
Of some one to explain so strange a case,
A peasant pass'd, who, spying us, repress'd
His steps, and from the solitary place,
In instant act to fly, turn'd back his frighted face

54. "But, chased and taken, to our stern demand
And inquisition, he at length replied,
That he, the day before, had seen a band
Of armed soldiers from the forest ride ;
One bore a head fresh sever'd at his side,
Grasp d by its golden gory locks ; his scan
Was keen—the visage clearly he descried,
And to his judgment (so his story ran)
'Twas of a beardless youth maturing into man.

55. "In shawl of satin soon the murderer slung,
And bore it pendent at his saddle-bow :
He knew them Christians by their foreign tongue
And red-cross habits, or he judged them so :

Weeping I stripp'd the body, nor was slow
To speak my apprehensions; paid the brave
The last sad rites, the best I could bestow;—
His dirge was chanted by the whisp'ring wave,
And the gray rustling woods sang requiem o'er his grave:—

56. "But if the corse be his whom I bewail,
A nobler tomb his relics should receive:"
Naught left untold of his mysterious tale,
Good Aliprando took his mournful leave.
Godfrey stood pensive, and the livelong eve
Sigh'd as the subject inly he discuss'd;
No clear assurance could his doubts relieve;
And much he wish'd, by signs of surer trust,
To know the mangled trunk and homicide unjust.

57. The night has risen, and silently unfurl'd
O'er heaven's blue infinite her brooding wings;
And sorceress Slumber, walking through the world,
On every eye her dulcet sirup flings;
Thou, Argillan, alone, by grief's sharp stings
Pierced to the quick, her blandishments dost slight,
Busying thy brain on mighty thoughts and things;
Nor giv'st to thy wild eyes and troubled sprite,
Mute quiet's peaceful calm, or slumber's soothing rite.

58. He, of a fervid and impetuous mood,
Active of hand, and turbulent of tongue,
Was on the Tronto born; in civil feud
Nursed by fix'd hatred, and exiled while young;
Thus, by strong passions to resentment stung,
In woods and wilds a robber he became,
And stain'd with blood the rocks from which he sprung;
Till, into Asia summon'd, he his fame
Bravely redeem'd in war, and gain'd a nobler name.

59. At length, tow'rd morn he closed his eyes and slept,—
No calm, sweet sleep, but the dull synonym
Of death;—through his thick blood deep stupor crept,
Possess'd each sense, and lock'd up every limb
In dreadful nightmare; then, delusions dim
Swarm'd to his brain, by cursed Alecto sent;
He slept, not rested; for the Fury grim,
In strangling dreams of terrible portent,
Her own alarming shape did darkly represent.

60. A headless trunk of monstrous size she feign'd,
Shorn of its better arm ; the left, the head
Fast by its horrent hair aloft sustain'd,
Disguised 'twixt livid pale and sanguine red.
The lips still breathed, and breathing spoke, though dead ;
Dripp'd the dark blood ; and many a doleful sigh
Shrill'd from the skull, as hollowly it said,
"Lo, Argillan ! 'tis daylight in the sky !
Fly, fly these dreadful tents ! their impious Chieftain fly.

61. "From his cursed frauds which kill'd me, but of late,
Who, comrades dear, shall keep you or defend ?
Th' insidious Traitor, in his rancorous hate,
Thinks to slay you, as late he slew your friend ;
But if that hand so eager to transcend
Th' undying fame which Brutus dared to seize,
Can on its own audacity depend,—
Fly not ; but let the tyrant's blood appease
My angry ghost, and give th' unquiet spirit ease

62. "I will be with thee, a pale shade, and yield
Arms to thy hand, and anger to thy breast ! "
She said ; and breathing, all his spirit fill'd
With a new fury not to be repress'd :
He broke from sleep ; and trembling roll'd distress'd,
While madness sparkled in each straining ball,
His poisonous eyes, of all the Fiend possess'd :
Arm'd as he was, he flew to summon all
Italia's fiery sons, obsequious to the call.

63. He led them where Rinaldo's arms were hung
In funeral pomp around his vacant tent ;
And thus, with pride and indignation stung,
His grief divulged, and gave his passion vent ;
"Shall then a vile tyrannic race, whose bent
No faith can bind, no reason can restrain,—
Kites, never gorged, though ever on the scent
For blood and gold, shall they with iron rein
Curb our proud necks, and tame our spirits to the chain ?

64. "What we have borne in suff'rings, shame, and tears
Six summers now, beneath their fatal spell,
Is such that Rome will, for a thousand years,
With anger burn, and with disdain rebel ;
I will not, no, brave souls ! I will not tell
How genius, prowess, arms were render'd void,

When Tancred triumph'd and Cilicia fell;
What wonted arts the traitor Frank employ'd,
When that which Valor won, usurping Guile enjoy'd!

65. "I will not tell, when need and time require
Firm thought, bold heart, and executing hand,
How through a thousand deaths we all aspire
With axe, mace, dagger, truncheon, blade, or brand;
First where the prize is fix'd, the peril plann'd,—
But when the palms, but when the prey they share,
The pride, the praise, the glory, gold or land,
These are not ours—'tis but for us to stare,
As they the trophies claim, the plunder homeward bear.

66. "Peace to the thought! there was perhaps a time
When serious and severe such wrongs would show;
Now let them pass—this last tremendous crime
Has made their seeming scarlet white as snow;
Rinaldo have they slain, insulting so
All laws divine and human; in his bloom
Cut off, the beautiful, the brave; and lo!
Flash not the skies? cleaves not, O earth, thy womb,
In its perpetual night the monsters to entomb!

67. "They've slain Rinaldo, of our faith the shield
And sword! and lies he unrevenged?—he lies
Yet unrevenged; and on the naked field,
Unhymn'd, untomb'd, beneath the freezing skies,
Laced o'er with wounds in terrible disguise;
Ask you what barb'rous ruffian smote him down?
Of him who can be ignorant? you have eyes!
Who marks not, jealous of our high renown,
Both Godfrey's damning praise and Baldwin's envious frown?

68. "But why debate? I swear by Heaven, that Heaven
Which not unpunish'd lets the perjured pass,
'Twixt light and dark, before my sight was driven
His wand'ring ghost, a pale and mangled mass;
A sight how wildly horrible! alas,
What frauds from Godfrey did it not divine!
It was no dream; my brain is as a glass,—
I see it yet; where'er my eyes incline,
There the red figure stalks, the eyeballs dimly shine.

69. "What shall we do? to that imperious hand
Which so unjust a death yet foully stains,
Submit for aye? or seek the far-off land,

Where rich Euphrates laves th' Assyrian plains,
And many a city, many a town sustains,
Held by a feeble and unwarlike race,
Soon to be tamed, I ween ! with little pains
This may we win ; no Frank shall there find place,
To share our hard-earn'd spoils, or brand us with disgrace.

70. "Yes, go, and let the guiltless hero lie
All unrevenged, if so it seemeth good ;
Though, if your chill and stagnant blood boil'd high,
Oh, boil'd it high and ardent as it should !
This poisonous snake that has devour'd for food
The flower and pride of our Italian clime,
Should to the rest of his accursed brood,
By his own pangs and death, of punish'd crime
A noted warning give, through long succeeding time.

71. "I, I, if courage serves your wish to dare
All that it should, will first assail his crest !
This very hour my dagger will I bear,
To probe his heart, malignant treason's nest !"
He said ; and on the spirits of the rest,
His wrathful genius and electric eye
Their own tumultuous energy impress'd ;
And, "Arm, O arm you !" was the madman's cry :
"Arm ! arm !" th' indignant youth in unison reply.

72. Midst them Alecto whirl'd her torch, and fire
Commix'd with poison in their bosoms blew ;
Th' infernal thirst for blood, the frenzied ire,
Each dreadful instant more controlless grew :
Forward the snaky witch dilating flew,
And to the Swiss from the Italians pass'd,
Storms in their fiery hearts alike to brew ;
Thence mid the British troops her plagues she cast ;
All lend a gaping mouth, and take th' infection fast.

73. Nor did the public loss and grief alone
Rouse in these foreign bands disdain so deep ;
They had old piques and grudges of their own ;
Whence, this new wrong but added to the heap
Fresh nutriment ; each scorn, long lull'd asleep,
Revived,—the Franks as tyrants were accursed ;
Their wrath and hate all limits overleap ;
Swell in proud threats, and, fix'd to dare the worst,
Loud as a roaring stream, restraint's strong floodgates burst.

74. So water, boiling in a brazen vase
With fire too fervent, gurgles, fumes, and glows;
Till, hot at heart, it lifts its raging face
Above the brim, frets, froths, and overflows.
No remedy remains; too few were those
Whose truth-illumined minds went not astray,
The headstrong crowd's distraction to compose;
Tancred, Camillo, William, were away,
And all whose sov'reign power their heat might else allay.

75. 'Tis uproar all; like tipsy bacchanals
The crowd to arms precipitately spring;
And now are heard fierce cries, seditious calls,
Shields clash, hoarse trumpets stern defiance fling,
And beardless boys heroic ditties sing:
Meanwhile swift messengers, on ev'ry hand,
To Godfrey warning of rebellion bring;
And armed Baldwin with his unsheath'd brand
Fast by his brother's side in silence takes his stand.

76. Hearing the charge, his eyes to heaven he turns,
And to his God for wonted succor flees:
"Lord! thou who seest how much my spirit spurns
Th' imputed crime—thy sight all spirits sees,—
Rend the dark mantle of the mind from these;
Their hearts illumine with thy light divine;
Rebuke the furies of the crowd to peace,
And give mine unstain'd innocence to shine,
Pure in the world's dim sight, as pure it beams in thine!"

77. He ceased; and felt new life and vigor dart
Warm thro' his veins, from heaven imbreath'd, which shed
Light o'er his face, and fortified his heart
With faith; surrounded by his friends, he sped
'Gainst those who thought t' avenge th' ideal dead;
Though bristling arms illumined all the place;
Though hate and rage in ev'ry glance he read;
Though there were some reproach'd him to his face,
Stately he still held on, with firm, unfalt'ring pace.

78. He had his hauberk on,—a vest of white,
Richly embroider'd, from his shoulders flow'd;
Bare were his hands and head; and, to the height
Of dignity sublimed, his features glow'd,
Bright as an Angel's from his blest abode

Sent sceptered forth : such was his port ; he trod
As on the winds ; no arms at need he show'd,
Dared them without,—but shook his golden rod ;
And when he spoke, all seem'd to hear the voice of God.

79. "What senseless threats are these that brave the skies ?
What idle clang of arms is this I hear ?
Who stirr'd these tumults ? is it in this wise
That your so-long-proved ruler ye revere ?
Godfrey of guile what whisp'rer in the ear
Arraigns ? who brings the accusation ? who
Abets the charge ? stand forth ! let him appear !
Ye look perchance that I with prayers should sue,
Number my proofs in plea, and mercy crave from you.

80. "No ! never shall the world that with my name
Resounds, to such debasement see me bend !
Me, Truth, the memory of my deeds, my fame,
And this starr'd scepter only shall defend :
Justice for once to grace shall condescend ;
For once remit the dues she should receive,
Nor o'er the guilty her just scales suspend ;
For former worth this error I forgive ;
Live, to regret your fault, for young Rinaldo live !

81. "Th' Arch-culprit only with his blood must wash
Away the treason—Argillan shall die ;
Who, moved by mere suspicion, base as rash,
Led the revolt, and bribed you with a lie !"
While thus he spake, his more than kinglike eye
In pomp of horror on the ruffian shook
Lightnings and frowns, as from a living sky ;
That Argillan, amazed, of force forsook,
Turn'd (who would think it ?) pale, o'ermaster'd by a look.

82. The crowd too, late so insolent, that roar'd
Such bold defiance forth of spite and pride,
Whose hands had been so swift to seize on sword,
Axe, torch, or javelin, as the fiend supplied
(Hush'd at his golden words), could not abide
His glance ; but cast their guilty eyes to ground,
While shame their cheeks to deepest crimson dyed;
And suffer'd Argillan, though bristled round
With all their ported spears, in fetters to be bound.

83. So when a lion, roaring in his rage,
Shakes high against the sun his frightful mane,
If he who tamed his wildness to the cage,
But knits his brows in visible disdain,—
His harsh rule fearing, fearing to sustain
His threats, he pays obedience to the spell,
Foregoes his fire, and crouches to the chain;
Nor can his teeth, arm'd paws, or malice fell,
Spirit him up with pride, or tempt him to rebel.

84. 'Tis famed that there was seen, of cruel look
And threat'ning gesture, but celestial mold,
A winged warrior, who with one arm shook
Before the pious prince a targe of gold;
And with his right hand, dreadful to behold,
Brandish'd the lightnings of a naked sword,
From which some recent drops of crimson roll'd;
The blood perhaps of realms on which were pour'd,
In his long-slumb'ring wrath, the vials of the Lord.

85. The tumult thus composed, they cast aside
Their arms and evil wills with one consent;
And Godfrey, slowly, and in decent pride
Return'd, admired, to his imperial tent:
On various cares and new engagements bent,
He now determines to attack the town,
Ere or the second or third day be spent;
And oft surveys the timbers late cut down,
That now in huge machines tremendous battle frown.

END OF CANTO VIII.

JERUSALEM DELIVERED.

CANTO IX.

ARGUMENT.

THE Fury spurs on Solyman to make
A sharp assault upon the Franks by night;
God, who beholds th' infernal spirit take
Part in the charge, to countervail their spite,
Sends Michael down to earth, who puts to flight
Their evil host; when freed from their array,
The troup inthrall'd by fair Armida's sleight,
Returning, aid the Franks; at dawning day
His loss the Soldan sees, and murmuring flees away.

JERUSALEM DELIVERED.

CANTO IX.

---

1. But Hell's great Plague, who saw her rule dissolved,
The heats allay'd, the passions lull'd to peace,
Immutable of mood, and still resolved
To war on fate and the divine decrees,
Departs,—and where she passes, the green trees
Fade, the sick sun turns pale, the living springs
Stagnate, and cankers blight the flowery leas ;
Charged with fresh furies, pond'ring fiercer things,
Headlong she shoots abroad, and claps her sounding wings.

2. She, knowing well how by the busy arts
Of her foul consorts, to the Camp were lost
Rinaldo, Tancred, and the rest whose parts
In war, were fear'd and celebrated most,
Exclaim'd : " What wait we for, since clear the coast ?
Now let our Solyman, when midnight lowers,
Unlook'd-for come, and slay the sleeping host ;
From a discordant camp, exhausted powers,
Surely (or much I hope) the vict'ry will be ours ! "

3. This said, to the Arabian bands she flew,
Where, made their captain, Solyman remain'd ;
Than whom no fiercer man the saber drew
In Christ's defiance, or his laws disdain'd ;
Not if the Titans were from hell unchain'd,—
Not if the earth were now to renovate
Her big-boned Giants ; o'er the Turks he reign'd,
And held his court in princely Nice of late,
In all the pomp and pride of oriental state.

4. He ruled the lands from Sangar's silver springs
To crook'd Meander and the Grecian shore,

Where the famed Phrygian and Bithynian kings,
The Mysians and the Lydians lived of yore,
With all who hear the stormy Euxine roar:
But when against the Turks, in Asian sky,
The pilgrim armies first their ensigns bore,
Conquer'd his realms, his Paynim chivalry,
Twice fought in tented field, were twice compell'd to fly.

5. When fortune oft he had in vain essay'd,
Forced to abandon the loved kingdom lost,
He to the Court of Egypt pass'd, in aid
Of its brave King, who proved a noble host;
Glad that a warrior so renown'd, the boast
Of Asiatic story, should combine
With him in plans which all his soul engross'd,—
To drive the Christian powers from Palestine,
And to their pilgrims still deny the sacred shrine.

6. But, ere he openly denounced on them
Decided war, to make success more sure,
He would that Solyman, with gold and gem
Giv'n for that use, the Arabs should secure;
While he the Asian and barbaric Moor
Bribed to his ported flag; at his desire
The Soldan went; and quickly to his lure
Attach'd the greedy Arabs' souls of fire,
Robbers in ev'ry age, and myrmidons of hire.

7. Thus made their Chief, he now with blade and bow
O'erran Judea, gath'ring ample prey;
So that he barr'd all access to and fro
Betwixt the tented camp and navied bay:
And brooding deep, from bitter day to day,
Over his ancient power, his present lot—
A ruin'd name, an empire pass'd away,—
Some greater deed his wrath resolved to plot,
Though yet he had not judged, or well determined what.

8. To him Alecto hurried, in the guise
Of a grave man right venerably old,
With bearded lip, smooth chin, and piercing eyes,
And wrinkled aspect, bloodless to behold:
Her head a Turkish shawl in many a fold
Wreath'd round; the vest across her shoulders flung
Flow'd to her heel; a cimeter in gold
Shone at her side; aback a quiver hung;
And in her martial hand she bore a bow unstrung.

9. "While we," she said, "but traverse empty plains,
A howling wilderness of sands forlorn,
Where now no rapine to be reap'd remains,
Nor conquest gain'd but such as we should scorn,
Godfrey to very heaven exalts his horn,
Smiting the City with his muster'd powers;
And now his engines to the walls are drawn;
And we must see, if unimproved the hours,
Fire ride the flaring wind, and scale her topless towers.

10. "Shall plunder'd herds, raped flocks, and hamlets burn'd
Be the sole spoils of Solyman? what then,
Are thus thy realms retrieved, thy wrongs return'd,
Rule reacquired, or grandeur thine again?
Rouse thee, arouse! lead forth thine armed men;
Let Dedanim awake; let Kedar rise,
And storm the Dragon in his midnight den!
Trust to thine own Araspes, whose advice
Has, both in good and ill, approved itself of price.

11. "He looks not for us, dreads us not, disdains
The naked Arab as a tim'rous slave;
Nor dreams that tribes whom custom only trains
To spoils and flight, would dare a deed so grave.
But thy brave worth shall make the rovers brave
Against an armed camp, which slumbers bind
Apt for the sword!" Her counsel thus she gave:
And breathing all her furies in his mind,
Mounted the passing cloud, and mingled with the wind.

12. He, lifting up his arm toward the skies,
Shouts to her,—"Thou, who fir'st my spirit so!
No man art thou, though under man's disguise;
I know thee—follow thee, behold! I go:
Where plains extended, mountains now shall grow,
Mountains of lifeless people gash'd and stark;
Where burn'd the desert, streams of blood shall flow;
Be now my Genius; lead me to the mark;
And rule my lifted lance to conquer through the dark!"

13. No dallying; no delay! he sounds his swarms,
Collects, harangues them, wins them to combine;
And with his own electric ardor warms
The Camp to second his matured design:
All stand prepared; Alecto gave the sign;—

With her own lips the sounding brass she blew,
And loosed the banner on its breezy pine;
Swift march the hosts, but still as falling dew,—
So still, so swift, they e'en the course of fame outflew.

14. Alecto led, then left them; she assumed
A courier's likeness and succinct array,
And at the time when check'ring twilight gloom'd,
And earth, 'twixt serious night and cheerful day,
Seem'd pond'ring which dominion to obey,
Entering the City, to the king's divan,
Through the mix'd multitudes she made her way;
And to his ear disclosed what Solyman
Purposed by night—the hour, the signal, and the plan.

15. But now black shadows, flush d with vapors red,
Curtain'd the moon; the weeping stars withdrew;
And the chill skies, in lieu of hoar-frost, shed
On earth the semblance of a bloody dew;
Pale meteors fell; malignant goblins flew
Through heaven; and groans that froze the soul with fright
Were heard, while from his grots of brimstone blue
The King of Ghosts let loose each damned sprite,
And from the void abyss spumed forth his densest night.

16. Through these drear glooms the fiery Solyman
Sought the devoted tents; but when Night's wain
Had measured half its journey, and began
Sheer down heaven's western steep to drive amain,
Within a mile of the pavilion'd plain,
Where the lull'd Christian in his martial cloak
Slept unsuspecting, he his barb'rous train
With food refresh'd; then, farther to provoke
Their souls to deeds of blood, thus eloquently spoke:

17. "Look on yon Camp, with thousand thefts and spoils
Dress'd out, more widely famed than strongly mann'd,
That, like a sea, into its greedy coils
Has gather'd all the wealth of Asian land!
This now boon Fortune offers to your hand,
The amplest booty with the slightest cost
And the least peril; all is at command,—
Steeds, clothed in scarlet, arms, with gold emboss'd,
Woo you, not profit them; all, all shall be engross'd!

18. "This is no more the host whose arms subdued
Imperial Nice, and clove the Persian's crest;
For in a war so long as hath ensued,
The greater part, of life lie dispossess'd:
Yet, grant it were entire,—in deepest rest
Is it not drown'd! the saber in the sheath?
Unlaced the hauberk? he is soon oppress'd
Who sleeps,—his life hangs by a slender breath;
Warriors! the cell of sleep is but the porch to death.

19. "On then, come on! I first will cleave a path
Through the grim guards within the enter'd wall;
Let all swords strike like mine! pattern your wrath
By mine; by mine your cruelty and gall!
Now let the Galilean's empire fall;
Now write you glorious in immortal gore;
And free your Asia from the tyrant's thrall!"
Thus he inflamed their spirits to the core;
Then to the deed of death moved stilly as before.

20. Lo, through the gloom the sentinels he spies,
By the faint twinkling of a casual lamp!
Nor can he longer hope in full surprise
To take the cautious Duke and slumb'ring Camp.
The sentries soon beheld his lion-ramp,
And, their alarum sounding loud, bear back,
Warn'd of his numbers by their sullen tramp;
So that the foremost guards were roused, nor slack
To seize their ready arms, and face the near attack.

21. Sure of discov'ry now, the Arabs wound
Their barb'rous horns, and raised their yelling cry,
"Lillah il Allah!" to the well-known sound
Neigh'd all their steeds—earth rang as they rush'd by,
Bellow'd the monntains, roar'd the rifted sky,
Roar'd the deep vales; th' abysses caught the tone,
And answer'd in drear thunder, while on high,
Alecto the blue torch of Phlegethon
Shook toward Zion hill, and sign'd her legions on.

22. First rush'd the Soldan on the guard, e'en then
In lax confusion, unarranged; less swift
Leaps the grim lion from his bosky den,
Shoots the fierce eagle from her mountain clift:
Floods, that pluck up and in their rapid drift
Roll down huts, rocks, and trees; lightnings that blast
Strong towers with bolts that leave a burning rift;

Earthquakes, whose motions turn the world aghast,
Are symbols weak to paint the force with which he pass'd.

23. His saber never through the grisly shade
Falls, but it smites ; nor smites without a wound ;
Nor wounds, but straight it kills ; should more be said,
The truth would like romance or falsehood sound.
Pain he dissembles, or he has not found,
Or scorns the blows which feebler arms imprint ;
Yet oft his burganet of steel rings round
Like loud alarm-bells with the lively dint
Of pole-axe, spear, or sword, and sparkles like a flint.

24. Just as his single sword to flight delivers
This foremost phalanx, a gigantic deed,
Like a sea swell'd with thousand mountain-rivers,
His rushing Arabs to the charge succeed.
Then the scared Franks flew tent-ward at full speed,
Th' audacious Victor following as they fled ;
And with them, rapt sublime on his black steed,
Ent'ring the camp-gate, he on all sides spread
Havoc, and grief, and pain ; loud wailings, rage, and dread.

25. High on the Soldan's helm, in scales of pearl,
With writhen neck, raised paws, outflying wings,
And tail roll'd downward, ending in a curl,
A rampant dragon grinn'd malignant things :
Its lips froth'd poison ; brandishing three stings,
You almost heard its hiss ; at ev'ry stroke
Heap'd on its crest, through all its livid rings
It seem'd the monster into motion woke,
Spit forth its spiteful fire, and belch'd Tartareous smoke.

26. Such and so Gorgon-like the Soldan's form
Show'd by those fires to the beholders' sight,
As Ocean tossing in a midnight storm
To sailors, with her million waves alight.
Some give their timid trembling feet to flight ;
Some, their brave hands to the revenging blade ;
And still th' infuriate Anarch of the Night
Increased the risks by dark'ning them in shade,
And to the midnight winds tumultuous discord bray'd.

27. Of those who show'd in this tremendous hour
The stoutest heart, was old Latinus, bred
On Tiber's banks : toils had not quell'd his power,—
He stood an oak with all its leaves unshed,
Green, though in age ; five sons to war he led,
Who, nobly envying his exploits sublime,
His steps attended with unequal tread ;
In iron armors, they their unripe prime,
And their yet growing limbs, clothed long before their time.

28. The sire's example whets their souls to slake
In blood their eager wrath · "And come," he cries,
"Come where ye see yon tyrannous proud Snake
Devour the crowd that from his fierceness flies.
Let not the sanguine crimes and butcheries
Which he on others perpretrate, unbrace
Your usual courage ; fame through peril lies ;
And honor, O my boys, itself is base,
Which no surmounted toils of jeopardy aggrace !"

29. So the fierce lionness her tawny whelps,
Ere mane invests their neck, or nails their paws,
Ere time with power their native malice helps,
Or teeth and whiskers jag their horrid jaws,
Leads sternly with her to the sylvan wars,
And by her own inflames their savage moods
Against the hunter who to flight o'erawes
The weaker beasts, and insolent intrudes
Upon the holy gloom and quiet of her woods.

30. At once before, beside him, and behind,
The sire and his imprudent little crew,
As though incited by one heart and mind,
In sudden impulse on the Soldan flew ;
Five long sharp lances they or thrust or threw ;
But his the eldest son in daring vein
Rashly abandon'd, and with ardor drew
The keen-edged sword, presuming, but in vain,
The warrior's prancing steed at vantage to have slain.

31. But as a cliff, exposed to storms, which towers,
Smit by a sea that ever howls and raves,
Firm in itself, sustains the wrath of showers,
Heaven's hail, fire, thunder, winds, and mountain waves :
So the strong Soldan lifts his front, so braves,
Unshaken in his seat, th' encounter weak

Of sword and spear : himself from harm he saves ;
And of the son that on his steed would wreak
Revenge, the head disparts, betwixt the eyes and cheek.

32. Fond Amarante, to aid the falling youth,
Stretch'd forth his pious arm ; O zeal misplaced,
Vain tenderness, and inconsid'rate ruth !
That to his brother's ruin he must haste
To join his own ! twined fondly round the waist,
That arm the Turkish saber from his side
Lopp'd off,—down sank embracer and embraced ;
And lip to lip, with melancholy pride,
Mixing their last faint sighs, like drooping roses died.

33. Then, having cut Sabino's lance in twain,
That vex'd him from afar, he spurr'd his horse,
Which, bounding on him with a loosen'd rein,
O'erturn'd and trampled so without remorse
On his fair breast, that from the youthful corse
In dreadful throes the spirit pass'd forlorn ;
Sorely repining at its foul divorce
From those delightful visions which adorn,
With such sweet hues, the birth of Boyhood's fresh
May-morn.

34. But Picus and Laurentes yet had life ;
Twins, born so similar in face and size,
Their persons oft set strangers at sweet strife,
And caused fond error in their parents' eyes :
Th' illusion now which with an art so nice
Nature had raised, Rage disenchants to dust ;
The saber harshly cancels all disguise ;
One through the heart the savage Soldan thrust,
And one he sunder'd quite, and left a breathless bust.

35. The father (ah, no father now !) bereft
Of his brave infants in so short a space,
Felt his own death in those five deaths, which left
To him no scion of his name or race :
In such sharp agonies how strength could brace
His aged heart, or reason aid his brain
Still to live on and combat face to face,
I know not ; but perhaps he saw not plain
The looks, the dying pangs, and paleness of the slain.

36. Perchance the Night with friendly pinions dim
Hid half their anguish from the parent's view ;
Still he felt conquest would be naught to him,

Unless with full revenge he perish'd too:
Then of his own blood prodigal he grew,
And of the Soldan's than a bird of prey
More greedily voracious; nor well knew
Which best his passionate desire would pay,—
Or to be kill'd outright, or suffer on, and slay.

37. But cried aloud: "Is then this arm so frail,
So scorn'd as old, or ridiculed as dead,
That all its efforts do not yet avail,
To call down wrath on my defenseless head?"
He said, and hurl'd with fury as he said,
His spear at the majestic homicide;
Straight to the mark the whizzing weapon fled,
Shiver'd both plate and mail, and pierced his side;
Whence the bright blood outgush'd, and all his armor dyed.

38. Roused by the wound, the Turk against him drove,
Sternly severe; his sword quick passage found
Through the knight's mail,—the target first it clove,
Which seven bull-hides in vain encompass'd round,
And in his bowels sheath'd its point profound:
The forcible assault from saddle push'd
The hapless knight; he sigh'd, and from his wound,
And from his mouth a purple vomit gush'd,
That all with blood the sands, with blood the herbage blush'd.

39. But as an Alpine oak which scorn'd the strength
Of Aquilo and Eurus, firm and sound,
By some unusual wind torn up at length,
Down tumbles, widely ravaging around
The pines and crashing cedars, so to ground
Latinus fell, and to destruction drew
More foes than one, round whom his arm she wound,
Fit end for one so brave! that overthrew,
E'en when o'erthrown himself, and e'en when slaughter'd, slew.

40. While, wreaking thus his inward hate, the Turk
Broke his long fast of battle, in their turn
His active Arabs in their barb'rous work
Make quick dispatch, and all resistance spurn!
Henry, the English knight, and Olopherne,
The proud Bavarian, stretch'd on earth supine,
Expire beneath thy hand, Dragutes stern!
Gilbert and Philip, Ariadene! by thine,
Born in fair castles both, beside th' enchanting Rhine.

41. Albatzar's mace Ernesto slew; the blade
Of Algazel, Engèrlan; but to tell
What various modes of death the field display'd,
And the ignoble multitudes that fell,
Mocks all attempt; at the first "Lillah" yell
And blast of trumpets, in his martial bed
Godfrey was woke, was up, was arm'd, in selle;
Gather'd a massy squadron; at their head
Placed himself; ranged their ranks; and on to battle led.

42. He, when he heard the uproar that was raised
Grow momently more wild, was well advised
That the marauding wand'rers of the waste
In sudden insult had the camp surprised;
Having by frequent message been apprised,
That they the regions round for spoil laid bare;
This well he knew; but never had surmised,
That such wild vagabonds would ever dare
To beard, in very deed, the lion in his lair.

43. But riding on, he heard alarum given
Elsewhere,—"To arms! to arms!" the trumpet jars
And barb'rous howls all horribly to heaven,
Loud as the clang and whirl of countless cars,
Ascend, and in loud thunder climb the stars;
This was Clorinda, who to battle hied
With the king's troops, and, terrible as Mars,
Argantes, breathing fury, at her side;
To Guelph, his viceroy, then the Captain turn'd, and cried:

44. "Hear what new war-cry swells from yonder part,
That lies toward the hills and city! there,
We need thy utmost courage, strength, and art,
The sallier's first insulting shocks to bear:
Go then! to guard that quarter be thy care;
And with thee half of these my troops array
In closest cube; while I myself prepare,
Where southward the hoarse horns defiance bray,
To front the hostile charge, and stand at desp'rate bay."

45. The plan mark'd out, to right and left they wheel'd,
By different paths, an equal risk to face,—
Guelph to the hills, and Godfrey to the field
Where now the Arabs hold his men in chase;
Proceeding, he gains strength; at ev'ry pace,

To his uplifted standard numbers throng:
Which, by the time he reach'd the special place
Where the grim Soldan slaught'ring pass'd along,
Had grown a mighty host, firm, massy, stout, and strong.

46. Thus, humbly gliding from his native mountain,
The Po at first fills not his narrow bed;
But aye the more, the farther from the fountain,
With added forces his proud waters spread;
O'er the burst banks his curl'd brows tower; with tread
Conqu'ring and swift, he takes his giant leap
Down the whelm'd vales, and with his horned head
Rebuts the Adrian waves: nor, in his sweep,
Seems to pay tax, but wage fierce warfare with the deep.

47. When Godfrey saw his troops affrighted fly,
He spurr'd, and shouted: "Shame! what new disgrace,
What dastard fear is this? tell me but why
You run, behold at least who gives you chase;—
A heartless crowd, irresolute and base,
Reeds shaken by a breeze; they neither know
To strike a gallant soldier to his face,
Nor take a stroke in front; your faces show!
That will alone suffice to scare the craven foe!"

48. This said, he spurr'd his horse, and onward flew
Where he beheld the Soldan's shining snake;
Through blood and dust, through sabers not a few,
And groves of spears his progress did he make;
With stroke and onset he dissolved and brake
Ranks the most strong, and masses most compact;
And everywhere to earth was seen to shake,
With a bold arm, attacking or attack'd,
Warrior and war-horse, shield and shielded cataphract.

49. O'er the mix'd heap of men and arms made black
With bloodshed, bounds his barb, of nothing shy;
Th' intrepid Soldan saw the coming wrack,
And neither fled, nor had the wish to fly;
But spurr'd abroad to meet him, and on high
Raised his Damascus cimeter to smite
The moment they should meet;—thus drew they nigh.

O what two Peers did Fortune there unite,
From the world's wide extremes, to prove their matchless might!

50. Fury in narrow lists with virtue strove
For Asia's boundless empire: who can tell
The fierceness of the fight! how saber drove
At sword! how swift and strong the strokes that fell
Their dreadful deeds I pass unsung; they dwell
With unessential Night, whose awful screen
Hid them from notice! they were deeds that well
Deserved a noonday sun, and to have been
By the whole world at once in cloudless glory seen.

51. The Christians, cheer'd by such a glorious guide,
Wax bold, and push the battle to the gate;
And round the dragon crested homicide,
Dense grows the crowd, arm'd best in proof of plate;
Foot press'd to foot, no ground repining hate
Concedes; nor this nor that side wins or quails;
Faithful and infidel alike elate,
The victor falls, the vanquish'd now prevails;
And life and grisly death are hung in equal scales.

52. As with like rage and strength to battle fly
Here the strong South-wind, there the ruffian North,—
They cuff, they rave, they clash; and sea and sky
To neither yield themselves, though lash'd to froth,
But cloud for cloud, and wave for wave send forth:
So fought both hosts beneath the hideous shade—
Unyielding, firm, sharp, obstinate, and wroth;
Front shocking front, in horrible parade,
Shield with shield, helm with helm, and blade loud clash'd with blade.

53. Nor toward the City shock the charging hosts
Meanwhile with less loud uproar; nor less dense
Glooms their array; a thousand thousand ghosts
And Stygian fiends the cope of heaven immense
Fill, and in Pagan bosoms breathe intense
Resolve and fortitude; that none desire,
Or even think to stir a footstep thence;
While with new rage Argantes they inspire,
Enough inflamed before with his accustom'd fire.

54. He too the guards repulsed, and at one bound
Clear o'er the deep fosse and high ramparts leap'd,—

Level'd the outworks, smooth'd the lofty mound,
And with the Franks he slew, the trenches heap'd;
So that his knights with ease pursuing, steep'd
The ground with gore, and to a purple red
Dyed the white tents; like praise Clorinda reap'd
Fast by his side, or following where he sped;
With much disdain that she th' assailants did not head.

55. And now the Christians were in flight, when Guelph
The field of slaughter opportunely gain'd;
He made them turn their faces; he himself
Bore the foe's onset, and his rage restrain'd.
Thus fought they; and on both sides the blood rain'd
In equal showers, and equally they earn'd
The dreary laurels of revenge distain'd:
His eyes meanwhile where hot the battle burn'd,
From his empyreal seat the King of Glory turn'd.

56. There He abides; there, full of truth and love,
Creates, adorns, and governs all that be,
High o'er this narrow-bounded world, above
The reach of reason and of sense; there He
Presides from all to all eternity,
Sublime on solemn throne, unbuilt with hands,
Three Lights in One! while in meek ministry,
Beneath his feet, with Fate and Nature stands
Motion, and He whose glass weighs out her golden sands:

57. With Place and Fortune, who, like magic dust,
The glory, gold, and power of things below,
Tosses and whirls in her capricious gust,
Reckless of human joy and human woe:
There He in splendor shrouds himself from show,
Which not e'en holiest eyes unshaded see;
And round about him, in a glorious bow,
Millions of happy souls keep jubilee,—
Equals alike in bliss, though diff'ring in degree.

58. As the loud harmony of angel hymns
Joyous through heaven's resounding palace roll'd,
Michael he summon'd, whose seraphic limbs
Sparkle and burn in adamant and gold;
And thus serenely spake: "Dost thou behold
How from th' abyss yon fiends are risen, to spoil
The faithful flock beloved of my fold?
Seest thou then, arm'd with malice, how they toil
In wrack and uproar wide those kingdoms to embroil?

59 "Go! bid them all avaunt, and leave the care
Of war to warriors, as is just and right;
Nor tempest and infect the earth and air
Longer, with their foul charms and evil flight;
But bid them back to the abyss of night,
Their merited abode of wail and pain;
There to torment themselves, and wreak their spite
On the lost spirits subject to their chain;
Lo, this my bidding is, and thus do I ordain!"

60. This said, the wing'd Archangel low inclined
In rev'rent awe before th' Almighty's throne;
Then spread his golden pinions on the wind,
And, swifter than all thought, away is flown:
He pass'd the regions which the Blessed own
For their peculiar home, a glorious sphere
Of fire and splendor; next, the milder zone
Of whitest crystal; and the circle clear,
Which, gemm'd with stars, whirls round, and charms his tuneful ear.

61. To left, distinct in influence and in phase,
He sees bright Jove and frigid Saturn roll;
And those five other errant fires, whose maze
Of motion some angelic spark of soul
Directs with truth unerring to the goal:
Through fields of endless sunshine he arrives
Where thunders, winds, and showers from pole to pole
Waste and renew, as each for mast'ry strives,
Green Earth, that fades to bloom, and to decay revives.

62. The horrors of the storm, the shadowy glooms,
With his immortal fans he shakes away;
The splendor falling from his face illumes
Night with a sunshine luminous as day:
So after rain in April or in May,
The sun with colors fine of ev'ry hue
Paints the most clouds, green, crimson, gold, and gray;
Cleaving the liquid sky's calm bosom blue,
So shines a shooting star in momentary view.

63. But when he came where the malignant Fiends
Inflamed the Turks, he check'd his swift career;
Balanced his vig'rous pinions on the winds;
Then spoke, and, speaking, shook his dreadful spear:

"Not yet, Accursed! have ye learn'd to fear
That God whose blazing thunderbolts of yore
Scorch'd your gay wings, and to the nether sphere
Smote you? have ages, spent in torments sore,
Left you rebellious still, and haughty as before?

64. "Lo! Heaven hath sworn, that to the Cross shall nod
Yon towers, and Sion ope her portal gates;
Who shall withstand the oracles of God;
Provoke his wrath, and fight against the Fates,
Depart, ye Cursed! to your native states,
The regions of perpetual death and pain,
To you devote; the fiery surge awaits
Your coming, and rears bright its blazing mane;
There urge your impious wars, your triumphs there ordain!

65. "There o'er the guilty tyrannize; there wreak
Your rage, and muster all the pangs ye know,
Mid racks of iron, shaken chains, the shriek
And gushing of interminable woe!"
This heard, they fled; whom he perceived more slow,
The Angel, with his fatal lance divine,
Goaded and drove: with sullen groans they go;
To realms of smiling light, and golden shine
Of the gay morning-stars reluctant to resign.

66. And spread tow'rd Hell their dragon wings, to tease,
And tear with sharper pangs the tortured ghosts;
Not swallows in such flocks pass o'er the seas,
Gath'ring to milder suns and warmer coasts;
Not leaves in woods, when Autumn's first night-frosts
Nip their sear'd beauty, in such numbers e'er
Heap the low valleys: freed from their foul hosts,
The joyous earth shook off her black despair,
And cheer'd with flowers the ground, with harmony the air.

67. Yet not for this the valor or the ire
In fierce Argantes' breast decay'd or sank;
Though there Alecto breathed not now her fire,
Nor with her whip of scorpions lash'd his flank;
But evermore, where frown'd the closest rank,
He keenly plied his sharp, vindictive blade;
He mow'd down Briton, Greek, Italian, Frank,
The proud, the mean, the potent equal made;
And the plumed liege beside his plumeless vassal laid.

68. Not far behind, the Camp Clorinda strow'd
With sever'd limbs, and with as keen a gust;
Through Berlinger's proud heart, the warm abode
Of life and sense, her cimeter she thrust,—
True to her wish, and to her aim so just,
Its red point issued from the back; she left
The hapless warrior grov'ling in the dust,
Then through the navel Albino bereft
Of life, and Gallo's skull, though helm'd, in sunder cleft.

69. Gernier's right hand, that gash'd her as she pass'd,
She cut sheer off; which yet did not abstain
From grasping with its quiv'ring fingers fast,
Half animate, the sword, and on the plain
Glid like a snake's lithe tail, that, cut in twain
By some stung passenger, twists to and fro,
And fiercely strives to reunite, in vain:
Thus lopp'd, he writhed; the Heroine left him so,
Then at Achilles flew, and dealt a nobler blow.

70. Betwixt the nape and neck the saber smit,
And cut the nerves and sinews that sustain'd
The head, which, falling, on the earth alit,
And in foul dust the beauteous face profaned,
Ere the trunk fell; erect the trunk remain'd
(A sight of horror!), nor its seat forsook;
Till the sagacious steed, no longer rein'd
By the strong hand that wont its pride to brook,
Rampant from off its back the useless burden shook.

71. While thus the dauntless Heroine gored and scourged
The Western Lords, and thinn'd their serried lines,
Her steed against her brave Gildippe urged,
Nor made less slaughter on the Saracines:
Their sex the same, the same wild beauty shines
In each; in each the fire of glory glows;
At her courageous rival each repines;
But face to face in battle thus to close,
Fate grants it not,—their lives are owed to mightier foes.

72. Here one, and there the other shock'd and charged,
Nor this nor that could clear the fighting crowd;
But gen'rous Guelph press'd forward, and discharged
At his fair foe, with broad-sword raised, a proud
Aspiring stroke; it linger'd not, but plow'd
Her side, and purple turn'd its purest white;
Heroic scorn her flashing smile avow'd,—

She with a thrust sharp answer made the knight,
And 'twixt the ribs his wound did passing well requite.

73. A second, stronger blow Lord Guelpho strook,
Which err'd as tall Osmida, passing by,
By chance upon his turban'd forehead took
The wound unmeant, gash'd deep from eye to eye.
But here, for glory fierce, the company
Which Guelph commanded, interposing, drew
In numbers round; while, fix'd to do or die,
Of the press'd Pagans crowds on crowds throng'd too,
So that the madd'ning fight more wild each moment grew.

74. Meanwhile Aurora sweet her roseate face
Shows from the balcony of heaven; and lo!
Burst from his bonds, and fervent from disgrace,
Where the press thickens and the tumults grow,
Comes Argillan, abrupt; from top to toe
Sheathed in such arms as chance for the assault
First offers,—good or bad, he cares not, so
They do but serve him to amend his fault,
And by new deeds to praise his tarnish'd name exalt.

75. As when a wild steed in the stalls of kings
Fed for the battle, from his manger breaks;
O'er vales, o'er mountains to his loves he springs,
Seeks the known meads, or to the river takes;
His curl'd mane dances on his back; he shakes
His haughty neck aloft; his broad hoofs sound
Like the black thunder; with the bright fire-flakes
Struck forth from his swift trampling, burns the ground
And with his neighings shrill he fills the world around;

76. So issues Argillan; his fierce eyes blaze,
Intrepid shows his brow, sublimely strong
His lifted arm; his swift feet leave no trace,
Scarce stir the light dust as they bound along:
And now, the turban'd multitudes among,
He lifts his voice like one that laughs to scorn
All jeopardy and fear: "O ye vile throng!
Dregs of the world! what impudence has drawn
You to a field of war, amidst wild asses born?

77. "'Tis not for you the shield and battle blade
To shake aloft, or wear the warrior's weed;
But to commit, half naked and afraid,

Wounds to the wind, your safety to the steed!
All your achievements and brave schemes, indeed,
Are wrought by night, blind Night your sole resource
And tower of strength! now she has fled, you need
Valor and arms of more efficient force;
To what kind guardian Power will you now have recourse?"

78. While thus he spoke, on Algazel's bare cheek
So fierce a stroke he took at bold surprise,
As clove his jaws, and, as he sought to speak,
Cut short his answ'ring accents; o'er the eyes
Of the poor wretch a misty horror flies;
An icy frost runs chill from vein to vein;
He groans, he falls, and in the agonies
Of death, still fill'd with fury and disdain,
Bites with his gnashing teeth th' abominated plain.

79. By various deaths then Agricalt he slew,
Strong Muleasses, stronger Saladine;
Then at Aldlazel exulting flew,
And clove the haughty Arab to the chine;
Next wounding in the breast bold Ariadine,
He beat him down, and with fierce vaunts of pride
Taunted the youth; he, stretch'd on earth supine,
His languid eyes uplifting ere he died,
Thus to his glorying words presagingly replied:

80. "Not thou, whoe'er thou art, shalt glory long
In this my death, short-sighted homicide!
Like chance awaits thee; soon a hand more strong
Shall stretch thee pale and breathless by my side!"
Grimly he smiled; and "Of my fate," he cried,
"Let Heaven take care; meanwhile die thou, and fill
The maw of birds and hounds!" then with a stride
Of haughtier vaunt, he press'd him with his heel,
And drew at once away the spirit and the steel.

81. Mix'd with the lancers rode the Soldan's page—
His fav'rite page, angelically fair;
On whose smooth chin the flowers that vernal age
Strews in its deep'ning ripeness yet were rare;
A poet's fancy would the pearls compare
That in moist silver his warm cheeks inchase,
To dews on April roses; to his hair,
Untrimm'd, the golden gather'd dust gave grace,
And even severe disdain show'd sweet in such a face.

82. His steed for whiteness match'd the snows that drift
On the high Apennines ; the lights that glance
In Arctic skies are not more lithe and swift
Than he to run, to twine, to wheel, to prance :
Grasp'd in the midst he shook a Moorish lance,
And a short saber graced his side ; with bold
Barbaric pomp, as in antique romance,
He shone in purple, glorious to behold,
Fretted with blazing gems, and damask'd o'er with gold.

83. While the fair boy whose mind the new delight
Of glory charm'd, with uncheck'd conquest warm,
Hither and thither in his childish sleight
Drove the bewilder'd crowd with little harm,
Like a grim lion couching cool and calm,
Fierce Argillano to his motions lent
Regard; watch'd well his time; then raised his arm,—
Loud whizz'd the lance, and, true to his intent,
At stealth the white steed slew, and down the rider went.

84. At his sweet face, where suppliant pity mild
For mercy, mercy, vainly made appeal,
The victor-churl struck, hoping to have spoil'd
That masterpiece of beauty ; but the steel,
Humaner than the man, appear'd to feel
Pain for the wrong, and lighted flat ; alas,
What could it serve him ! soon his cruel skill
The fault retrieved,—he made a surer pass ;
Deep gash'd the sword his cheek, and stretch'd him on the grass.

85. The Soldan, who at no great distance fought,
By Godfrey in the battle kept at bay,
Turn'd his spurr'd steed the moment he had caught
Sight of the risk, and through the wedged array
Of charged and charging squadrons clove his way,
And came in time—for vengeance, not for aid ;
O grief ! O anguish ! he beheld his gay
And late so smiling Lesbin lowly laid,
Like a fine flower cut down, and drooping undecay'd.

86. His graceful head fell with an air so meek ;
Life's flitting sunshine languish'd into night
O'er his blue eye, and on the suff'ring cheek,
Strew'd by Death's Angel in his love, the white
Rose breathed so sweetly, that, in pride's despite,
His marble heart was touch'd ; and from his brain,

In midst of rage, the tears gush'd big and bright:
What! can he weep, who saw his ancient reign
Pass by without one tear to mark his parting pain?

87. He weeps! but when the smoking sword he views
In Lesbin's blood imbrued, all softness dies;
His spirit is ablaze; his rage renews;
The scorch'd tears stagnate in his stormy eyes,
That flash with fire; on Argillan he flies,
Lifts his drawn sword, and splits from thong to thong,
First the raised buckler with its proud device,
And next his helmed head—a stroke most strong,
Worthy a Sultan's scorn who writhed beneath such wrong.

88. Nor thus content, he from his steed alights,
And makes fierce battle with the corse he slew;
Like a struck mastiff, that in vengeance bites
The stone some passenger in anger threw:
O vain relief of anguish! to pursue
With rage the dust insensible to pain:
But meanwhile Godfrey and his circling crew
Of chevaliers, against the Soldan's train
Spent not in vain their powers, struck not their blows in vain.

89. A thousand Turks were there from head to heel
Sheathed in fine mail, with plated shields; their frame,
Untired by toil, was stubborn as the steel
That arm'd their limbs; their daring souls the same,—
Versed in all movements of the martial game:
The Soldan's ancient body-guard, they pass'd
With him to the Arabian wilds, when came
His evil hour, and to his fortunes fast
Adhered through bright and dark, confed'rates to the last.

90. These, press'd together close in firmest rank,
Little or nothing to the Franks gave place;
Among them Godfrey charged, and in the flank
Wounded Rostene, Corcutes in the face;
From Selin, lifting high his Moorish mace,
He shore the head; then to Rosseno drew,
Lopp'd off both arms, and in that piteous case
Left him to die, while on the rest he flew;
And many a Paynim maim'd, and many a Paynim slew.

91. While thus he strikes, and on his moony shield
Takes all their strokes, invincible as bold,
Nor in one point the gruff barbarians yield,
Their hopes yet ardent, nor their courage cold,
Fresh clouds of drifted dust ride nigh, that hold
Lightnings of war within their womb ; and lo !
Nearer and nearer as their skirts are roll'd,
A sudden shine of arms moves to and fro,
That fills with deep alarm the bosoms of the foe.

92. Here fifty knights to battle came, who bore
In argent field the Red-cross of their Lord ;
Had I a hundred mouths and tongues, yea, more,
Throat, lungs, and breath of brass to sound abroad
Their deeds, I could not fittingly record
What numbers lifeless sank upon the plain
In their first charge ; the valiant Turk that warr'd,
And Arab that warr'd not, but sought to gain
The gates for flight, alike was met, was pierced, was slain.

93. Grief, Scorn, Pain, Horror, Cruelty, and Fear,
Ran shrieking on all sides, and you might see
Death the Destroyer stride from van to rear,
In thousand guises, butch'ring those that flee ;
Conqu'ring the brave ; and with a bloody sea
Billowing the ground :—the king with many a knight
Had issued from the walls, in certainty
Of full success, and with the morning light
Beheld the subject plain and uncompleted fight.

94. But when, no longer dubious of th' event,
He the main army saw in disarray,
He bade the trumpet sound retreat, and sent
Repeated heralds to command and pray
Argantes and Clorinda back ; but they,
Intoxicate with blood, and blind with ire,
Long time refuse his message to obey ;
At length they yield, but jointly still aspire
To orb their scatter'd troops and in firm rank retire.

95. But who a coward host can rule or guide ?
The flight is taken, and the fierce foe nigh ;
One casts his shield, and one his sword aside,
As more encumber'd than defensed thereby :
Stretch'd from the South toward the Western sky,
A rugged valley winds, abrupt and deep,
Near Salem,—thither do the many fly,

In crowds on crowds rude rushing down the steep,—
Dark clouds of dust arise, and to the city sweep.

96. While down the hill precipitate they ran,
The Christian host vast slaughter of them made ;
But when they cross'd the valley, and began
To climb the rocks in bowshot of the aid
Sent by the king, his forces Guelpho stay'd ;
For, at such disadvantages of height,
He would not risk th' uncertain escalade ;
Thus safe within the walls, the king from flight
Received the small remains of that unprosp'rous fight.

97. All that to human efforts Nature grants,
The Soldan now had done ; with sweat and gore
His members are bedew'd ; he gasps and pants,
Sharp anguish shakes his frame, he can no more.
Weak grew his arm beneath the shield it bore ;
His red right-hand, with slaughter overspent,
Scarce waved the sword; that sword, so sharp before,
Now only bruised, so blunted, hack'd, and bent,
It long had lost the use for which the shape was lent.

98. Feeling thus faint, he hesitating stands
In dubious mood, 'twixt warring counsels toss'd,—
Or should he perish by his own proud hands,
Since hope afresh was wreck'd and honor lost,
So none the glory of his death could boast,
Or, should he care to save his life, and flee
Far from the field where lay his vanquish'd host?
"Fortune," at last he cried, "I yield to thee ;
And let my flight the seal of thy scorn'd conquest be:—

99. "Let Godfrey view once more, and smile to view
My second exile ;—soon shall he again
See me in arms return'd, to vex anew
His haunted peace and never stable reign.
Yield I do not ; eternal my disdain
Shall be as are my wrongs ; though fires consume
My dust, immortal shall my hate remain ;
And aye my naked ghost fresh wrath assume,
Through life a foe most fierce, but fiercer from the tomb !"

END OF CANTO IX.

A rude Silenus oft the days of old
Have seen unclose, and yield some Goddess fair,
But never yet did sylvan image hold
Charms such as issued from the myrtle rare:
For forth a Lady stept with golden hair,
With angel beauty, angel mien and grace;
In whom, albeit of visionary air,
Rinaldo starts Armida's form to trace,
The same expressive eye, fond smile, and radiant face.

STANZA XXX; CANTO XVIII

JERUSALEM DELIVERED.

CANTO X.

ARGUMENT.

BEFORE the Soldan, as he sleeps, Ismen
Presents himself, and secretly conveys
The Prince to Sion, where his courage keen,
And the unbending firmness he displays,
Soon cheers the drooping Tyrant ; Godfrey prays
Of his stray knights the story of their woes ;
And when the fear which on his spirit preys
For lost Rinaldo finds a happy close,
His sons' renown and worth the gifted Seer foreshows

JERUSALEM DELIVERED.

CANTO X.

---

1. WHILE yet he spoke, a steed, from battle stray'd,
Came bounding up to him, on whose free rein
A hot and hasty hand the Soldan laid,
And leap'd across him, faint with toil and pain:
The dragon crest, that with such length of train
Of late in air rose dreadful, shorn away,
Leaves the proud helm undignified and plain;
Rent are his glorious robes, his trappings gay;
Nor has he left one sign of pomp or kingly sway.

2. As from the wattled pens the villain wolf
Chased out, scuds darkling to the forests hoar,
Which, though he well has fill'd the rav'nous gulf
Of his vast stomach with the flesh and gore
Of many a victim, thirsting yet for more,
Laps off the bloody froth his jaws distil,
With greedy tongue; e'en so the Soldan bore
From that night's slaughter an unsated will,
For boundless fields of blood athirst and hung'ring still.

3. As was his fortune, from the drizzly cloud
Of sounding arrows that around him flew,
From groves of lances, ranks of swords, a crowd
Of hostile knights, securely he withdrew;
And ever as he rode, unknown to view,
The most untrod and wildest ways he sought;
While, unresolved what measure to pursue,
With each fresh billow of conflicting thought,
Fluctuates his stormy mind, still fixing, fix'd on naught.

4. At length to Egypt he resolved to hie,
Where now the Caliph his vast hosts array'd;
And, join'd with him, the arms and fate to try

Of a fresh conflict ; this decision made,
In his mid course no longer he delay'd,
But with the speed his urgency demands,
Rode for the South ; he needed none in aid,
To show the way where on the seashore sands,
Right strongly tower'd, the town of antique Gaza stands.

5. Nor, though sharp pangs upon his members seize,
And his weak frame grows weary, will he lay
His arms aside to taste the bliss of ease,
But in sore travel spends the total day,
Till from his sight the landscape swims away,
And shadows tinge the sky's sweet colors brown ;
He then alights ; then swathes, as best he may,
His thrilling wounds ; and from the lofty crown
Of overnodding palms ambrosial fruit shakes down.

6. And, thus refreshed, on the bare earth he sought,
His head reclining on his shield, to gain
Rest to his wearied side, and still the thought,
The restless thought that tired his busy brain :
But every moment miserable pain
Stung the sick slumb'rer on his couch of thorn ;
Oft a swift horror shot from vein to vein ;
While by the inward vultures, Grief and Scorn,
His sad heart still was pierced, his liver fiercely torn.

7. At length, when Night had reach'd her deepest noon,
And lull'd in solemn trance all things around,
Conquer'd with weariness, in softest swoon
His vexing mem'ries and regrets he drown'd :
Brief languid quiet his shut eyelids crown'd,
And a benumbing torpor, dull but dear,
Its soothing coils about his members wound ;—
While yet he slept, a sudden voice severe,
Toned like the thunder, thus resounded in his ear :

8. "Solyman ! Solyman ! this lazy rest
To a more suited time reserve ; still groans
The land thou'st ruled—a weeping slave, oppress'd
Beneath the yoke of foreign myrmidons :
And sleep'st thou here, upon a soil that owns
So deep a vestige of thy late disgrace ?
Hast thou the sad remembrance lost, whose bones
Untomb'd it holds ? is it in such a place
That thou must idly wait to give the morning chase ?"

9. The Soldan, waking, raised his eyes, and view'd
A man beneath a hundred winters bent;
Who, with a writhen staff from the wild wood,
Guided his feeble steps where'er he went;
"And who art thou?" he utter'd, malcontent,
"Officious goblin! whose ill ministry
Is thus to haunt lone passengers o'erspent,
And scare off their brief sleeps? take wing, and flee
What is my proud revenge, what my disgrace to thee!"

10. "I," said the bearded Sire, "am one to whom
Is known in part the scope of your new scheme;
And as a friend more watchful of your doom
And cherish'd int'rests than you yet may deem,
I come; nor let my bitter sarcasm seem
Severe in vain; scorn is the quick'ning spur
Of virtue and ennobling self-esteem;
Let not my accents then, which serve to stir
The latent fire to flame, your anger thus incur.

11. "Though now (if I your purpose read aright)
Your steps to the Egyptian Court incline,
A dang'rous journey and a fruitless flight,
If yet you pause not in your rash design,
My mystic art, from many a hostile sign,
Predicts; since, whether you remain or go,
No less the forces of the Saracine
Will march; and there, what valor can you show,
Or how your genius use against our common foe?

12. "But, if you trust to me, within those walls
Which fast the Latin arms in leaguer gird,
In open day, and to the inmost halls
Of Salem, without sword, I pledge my word
To bring you safe, unnoticed and unheard;
There take your fill of glory and delight:
With arms and zeal to fit exploits transferr'd,
Defend her towers, till, to renew the fight,
The hosts of Egypt come, and conquest crowns your right!"

13. While thus he spoke, the fierce Turk with amaze
The ancient man's electric aspect eyed;
His voice was like a spell; and from his face,
And from his savage mind all signs of pride
And rage he banish'd: "Father!" he replied,
"This instant I am ready, I am swift
To follow wheresoe'er thy will may guide;

That counsel's best which promises to lift
My steps with most of toil to Danger's loftiest clift !"

14. The Ancient praised his zeal, and straightway pour'd
Into his smarting wounds, which Night had chill'd,
A sov'reign juice that soon his strength restored,
Stanch'd the red ichor, the sore bruises heal'd ;
And, seeing now the sun begin to gild
The orient clouds yet purple from their play
Round young Aurora, "Rise from off thy shield !"
He said, "'tis time to go ; since breaking day,
Which calls the world to toil, already lights our way."

15. His magic car stood ready at command ;—
They mount ; the Stranger, shunning all delay,
Shook the rich reins, and with a master's hand
Lash'd the black steeds, that, ramping, scour'd away
So swift, that not the sands a trace betray
Of hoof or wheel ; they vanish as they come,
Proudly precipitant, and snort, and neigh,
Paw the parch'd soil, and, ardent for their home,
Champ their resplendent bits all white with fleecy foam.

16. Away ! away ! and still as fast and far
They fly, the air to clouds condensing roll'd
In heaps around, and draped th' enchanted car ;
Yet not a wreath could human eye behold ;
Nor stone nor rock, (surprising to be told),
Hurl'd from the most magnificent machine,
Might of its crapelike volume pierce the fold !
Yet by the two within were all things seen—
The clouds, air, earth, and sky, all rosily serene.

17. With wrinkling forehead and arch'd brow, the knight
On cloud and car gazed stupidly intent,—
Its wheels seem'd wings, and its career a flight,
So swift and soundless on its way it went
O'er the smooth soil ; the Sage plenipotent,
Who saw his raptured spirit stand aghast
At the sublime and mystical portent,
From his abstraction roused him ; voice at last
Came to his lips, from which these eager questions pass'd.

18. "Whoe'er thou art that, passing mortal man,
Mak'st pliant Nature thus thy freaks fulfill,
Who, reading thought and purpose at a scan,
The heart's close chambers rangest at thy will ;
O ! if it be within thy gifted skill,

Far peeping into Time, to see the shows
Of things yet dark, and spell their good or ill,
Say, prophet, say, what ruin or repose
Do the mysterious stars foredoom from Asia's throes?

19. "But first thy name declare, and by what art
Thou work'st things thus beyond weak Fancy's reach;
For, in this stupor of the mind and heart,
How else can I attend thy wondrous speech?"
The Wizard smiled; "Of that which you beseech,
Part I, at least," said he, "will grant; one page
We may turn over, and its secrets teach;
Ismeno I, the Syrian Archimage,
Named from the magic arts in which I love t' engage.

20 "But, Prince, to glance through dark futurity,
And of far fate th' eternal leaves to read,
Were an attempt too arrogant and high;
Nor do the Heavens to man such power concede
To face the ills and suff'rings here decreed,
All spirit, wisdom, strength, let each assume;
For oft the valorous and the wise succeed
In striking brightness from the deepest gloom,
And from the spheres shape out their own triumphant doom.

21. "For thee 'twill be a little thing, the powers
And pillars of Frank rule to shake; prepare
Not to flank only, nor to shield the towers,
Which those fierce hosts with such unceasing care
Strongly inclose,—'gainst steel,—'gainst fire lay bare
Thine all unconqu'rable arms; be bold;
Hope all things, suffer all things, all things dare;
Myself hope much; to thee shall now be told,
What through the mist of years obscurely I behold.

22. "I seem to see, ere many an annual round
Yon dancing planet runs, a Chief arise,
Who shall grace Asia with his deeds renown'd,
And with the scepter of the Ptolemies
Rule fruitful Egypt; on the policies,
Industrious arts, and blessings of his reign,
I'm mute,—their number pains my straining eyes:
This be content to know, the Christian chain
With equal scorn and strength his hand shall shake in twain.

23. "Yea, from its very base their rule unjust
Shall in his last proud field uprooted be;
And the lone remnant for their safety trust
A petty rock beside the howling sea,
Protected only by its waves; from thee
This Chief shall spring!" here hush'd the prophet's voice;
"And O!" the Turk replied, "thrice happy he,
Destined to such a noble task!" the choice
His vulture thoughts half grudge, yet, while they grudge, rejoice.

24. "Let Fortune," he subjoin'd, "for good or ill
Come or come not, as is prescribed on high;
She sways not me, but shall behold my will
Unconquer'd aye, and steadfast as the sky:
First shall the moon from her blue circuit fly;
First shall the stars' immortal footsteps reel
From the path fix'd for them to tread, ere I
Swerve but a step to shun her whirling wheel!"
He said, and crimson turn'd, with scorn and fervent zeal.

25. Thus commune they; and now the plain they pass,
Near which their domes the white pavilions rear;
There what a cruel sight was seen! alas,
In what unnumber'd shapes did death appear!
To Solyman's stern eyes a troubled tear
Of grief and passion rose at the survey,
And fill'd his face with gloom; afar and near,
In what wild havoc, how insulted, lay
His arms and ensigns, fear'd, so fear'd of yesterday!

26. He saw the Franks in carnival o'erspread
The field, oft trampling on the faces pale
Of his slain friends, as from th' unburied dead
They tore the gorgeous vests and shirts of mail,
With rude insulting taunts: down the far vale,
In long, long order, many a fun'ral choir
Was seen attending with the voice of wail
Bodies beloved, while some brought careless fire,
And Turks and Arabs heap'd in one commingling pyre.

27. He deeply sigh'd, he drew his sword in rage,
And from his seat leap'd, eager in their blood
T' avenge the insult; but the Archimage
His mad resolve inflexibly withstood;
And, curbing by rebuke his furious mood,
Made him perforce resume the seat resign'd;

Then to the loftiest hills his course pursued,
Baffling the rival pinions of the wind,
Until the hostile tents in distance sank behind.

28. Alighting then, the chariot disappear'd,
And side by side on foot the trav'lers went;
Still curtain'd in the cloud, their course they steer'd
Down a deep vale of difficult descent,
Till they arrived where to the Occident
Sublime Mount Sion turn'd its shoulders wide,
In rocks and cliffs fantastically rent;
There paused the Sorcerer, and its fissured side
Coasting from steep to steep, in close perusal eyed.

29. Scoop'd in the bosom of the living stone,
Time immemorial, yawns a hollow grot,
Whose mouth, from long disuse, was overgrown
With briers and herbs that mantled all the spot,
By all but the Magician long forgot;
He clear'd the way, the entrance he explored,
And, bending low his body, scrupled not
Darkling to creep into the cave, unawed,
Holding his right hand out to guide the Turkish lord.

30. Out then spake Solyman: "What uncouth cave
Is this, through which my stealing steps must glide?
Far nobler passage with my trusty glave
Would I have cleft, if thou hadst not denied:"
"Reluctant soul!" the Archimage replied,
"Let not thy proud feet spurn the gloomy ways,
Which potent Herod has so often tried,—
Which Herod ofttimes trod in ancient days,
Whose deeds in arms are yet the theme of Syrian praise.

31. "This cave the monarch scoop'd, when with a power
More strict his froward Jews he wish'd to bend;
By this he could with ease from yonder tower,
(Then named Antonia from his noble friend,)
Either, invisible to all descend
To the grand Temple, and secure his flight,
If aught of tumult threaten'd to impend
In the rebellious city, or, by night
Fresh forces introduce, nor shock the public sight.

32. "This dark and solitary cave, of all
Existent beings but to me is known;
It now shall be our usher to the hall,
Where in divan the mightiest of his throne,

Emir, and sage, and Persic Amazon
Are gather'd by the King, who seems to fear,
Somewhat too much, misfortune's angry frown ;
Much needed shalt thou come ; stand still, give ear,
Then move, at suited time, bold words of lively cheer."

33. He said : the Prince no longer now disdains
To enter the strange cavern ; but by ways
Where ever-during night, and silence reigns,
Follows the Wizard through the winding maze ;
At first low stooping, but the grot in space
Loftier dilates, the farther they explore
Its labyrinthine depths, until they pace
At utmost ease of height the chisel'd floor,
And midway, soon approach a little grated door.

34. Ismeno shot the lock ; and to the right
They climb'd a staircase, long untrod, to which
A feeble, glimm'ring, and malignant light
Stream'd from the ceiling through a window'd niche.
At length by corridors of loftier pitch
They sallied into day, and access had
To an illumined hall, large, round, and rich ;
Where, sceptered, crown'd, and in dark purple clad,
Sad sat the pensive King, amid his Nobles sad.

35. The Turk, unseen within the hollow cloud,
His eager eyes around th' assembly roll'd ;
And heard meanwhile the monarch, from his proud
Enamel'd seat of elephant and gold,
His changed imaginations thus unfold :
"Oh, ruinous indeed the day gone by
Proved to our rule ! my eagle heart is cold ;
Cold, O my friends ! and, cast from hopes so high,
Egypt is now the all on which we can rely.

36. "But well ye see how distant are her arms
From our so pressing exigence, alas,
Our risks ! for your advice in these alarms
We all are met,—each speak the thoughts he has :"
He ceased ; sad sounds around repining pass,
Like hollow winds in woods when dark the year
Weeps into winter ; but, with front of brass,
Lively of look and confident of cheer,
Argantes straight uprose, and hush'd each whisp'ring
peer.

37. "What, most magnificent of Kings! what now?"
Were the first words of the undaunted Knight;
"What trial's this? who does not know that thou
Need'st not our judgments to decide aright?
Yet will I say, be all our hopes in fight
Placed in ourselves; and if, as schoolmen tell,
No ills can harm true Virtue, nor affright,
Be that our spear, our shield, our citadel,—
Let us her dictates use, nor love our lives too well.

38. "I say not this as hopeless of the aid,
The most sure aid our Court did late decree;
To doubt the promises my lord has made,
Were neither just in you, nor right in me:
But this I say, because I wish to see
In some of us an energy more brave;
A soul prepared for whatsoe'er may be—
To scorn the chance that guides us to the grave,
And look on vict'ry still as our predestined slave."

39. Thus spoke Argantes; nothing more he chose
To say, as useless in so clear a case;
When with an air of state Orcano rose,
A peer descended from a princely race:
With warriors once he held respected place;
But, married to a young and beauteous bride,
His courage melted in her sweet embrace;
And in his babes now placing his chief pride,
Sad o'er the risks of war the sire and husband sigh'd.

40. "My Prince," he thus began, "I ne'er can blame
The warmth of words magnificent, that start
Bright with the impress of young Glory's flame,
Which will not be confined in the close heart;
And if the good Circassian, in the smart
Of ardent feeling, oft in speech exceeds
Cool caution's bounds and overplays his part,
This let him claim; for, hotly as he pleads,
His glorying words are match'd by no less glorious deeds.

41. "But it behooves thee, whom the wider ken
Of times and actions so discreet has made,
Such spirits by thy wisdom to restrain,
When by enthusiast heat too far betray'd:
To balance with thy hopes of distant aid
Our present perils—what may yet befall,—
And to contrast, in this their fierce crusade,
The arms, the zeal, the genius of the Gaul,
With each new builded work and immemorial wall.

42. "Our town (if freely I may speak my thought)
Is strong by nature, stronger yet by art;
But what sublime and strong machines are brought
Against its bulwarks, on the adverse part!
What is to happen, I know not,—my heart
Both hopes and fears the issue, as the scale
Vibrates of war; but hope must soon depart,
Hope must depart, for sustenance will fail,
If they in stricter siege invest us, and assail.

43. "But, as respects the store of herds and grain
That yesternight within the walls was brought,
While the press'd Franks, in yon pavilion'd plain
Crimsoning their swords, on conquest only thought,
(And at the greatest hazard it was wrought,)
What will it be in this large town? at most,
Scant for our need, if the siege lasts; nor short
The siege must prove, e'en though the Egyptian host
Come punctual to the day and hour at first proposed.

44. "But what, if longer they delay? or grant
That they our hopes outstrip, and well fulfill
Their plighted promise, is there naught to daunt?
Is the war-storm roll'd back from Zion hill?
Is vict'ry ours?—No, King! we must fight still
With this redoubted Godfrey, as at first;
With the same captains, the same hosts, whose skill
So oft has baffled the fair hopes we nursed,
And Arabs, Persians, Turks, in utter rout dispersed!

45. "Their bravery, brave Argantes! thou hast known,
Who oft in field hast yielded quick retreat,
Oft to the conqu'ring foe thy shoulders shown,
Oft turn'd for safety to thy wind-swift feet;
Coupled with thee in danger and defeat,
This knows Clorinda, this know I; not one
In the divan has cause for self-conceit
Above the rest; my lord, I censure none;
All that the might of man can do, ourselves have done.

46. "Yet will I say, though he should frown to hear
The truth, and fiercely take the dues of hate,
I see, alas, by tokens but too clear,
The dreaded Franks led onward by a fate
Not to be shunn'd! no force, however great,
Nor harnessries of steel, nor towers of stone
Will bar their final conquest; this I state,
(Bear witness, righteous Heaven!) from zeal alone,—
Zeal for my country's good, and duty to the throne.

47. "How wise the King of Tripoli! he knew
How with calm peace his kingdom to retain,
While by his stubbornness the Soldan drew
Their vengeance down, and either now lies slain,
Or vilely groans beneath the victor's chain;
Or into exile, of each face afraid,
Flies, ekeing out a life of care and pain;
He too, had he but yielded part, and paid
Tribute or gifts of price, might still his realms have sway'd."

48. In these ambiguous words the Syrian gave
A dubious glimpse of his oblique device;
For, to buy peace and live a feudal slave
He durst not openly the king advise:
But the impetuous Solyman of Nice,
With deepest scorn and indignation stung,
No longer could endure such calumnies;
And first the Wizard whisper'd him, "How long
Art thou disposed to bear the taunts of such a tongue?"

49. "Against my will," he answer'd, "well you wist,
Keep I thus mute; I burn with rage and scorn!"
Scarce had he said, than the gross web of mist
That like a garment mantled them, was torn,
And into open heaven dissolving borne;
At once refulgent from the rending cloud
The Prince stood forth in the clear light of morn;
With fiery eye, magnificent and proud,—
Into the hall he strode, and sudden spake aloud:

50. "Lo, I of whom ye prate before you stand,
No tim'rous wretch that into exile flies,
But ready e'en with this war-wearied hand,
To prove how foully yon pale craven lies!
And is it I, who shed in all men's eyes
Such streams of blood; who fought, the livelong night,
Till the smooth plain did into mountains rise,—
I, who with thousands still sustain'd the fight,
Of every friend deprived—am I accused of flight?

51. "But mark me well! if he, or any such,
False to his faith, his country, and his kind,
Dares on so base a theme again to touch,
This sword shall stab the mischief in his mind:
First lambs and wolves shall in one fold be join'd;
First doves and snakes shall in one nest embrace;
Ere on one soil affianced peace shall bind

Our hands in friendship with this hated race ;
No ! first the stable globe shall perish from its place."

52. While speaking, he his terrible right hand
Laid on his sword in threatful attitude ;
As statues mute, the Magnates of the land
Sate, by his words and Gorgon face subdued ·
Then with a gentler tone, in milder mood,
He greeted courteously the King, and said :
" No more, my lord, on past reverses brood,
Since I am here, who bring no trivial aid ;
Let this to livelier hopes thy fainting heart persuade."

53. He, rising to salute him, made reply :
" Oh with what joy do I behold thee here !
Now, neither of my slaughter'd chivalry
Feel I the loss, nor for the future fear ;
Thou of a truth art come, companion dear !
My power to fix, and in good time renew—
Unless the flatt'ring stars prove insincere—
Thine own ;" thus saying, to the Prince he drew,
And round his neck his arms in strict embracement threw.

54. Their greetings paid, his own rich chair of state
The King conceded to the brave Nicene ;
Then on a damask throne beside him sate,
And on his left hand placed the sage Ismene :
While of their wondrous coming unforeseen
Curious the King for explanation press'd
The Archimage apart, Clorinda sheen
Came from her seat and to the royal guest
Respectful homage paid ; him honoring, rose the rest :

55. And with them brave Ormusses, who, indued
Of late by Solyman with powers to guide
A troop of Arabs to the town, pursued
Ways long disused, and while the fight was plied
With sternest resolution, undescried
Through the dark midnight, had the skill to gain
The straiten'd town in safety ; and beside
His armed force, brought store of herds and grain ;
Aids, which the pining host had look'd for long in vain

56. Sole with an aspect full of surly scorn,
Silent the piqued Circassian kept his place ;
Like a grim lion, that at sound of horn
Rolling his eyes, disdains to stir one pace :

Abash'd Orcano durst not e'en upraise
His eyes; but, prick'd by shame's compunctious sting
Shrunk from his wrong'd opponent's angry gaze:
The Soldan thus and nobles in a ring
Leave we in deep divan, around the Syrian King.

57. But Godfrey, following fast as victory led,
Had clear'd the ambush'd straits, the guarded heights,
And paid meanwhile to his lamented dead
The last funereal pomps and pious rites:
And now he gives command that all his knights
Be ready, when the matin trumpet calls,
To move th' assault; their ardor he incites;
And wheeling round, in prospect of the walls,
Yet mightier rams and towers, the townsmen more appals.

58. And when he knew the noble troop that came
In the last fight so timely to his aid
For his own knights, who, through their amorous flame,
Had follow'd late the fair insidious maid,—
And with them Tancred, whom we saw betray'd
To powerless bondage in Armida's cage,
After his fancied Lady as he stray'd,—
Alone before the Solitary Sage
And his chief friends, he sent, their presence to engage.

59. Soon as they came, "Let one of you," he said,
"Of your brief wand'rings the events relate;
And by what turn of fortune you were led
To bring such succor in so sharp a strait:"
They blush'd; since, e'en for venial errors, great
Is the remorse of virtue; each would shun
The task, and downcast stood with looks sedate;
Raising his eyes at length, th' illustrious son
Of British William rose, and bashful thus begun.

60. "We, whose void lots remain'd undrawn, while night
Favor'd us, secretly from camp withdrew;
Following, I do not deny, Love's meteor light,
And a fair face insidious to undo;
We went by crooked by-ways, trod by few,
In discord, jealousy, and fierce debate;
And oft the witch impassion'd glances threw,
Sweet words, and sweeter smiles, (seen through too late!)
Which, while they fed our love, increased our mutual hate.

61. "At length we reach'd th' accursed spot, where Heaven
Rain'd down its flaky fire in ancient time,
Revenging outraged Nature on the leaven
Of foul Gomorrah and her coasts of crime:
Once fruitful was the land, and pure the clime;
Where odious winds now fret, and billows yell,
Roll'd on a wild lagoon of bubbling slime
Bituminous, that, smoking as they swell,
Breathe in gross air the hue and sulph'rous scent of hell.

62. "This is the pool in which whate'er is thrown
Will never sink, but on the surface float;
Men, iron, marble, brass, and solid stone,
All that has weight, is buoy'd up as a boat;
A castle crowns the flood, and o'er its moat
A narrow bridge gives access to the pile;
Thither we went; within, sweet mysteries smote
Our senses,—Nature wore her brightest smile;
Gay shone the summer sea, and laugh'd th' enchanted isle.

63. "The air was mild, Heaven calm, the joyous bowers
Fresh, the woods green, the waters bright and blue;
Midst myrtles, lilacs, and divinest flowers,
A fountain to the sun in silver flew;
The crisp leaves made soft music, as to woo
Tired eyes to slumber in the shaded grass;
Heard was the bee to hum, the dove to coo,
Nor mute was Heavenly Philomel; I pass
The glorious structures wrought in marble, gold, and glass.

64. "On the smooth turf, near the melodious wave,
In brownest shade were ivory tables set;
With sculptured vases deck'd and viands brave
Of every clime and season,—all that yet
Art dress'd, or taste purvey'd, or rifling net
Snared from the leafy wood or billowy sound,
With every flavorous wine and rich sherbet;
A hundred charming nymphs, with roses crown'd,
Skillful as Hebe, served, and sped the banquet round.

65. "With radiant smiles and fond engaging speech
She brew'd enchantments fatal to our fame;
While at the feast, from Love's full goblet each
Quaff'd off a long forgetfulness to shame,

She, rising, said, 'I soon return;' she came,—
But with a face less tranquil than before;
Her cheek's rose-hues were deepen'd into flame;
A small enchanting wand her right hand bore,
Her left a book, whence she strange mysteries murmur'd o'er.

66. "Fast as she read, I felt a secret change
Invest at once volition, sense, and thought;
I long'd the watery element to range,
Leap'd from my seat, and flounced in amorous sport
Through the smooth wave,—so wonderfully wrought
Her spell! my legs combined; my arms began
T' incorporate; my tall form grew spare and short;
O'er all my skin bright scales of silver ran;
And the mute fish possess'd the late majestic man.

67. "Changed like myself in form and instincts, all
Swam the clear silver of the living stream;
What then my feelings were I now recall
As through the medium of a brain-sick dream:
At length it pleased the enchantress to redeem
Our spirits from the spell; our shapes we took,
But wonder kept us dumb, and awe supreme;
When, still some anger lowering in her look,
She, threat'ning thus, our hearts with fresh commotion shook:

68. "'Lo, now at length ye know my height of power,
My empire o'er you! in my will it lies,
To shut you up forever in yon tower,
Dead to the sunshine of the cheerful skies;
Or rib you into rocks of stone or ice,
To bear the fury of all winds that blow;
To wing you into birds; or, in a trice,
Root you in earth to germinate and grow;
In shaggy hides to howl, or in cold fountains flow.

69. "'You yet may shun my anger, if ye choose
T' adapt your conduct to my sov'reign will;
Change but your faith, and in our service use
Your swords the impious Lorrainer to kill:'
All scorn'd the cursed conditions to fulfill,
Save base Rambaldo; him, and him alone
She won,—while we (for 'gainst her magic skill
What could avail?) in darksome cells were thrown,
Beneath a weight of chains, for long, long moons to groan.

70. "To the same castle came in evil hour
Bold Tancred, who by guile was captured too:
But the fair, false Enchantress in her tower
Not long detain'd us; for, if fame say true,
An envoy with an armed retinue
Came with Prince Idraotes' signet ring
From rich Damascus,—of the maid to sue,
That he our troop, disarm'd and chain'd, might bring
As an obliging gift before th' Egyptian king.

71. "Watch'd by a hundred guards we went our way;
When, as the providence of Heaven decreed,
The good Rinaldo, who from day to day
Goes adding by some new heroic deed
Fresh grace to glory, on his sprightly steed
Met us, nor paused a moment to assail
The knights our guard;—most nobly did he speed;
Victorious from the foe our shirts of mail
Stripp'd, and to us restored, attest the certain tale.

72. "I saw, all saw him! to his robes we clung,
Heard his kind voice, and grasp'd his hand; thus then,
False is the rumor that from tongue to tongue
Sounds through the Camp, which misreports him slain;
The youth is safe; but thrice the sun's bright wain
Has circled Heaven, since, with a pilgrim guide
Parting from us, he took the sandy plain
That leads to Antioch; having first aside
His shatter'd armor cast, to deepest crimson dyed."

73. He ceased; meanwhile his eyes the hermit raised
To Heaven,—his color changed, diviner grew
His sainted form; quick feelings feelings chased,
And all his features into sunshine threw;
Full of the Deity, his spirit flew
On rapture's glowing wings, in glorified
Trance to the sanhedrim of Angels,—drew
The curtains of the sanctuary aside,
And the eternal march of unborn years descried.

74. Unlocking then in more than mortal sound
His lips, of things to come the Prophet tells;
The rest in wonder at the change stand round,
Attentive to his thunder'd oracles:
"He lives," he cried, "Rinaldo! and all else
Are but the wiles of feminine deceit;
He lives; and God, the living God that dwells

In splendors beaming round the Mercy-seat,
Reserves his unripe youth for glories more complete.

75. "Trivial as yet and infantile appears
Each feat of his wherewith awed Asia rings;
I see, I see him with the rushing years
Tame the strong crimes of Cæsars and of kings;
And with the mild shade of its silver wings,
I see his brooding Eagle overspread
Th' Eternal City and the Church, that springs
From the wolf's paw, redeem'd as from the dead,
And many a worthy son shall bless his happy bed;—

76. "Children, and children's sons, who shall be styled
Illustrious patterns of their sires' renown;
And guard from wicked courts and traitors viled
The papal miter and the ducal crown,
With the religious temples; to strike down
The haughty, raise the weak, the guilty goad,
And shield young merit from misfortune's frown—
These be their arts; and in this glorious mode
Shall Este's Eagle soar beyond the Solar road.

77. "And just it is, that, as by power unawed
She strikes for truth, rejoicing in the light,
From Peter's hands her pounce should bear abroad
The mortal thunders; wheresoe'er the fight
Waxes for Christ, her baffling pinions bright
With triumph aye shall spread; this brilliant track
Heaven, and her inborn virtue to her flight
Accord;—thus, home to the sublime attack
Whence she hath flown, 'tis will'd the trumpets call her back!"

78. The griefs and fears that each had entertain'd,
Wise Peter's words did wholly dissipate;
Sole in the general joy the Duke remain'd
Silent, giv'n up to themes of gravest weight:
Meanwhile the sun had reach'd Eve's golden gate;
Still Night o'er earth her solemn mantle throws;
Home to their several tents the Chiefs of state
Return, and give their members to repose;
But Godfrey's studious mind no rest in slumber knows.

END OF CANTO X.

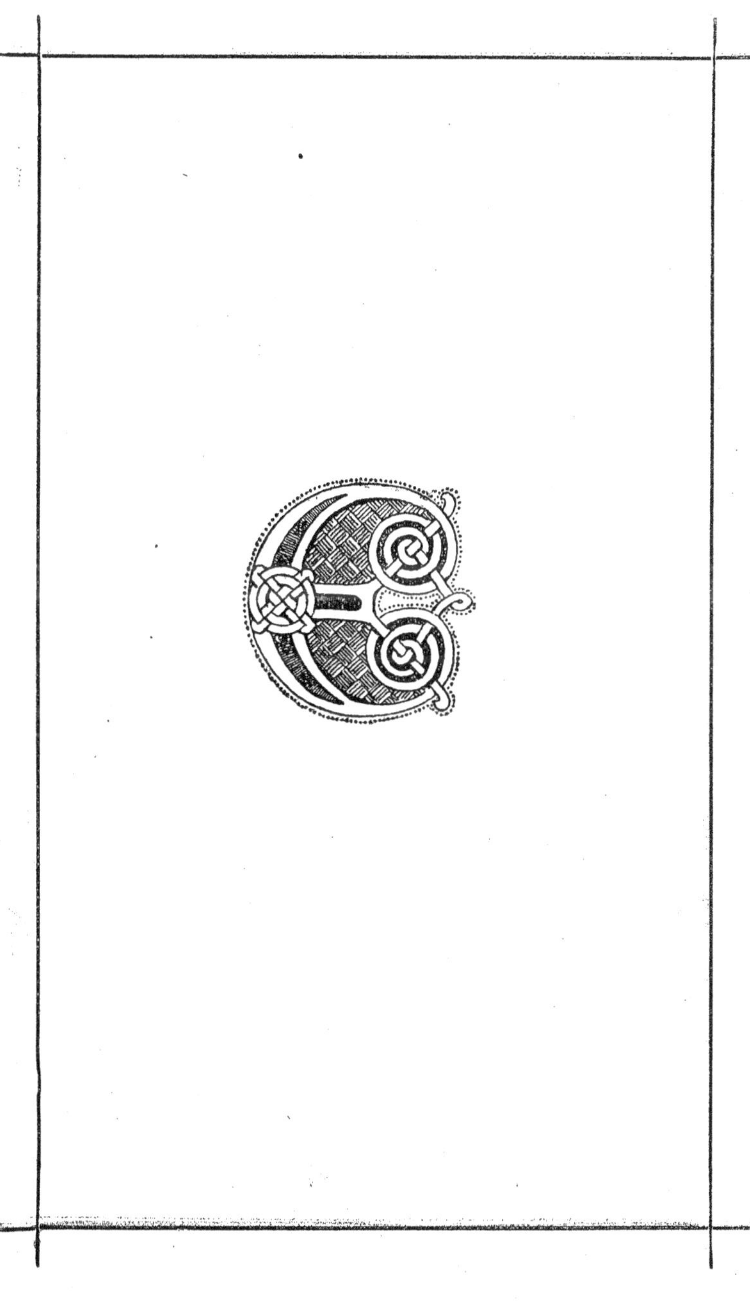

JERUSALEM DELIVERED.

CANTO XI.

ARGUMENT.

WITH holy hymns, pure sacrifice, and prayer,
The Christian hosts invoke celestial aid;
Then storm the town; and to their rage lay bare
The yawning walls,—some tempt the escalade;
The breach is widen'd, when the Persian maid
Shoots at the Captain from her mural height;
With the sore wound his high success is stay'd:
Cured by an Angel, he renews the fight,
But the sun soon rolls down, and Mars gives place to Night.

JERUSALEM DELIVERED.

CANTO XI.

1. While thus the Captain of the Christian nations,
   Whose constant thoughts on the assault were bent,
   Prepared to shake to their most deep foundations
   The city walls, each warlike instrument—
   Forth came the Hermit from his morning tent;
   And, taking him aside with solemn air,
   In these grave words arrested his intent:
   "Arms of this world, O Chief, dost thou prepare?
   Know, 'tis celestial aid that first should claim thy care.

2. "Begin from Heaven; invoke with holy hymn,
   With public prayer and reverential deed,
   The armed host of Saints and Seraphim,
   By whose bless'd aid success may be decreed;
   In sacred garments let the Priests precede,
   And tuneful psalms with suppliant voices raise;
   While thou and thy illustrious Nobles lead
   The multitude along, that, as they gaze,
   Shall catch from you the flame of piety and praise."

3. Severely spake the army's ghostly guide,
   And virtuous Godfrey own'd the words were wise;
   "Servant approved of Jesus!" he replied,
   "Well pleased I follow thy inspired advice;
   Thus then, while I to these solemnities
   My captains, lords, and chevaliers invite,
   Seek thou the ministers of sacrifice,
   William and Ademar; with them unite,—
   The sacred pomp prepare, and ceremonial rite."

4. The Seer, the bishops, and the monks next morn,
   With all the canons of inferior class,
   Meet in a valley far from camp withdrawn,

Where, round an altar on the hallow'd grass,
The Priests were wont to solemnize high mass;
White robes they wear; the Pastors of the flocks
Have on their sacerdotal albs, which pass
In front divided o'er their golden frocks,
Clasp'd with aigraffes of pearl; starr'd miters crown their locks.

5. Peter alone, before, spread to the wind
The sacred sign which Seraphim revere;
The choir with slow and solemn steps behind
In two long ranks, apart, their voices rear
In Heavenly hymns and anthems, that insphere
The spirit of sweet praise and humble prayer,
Sung in alternate chorus; last appear
William and Ademar,—the reverend pair
Bring up their arriere bands in order passing fair.

6. Great Bouillon next, without companion, pass'd,
As kings and princes use; by two and two
The Captains follow'd, in his steps; and last,
The total host in distribution due,
Arm'd for defense; thus marshal'd, they march'd through
The portal-gates; all tumult far was flown;
Nor brazen horn ferocious clamors blew,
Nor war-cry shrill'd; to Heaven arose alone
Piety's suppliant voice in music's melting tone.

7. Thee, Father! thee they sing, coequal Son!
And thee, bless'd Spirit! in whom both combine;
All-pitying, saving, all-consoling One!
Thee, Virgin-Mother of the man Divine!
And ye, who o'er the bright-wing'd hosts that shine
Around, in triple orbs vicegerence have,
Princedoms! your succor they invoke; and thine,
Baptist beloved! that in the less pure wave,
Pure Mary's sacred Son immaculate didst lave.

8. Thee too they hail, the strong, the stable rock
Whereon the Church is built; whose gentle pleas
Win now thy new successor to unlock
The gracious gates of pardon and of peace;
And the twelve heralds who o'er lands and seas
Advent'ring, publish'd with their latest breath
Their Lord's triumphant apotheosis;
And those who, seized, tormented for the Faith,
Proved with their blood its power, and seal'd its truth with death.

9. To saints whose writings point the path to truth
And bliss, no less soft supplications swell;
To Christ's dear handmaid, who in bloom of youth
The nobler part of life selected well;
To the chaste virgins that in cave or cell
With solemn nuptials were espoused to God;
And those, who, braving kings and nations fell,
The lictor's axe, the prætor's torturing rod,
Strait Virtue's thorny path magnanimously trod.

10. Thus worshiping, thus chanting in their zeal,
Circling the long, long plain, the people came
With easy pace to Olivet, a hill
Fruitful in olives, whence it takes its name:
A hill long signalized by sacred fame
Through the wide world; like a majestic queen
East of the town it soars, as if to claim
Th' ascendant, parted only by the green
Vale of Jehoshaphat, which fills the space between.

11. Thither the tuneful army tends, and fills
The Heaven with melody; the vales ring round,
And answ'ring Echo from her haunted hills,
From secret caves, and hollow glens profound,
A thousand times repeats the charming sound;
You would have thought a choir of Dryads near
Sang from the groves and grottoes underground:
So variously, and aye so sweet and clear,
Jesu, Maria's name rewarbled back they hear.

12. On the town walls the curious Pagans stand,
Silent as summer night; in much amaze
At rites so strange, unwonted pomps so grand,
Their solemn march, and humble hymns of praise;
Long on the sacred spectacle they gaze;
But when the novelty of show is o'er,
A scornful yell the wicked miscreants raise,
That with loud blasphemies the mountains hoar,
Woods, torrents, towers the rocks and winding valleys roar.

13. But not for this their pure, melodious song
The Christians cease; the clamors of their foes
Unmoved they slight, as they would slight a throng
Of chatt'ring swallows or loquacious crows;
Nor can the arrows which their strong cross-bows
Loose, at such distance, from the dancing string,
Their orderly array to discompose,

Strike them with fear, or mar the notes they sing ;
Full to their purposed close the hymns commenced they
bring.

14. Next, for communion, on the mountain's height,
The sacramental altar beautified
With sculptured images they raise, and light
The golden lamps that stand on either side ;
Then other vestments more divinely dyed,
With gold ingrain'd, the pontiff William wears ;
And, after silent thought, to God their guide
Lowly he bends, and asks, in fervent prayers,
Peace for sins past, and grace against impending snares.

15. While humbly round the near spectators bend,
The more remote attend with steadfast eyes
His speaking lips ; when now there was an end
Of the pure rites and mystic sacrifice,
The Bishop turn'd, and lifting tow'rd the skies
His sacerdotal hands, the armies bless'd ;
Then cried to them "Depart!" the companies,
With silent pomp slow wheeling to the West,
By the same path return'd which they before had press'd.

16. Th' intrenchments enter'd, people, duke, and prince,
Fill'd with sweet peace to their pavilions went ;
While thousands, proud their homage to evince,
Escorted Godfrey as with one consent
E'en to the threshold of his curtain'd tent,
Parting with fond farewells : but he recall'd
The captains, and, as midnoon now was spent,
To a plain feast the party seneschal'd,
And in the second seat the Count Toulouse install'd.

17. When they with drinks and viands had appeased
Nature's keen appetites, the General rose,
And thus his knights address'd: "When next the East
Shows morning, all things for th' assault dispose ;
'Twill be a day of bloodshed and of blows,
Havoc, and sweat, and toil, as this is one
Of preparation, quiet, and repose ;
Go then, prepare yourselves and troops ; that done,
Rest all,—the dial's shade has yet some hours to run."

18. This said, they take their leave ; the heralds then
By blast of trumpet give commands, that all
Stand ready under arms when first they ken
The breaking day, to storm the Northern wall :

Brisk was the tending of the steeds in stall,
Hamm'ring of armor, trimming of the crest,
And deep the hum of wassail, till the call
To vespers, and still Night, the friend of rest,
Giving new truce to toil, all eyes in slumber bless'd.

19. Dubious and dusk, the Lady of the dawn
Not yet had ris'n to walk her rosy round;
The shepherd sought not yet his custom'd lawn,
Nor shining share turn'd up the fallow ground;
Still in their nests the blithe birds slumber'd sound;
Not yet the lark upsoar'd on flick'ring wing,
Nor forest echo'd to the horn or hound;
When first the matin trump was heard to sing,
"To arms!"—"to arms!" the skies and misty valleys ring.

20. Ten thousand tongues take up the welcome words,
"To arms!" and still "to arms!" is all their cry;
Godfrey awakes, but not this morning girds
The wonted cuishes on his martial thigh;
His greaves and iron mail are hung on high,
And on his back is borne a suppler suit,
Of lighter make and less validity,—
Arms, only worn by such as fight on foot;
When in good Raymond comes, to pay the morn's salute.

21. The Count, perceiving him arm'd thus, soon guess'd
His purpose, and exclaim'd: "How's this, my lord?
Where is your solid breastplate? where the rest
Of your steel armors, hard and strong to ward
Strokes, that may else prove fatal? what! abroad
But half array'd, in a juppon so weak!
This negligence we never can applaud;
It would appear our Chief was bent to seek
Mean glory's course; of such these habits seem to speak.

22. "What! look you for the private palm of those
That mount the breach? to others leave the task,
And some less serviceable souls expose
To risks adapted to the meed they ask;
Resume, my lord, your customary casque,
Vant-brace, and hauberk; know your proper post;
For ours, if not for your protection, mask
Your face; for Heaven's sake, go not thus exposed!
You are the soul, the strength, the life-blood of the host."

23. "When," said the Chief, "Pope Urban girt this blade
On me in Clermont, and the holy Seer
Bade me perform in this divine crusade
The duties of a gallant chevalier,
I made a secret vow to God, that here
I would not act on this eventful day,
Come when it might, as Captain or as Peer;
But thus assume the arms and plain array
Which simple soldiers use, and combat e'en as they.

24. "When, therefore, these my armies marshal'd stand
In war-bravade against the town,—when I
Have fully seen to all points that demand
The Chief's consid'rate head and judging eye,
Reason it is, nor thou the need deny,
That, faithful to my vow, I strive to reap
A soldier's laurels, to the walls draw nigh,
And, sword in hand, upon the ramparts leap;
Heaven will my ventured life in safe protection keep."

25. He ceased; and the Frank knights with loud acclaim
Th' example took; his brothers and the rest
Of the confed'rate barons did the same,
And in light mail their limbs as footmen dress'd:
Meantime the Pagans to the quarter press'd
That fronts Arctóphylax, the icy Bear,
And thence wheels round toward the golden West:
For more accessible the site, and there
Less stubborn show the walls, impregnable elsewhere.

26. Elsewhere, the crag-built town would scorn the war
Of hosting millions; thither not alone
Does the fierce tyrant the strong burghers draw,
The hireling aids, and satraps of his throne,
But them o'er whom advancing Age has strown
Its chill snows—bearded sires and boys—he calls
To dangers and fatigues till now unknown;
These hie and serve the warriors on the walls
With stones, bitumen, lime, oil, darts and brimstone balls.

27. With bristling arms and many a fix'd machine,
Lined are the walls that overlook the plain;
Breast-high above them is the Soldan seen,
Like a grim Giant, while, with fell disdain
Forever working in his fretful brain,
Elsewhere, far-off discern'd, Argantes rears
His bulk enormous; and, betwixt the twain,

High on the topmost tower, Clorinda fierce,
Known by her silver arms, conspicuously appears.

28. Her costly quiver, with sharp arrows stored,
Hangs at her back,—the bow is in her hands,
Bent,—the shaft dances on the chord, the chord
Is ready drawn, and oft her eye demands
The instant coming of the Christian bands:
Burning to twang the string against the crowd,
With lips apart the lady archer stands
As Dian stood, when from the radiant cloud
She loosed her vengeful darts at Niobe the proud.

29. Below, on foot, the aged Monarch hies
From gate to gate, upon the walls surveys
His first arrangements with observant eyes,
And cheers his troops with speeches full of praise;
Here he recruits their ranks, and there displays
Store of fresh arms and engines, and with care
Provides for all; but, in the public ways,
Throngs of sad matrons to the mosques repair,
And to their Prophet false bend low in senseless prayer.

30. "O Mahmoud! with thy strong and righteous hand
In twain the spear of this Frank spoiler break!
Check, and confound, and stretch him on the sand
Beneath our walls, for thine own glory's sake,
Which he so much has outraged!" thus they spake;
But their words reach'd not him, who, pierced with pains
Eternal, tosses on the fiery lake;—
While for defense each nerve the City strains,
Musters the Christian Chief his army on the plains.

31. And first from camp his infantry he guides,
With wondrous providence and art disposed,
And 'gainst the walls to ruin doom'd, divides
Transversely into two the massy host:
In center the wheel'd engines take their post,—
Structures of unimaginable powers,—
Scorpions and strong ballistæ; whence are toss'd,
Like lightning and like thunder on the towers,
Lances, and quarried rocks, and sleet of arrowy showers.

32. His heavier-arm'd he places in the rear
For surer guard, his light-horse in the wings;
Then gives the word, and instant in the ear
Of either host the signal-trumpet rings:

Tremendous is the cast of stones from slings,
Javelins from engines, quarrels from cross-bows,
And mortal arrows from resounding strings;
Some fall, some flee; and thinn'd and broken shows,
On the defended wall, the phalanx late so close.

33. Then with all speed the eager Franks impel
Their progress; part into a tortoise form,
Shield lock'd with shield, beneath its iron shell
Secure; while part slink from the sounding storm
Of stones and raining darts, in cubiform
Battalia underneath the vines; they gain
Thus screen'd, the counterscarp, and ceaseless swarm
Fervent as summer-emmets, nor in vain,
The hollow depth to fill, and equal with the plain.

34. The circling moat was not of marshy sward,
(This the dry soil forbade,) nor soft with mud;
So that they fill'd it soon, though large and broad,
With turf, stones, timber, and fascines of wood:
Daring Adrastus was the first that stood
From forth the shell of shields; he raised sublime
A scaling-ladder, and, despite the flood
Pour'd from above, of boiling pitch and lime,
Dauntless his crest advanced, and stood resolved to climb.

35. The fiery Switzer in his rash neglect
Of life, on high with wonder they survey,
Mark to a thousand arrows, and uncheck'd
By all that would his course audacious stay;
Half had he finish'd his aërial way,
When sudden, by the strong Circassian thrown,
A huge round rock with quick tempestuous sway,
As from a mortar shot, upon his crown
Alit, and rudely beat th' heroic soldier down.

36. Not mortal is the stroke; but still the fall
Stuns him, and mute and motionless he lies;
Loud shouted then the victor on the wall,—
"Fall'n is the first! who next the venture tries?
Why not assail us in the open skies?
Come from your caves; skulk not like foxes there,—
I skulk not; nothing shall your strange device
Save you, but like the badger and the bear
Die in your dens ye shall; by Mohamet I swear!"

37. Not for his taunt the Franks their toil refrain,
But, close in curtain of their sheds conceal'd,
Safe the barb'd darts and heavy weights sustain,
Man link'd with man, and shield compact with shield,
While to the basis of the walls are wheel'd
Batt'ries, of beams immeasurable, with plates
Of hammer'd iron thrice with fire anneal'd,
Fronted like rams; at whose assailing threats
Tremble the lofty walls, and shake the echoing gates.

38. Meanwhile a hundred hands upon the walls
Have heaved, and hung in terrible libration
O'er the blind tortoise a huge crag; as falls
The loosed lavange from its aërial station,
Down, down it roll'd,—in thund'ring dislocation
Crush'd the dense shell of shields, crush'd helm and head,
And left the batter'd ground, in agitation
From the o'erwhelming mountain, overspread
With blood, with brains, with bones, and arms of sanguine red.

39. No longer now beneath the shelt'ring roof
Of their machines the Franks themselves confine,
But from the latent risks to open proof
Of danger rush, and give their light to shine;
Some raise scalados, nor to mount decline,
Though in the face of peril and mishap;
Others the deep foundations undermine;
Then rock the walls, and many a glorious gap
Starts in the shrinking base and buttresses they sap.

40. And fall'n they had, so fast its boist'rous blows
Thereon the huge bombarding ram repeats,
But from the battlements the Turks oppose
The wonted artifice that most defeats
Its horned might; where'er the vast beam beats,
Packs of soft wool elastic they suspend;
With which, when as the butting engine meets,
The substance yields, the pliant swathes distend,
Break the rude shock, and safe th' endanger'd wall defend.

41. While in this valiant mode the daring bands
Round the climb'd walls in clusters fight and bleed,
Seven times Clorinda bends, seven times her hands
Twang the tough bow, and loose the eager reed;
As many shafts as from the ivory speed,

So many stain their points and gray-goose wings,
Not in plebeian blood—so mean a deed
Her spirit had disdain'd,—but that which springs
In the more noble veins of heroes, chiefs, and kings.

42. The first brave knight that by her arrow bled,
Was the young heir of Britain's happy land ;
Scarce from the tortoise had he raised his head,—
The shaft came down, and pierced his better hand ;
His glove of steel avail'd not to withstand
The deadly weapon,—from the wounded vein
Gush'd the bright blood, and purpled all the sand :
Disabled thus for fight, he left the plain,
And, groaning, gnash'd his teeth, but more from rage than pain.

43. The good Count Amboise on the fosse's bank,
And in the high scalade Clotharius died ;
The former pierced from breast to back, the Frank
More dreadfully transfix'd from side to side ;
Again she shot ; and as the Flemings' guide
Swung the huge ram, her arrow cut the wind,
And pierced his arm : to draw the dart he tried ;
But ill the shaft obey'd his ardent mind,
The shaft indeed he drew, but left the head behind.

44. As too rash Ademar, the grave and good,
Watch'd the assault far off, the fatal cane,
Charged with hot wrath, came whizzing where he stood,
And grazed his brow ; impatient of the pain,
He clapp'd his hand upon the wounded vein,
When lo, a second nail'd it to his head,
And quiv'ring fix'd in his bewilder'd brain !
He falls—his holy blood, by woman shed,
Floats o'er his priestly robes, and dyes the sable red.

45. As Palamed, the young, the bold, and brisk,
Climb'd the tall steps, and on the steep tower's height
Just placed his foot, disdaining every risk,
To his right eye the seventh shaft took its flight ;
Pass'd its orb'd cell, and through the nerves of sight
Issued, vermilion, at the nape ; he fell,
Blind with the shadows of fast-hasting night,
And sigh'd out life beneath the citadel
Which he had hoped to win, and had assail'd so well.

46. Thus shot the maid ! the Duke meanwhile oppress'd
In fresh assaults, beside the Northern gate,
Th' embattled guard ; and to the walls address'd
The most colossal of his engines great,—
A tower of cedar, built sublime to mate
The topmost walls, stupendous to behold !
Pond'rous with ported arms, and fraught with fate,
With half a squadron in its spacious hold—
On thund'rous wheels it moved, and near the turrets roll'd.

47. Onward it came ; far shooting, as it drove,
Lightnings of arrows at its facing foes ;
And, as ships use with ships in sea-fights, strove
By instant grappling with the walls to close :
But this the Pagans at all points oppose ;
Now pushing back the fabric, batt'ring now
Its front and timber'd sides with clubs, with crows,
And Moorish maces ; with the rocks they throw,
Creak the huge beams above, the heaving wheels below.

48. Such was from this part, such from that the flight
Of stones and darts, that Titan seem'd to shroud
His face, blue Heaven show'd brown as summer-night,
And cloud, rebounding, clash'd in air with cloud,
Like two thwart tides : as leaves from forests bow'd
By showers congeal'd in winter's icy hall
To hail,—as apples shook by whirlwinds loud
In unripe greenness from the stalk,—so fall
In heaps the Moslem foe from the dismantled wall.

49. For 'twas on them the shot most havoc made,
As less defensed and shelter'd from its power ;
Of the forlorn survivors, numbers fled,
In utter terror of the fulmined shower,
And thunder of the strong stupendous tower ;
But still the Soldan stay'd, and round him drew
A few bold spirits unalarm'd, the flower
Of Syrian bravery ; Argantes too,
Arm'd with a pond'rous beam, against the fabric flew

50. Back with vast force, the length of all the pine,
He push'd, and kept it distant ; to his side
Came from her tower the Lady palatine,
With them in glory and in risk allied ;
Meanwhile the Christians with long scythes divide
From the wall's headlong perpendicular,

The ropes to which the pendent bales were tied ;
Which, down descending, leave the ramparts bare
To all the rude affronts and thunder-strokes of war.

51\. And thus the tower above and ram below
Play with such fury now, that they begin,
Crush'd, cleft and undermined, to yawn, and show
The houses, mosques, and peopled streets within
Thither the army swarms with lively din,
By Godfrey led beneath the battled marge ;
Who, fully bent the tott'ring wall to win,
Moves under compass of that ampler targe,
Which never loads his arm, but on some desp'rate charge.

52\. Thence he perceives Prince Solyman descend
Down to the gaping beach, and, sword in hand,
Th' attempted pass at all risks to defend,
With fix'd resolve, imperatively grand,
Amidst the ruins take his haughty stand ;
Leaving on guard, with providence discreet,
Clorinda and Argantes, to command
The walls ; he sees, and feels his bosom beat
With gen'rous scorn of life, and glory's fervent heat.

53\. And to the good Sigiér, who bore behind
His bow and buckler, he directs his speech :
"Give me, my friend, that lighter shield refined,
Whose temper axe nor saber can impeach ;
Quick ! to yon ruin'd rocks I mean to reach ;
And of these multitudes the first to be
That pass victorious through the guarded breach ;
High time it is, that of my chivalry
Some such transcendent proof the host at length should see !"

54\. Scarce, changing shields, had he said this, than swift
A barbed arrow on sonorous wing,
Shot from the summit of the mural clift,
Transfix'd his leg, where keenest was the sting,
The nervous region whence its sinews spring ;
'Twas thou, Clorinda, if report say true,
Sent the fell shaft, and 'tis thy praise we sing ;
From thrall, from death, if then thy Pagan crew
Escaped, to thee alone the laurel-leaves are due.

55\. But the brave Chief, as though he did not feel
The deadly anguish of the hurt he bore,

Ceased not his course, but climb'd with daring zeal
The breach, and down fresh rocky fragments tore,
Cheering his party on ; but stiff and sore
The wound soon wax'd ; and the encumb'ring foot
His active labors can sustain no more ;
Through all the limb keen shiv'ring horrors shoot ;
Forced, he at length gives o'er, and quits the wish'd pursuit.

56. Beck'ning Guelph therefore to his side, he said :
" Withdraw I must ; sustain, my friend, I pray,
The Captain's place and person in my stead,
Supply mine absence in this sharp assay ;
Short, at the worst, will be the time I stay ;
I do but go and come,—my hurt bites keen,
Though but a bruise ; " this said, without delay,
On a light steed he leap'd, and o'er the green
Rode to the Camp, but not, as he supposed, unseen.

57. With him good fortune from his host departs
In favor of the foe, whose hopes rose high ;
Strength and fresh spirits lift their dancing hearts,
Knit the slack arm, and fire the languid eye ;
But with the Franks all strength and ardor die ;
Weak grow their onsets ; they maintain their ground,
But short of blood their darted weapons fly ;
The sword still strikes, but strikes without a wound ;
And e'en th' appealing trumps more languishingly sound.

58. And now again the crowded ramparts show
Those who in panic late were scatter'd thence ;
The very women, with the genuine glow
Of patriotic rage and martial confidence
Caught from Clorinda, rush to their defense ;
With robes succinct and loose locks they appear,
Ranged all along the spacious ramparts, whence
They toss the dart, nor show the slightest fear
T' expose their beauteous breasts for fortresses so dear.

59. But that which most dismay'd the Franks, and most
Revived the guardians of the sacred town,
Was, that a rock, in sight of either host,
Came from afar, and struck Lord Guelpho down ;
Amidst a thousand as he climb'd, the stone
Fell where the sinews of the knee were knit,
And ground its shiv'ring armor to the bone ·

At the same moment, a like mass alit
On Raymond's morion'd brows, and him too backward
smit.

60. Eustace is next hurt sore, as from the bank
Of the broad fosse he purposes to spring;
Nor in this hour so adverse to the Frank,
Was there one weapon sent upon the wing,
From horn or hand, from catapult or sling,
That did not, to their cost, or tear apart
Spirit from flesh, or bruise, or keenly sting;
In this success, wild wax'd Argantes' heart,
And thus he roar'd in sounds that made both armies start.

61. "This is not Antioch, nor is this the night
Friendly to Christian guile; look up! survey
The shining sun, troops wakeful, and the fight
Of a far diff'rent nature and array:
Is then your ancient love of praise and prey
Quite gone? extinct each spark of former fire?
That ye with such admired address give way,
And, spent so soon, from the assault retire,
O foemen!—nay, not men, but maids in men's attire."

62. By such-like taunts the haughty Chevalier
To such excess of rage his temper wrought,
That the large city seem'd too small a sphere
For his hot spirit and capacious thought:
Up, with a shout, his strong beech-spear he caught:
Down leaping from the ramparts, made more wide
The ruin of the breach; and, as he brought
His bulk beneath it, seeing at his side
The dauntless Soldan, thus magnanimously cried:

63. "Lo, Solyman, the place! and lo, the time,
That may at length decide our proud dispute!
What wait you for? what fear? now first let him
Leap forth, who most the laurel and the fruit
Of sov'reignty desires!" with this salute,
Out at once rush'd they through the broken wall,
Their daring deeds to their demands to suit;
That, headstrong rage provoked and native gall,
This, rival honor much, and much the rival's call.

64. Sudden and unforeseen upon the Franks,
In desp'rate rivalship, with shouts they flew;
And from amidst their dissipated ranks
So many soldiers pierced, so many slew,

And bucklers split, and helmets cleft in two,
And ladders broke, and swinging rams cut down,
That it might seem a second rampart grew,
On failure of the first, hill-high, to crown
The ruin'd heap, and fend afresh th' endanger'd town.

65. The crowds that late were ardent to ascend
The walls, to danger urged by the desire
Of mural crowns, now scarce themselves defend,
Much less to climb the rifted breach aspire,
But from the fierce assault, dismay'd, retire;
Their rams, their vines, their catapults they quit;
Which, left a prey to the revenging ire
Of the two Pagans, batter'd, crush'd, and split,
Are for all future use soon render'd quite unfit.

66. Like rapt Demoniacs loose, the dreadful pair
Wide and more wide the field of battle scour;
Call to the citizens for fire, and bear
Two blazing pines against the cedarn tower:
Forth from the gates of their Tartarean bower,
So cursed Megara with Alecto breaks,
To set the world in uproar, with the power
Of Dispossess'd; so each fell Sister shakes
Abroad her sparkling brand and bacchanalian snakes.

67. But Tancred, who elsewhere, yet unrepell'd,
Cheer'd on his troops forth issuing from the vines,
Soon as that bold achievement he beheld,
The double brandish'd flames, the burning pines,—
Broke short his speech, and to the Saracines
Rush'd, to chastise their rage and stay their wrack;
And of his prowess gave such pregnant signs,
That they who late as conqu'rors press'd th' attack,
Forbore the chase, and fled themselves affrighted back.

68. Fled the grim Soldan, fled the Mamaluke;
With humbler crests the way they came they went;
Thus changed the war! meanwhile the wounded Duke
Had reach'd with pain the threshold of his tent;
And now 'twixt Baldwin and Segiér stood bent
On instant succor; crowds on crowds succeed,
Who fill the air with sighing and lament:
He, while endeavoring from the flesh with speed
To draw at once the steel, broke short the rooted reed.

69. Thus baffled, careless of the coming smart,
He bade them take at once the shortest way

For cure, to largely lance the wounded part,
And bared to sight the barbed weapon lay :
"Send me but back to war, ere closing day
Invalidate our arms, or cool our zeal!"
He said ; and straight, forbidding all delay,
Propp'd on his lance, to the physician's steel
Stretch'd out the afflicted limb, firm resting on his heel.

70. Gray Erotimus, born beside the Po,
Came to his aid : a sage, who knew the use
And secret virtues of all springs that flow—
Of all green herbs the hills and woods produce ;
He too was smiled on by the partial Muse,
But valued sweet Castalia's warbling wave
Less than the mute fall of Pœonian dews ;
His science wounded men from death could save,
And cancel'd names in verse immortally engrave.

71. Supported stands the Chief, serene ; he grieves
But to behold his friends lamenting round ;
The ready leech tuck'd up his long loose sleeves,
And with a belt his flowing tunic bound ;
With sov'reign herbs attractive, he the wound
Sooth'd, with kind hand soliciting the dart,
Which yet stirr'd not ; when this the Ancient found,
With nipping pincers he perform'd his part ;
Still the vex'd steel adhered, and mock'd his nicest art.

72. No way seems Fortune willing to assist
His purpose or his skill ; and Godfrey shows
Signs of sharp agony,—a deathlike mist
Swims o'er his sight, and from his members flows
A dead cold sweat : but piteous of his throes,
His guardian Angel from Mount Ida flies
With gather'd dittany : an herb that blows
With purple flowers, delightful to the eyes,
In whose young downy leaves divinest virtue lies.

73. The secret powers of this celestial plant,
Maternal Nature to the mountain goat
Suggests, when, wounded in its healthy haunt,
The shaft adheres within its shaggy coat ;
This now, though from a region so remote,
The winged Angel in a moment bears ;
And, so that none the Heavenly succor note,
In the warm bath which next the sage prepares,
Distills the sprightly juice, nor other med'cines spares.

74. Dews from the Lydian well, ambrosial oils,
And odorous panacea therein he flings:
The Sage with this the thrilling wound embroils.
And, thus fomented, the barb'd steel outsprings
With voluntary impulse,—pain's sharp stings
Cease, the blood stanches, the cleft parts combine
And a fresh vigor each lax tendon strings:
"Lo!" cried the leech, "this is no cure of mine:
This is not art's effects but done by hands divine.

75. "Some Angel, shooting from the stars unspied,
Has been thy surgeon; of his Heavenly hand
I see the tokens; arm then, arm!" he cried,
"Why linger? back, the battle to command!"
His leg the Chieftain with a purple band
Wrapp'd round, and, ardent for the war, in haste
Seized his ash-spear immeasurably grand,
Again upon his arm his buckler braced,
And on his cheerful brows the glist'ning helmet laced.

76. And from his tent toward the shaken town,
Turn'd with a thousand knights, and left the camp;
Clouds of raised dust the sapphire skies embrown,
In Heaven's bright temple fades th' immortal lamp;
Trembles the firm earth underneath their stamp;
And, far-off as the foes his coming spy,
Chill flows their blood; their zeal faint horrors damp,
And through their bones fear's shiv'ring lightnings fly;—
Loud shouted Godfrey thrice, loud thunder'd thrice the sky.

77. Well knew his men the tones, which in them breathe
Zeal for the strife, and sorrow for their fault;
Their faintness, fears, they to the winds bequeath,
And rush, renew'd like lions, to th' assault:
Press'd home, the two ferocious Pagans vault
Into the mural breach; thence quick protend
Their poignant spears, their moony shields exalt,
And stubbornly the rifted pass defend
From Tancred's knights, that thick as buzzing bees ascend.

78. Hither came Godfrey, gloriously emboss'd
In arms, wrath flashing from his looks severe;
And the next moment at Argantes toss'd
The Jove-like lightnings of his awful spear;
Never from town or tower did engineer

From the strong scorpion rock or javelin cast
With more consummate force or swift career,—
The knotty beam e'en thunder'd as it pass'd;
Up raised the knight his shield, to meet it naught aghast.

79. The poignant ash his shield in sunder clove,
Nor could his coat of mail its flight restrain;
Through shield, belt, corselet, ruining it drove,
And in pure vermeil did its point ingrain;
But the fierce knight, impregnable to pain,
From his pierced veins and shatter'd brigantine
Pluck'd the fix'd steel; and, hurling it amain
At Godfrey, cried: "To thee I re-consign
The gift; look thou thereto; it is no toy of mine!"

80. Back on its mission of revenge, the spear
Through the known path careering flew, but now
Struck not the mark at which 'twas aim'd; the Peer
Its flight foreseeing, bent his plumed head low
And fairly shunn'd the meditated blow:
Yet void it fell not! deep the weapon lies
In Sigiér's throat; he dies, but not in woe;
Since in the stead of his loved lord he dies,
Glad from its cherish'd shrine the faithful spirit flies.

81. At the same instant, with a pointed rock,
The powerful Soldàn smote the Norman lord;
Who stagg'ring, reeling, dizzied with the shock,
E'en like a whirling top from the child's cord,
Spun round, and senseless sank upon the sward:
Godfrey no longer could his wrath command;
But, brandishing his unsheath'd blade abroad,
Clamber'd high up the ruin'd heap, where stand
The two colossal knights, and braved them, hand to hand.

82. Then glorious deeds he did, and would have done,
For sharp and deadly were the strokes he gave;
But, curtain'd in red clouds, the slumb'rous sun
Went down, and from her dark Cimmerian cave
Night came, pacific, o'er the world to wave
Her arbitrary scepter, and allay
The rage of wretched mortals; Bouillon brave
Thus ceased from fight, and through the shadows gray
Led back his hosts to camp: so pass'd that bloody day.

83. But, ere the pious Chief forsook the field,
He saw the wounded borne in spacious car
Safe to the tents, nor to the foe would yield
In prey an atom of his works of war;
The tower that did with most of havoc mar
The marble walls, and scared with most affright,
Remain'd entire, though seam'd with many a scar;
The dreadful storm and thunders of the fight,
Though they had bruised its frame, had left the timbers tight.

84. Scaped the dire perils of the strife, it leaves
For a safe spot the scene of enterprise;
But, as a vessel crowding sail, that cleaves
The roaring sea and its vex'd waves defies,
Just as its wish'd-for port the captain spies
Clear through his optic tube, in sudden squall,
Strikes on hid rocks,—or as a steed, that plies
With sure-foot speed his journey safe through all
The rugged lanes, drops down, in sight of his sweet stall;—

85. So the tower struck, so stumbled! on the side
Which had sustain'd th' artillery of the foe,
Two wheels broke down whereon the piece should slide,
Already crazed by some tempestuous blow;
That the huge engine stay'd its motion slow,
And overhead hung ruinous in air;
But they with beams support it from below,
Till the prompt architects with skillful care
Uprear th' enormous bulk, its breaches to repair.

86. Thus Godfrey bade, that the stupendous mass
Might be refitted, ere the morning smile;
Then with his soldiers occupied each pass,
And station'd guards around the spacious pile;
But with the shrill sound of the saw and file,
Commingling rumors of the Chief's designs
Are by the townsmen clearly heard; the while
A thousand lights around the structure shine,
Whereby the work they watch, the latent scheme divine.

END OF CANTO XI.

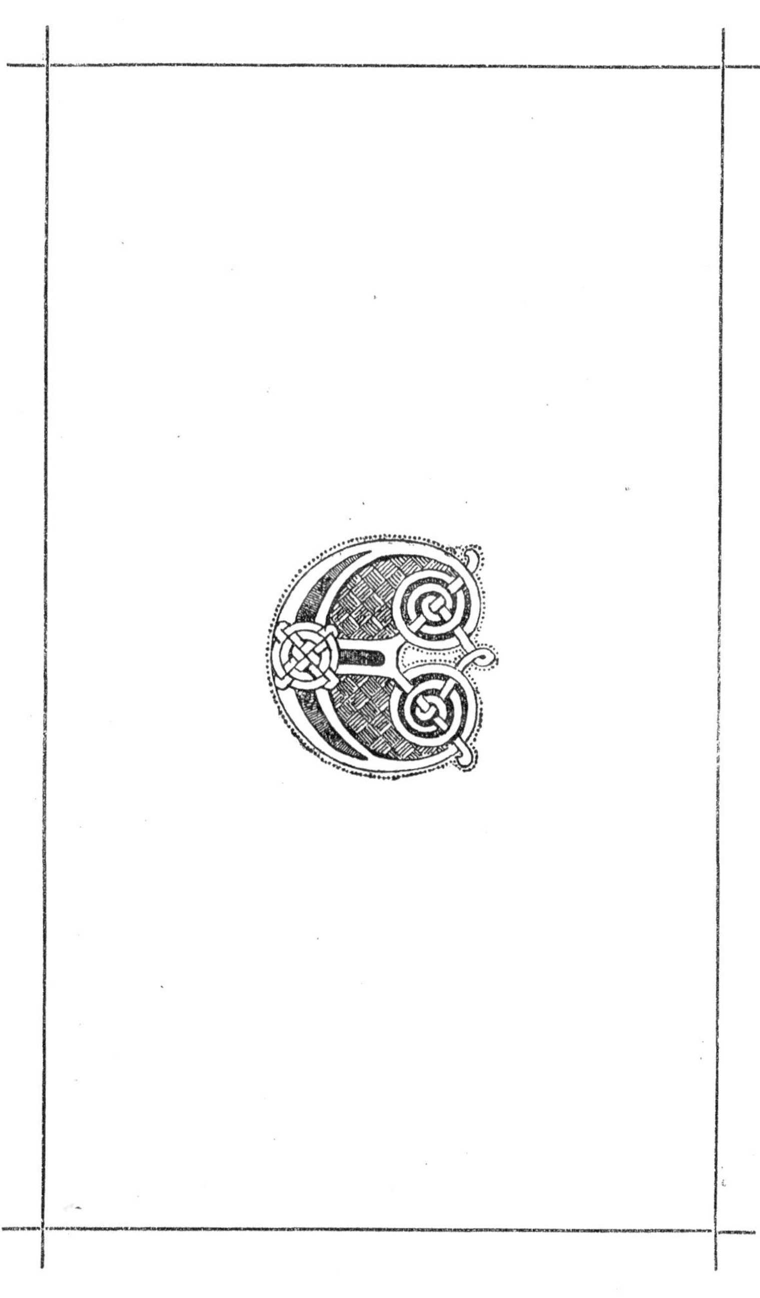

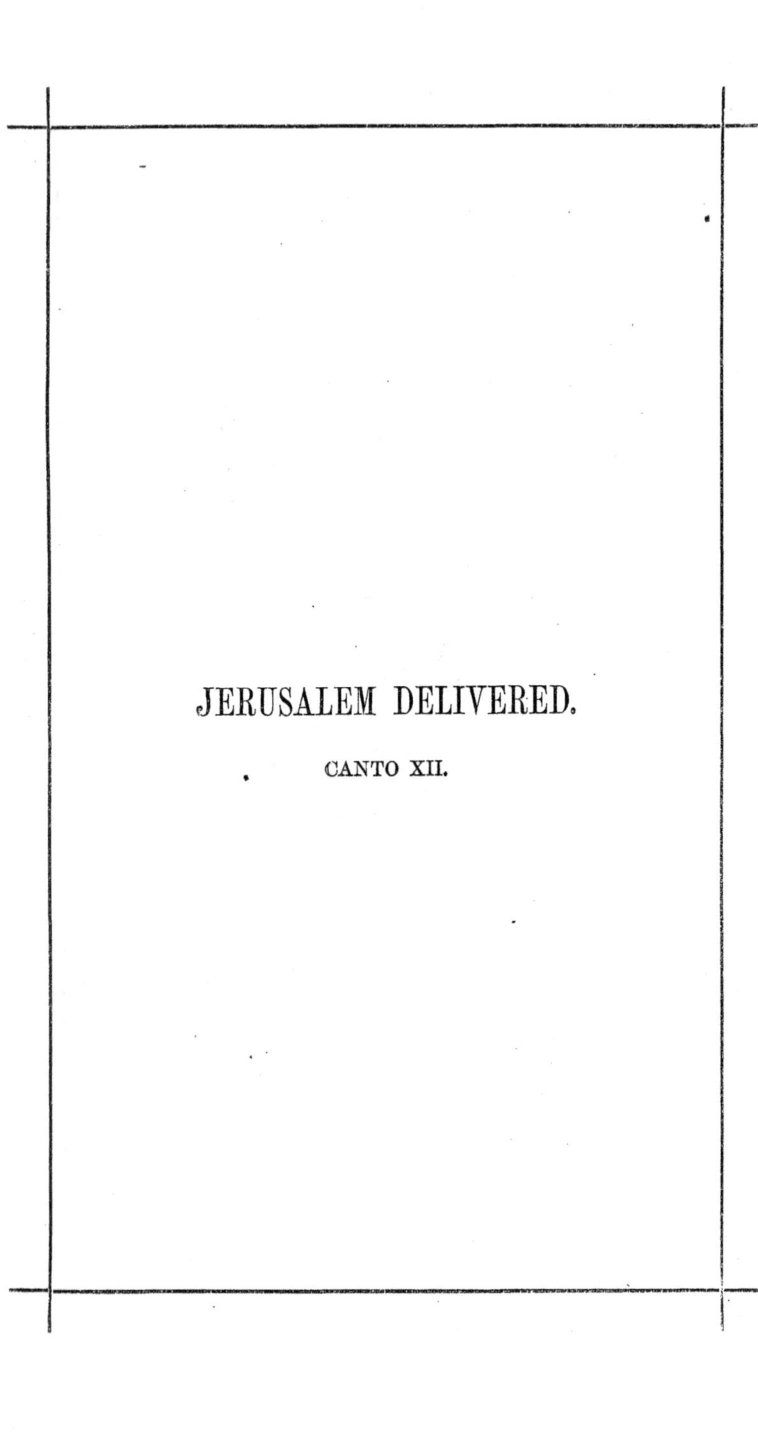

JERUSALEM DELIVERED.

CANTO XII.

ARGUMENT.

First from her faithful slave Clorinda learns
The secret story of her birth; then goes,
Mask'd, on a high adventure, and returns
Safe to the gates, successful o'er her foes;
But, chased by Tancred to the vales, they close
In mortal battle, and she falls; yet ere
She dies the right of baptism he bestows;
Sorely the Prince bewails his slaughter'd fair;
Argantes vows revenge, and soothes the crowd's despair.

JERUSALEM DELIVERED.

CANTO XII.

1 'TWAS night; nor yet had either wearied host
Found soft refreshment in the arms of sleep;
But here the Christians, wakeful at their post,
Guard o'er the workmen round the engine keep;
And there the Pagans their defenses steep,
Trembling and nodding to their fall, repair;
And, to build up the breaches wide and deep
Of the dismantled walls, no labor spare;
And each their wounded tend, with like consid'rate care.

2. At length the wounds are bandaged, and complete
Is every one of their nocturnal tasks;
The rest they leave; and, woo'd to slumber sweet
By gentler quiet, and the gloom that masks
The world at noon of night, their cumbrous casques
They cast aside; not so the Warrior maid:
Hung'ring for fame, she still for action asks,—
Action, from which fatigues all else dissuade;
With her Argantes walk'd, and inly thus she said:

3. "Deeds rare and wonderful indeed this day
Have the bold Soldan and divine Argaunt
Accomplish'd, by themselves to take their way,
Huge towers beat down, and hostile millions daunt;
While I, (the utmost merit I can vaunt,)
Coop'd in on high, with distant shafts but check'd
Their eager escalade; my shafts, I grant,
Flew fair enough, some fatal, I suspect;
But is this then the whole we women can effect?

4. "Better it were in woods and wilds again
To stags and wolves my arrows to confine,
Than trifle thus, a damsel, in the train

Of knights whose actions so superior shine ;
Why not the cuirass and the sword resign ?
Resume my woman's weeds, and live dissolved
In careless ease ? " thus mused she ; but in fine
A daring project in her breast revolved,—
Turn'd to the knight, and thus broke forth with soul resolved :

5. "I know not what blest ardor sets ablaze
My restless mind,—or do the Gods inspire
The daring thought that on my spirit preys ?
Or make we Gods of each sublime desire ?
Far lie the Franks encamp'd : look forth ; admire
The twinkling lights that burn toward the West ;
There will I go with torch and sword, and fire
Their rolling fort ; this passion of my breast
Let me but see fulfill'd, and Heaven arrange the rest !

6. "But, if I chance to be by Fate debarr'd
From measuring back my steps to thee, my friend,
The man that loves me with a sire's regard,
And my devoted damsels I commend :
Each kind protection to their griefs extend,
And back to Egypt, with the dear old sage,
Th' inconsolable girls in safety send ;
Promise me this ! their sex and his great age
May well thy care demand, thy sympathies engage."

7. Argantes stood amazed ; touch'd in his breast
Were all the springs of glory, and he cried :
"Wilt thou do this ? and leave thy friend, disgraced
Here with th' inglorious vulgar to abide ?
Safe from the risk, shall I with joy or pride
See the fire kindle ? no, Clorinda, no !
If I have ever been in arms allied
With thee, with thee this night too will I go,
And all thy fortune share, betide me weal or woe !

8. "I have a heart too can scorn death, and feel
The bauble life well flung for fame away : "
"To this," she answer'd, "an eternal seal
Didst thou in thy brave sally set to-day ;
But I am a mere woman in the way ;
Feeble indeed are my poor powers, and small
The aid I lend ; my death would none dismay ;
But (Heaven avert the omen !) shouldst thou fall,
Who will remain to guard the sacred wall ?"

9. "Why these excuses vain?" the knight replied;
"Fix'd is my will, and settled mine intent;
Allow'd, I follow; but, if once denied,
I go before thee, and thy zeal prevent:"
Thus overpower'd, Clorinda gave consent,—
They seek the King, with Emir, prince, and peer
Engaged in high and serious argument;
Then thus the Virgin spoke; "O Sire, give ear,
And what we wish to say with kind acceptance hear!

10. "Argantes swears (nor vain will be the boast)
To fire yon rolling fort,—the same swear I;
We wait alone till on the guardian host
Deep sleep falls heavy; those who wake shall die!"
The hoary King held up his hands on high;
A tear of joy stream'd down his wither'd cheek;
"And praised," he said, "be Thou, who yet dost eye
With gracious care thy worshipers, and seek
Still to preserve my crown, and guard these kingdoms weak!

11. "Fall they shall not, while in their sure defense
Two such undaunted demigods are found;
To your deserts what equal recompense
Can I decree? O, evermore renown'd!
Let Fame her golden trumpet take, and sound
Your glory, tuned to music's loftiest pitch,
And fill th' enchanted Universe around!
The deed itself be your reward; to which
No trifling part I add of realms esteem'd as rich!"

12. He said, and fondly to his bosom strain'd
Now him, now her; to equal transport charm'd,
The Soldan stood, nor in his heart contain'd
The gen'rous envy that his spirit warm'd;
But cried: "And not for nothing am I arm'd
With this good sword, nor shall I be less slow
To toss the fires!" the Amazon, alarm'd
For her endanger'd fame, replied, "Not so;
Are all to make th' attempt? who stays, if thou shouldst go?"

13. Argantes too, with features full of pride,
Stood ready to reject his scorn'd request;
But this the King forestall'd, and first replied
With placid aspect to his regal guest:
"Forward thou ever art to manifest
Thyself emphatically great, a knight

Prompt to dispute the laurel with the best,
Consistent with thyself, untired in fight,
Whom no new shape of death or danger can affright!

14. "I know that, sallying forth, thou deeds wouldst do
Worthy the Soldan; but for all to quit
Your wonted stations in the town, of you,
My bravest heroes, were a thing unfit,
Fraught with alarm; I would not e'en permit
These to depart, with such a jealous care
Guard I their lives, if I could well commit
To other hands the enterprise they dare,—
Or if the deed itself of less importance were.

15. "But since around th' immeasurable tower
The guards so thick are station'd that a few
Would not suffice, and numbers at this hour
Could not conveniently be spared on new
Fatiguing services, e'en let the two
That, to such risks accustom'd, first proposed
The noble task, with prosp'ring stars pursue
Their schemes alone, and realize a boast
Made in no idle mood; they are themselves a host.

16. "Do thou, as best becomes a king, remain
As regent of the gates; and when the pair,
Of whose success sure hopes I entertain,
Have fired the pile and back their footsteps bear,
Press'd by the Christians, with thy Turks repair,
Beat off the fierce pursuers, and prevent
The harms which else revenging rage may dare."
Thus spoke the King; the Soldan, ill content,
Said not another word, but smiled a sour assent.

17. "Yet go not," said Ismeno, "till I mix,
Of various grain impregn'd with fiery spume,
Tartareous balls, that where they strike shall fix,
Fixing ignite, and blazing, soon consume
The tower to dust; the witching hour of gloom
Draws nigh; by then the soldiers may remit
Their watch, o'erpower'd by languor, and the fum
Of sleep;" all praise the sorcerer's pregnant wit,
And parting wait the hour by him determined fit.

18. Her sculptured helm, her greaves of silver plate
And burnish'd mail aside Clorinda laid;
And in a suit prophetic of her fate,
Sable, and rough with rust, her limbs array'd,

Where no bright jewel flash'd, nor plumage play'd :
For thus she thought unseen to leave beguiled
The watch, swift stealing through the friendly shade ;
'Twas then her eunuch came, Arsetes mild,
Who had her cradle rock'd, and nursed her from a child.

19. All careless of fatigue, the good old man
Tended her still ; and, chancing now to see
The surreptitious arms, he soon began
To comprehend her risk ; and on his knee
Sore weeping, by the pious memory
Of his past offices, by locks grown gray
In her dear service, and by every plea
Of love and pity, did he long time pray
Her to resign th' attempt, and still she answer'd nay.

20. At length he said : " Since in its wrong thy mind
Is obstinate, since to my feeble years,
Since to my silver tresses thou art blind,
Blind to my love, and proof to all my tears,
My piteous prayers, and too prophetic fears,—
Lo, from thy hitherto unknown descent
I rend the veil ! that known, do what appears
Good in thy sight ;"—amazed, Clorinda bent
On him her large dark eyes, and thus the story went.

21. " In former days o'er Ethiopia reign'd—
Happy perchance reigns still—Senapo brave ;
Who with his dusky people still maintain'd
The laws which Jesus to the nations gave :
'Twas in his court, a Pagan and a slave,
I lived, o'er thousand maids advanced to guard,
And wait, with authorized assumption grave,
On her whose beauteous brows the crown instarr'd ;
True, she was brown, but naught the brown her beauty marr'd.

22. " The King adored her, but his jealousies
Equal'd the fervors of his love ; the smart
At length of sharp suspicion by degrees
Gain'd such ascendence in his troubled heart,
That from all men in closest bower apart
He mew'd her, where e'en Heaven's chaste eyes, the bright
Stars, were but half allow'd their looks to dart ;
While she, meek, wise, and pure as virgin light,
Made her unkind lord's will her rule and chief delight.

23. "Hung was her room with storied imageries
Of martyrs and of saints ; a Virgin here,
On whose fair cheeks the rose's sweetest dyes
Glow'd, was depicted in distress ; and near,
A monstrous dragon, which with poignant spear
An errant knight transfixing, prostrate laid :
The gentle Lady oft with many a tear
Before this painting meek confession made
Of secret faults, and mourn'd, and Heaven's forgiveness
pray'd.

24. "Pregnant meanwhile, she bore (and thou wert she)
A daughter white as snow ; th' unusual hue,
With wonder, fear, and strange perplexity
Disturb'd her, as though something monstrous too ;
But, as by sad experience well she knew
His jealous temper and suspicious haste,
She cast to hide thee from thy father's view ;
For in his mind, (perversion most misplaced !)
Thy snowy chasteness else had argued her unchaste.

25. "And in thy cradle to his sight exposed
A negro's new-born infant for her own ;
And, as the tower wherein she lived inclosed,
Was kept by me and by her maids alone,—
To me whose firm fidelity was known,
Who loved and served her with a soul sincere,
She gave thee, beauteous as a rose unblown,
Yet unbaptized ; for there, it would appear,
Baptized thou couldst not be in that thy natal year.

26. "Weeping she placed thee in my arms, to bear
To some far spot ; what tongue can tell the rest !
The plaints she used ; and with what wild despair
She clasp'd thee to her fond maternal breast :
How many times 'twixt sighs, 'twixt tears caress'd ;
How oft, how very oft her vain adieu
Seal'd on thy cheek ; with what sweet passion press'd
Thy little lips ! at length a glance she threw
To Heaven, and cried : 'Great God, that look'st all
spirits through !—

27. "'If both my heart and members are unstain'd,
And naught did e'er my nuptial bed defile,—
(I pray not for myself ; I stand arraign'd
Of thousand sins, and in thy sight am vile ;)
Preserve this guiltless infant, to whose smile
The tend'rest mother must refuse her breast,

And from her eyes their sweetest bliss exile !
May she with chastity like mine be bless'd ;
But stars of happier rule have influence o'er the rest !

28. " ' And thou, bless'd Knight, that from the cruel teeth
Of the grim dragon freed'st that holy maid,
Lit by my hands if ever odorous wreath
Rose from thy altars ; if I e'er have laid
Thereon gold, cinnamon, or myrrh, and pray'd
For help through ev'ry chance of life display,
In guardianship of her, thy powerful aid !'
Convulsions choked her words,—she swoon'd away—
And the pale hues of death on her chill temples lay.

29. " With tears I took thee, in a little ark
So hid by flowers and leaves that none could guess
The secret, brought thee forth 'twixt light and dark,
And, unsuspected, in a Moorish dress,
Pass'd the town walls : as through a wilderness
Of forests horrid with brown glooms, I took
My pensive way, I saw, to my distress,
A tigress issuing from a bosky nook,
Rage in her scowling brows, and lightning in her look.

30. " Wild with affright, I on the flowery ground
Cast thee, and instant climb'd a tree close by ;
The savage brute came up, and glancing round
In haughty menace, saw where thou didst lie ;
And, soft'ning to a mild humanity
Her stern regard, with placid gestures meek,
As by thy beauty smit, came courteous nigh ;
In am'rous pastime fawning lick'd thy cheek ;
And thou on her didst smile, and stroke her mantle sleek.

31. " With her fierce muzzle and her cruel front
Thy little hands did innocently play ;
She offer'd thee her teats, as is the wont
With nurses, and adapted them, as they,
To thy young lips ; nor didst thou turn away,—
She suckled thee ! a prodigy so new
Fill'd me with fresh confusion and dismay :
She, when she saw thee satisfied, withdrew
Into the shady wood, and vanish'd from my view.

32. " Again I took thee, and pursued my way
Through woods, and vales, and wildernesses dun ;
Till in a little village making stay,
I gave thee secretly in charge to one

Who fondly nursed thee till the circling sun,
With sixteen months of equatorial heat,
Had tinged thy face ; till thou too hadst begun
To prattle of thy joys in murmurs sweet,
And print her cottage floor with indecisive feet.

33. "But having pass'd the autumn of my years,
As sprightly vigor fail'd and life declined,
Rich in the gold that with her farewell tears
Thy bounteous mother to my hands consign'd,
I for my native country inly pined ;
After my many toils and wand'rings wide,
I longed amidst old faces left behind
In my dear birthplace tranquil to reside,
And spent life's wintry eve at my own warm fireside.

34. "To Egypt then, where first my eyes unclosed,
I took, conducting thee, a secret road,
And reach'd a flood, to equal risks exposed,—
Here robbers chased me, there the torrent flow'd :
What should I do ! resign my cherish'd load ?
No ! yet how shun the meditated theft ?
A moment's thought hereon when I bestow'd
I braved the stream ; with one bold arm I cleft
Venturous the roaring waves, and bore thee in my left.

35. "Swift as an arrow flow'd the flood ; midway,
The jangling tides forever boil and spin ;
There, as a curling snake devours its prey,
The volumed whirlpool gaped, and suck'd me in ;
Giddy, toss'd round, distracted with the din,
Thee then I miss'd ; but the wild waves upbore,—
Propitious breezes caught thy garments thin,
And laid thee safe on the smooth sandy shore ;
Which I at length too reach'd, when hope almost was o'er.

36. "With joy I took thee up ; eve's dusky light
The landscape veil'd, when, slumb'ring on the sand,
Methought the figure of a frowning knight
Came near, and pointing at my breast his brand,
Imperiously exclaim'd : 'No more withstand
The solemn charge with which thou long hast striven,
A mother's precept ! christen, I command,
This babe, the choice inheritant of Heaven ;—
To my peculiar care the orphan child is given.

37. "'Twas I gave mercy to th' infuriate brute,
Life to the wind, and mildness to the stream;
And woe to thee, if thou my words dispute,
Or as a vacant phantom disesteem
The Heavenly form I am;' with morn's first beam
I woke, and, shaking off the dews of night,
Went forward; but, as false I judged the dream,
And true my faith, I scrupled not to slight,
The angel's threat, and still withheld the sacred rite;—

38. "But as a Pagan bred thee, nor reveal'd
The secret of thy birth; while thou hast grown
Valiant in arms, the phœnix of the field,
And o'er thy sex and Nature's self hast shown
Thyself victorious; hosts hast thou o'erthrown;
Won riches, realms, and palms forever green;—
What since has happen'd, thou thyself hast known,
And how in peace, in battle, I have been
Thy sire at once and slave, through each succeeding scene.

39. "Last morn a sleep, the simile of death,
Ere yet the stars had faded from the sky,
Sank on my soul, and by our holy faith
Again thy Genius in my sleep pass'd by;
But haughtier was his look, more fierce his cry,—
'Traitor!' he said, 'the hour to disunite
Clorinda from the bonds of earth draws nigh;
Mine shall she yet become in thy despite;
Be thine the woe!'—he frown'd, and Heavenward took his flight.

40. "Thus, then, be warn'd! for sadly I suspect
O'er thee, my love, strange accidents impend;
Perhaps the Heavens are wroth when we reject
The faith our wise forefathers did commend;
Perhaps that faith is true; oh, condescend,
Deign, I entreat thee, to put off this vest
Of sable, deign thy purpose to suspend!"
He ceased, and wept; fear thrill'd her pensive breast,
For on her heart a like remember'd vision press'd.

41. But soon her aspect she serened, and said:
"This faith, which surely strikes my mind as true,
Which thou wouldst have me doubt in thy vain dread,
The faith that with my nurse's milk I drew,
Still will I keep; nor yet resign, (beshrew
The soul that would!) my old heroic spear,

And plighted purpose ; no, not if I knew
That Death, with that fierce visage which strikes fear
Into the hearts of men, would dog me as a deer ! "

42 She soothes him, smiles on him, and straight retires,
For now the hurrying hours to action call ;
And with the dauntless hero who desires
To share her hazard, seeks the palace hall ;
Ismeno joins them, and with words of gall
Spurs on the daring hearts that little need
Renew'd excitements ; gives to each a ball
Of pitch and sulphur ; in a hollow reed
Shuts up the fatal flame, and bids them do the deed.

43. Charged, they depart ; and over dale and hill
Circling the valleys, through the darkness scud
With speed incessant, side by side, until
They near the spot where the vast engine stood ;
There high their spirit rises, hot the blood
Boils in their veins ; desire and scorn combine
To cheer them on, and in their madding mood,
Drawn are their swords ; the watch behold the shine
Of coming arms, and loud demand the passing sign

44. Mute they move on; "To arms !" exclaim the guard.
Their sudden shouts the valiant couple stun,
But naught their gen'rous enterprise retard,—
They bound abroad, and all concealment shun ;
As from th' electric cloud or level'd gun,
At the same instant comes the flash, the thunder,
And bolt of ruin ; so for them to run,
Arrive, strike, penetrate, and cleave asunder
The phalanx, is but one, one moment's work of wonder.

45. Through thousand arms, amidst a thousand blows
They pass, and execute their glorious aim ;
Their glimm'ring lights secreted they disclose,
And tip the black combustible with flame :
Toss'd, to the tower it fixes ; words are tame
To picture how it creeps, expands, aspires ;
How soon it runs o'er all the timber'd frame ;
How thick the smoke, and in what billowy gyres,
Climbs to the lofty stars, and cloaks their shining fires.

46. Vast globes of fire amid the ceaseless whirl
Of smoke voluminous, now dim, now bright,
As the cloud fluctuates, high to Heaven upcurl,—
The blust'ring winds add fury to their flight :

Then join the scatter'd flames ; a sudden light
Strikes the awed host,—they arm in mute amaze ;
'Tis done ! the pile so terrible in fight,
Sinks in a lofty, broad, columnar blaze ;
And one brief hour destroys the workmanship of days.

47. Two bands meantime to where the pile is burning
Haste from the Camp ; which when Argantes sees,
He shouts, "Your blood shall quench the fire !" and turning
His sword against them, with wild menaces
Keeps them at bay ; but, yielding by degrees,
With fair Clorinda to the brown hill's bent
Retires, while fast behind the crowds increase,
Like headlong floods which August rains augment ;
Hotly they press the chase, and climb with them th' ascent.

48. The Golden Gate turns on its hinge ; and there,
With his arm'd people stands the Turkish King,
Ready to welcome back the dauntless pair,
If favoring fortune should them homeward bring ;
High o'er the ruins of the fosse they spring
Before a grove of spears,—the Soldan stout
Gives the known word, the portals wide they fling,
Drive back the Franks, and, wheeling swift about,
Close the strong gates,—alas ! these shut Clorinda out.

49. For at the moment when the Turks let fall
The pendulous portcullis, forth she flew
To wreck her ire on Arimon the tall,
Whose daring sword had cut her hauberk through ;
This she revenged, nor yet Argantes knew
That she was separate from his side ; the glare
Of steel, the anarchy of fight, the crew
That press'd behind, and denseness of the air,
Wholly his sight confused, distracting every care.

50. But when her sultry anger she had quench'd
In the proud blood of dying Arimon,
Saw the gates closed, and how she stood intrench'd,
She deem'd Clorinda utterly undone,
And look'd alone for death ; but soon, as none
Pierced her disguise, fresh hopes of safety rose.
With other turns of wit, she feigns her one
Of the same troop, a bold demeanor shows,
And with cool unconcern slips in amidst her foes.

51. Then, as the still wolf glides to the green wood,
Conscious of crime, and in close ambush lies:
So, by the tumult favor'd, and unview'd,
Through the dun shade of the nocturnal skies,
Dissever'd from the press, Clorinda flies:
Tancred, alone, it seems, the secret knew
Both of her fatal chance and sly device;
Arriving there as Arimon she slew,
He saw her, mark'd her out, and kept in constant view

52. Her would he fight with, deeming her a man
Glorious in arms as lively in address;
Around the winding ramparts swift she ran,
In at some other gate to gain access;
As swift behind her did th' avenger press:
Nor was it long, ere on the gusty breath
Of the night-wind she heard, with some distress,
The sound of arms; whence, turning, "Halt!" she saith;
"What fleet foot news bring'st thou?" He answer'd, "War and death!"

53. "War shalt thou have," said she, "and death, if these
Are thy request;" and here her step she stay'd;
Tancred his steed abandons, when he sees
His foe on foot, by lonely hills embay'd:
Then she her saber, he his poignant blade,
Draws from the sheath; they stand as mortal foes;
Wrath nerves the hero, haughtiness the maid;
Like two young bulls, each smarting with the throes
Of envy, rage, and love, in desp'ra.e strife they close.

54. Worthy of royal lists, and the clear shine
Of suns would be the battle, if descried;
Dark Abbess! thou that in thy Gothic scrine
The mold'ring relics of their tale dost hide,
Grant me to lift thy cowl, to waft aside
The curtain, and in radiant numbers braid
Their deeds, for endless ages to abide;
So with their glory, glorious shall be made,
In page of high Romance, the mem'ry of thy shade.

55. They shrink not, trifle not, strive not to smite
By artificial rules with wary will;
Stand not on postures or on points, the night
And their blind rage forbid the tricks of skill;
But swords clash horribly with swords, and shrill
The mountain echo shrieks along the plain;

Not a foot stirs,—where stood, there stand they still ;
But aye their hands in motion they maintain ;
And not a lounge, or foin, or slash descends in vain :

56. Shame stings disdain to vengeance, vengeance breeds
New shame,— thus passion runs a ceaseless round :
To spite despite, to rage fresh rage succeeds,
The agony to strike, the lust to wound
And now the battle blends in narrower ground ;
No room have they to foin, no room to lash ;
Their blades flung back, like butting rams they bound,
Fight with the hilts, wild, savage, raging, rash,
And shield at sounding shield, and helm at helmet dash.

57. Thrice in his boist'rous arms the maid he press'd,
And thrice was forced to loose his sinewy clasp ;
She had no fancy to be so caress'd ;
Impassion'd Love is not an angry asp.
Again with eagerness their swords they grasp,
And tinge them ruddy as Vesuvian fire,
In blood of many wounds ; till, tired, they gasp
For very breath,—some paces back retire ;
And from their long fatigues all pantingly respire.

58. Faint on their swords, with like exhausted frame,
Alike they rest, and echo gaze for gaze :
Fades the last star ; Aurora, robed in flame,
Unbars Elysium, and the morning plays ;
Tancred perceives, beneath its grateful rays,
From her the trickling blood profusely rain,
And glories in the languor she displays ;
Oh man, vain man ! poor fool of pride and pain !
Puff'd up with every breath from Fortune's wav'ring vane !

59. Why that proud smile? sad, O how sad, shall be
Thy acted triumphs when th' illusion clears !
Thine eyes shall weep, if still the light they see,
For every drop of blood a sea of tears !
Thus resting, gazing, full of hopes and fears,
The bleeding warriors, silent as the dead,
Stood for a space ; at length some feelings fierce
Tancred deposed,—kind thoughts rose in their stead;
He wish'd her name to know, and breaking silence, said :

60. "Hard is our chance, our prowess thus to spend
On deeds which silence and these shades conceal ;
To which thwart Fortune yields no praise, no friend

On our view'd acts to set his speaking seal!
Yet, if amid the sullen shock of steel
Prayers may have access, courtesies find place,
Thy name, thy country, and thy rank reveal;
That I, whatever issue crown the case,
May know at least who gives my death or victory grace."

61. Sternly she said: "Thy prayer no access wins;
Custom forbids; but whatsoe'er my name,
Thou seest before thee one of those brave twins
Who gave your towering structure to the flames."
Fired at her answer, Tancred made exclaim:
"In evil hour hast thou thy guilt avow'd;
Thy speech and silence are to me the same,
Discourteous wretch, contemptible as proud!
Both chide my sloth, and both for vengeance plead aloud."

62. Rage to their hearts returns, and spurs them on,
Though weak, to war; dire war! from which the sleights
Of art are banish'd, whence all strength is gone,
And in the room of both, brute fury fights:
Oh, sharp his falchion, sharp her saber smites!
What bloody gaps they make through plate and chain,
In their soft flesh! revenge, revenge requites;
If life parts not, 'tis only that disdain
Knits it in pure despite to the rebellious brain.

63. As the deep Euxine, though the wind no more
Blows, that late toss'd its billows to the stars,
Stills not at once its rolling and its roar,
But with its coasts long time conflicting jars;
Thus, though their quickly ebbing blood debars
Force from their blades as vigor from their arms,
Still lasts the frenzy of the flame which Mars
Blew in their breasts; sustain'd by whose strong charms,
Yet heap they strokes on strokes, yet harms inflict on harms.

64. But now, alas, the fatal hour arrives
That must shut up Clorinda's life in shade;
In her fair bosom deep his sword he drives;
'Tis done—life's purple fountain bathes the blade!
The golden-flower'd cymar of light brocade,
That swathed so tenderly her breasts of snow,
Is steep'd in the warm stream: the hapless maid

Feels her end nigh ; her knees their strength forego :
And her enfeebled frame droops languishing and low.

65. He, following up the thrust with taunting cries,
Lays the pierced Virgin at his careless feet ;
She, as she falls, in mournful tones outsighs
Her last faint words, pathetically sweet ;
Which a new spirit prompts, a spirit replete
With charity, and faith, and hope serene,
Sent dove-like down from God's pure Mercy-seat,
Who, though through life his rebel she had been,
Would have her die a fond, repentant Magdalene.

66. "Friend ! thou hast won ; I pardon thee, and O
Forgive thou me ! I fear not for this clay,
But my dark soul—pray for it, and bestow
The sacred rite that laves all stains away :"
Like dying hymns heard far at close of day,
Sounding I know not what in the soothed ear
Of sweetest sadness, the faint words make way
To his fierce heart, and, touch'd with grief sincere,
Streams from his pitying eye th' involuntary tear.

67. Not distant, gushing from the rocks, a rill
Clash'd on his ear ; to this with eager pace
He speeds—his hollow casque the waters fill—
And back he hurries to the deed of grace ;
His hands as aspens tremble, while they raise
The lock'd aventayle of the unknown knight ;—
God, for thy mercy ! 'tis her angel face !
Aghast and thunder-struck, he loathes the light ;
Ah, knowledge best unknown ! ah, too distracting sight !

68. Yet still he lived ; and, must'ring all his power
To the sad task, restrain'd each wild lament,
Fain to redeem by those baptismal showers
The life his sword bereft ; while thus intent
The hallowing words he spoke, with ravishment
Her face transfigured shone, and half apart
Her bland lips shed a lively smile that sent
This silent speech in sunshine to his heart :
"Heaven gleams ; in blissful peace behold thy friend depart !"

69. A paleness beauteous as the lily's mix'd
With the sweet violet's, like a gust of wind
Flits o'er her face ; her eyes on Heaven are fix'd,
And Heaven on her returns its looks as kind ;

Speak she can not; but her cold hand, declined,
In pledge of peace on Tancred she bestows;
And to her fate thus tenderly resign'd,
In her meek beauty she expires, and shows
But as a smiling saint indulging soft repose.

70. But when he saw her starlike spirit set,
The self-possession which had mann'd his soul
Bent to the storm of anguishing regret
That o'er his bosom burst beyond control:
Pangs of despair convulsed his heart; life stole
As to its last recess; death's icy dew
Bathed his pale brow; his blood forebore to roll;
Till like the breathless dead the living grew,
In chillness, silence, air, and attitude, and hue.

71. And sure his life, impatient of the light,
Struggling had burst in its rebellious scorn
From its weak chain, and follow'd in its flight
The beauteous spirit, that, but just reborn,
Had spread its wings in sunshine of the morn,—
Had not a party of the Franks, dispread
In search of water o'er the gleaming lawn,
By providential guidance thither led,
Seen where he lay supine, the dying by the dead.

72. Their Chief, though distant, by his armor knew
The Latin Prince, and hasten'd to the place;
The lifeless beauty he remember'd too
For Tancred's love, and mourn'd her fatal case;
He would not leave a form so full of grace,
Albeit a Pagan, as he deem'd, a prey
To wolves, but lifting, in a little space,
To others' arms both bodies whence they lay,
Took straight to Tancred's tent his melancholy way.

73. Not yet the knight, so equably and slow
They march'd, from his dark trance awaken'd was,
But feeble groans at intervals might show
Some sands still glided in his vital glass;
The Lady lay a mute and stirless mass,
Nor breath, nor pulse gave hope that life was there
Incorporate with its beauty: thus they pass;
Thus, side by side, the two, lamenting, bear;
And in adjoining rooms dispose with silent care.

74. His pitying squires drew nigh; with busy pain
Chafed his chill temples, and his mail unbound;

His languid eyes at length he oped again,
Felt the physician's hand, the smarting wound,
And heard, yet dubious of his sense, the sound
Of whisp'ring lips,—where was he, and with whom?
Long with bewilder'd gaze he look'd around;
At length his squires, at length he knew the room,
And in low feeble words lamented thus his doom:

75. "Yet do I breathe? yet live to view the beams
Of this cursed day, more odious than the shade?
Clear witness of my blind misdeed, it streams
T' accuse my rashness, and my guilt upbraid:
Ah, coward hand! why now art thou afraid,
Thou, so well versed in all the turns of strife,
The impious minister of death repaid
In infamy, to grasp the vengeful knife,
And cut the pall-black thread of this opprobrious life!

76. "Take the fell steel, and hide it to the hilt
Within me,—my sad heart in sunder cleave!
But thou, perhaps, inured to deeper guilt,
May'st deem it mercy such quick ease to give:
Then as a dire example let me live,
Monster of luckless Love! a mark for men
To point at, and abhor; this base reprieve
To shameful life will be th' alone fit pain
For such enormous guilt, and of so dark a grain.

77. "Vex'd by just Furies, anguish, grief, and care,
A wand'ring maniac must I live—to run,
Shrieking, from phantoms with which sleep shall scare
My soul, when Night her orgies has begun;
To hold in horror and in hate the Sun,
That did my fatal error show; to eye
Myself with fear, and strive myself to shun;—
Evermore flying, evermore to fly,
While hell's pursuing fiends are ever howling nigh!

78. "But where, alas, where lie the relics chaste
Of my slain angel? what my cruel scorn
Left whole, perchance some savage of the waste—
The lion mangles, or the wolf has torn;
Ah spoils for them too rich! dear beauty, born
To different end! too sweet, too precious fruit!
Poor injured maiden! whom the shades forlorn
And lone hills have betray'd, first in dispute
To me, and next in prey to some ferocious brute.

79. "Yet will I go, and the loved spoils collect;
Dear limbs! where late the hues of beauty bloom'd;
But if the wolf, in hungry disrespect,
Those virgin relics has indeed consumed,
In the same cavern let me be intomb'd,
Let the same jaws ingulph me! hail'd by me
Will the stroke come; but, prey'd on or inhumed,
A glorious sepulcher, my love, 'twill be,
Where'er thy bones are cast, to be inurn'd with thee!"

80. But being told that her lamented form
Lay in his tent, a beam of joy appear'd,
Like lightning flashing through a sable storm,
To light his aspect, and the darkness clear'd;
Straight from the couch of his repose he rear'd
The heavy burden of his limbs, and slow—
Weak as an infant, full of pain, but cheer'd
By her dear image, thither strove to go,
On frail unsteady steps, loose staggering to and fro.

81. But when he came, and in her beauteous breast
Saw the red gash his murd'rous hand had made,
And her late radiant aspect calm'd to rest,
Like a nocturnal sky, in livid shade,—
His height'ning color was perceived to fade;
A trembling ague rock'd his frame; and there
Would he have sunk, but for immediate aid;
"Sweet face!" he sigh'd, "thou canst make death look fair,
But has not power to soothe, or sweeten my despair!

82. "Fair hand! dear pledge of pard'ning amity!
Late forceful pleader, utt'ring love's farewell!
What do I find thee now? ah, what am I!
And you, light limbs, that did in flight excel
The graceful motions of the fleet gazelle,
What but upbraiding vestiges are ye
Of my irreparable rage? too well
My stony eyes and cruel hand agree,
When, what the one destroy'd, the other brooks to see;—

83. "And see without a tear! then weep, my blood,
Since my remorseless eyes to weep forbear!"
Frantic he spoke; and in his madding mood,
Strong with desire of death, began to tear
His hands away, and to his nails laid bare
Each irritated wound,—the blood like rain
Gush'd forth, and in this fit of wild despair

He must have died, had not excess of pain
Caused him to swoon away, and life perforce retain.

84. Borne to his bed again, his flutt'ring sprite
Back to its hated mansion they reclaim ;
The dire mischance and anguish of the knight
This while was widely spread by babbling fame ;
And thither came the Chief, and thither came,
With his loved friends, the Solitary Sage ;
But neither grave admonishment could tame,
Nor pity soothe, nor gentlest prayers assuage
Of his distracted grief the stubbornness and rage.

85. As in a tender limb the serpent's sting,
With oils fomented, doth the keener smart :
So their kind solaces of love but bring
Acuter pangs to his afflicted heart !
But reverend Peter, who the faithful part
Of a good shepherd ever undertook
With his sick flock, bless'd counsels to impart,
His long romantic passion would rebuke,
And from its frenzied trance his willful spirit shook :

86. "O Tancred ! Tancred ! how unlike that mind,
Whose first unfoldings did so bright appear !
What cloud, what darkness does thy vision blind ?
What sorcery shuts thy intellectual ear ?
This thy sore trouble is instruction clear
Sent from the Lord ; dost thou not see the ray
That would direct thy feet ? dost thou not hear
The voice that calls thee to the safer way,
Wherein thou first didst walk, whence now thy footsteps stray ?

87. "To actions worthy thy first love, his voice
Recalls thee, vow'd to this divine crusade ;
Which thou hast left (unwise, unworthy choice !)
For the blind worship of a Pagan maid.
Happy misfortune ! Heaven on thee has laid
In tend'rest clemency its chast'ning rod ;
Thy fault, thyself has it the agent made
Of thine own good ; and is it in this mode
That thou the gift receiv'st, and own'st the grace bestow'd ?

88. "Scorn'st thou then, ingrate, the salubrious gift
Of God, with God incensed ? unhappy ! think
Whither this angry whirlwind bears thee—swift

O'er dark Eternity's tremendous brink ;
Down the deep precipice about to sink,
Thou hang'st at mercy of the slenderest breath ;
Call, I entreat, call back thy senses, shrink
From the momentous danger, look beneath,
And curb this impious woe, that leads to endless death!

89. That second death the sufferer's soul alarm'd,
And, all relinquishing his wish to die,
Their soothing words he entertain'd, and calm'd
The hurricane within ; yet still a sigh—
A groan at times escaped ; by fits his eye
Would weep, and his sad tongue lament aloud,
Now holding with himself wild colloquy,
Now with his love, who from some rosy cloud
To his fond plaints perchance an ear of pity bow'd.

90. On her at smile of morn, for her at frown
Of eve he calls, he murmurs, and complains ;
Like a lorn nightingle when some rude clown
Has stol'n her plumeless brood ; in piercing strains
She fills the dying winds, and woods, and plains
With her sweet quarrel ; all night long she weeps,
And to the list'ning stars repeats her pains,
Till morn with rosy tears the forest steeps ;—
Then on his streaming eyes awhile calm slumber creeps.

91. And, clad in starry robes, the maid for whom
He mourn'd, appears amid his morning dreams ;
Fairer than erst, but by the deathless bloom
And Heavenly radiance that around her beams,
Graced, not disguised ; in sweetest act she seems
To stoop, and wipe away the tears that flow
From his dim eyes : "Behold what glory streams
Round me," she cries ; "how beauteous now I show,
And for my sake, dear friend this waste of grief forego:

92. "Thee for my bliss I thank ; Earth's sordid clod
Thou by a happy error forced to quit,
And for the glorious Paradise of God
By sacred baptism mad'st my spirit fit :
There now midst angels and bless'd saints I sit,
In rapturous love and fellowship divine ;
There may our souls together yet be knit,
And there in fields where suns eternal shine,
Shalt thou at once enjoy their loveliness and mine ;—

93. "If by thy passions unseduced, if thou
Grudge not thyself the bliss ; live then, Sir Knight,
Know that I love thee, far as Love can bow
For aught of earthly mold a Child of Light!"
As thus she spoke, her glowing eyes shone bright
With an immortal's fervor,—rosy red,
She in the mild irradiance shut from sight
Her face, like a sweet flower, her fans outspread,
And in his drooping soul celestial comfort shed.

94. Soothed he awoke, and to the hands discreet
Of skill'd practitioners his wounds resign'd;
The while his friends interr'd, with spices sweet,
The limbs late vital with so great a mind;
And if the tomb to which they were consign'd
Was not of pure Pentelican, nor graced
With sculptures plann'd by architects refined,
The stone was choice, and wrought with all the taste
The urgent time allow'd, in form antiquely chaste.

95. There by bright lamps that in long order shine,
With many a dirge, her bones in earth they lay;
And on the smooth trunk of a leafless pine
Her arms, hung round with cypress and with bay,
In trophy to her fame aloft display;
And thither did the Prince his footsteps turn
All languid as he was, at break of day,
With awe and melancholy calm concern,
Unseen her grave to view, and clasp her reverenced urn.

96. When reach'd the tomb, his spirit's dolorous jail,
Prescribed by Heaven's inscrutable decree,
Long on the pile, mute, motionless and pale,
His hollow eyes in absent reverie
He fix'd: at length to his relief a sea
Of tears gush'd forth; and, gath'ring voice, he said,
His accents prefaced with a sigh: "O ye
So lov'd, so honor'd tablets of the dead,
In which my soul abides, o'er which my tears are shed!—

97. "Not of unliving dust are ye the shrine,
But Love's quick ashes, canonized by woe;
From you I catch his wonted fires divine,
Less sweet, less grateful, but as warm they glow;
Take the sad sighs and kisses I bestow,
Bathed in the fondest tears that ever bless'd
The grave of luckless beauty; take, and O
Convey each sigh breathed forth, each kiss impress'd,
To the beloved remains that in your bosom rest!

98. "For if to her fair spoils that fairest Saint
E'er gives a glance, thy pity and my love
Will not offend; since, neither can the taint
Of scorn or hatred reach the blest above;
She who forgave my crime, can ne'er reprove
My zeal,—this hope alone my tears can dry;
It was, she knows, my hand alone that drove
The murd'ring sword; nor can it irk that I,
Who lived adoring her, adoringly should die.

99. "And die adoring her I shall; blest day,
Whenever it arrives! but far more blest,
If as now round thy polish'd sides I stray,
I then be taken to thy sacred breast!
Ah! let our blending souls together rest
In Heaven, our ashes in the self-same tomb:
If I by death be of the bliss possess'd
Which life denied me,—might I but presume
This, this to hope indeed, delightful were my doom!"

100. Meanwhile in Salem, of Clorinda's fall
At first confused and floating whispers rise;
Till, ascertain'd and soon divulged, through all
Th' astonish'd City the loud rumor flies,
Mingled with tears, and shrieks, and women's cries:
As though the town itself, the sacred town,
Were now by storm become the victor's prize;
And in the rage of flying flames went down
Their temples, spires, abodes, and towers of old renown.

101. But every eye was on Arsetes turn'd,
Who stood, a piteous spectacle of care;
He not as others his dear mistress mourn'd;
His eyeballs, stony with supreme despair,
Shed not a tear; but fiercely did he tear
His face, his bosom, and with ashes strow'd
The hoary honors of his silver hair:
As thus he drew th' attention of the crowd,
Midst them Argantes came, and thus harangued aloud.

102. "Much did I wish, when conscious that the gate
Was closed against th' incomparable maid,
To follow straight,—I ran to share her fate,
Protect her life, or be beside her laid;
What did I not? what said I not? I pray'd,
Adjured the King, by all that was most dear,
T' unbar the gates: he, of the Franks afraid,
Denied my suit, though tender'd with a tear;
And, men of Syria! he has sole dominion here.

103. "Ah! had I then gone forth, or safe from strife
I the brave heroine had brought off, or closed
Where she has made earth purple, my sad life
In memorable decease, a glorious ghost!
But what could I do more? the starry host,
And counsels both of Gods and men were set
In adverse influence, to my wish opposed;
Cold in her grave the Virgin lies; but yet,
There are some mournful dues which I will ne'er forget.

104. "Hear, all Jerusalem, my vow! Heaven, hear!
And, if I fail my promise to fulfill,
Blast me with fire! deep, deep revenge I swear,
On the base Frank that did Clorinda kill!
Never from battle shall my sword lie still,
However fully flesh'd upon the foe;
Ne'er be dissever'd from my side, until
I stab cursed Tancred to the heart, and throw
His ruffian carcass out, to feed the hound and crow!"

105. The warrior ceased; and to his fierce harangue
From the soothed crowds applauding shouts succeed:
Hush'd their sore weeping, lost is every pang
In the mere fancy of th' expected deed.
O blind, presumptuous vow! far different seed
Than flow'ring hope imagines, to his scythe
Time will devote; thyself, thyself shalt bleed,
In equal battle bleed, and dying writhe
Beneath his sword o'er whom thou now exultest blithe!

END OF CANTO XII.

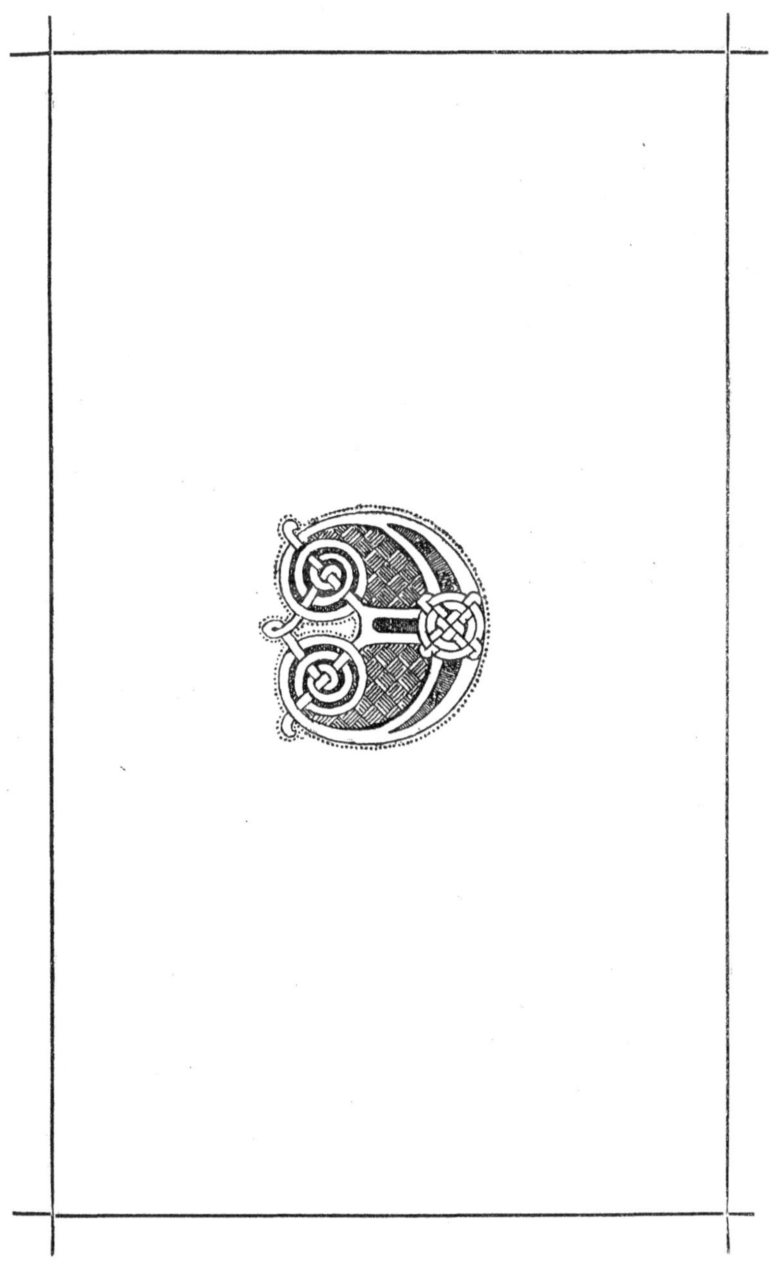

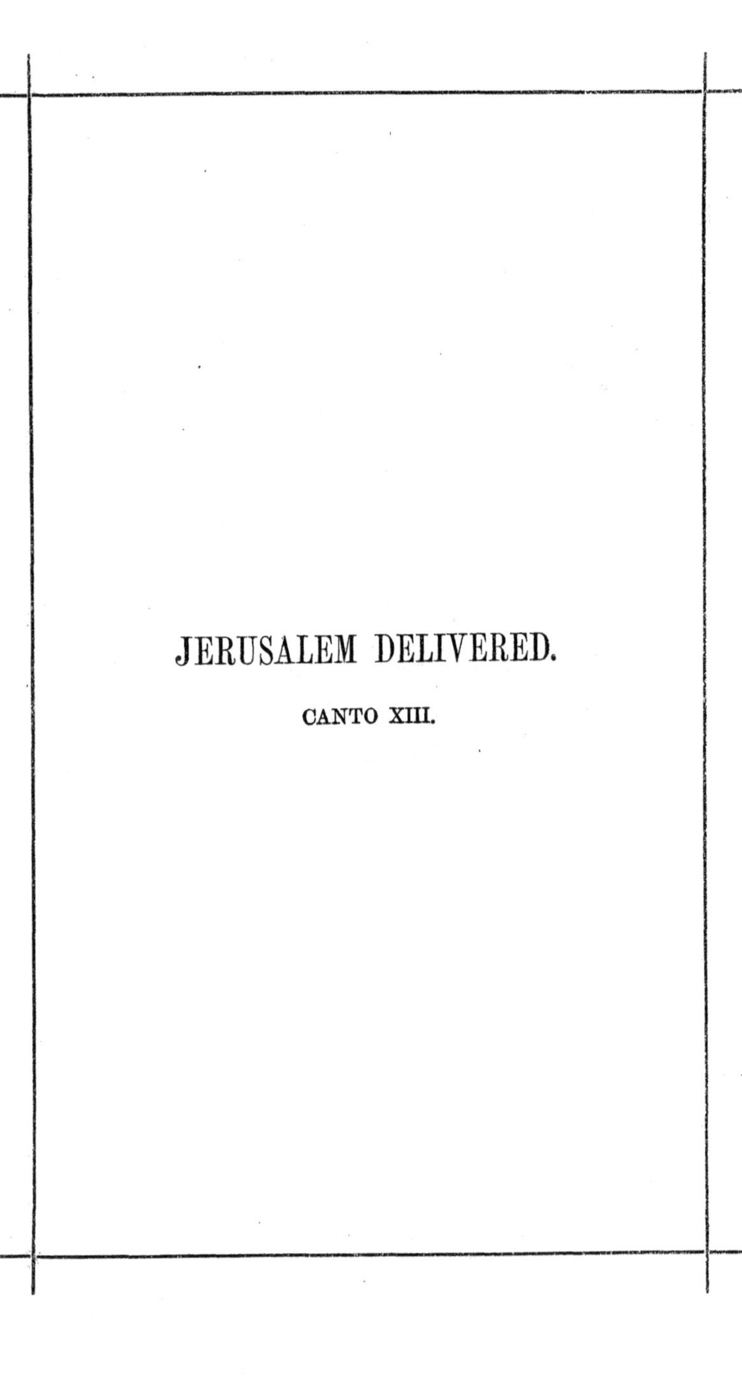

JERUSALEM DELIVERED.

CANTO XIII.

ARGUMENT

ISMENO frees the Demons of the Deep
To guard the forests ; the mere sight of these,
Scares from the regions they are set to keep,
The men who come to cut the shady trees :
There Tancred boldly ventures, and with ease
Enters the grove, but foolish love o'erpowers
His show of courage; meanwhile not a breeze
Stirs,—heat, excessive heat the earth devours,
And the sick camp decays, till blest with copious showers.

JERUSALEM DELIVERED.

CANTO XIII.

1. Scarce was the vast, tower-tempesting machine
   To ashes sunk, than, further to secure
   The City, respited from storm, Ismene
   New artifices plann'd, by rites impure,
   And added spells tremendous, to insure
   The army's ruin, and prevent the fall
   Of fresh materials from the groves obscure:
   That sò, no second store of engines tall
 Might Sion's gates bombard, or rend her sacred wall.

2. Near the encampment of the Christians, grows,
   Mid solitary valleys, old and vast,
   A forest, thick with mossy trees, whose boughs
   A solemn horror far in compass cast:
   There, when the golden sun at noon rides past
   In clearest glory, a discolor'd light,
   Malignant, such as falls from skies o'ercast,
   When night with day, or day disputes with night,
 Streams through its hoary glades, and daunts th' uncertain sight.

3. But when the sun departs, immediate clouds,
   And horror, black as hell, the place invade;
   Darkness which blinds the vision, and which crowds
   The heart with fears; for pasture or for shade,
   There never goat-herd drives his goats, dismay'd,
   Herdsman his herds; there never shepherds sound
   Their lively reeds; nor in its nodding glade
   Enter faint pilgrims, but with awe profound,
 Point as they pass, and shun far off th' unlucky ground.

4. Here at deep midnight, borne on clouds and storms,
   Foul witches gather to their blasted green,

Each with her mate, and take the frightful forms
Of dragon, pard, or bearded goat obscene ,
A council loathesome, infamous, unclean ;
That oft with false presentments and delights,
Allure from goodness : hither they convene,
To hold in pomp, by Hecate's pale lights,
Their impious marriage feasts and bacchanalian rites.

5. So goes belief ; and from its haunted bowers
Nor bough nor twig the natives ever rent ;
But these the Franks, since for their rams and towers
None others served, invade with one consent.
Here now the Sorcerer came, malevolent,
At next dead noon of night,—the hour that best
Suits his black science : not a whisper went
Through the wild woods, when, wrapp'd in coal-black vest,
His magic rounds he traced, his mystic signs impress'd.

6. One naked foot he in the charmed ring
Set, murm'ring mighty rhymes ; nor fail'd to turn
Thrice to the clime whence first the sunbeams spring;
Thrice to the region gaped where last they burn :
Thrice shook the wand that from the dreary urn
Calls buried phantoms to walk forth again
Incorporate ; three times gloomily and stern,
Stamp'd with his foot unshod : then spake he ; then,
Ran these tremendous words through each rebellowing glen.

7. "Hear ! hear, O ye, whom from the stars of yore
God's flashing thunders smote to deepest hell !
Hear, ye that walk the clouds ! hear, ye that pour
The storms abroad, and in the whirlwinds yell !
And you, dark elves of fog, of fire, and fell
Demons, and ghosts, and demogorgons dire !
Hear, all ye devils that in Avernus dwell,
Grim torturers of the damn'd ! and thou, their sire,
King of lost kings, that rul'st the shadowy world of fire.

8. "Guard well these groves : elm, cedar, ivy, oak,
I give you told and chronicled aright ;
As souls of men in bodies, I invoke
You so to haunt their branches, every sprite ;
Chase back with fury, or at least affright
Th' insulting Christians, soon as they essay
To reach and fell them !" many an impious rite,
Fell charm, and dreary spell the Wizard gray
Join'd, which 'twere sin to hear, and blasphemy to say.

9. At these fell words each bright star that adorns
The blue of midnight, quench'd its fires divine;
The moon, disturb'd, drew in her golden horns,
Cloak'd in black clouds, nor after dared to shine:
Incensed he turns, with aspect more malign,
And stamping shouts: "Not yet do ye appear,
Charged spirits? each to his appointed shrine!
Why this delay? perchance ye wait to hear
Voices more potent yet, and curses more severe!

10. "I have not yet forgot, from long disuse,
My cruel arts of more effectual fame;
This tongue, I know, can, blooded o'er, break loose
With perfect ease from its control, and frame
That so tremendous sound, that mighty Name,
Which heard, e'en Pluto must start up dismay'd,
And hither hurry from his throne of flame;
Which! oh, which if—" more yet he would have said,
But that he inly knew the summons was obey'd.

11. Infinite spirits numberless come down;
All that through air on Hell's drear errands flee,—
Ghosts of th' abyss, and elves from forests brown,
From cave, mine, fountain, fire, and roaring sea:
Slow, and still trembling at the late decree
Prohibiting from battle, comes and grieves
The universal swarm; but, bound to be
Seals of th' enchantment, each his charge receives,
Shrined in the mossy trunks, gray boughs, or flutt'ring leaves.

12. Straight to the King the Sorcerer, when aware
That the protecting charm was now complete,
Hied and exclaim'd: "Leave every doubt and care;
Thy heart refresh, and of enjoyment treat!
Henceforth in safety stands thy regal seat;
For never shall the Franks have power or heart
Their engines to renew,—so brave a feat
Have I perform'd;" thus glorying, part by part
He the success narrates of his mysterious art:—

13. Then thus continues: "With my spell the stars
Themselves are charm'd, to my no less delight;
Know, that in Heavenly Leo raging Mars
Must with the splendid sun erewhile unite
In blest conjunction, and with fever smite
The hostile armies; naught shall cool the glow,—
Winds, airs, nor rains by day, nor dews by night;

Since all the Influences in Heaven foreshow
A time of burning heat,—pain, wailing, want, and woe.

14\. "Drought more intolerable than e'er distress'd
Ind, or adust Zahara! us the heat
Will little harm, within a town so blest
With cool delights—fresh shades, and fountains sweet,
But most the sunbeams on our foes will beat;
Who, stretch'd on sands insuff'rable as they,
Denied refreshment, hopeless of retreat,
Will to th' Egyptians fall an easy prey,
First smit by Heaven, then swept like locusts clean away.

15\. "Thou, sitting still, shalt conquer; 'twere not wise
To tempt of Fortune then the doubtful smile;
But if the rash Circassian, who decries
All, even hon'rable repose, revile,
And importune thee in his usual style,
Find thou the means his willfulness to rein;
Since Heaven's kind Sov'reign shall to thee erewhile
Send peace, and to thy foes, consumed with pain,
The sword which, smiting once, need never smite again."

16\. Soothed by this speech, the King recovers heart,
And the whole force of Godfrey inly mocks;
He had already well repair'd in part
The walls late shatter'd by the ram's rude shocks;
The rest with iron cramps and mortised blocks
He now sécures; nor yet his cares relax;
Round him the total population flocks,—
Freeman, liege, slave,—on all he lays the tax
Of hard, unceasing toil; and warm their labors wax.

17\. Meantime the pious Prince resolved no more
To storm by force of arms the strengthen'd town,
Till rams and towers yet mightier than before,
Should with more sure success his prospects crown;
He therefore sent his soldiers to cut down
Fresh timber for the work: at morning light
They go; in mist the silent forests frown,—
But scarce their sable skirts appear in sight,
Than awe arrests their steps, and fills their souls with fright.

18\. As boys on ivied towers and haunted rooms
At fall of twilight dare not cast an eye,

Fancy a ghost in every thing that glooms,
And, hair on end, from the grim fancy fly:
So when beyond the hills these men descry
The hoar wood nodding to the wind's light wings,
Alarm'd, they turn and flee; unconscious why,
Unless that fear before their senses brings
Goblins, chimeras, ouphes, and all unholy things.

19. Back they return, sad, timid, trembling, pale,
Their words confused and various as their fears;
That not a soldier entertains their tale,
But turns to mirth the monstrous things he hears.
Indulgent Godfrey of his cavaliers
Sends a choice troop, in shining arms array'd,
Who, faced with boldness, strength'ning with their spears
The men from harm, might their faint souls persuade
To do his late commands, and pierce the tangled shade.

20. Approaching where, in blackest seats embower'd
Of savage shade, the wicked fiends fulfill
The wizard's charge, the gloomy forest lower'd
In sight,—they tremble, and their blood runs chill;
Yet onward they proceed, concealing ill
Their vile dismay beneath a lively face;
In sinuous windings they descend the hill;
And have so far advanced, that little space
Sep'rates their footsteps now from off th' enchanted place.

21. Sudden a sound comes from the wood, as when
Earth yawns, towers tremble, steadfast mountains quake,
South winds repine in Autumn's yellow glen,
And murm'ring billows on the shingles break:
The lion's roar, the hissings of the snake,
The night-wolf's howls are heard, the bear's low moans:
Trumpets and thunders, whisp'rings that awake
Hideous alarms, and melancholy groans—
All speak in that one sound, though under various tones.

22. The cheeks of all grew pale as death; their fear
A thousand guilty signs declared too plain;
Nor discipline could nerve, nor reason cheer,—
They neither could advance, nor durst remain:
Weak were their efforts, their protection vain
Against the secret influence that confused

Their pride, their courage, and their self-disdain ;
At length they fled : their boldest, introduced
To Godfrey's presence, spoke, and thus their flight excused :

23. "Signior ! not one of us can longer vaunt
The power or will those guarded woods to fell :
Spirits I swear posses each moving plant ;
There grisly Pluto has transferr'd all hell.
The heart that fearless ventures where they dwell,
Must be of diamond, diamond to the core ;
But none save madmen, scornful of the spell
That guards the entrance, would the depths explore,
So loud the savage grove rebellows to their roar."

24. Thus went his tale. Among the curious crowd
That gather'd round, by chance Alcasto stood,
Who both at death and danger laugh'd aloud,
Rash, stupid, stern, and obstinate of mood ;
Not the wild lion roaring o'er his brood,
Nor aught that seems tremendous to mankind,
Ghost, dragon, murd'rer, wizard of the wood,
Lightning, nor earthquake could appall his mind,
Nor aught that haunts the flood, or walks the roaring wind.

25. He toss'd his haughty head, and smiling cried :
"Thither whence this man shrinks let me repair ;
I will invade the peopled wood with pride,
Despite its hollow sounds and shapes of air :
No grinning goblin shall my spirit scare,
Nor roar of boughs around, nor scream o'erhead
Of savage birds ; most freely will I dare
Its frightful glooms and tangled paths to tread,
Though through the throat of hell descending to the dead."

26. He waved his armed hand, and with a proud
Contempt stalk'd off ; the wood was soon in view ;
Soon the strange roar was heard, rebellowing loud,
The timbrels rang, the dreary trumpets blew ;
Yet not a step th' audacious man withdrew ;
Secure and scornful as at first, he sought
An open glade of pine and spreading yew ;
The charmed soil he trod,—when, swift as thought,
Upsprang a guardian fire, and with th' intruder fought.

27. Wide and aloft the smoking fires extend,
And, in the form of high embattled walls,
Gird the green wood and from his blade defend,
That not the slend'rest branch or sapling falls;
The loftier flames roll into gorgeous halls
Fantastically tower'd, and fortified
With warlike engines darting sulph'rous balls,
To guard this new Gehenna; while, more wide,
Rocks climb'd the clouds, with gold and burning crimson dyed.

28. O, what strange monsters, arm'd, in guard appear
On the tall battlements! a hideous row!
Glare with their Gorgon eyes, and frequent rear
Their clashing arms, with many a menaced blow!
At length he fled; and though his flight was slow
As the grim lion's when in distant chase
Held by the hunter, still he fled the foe:
Sad fear—till then a thing unknown, found place
Within his boist'rous heart, and paled his daring face.

29. Nor was he conscious that he fled, e'en yet;
But when to distance he had gone, disdain—
A wild amazement, anguishing regret,
And deep repentance stung his fretful brain:
Crimsoning 'twixt shame and grief, he pass'd the plain
Turn'd from the crowd his devious steps aside;
And, stealing to his tent, essay'd in vain
From human eyes his downcast face to hide—
That face, so late the seat of all-despising pride.

30. To Godfrey call'd, he lingers, makes delays,
And tries to shun the summons, all he can;
Forced, he at length arrives, but nothing says,
Or wildly babbles like a sleeping man:
Well in his falt'ring speech, and face now wan,
Now flush'd with shame unusual, Godfrey saw
Flight and defeat; and "How," he thus began,
"Is this? or is it witchcraft strikes this awe,
Or Nature's high portents, transcending Nature's law?

31. "But if there yet be one whose noble breast
To pierce the grove with brave ambition beats,
Free let him try th' adventure, and at least
Bring news more certain from its dark retreats."
Thus spake the Duke: and thrice those savage seats
Were tried, successive days, at his desire,
By chiefs most famed for high romantic feats;

Yet forced, yet fain was each one to retire,
Scared by the sounds, the sights, the monsters, and the fire.

32. This chanced while Tancred paid the last sad rite
To his loved lady: weak he was, and pale;
His eyes still sicken'd at the cheerful light,
His steps were feeble, and his members frail;
Ill could he bear the weight of helm or mail;
Yet now, since all his wish'd assistance claim,
Nor toil deters him, nor can danger quail;
Warm to his heart fresh life with courage came,
New strung his sinewy joints, and fortified his frame.

33. He, silent, calm, collecting all his soul,
Fearless, yet heedful, sought the forest vast;
And the drear aspect of the wood, the roll
Of thunder, clouds, the earthquake and the blast,
Firmly sustain'd, amazed, but not aghast;—
His heart a little moment beat more high,
But sank as soon; and forward still he pass'd:
When, sudden, in the sylvan region nigh,
The fiery city rose, whose turrets touch'd the sky.

34. Back stepp'd the Prince, and made a moment's pause,
Inly debating: "What will arms serve here?
In the devouring flames and monsters' jaws
Shall I leap headlong then? yet wherefore fear!
Ne'er will the brave man count his life too dear,
When public good the sacrifice demands;
But neither will he draw too rashly near
The scene where Ruin with a hundred hands
Deals death; and surely such is this which here expands.

35. Yet, if I fly, what will our armies say?
What other forest can they hope to fell?
Will Godfrey cease th' adventure to essay?
And shall another break th' unholy spell?
This fire, although the simile of hell,
May be in fact less fierce, by fiends prepared
To daunt, not harm;—whichever way, 'tis well;
Let the worst come!" this said, with blade unbared,
He through th' eruption leap'd,—O, risk divinely dared.

36. He felt no raging heat, no fervent glow,
His arms undimm'd, unscorch'd his naked face;
If real flame, or glitt'ring fairy show,

He knew not rightly, in so short a space;
For, soon as touch'd, the visionary blaze—
Turrets, domes, towers, and apparitions drear,
Melted in mist, blue mist, that in their place
Brought glooms and clouds; the wind and tempest near
Hail'd, thunder'd, howl'd,—dispersed, and Heaven again shone clear.

37 Amazed, but still intrepid, Tancred stood;
And, when the echoing storm at distance died,
Trod with slow steps secure th' unhallow'd wood,
And all its hoary scenes and secrets eyed;
No farther signs or prodigies he spied;
Nor elf before, nor goblin glared behind;
Naught gave prevention, access naught denied,
Save the gray trees, that, thickly intertwined,
His steps entangled oft, and oft his sight confined.

38. He reach'd at length a fair and spacious plot,
Shaped like a circus; in whose center waved
One single tree—a cypress, that upshot
Like a green pyramid to Heaven, and braved
The winds with beauty; sweetest flow'rets paved
The mossy floor: the prospect he perused;
Advanced, and saw on the smooth rind engraved,
Symbols like those mysterious Egypt used,
Long ere her graphic art young Greece had introduced.

39. Mid these dark types, some Syriac words appear'd,
A tongue to him familiar,—thus they ran:
"O thou, who in these aisles of death hast dared
To place thy glorying foot, audacious man!
Ah! if thou be not under pity's ban,
Cruel as bold, disquiet not, nor tread
This secret seat; but, if thy spirit can,
Pardon the hapless souls to darkness wed;
Why shouldst thou come to fight,—the living with the dead!"

40. Thus spake th' inscription: while in pensive mood
He sought their mystic sense, he heard behind,
Amidst the leaves of the enchanted wood
And weeping boughs above, the serious wind
Frame a low melancholy dirge, that pined
Sadly harmonious, sounding in his ear
Like human sighs; a sound, that in his mind
Instill'd I know not what confusedly dear
Of pity, pain divine, sweet grief, and sweeter fear.

41. He drew his sword at length, and with full force
Struck the tall tree; O wonderful! the wound,
As bursts a fountain from its sylvan source,
Gush'd forth with blood, and crimson'd all the ground.
Chill horror seized the knight: yet, fix'd to sound
The mystery to its depth, and desp'rate grown,
Again he struck; when, hollow and profound,
As from a vaulted grave, in piteous tone,
Murm'ring within he heard a spirit deeply moan.

42. "Too much already, Tancred, has thy blade
Wrong'd me!" the sad voice feebly made exclaim;
"My late so happy home didst thou invade,
And rudely drive my spirit from the frame,
In and through which it lived: why wilt thou maim
Still the poor trunk to which my doom unbless'd
Binds me? can wrath so far the heart inflame,
Cruel! that in their shrouds thou must molest
Thy foes, when Death has seal'd, and reverences their rest?

43. "I was Clorinda: nor does her sad sprite
Alone in heart of oak or cypress dwell.
But ev'ry other Frank or Pagan knight,
That before Salem in proud battle fell,
Is here by magic's most mysterious spell
Immanacled, I know not if to say
In vital body, or funereal cell;
With sense the trunks, with life the branches play:
And thou a murd'rer art, if thou one sapling slay."

44. As a sick man, that in his sleep perceives
Some fiery dragon or chimera grim;
Though he suspects, or firmly e'en believes
That the whole show is but a feverish dream,
Yet strives to fly, with many a shriek and scream,
Such fright the dire and horrid semblance breeds!
So, though th' enamor'd knight cannot but deem
False the sad voice that for his pity pleads,
He yet th' illusion fears; and trembles, and recedes.

45. At once pain, pity, love, fear, grief, surprise,
Rush o'er his heart; half frenzied and unmann'd,
Cold on his brow the dew of horror lies,
And the sword falls from his relaxing hand:
He sees in thought his murder'd lady stand,
Weeping, imploring him with groans to spare
Her suff'ring tree, and sheath his dreadful brand;

Nor can his harrow'd fancy longer bear
To view her gushing blood, and hear her piteous prayer.

46. Thus he on whose brave heart no blind alarm
Of danger or of death could e'er intrude,
Powerless and soft alone at Love's deep charm,
A spirit false did with vain plaints delude :
Meanwhile a whirlwind, roaring from the wood,
Caught up his sword, and bore it out of ken
Through the dark grove ; the warrior, thus subdued,
At length retired ; and from the bosky glen
Issuing, his falchion found, and gladly grasp'd again.

47. Yet durst he not return, to pierce anew
Of these mysterious bowers the shadowy screen,
But as to Godfrey's presence near he drew,
Call'd back his spirits, and composed his mien ;
Then thus address'd him : " Listen ! I have seen
Things passing all belief ; things which to you
Will sound like fables ! of the forest green
The tales you have been told—the dreary view,
And loud appalling sounds, in ev'ry point are true.

48. " First rose a wondrous fire, self-kindled, bright,
Rose in an instant, building high and wide
Towers, whereon, arm'd and shielded for the fight,
Whole hosts of monsters all access denied :
Yet these I pass'd, unharm'd, unterrified
Or by the brandish'd blades, or volumed train
Of the fierce flames,—they vanish'd, when defied :
Night fell, winds roar'd, rain dash'd ; but straight again
Day smiled, the winds were hush'd, and sunshine chased the rain.

49 " Yet more ! with feeling, life, and speech indued,
A human spirit in each tree is shrined ;
I heard one feebly wailing in the wood,
That wild, sad voice, still, still it haunts my mind :
While, as though actual flesh the members lined
Of ev'ry hoary trunk and sapling spray,
Blood at each stroke ran trickling from the rind ;
I own myself subdued, nor dare essay
Again the bark to strip, or rend one branch away."

50. While thus he speaks, a tide of tossing thought
Absorbs the soul of Godfrey ; what if he
In his own person the enchantment sought,

And with his scepter made those demons flee,
Which, as he judged, by power of sorcery
Possess'd the forest! or should he provide
Elsewhere his timbers, which perchance might be,
If from a distance, with more ease supplied?
Him from this trance of thought the hermit roused and cried:

51. "Forego thy daring fancy: other hands
Must from yon forest cut the charmed trees;
Lo, on the far, the solitary sands
Grates the doom'd bark, and gathers from the breeze
Her golden sails! from loose inglorious ease,
Love's siren chains and zoneless Beauty's bribes,
Th' expected Knight his captive spirit frees;
And soon will come the time which Heaven prescribes
For Sion's destined fall, despite her guardian tribes!"

52. He spake with voice seraphic; while his face
Shone with a light approaching to divine:
Godfrey to his prophetic words gave place,
And turn'd his thoughts, which never lie supine,
To other projects; but the radiant sign
Of Cancer now receives the sun, which foils
His schemes, and traverses each wise design:
Heat, unremitted heat the clime embroils,
And wearying, quite unfits his host for martial toils.

53. Th' Elysian Pleïads quench their friendly lamps;
In Heaven's blue sphere swart planets tyrannize;
Whence streams an influence, that informs, and stamps
On air th' impression of their baleful dies;
More and more sultry grow the noxious skies;
Yet wide and wider sickness sheds its seeds;
More mortal heats descend, and vapors rise;
To torturing day more torturing night succeeds;
And still the next, and next, superior mischief breeds.

54. The glimm'ring Sun ne'er issues from the deep,
But roseate mists his angry face inclose;
Ne'er sets, but tears of blood his eyeballs weep, —
Tears, of a tincture that too well foreshows
A melancholy morrow doom'd to close
With the like drops, sweat from his sanguine veins,
Threat'ning to rise more fierce than last he rose,
And sharp'ning thus the sufferings each sustains,
With long foretasted griefs, and dread of future pains.

55. Then when at noon he darts his radiance down,
In compass far as mortal eye surveys,
The fair flowers languish, the green turf turns brown,
The leaves fall yellow from their sapless sprays ;
Earth gapes in chinks ; th' exhausted fountain plays
No more its music ; shrunk the streams and lakes,
He subjects all things to his ardent rays ;
The barren cloud, in air expanded, takes
Semblance of sheeted fire, and parts in scarlet flakes.

56. Heaven seems a sable furnace : not a thing
Speaks freshness to the sight ; the frolicsome
Sweet Zephyr, silent, waving not a wing,
His grotto keeps ; mellifluous air is dumb.
Not a bird's flutt'ring, not an insect's hum,
Breaks the still void ; or on its sultry gloom
If winds intrude, 'tis only such as come
From the hot sands, Sirocco or Simoom,
Which, blown in stifling gusts, the springs of life consume.

57. Nor brings the Night more comfort : on her shade
The glowing Sun his radiant impress leaves ;
With comets, lightnings, and the golden braid
Of other kindling fires her veil she weaves ;
Thee too, sad Earth, the niggard Moon bereaves
Of her delightful dew-drops ! not as erst
In amorous song her Druid minstrel grieves ;
And all the wild-wood bells and blossoms thirst
For the moist juice which late their fragrant spirits nursed.

58. Through these unquiet nights, sweet Sleep, exiled,
Fled from the languid lids of weeping men ;
Nor would by amorous courtship be beguiled,
Or flatt'ring words, to spread his wings again :
But yet their worst of evils was the pain,
The rage of thirst : Judea's impious king
With secret herbs, and drugs of deadlier grain
Than Styx or sable Acheron could wring
From their malignant waves, had poison'd every spring.

59. And Siloa's brook, that, gliding clear and swift,
Gave affluent beverage to the Franks before,
Has now no fresh'ning virtue in its gift,
Scarce with warm waves o'erspreads its sandy floor.
Not the broad Po in May, when amplest pour
His floods, nor Ganges, which the Indian deems

A God, nor seven-mouth'd Nile, when floating o'er
Green Egypt's boundless plains with even streams,
To their inflamed desires at all superfluous seems.

60. If any e'er 'twixt shady woods had seen
Cool glassy lakes in liquid silver sleep,
Quick fountains, bubbling up from mosses green,
Slide down smooth hills, brooks querulously creep
O'er lustrous stones, or Alpine torrents leap
Roaring from Heaven, he paints them o'er and o'er
To his enamor'd wish, sweet, icy, deep,
And, tasting them in fancy, tortures more
A heart already fired, tormented to its core.

61. Warriors robust, whose frames of sturdiest mold,
Not the long march through asp'rous regions rude,
Nor iron mails that aye their limbs infold,
Nor weapons thirsting for their death, subdued,—
Tamed by the sultry heat, with sweat imbrued,
Lie both a burden to themselves, and prey;
Faint, weak, dissolved in idlest lassitude,
A secret fire lives in their veins, whose ray
Eats by degrees their flesh, and melts their bones away.

62. Sickens the late fierce steed; untasted, loathed,
Stands his once relish'd, once saluted corn;
The dancing mane and neck with thunder clothed,
But late superbly in the battle borne,
Droops to the ground; the pride of laurels worn
No more dilates his nostrils, swells his veins;
Glory his hatred, vict'ry seems his scorn;
His rich caparisons, embroider'd reins,
And sumptuous trophies, all—as baubles he disdains.

63. Sickens the faithful dog, and for his lord
And once beloved abode no longer cares;
Couchant he lies, by inward furies gnaw'd,
And, scorch'd, gapes momently for lighter airs;
But respiration, though it oft repairs
Nature's disorders, and corrects the fire
In feverish bosoms, charm'd from healing, bears
Not now the cool refreshment they require;
So hot and stifling blow the breezes they inspire.

64. Thus languishes the earth; in this estate
The wretched troops lie sick'ning in their tents;
And, desp'rate grown of vict'ry, meditate
What deadlier ills must crown these dire events:

On every side the spacious camp presents
Some dreadful scene ; on every side the noise
Is heard of murmurs, weepings, and laments ;
"What more hopes Godfrey?" cry they with one voice ;
"Waits he till hasting death the total camp destroys?

65. "Ah! with what forces does he hope to be
Lord of these towers? whence now his rams and vines
Can he expect? does he alone not see
Heaven's wrath reveal'd against our rash designs?
By thousand prodigies and thousand signs
To us its adverse spirit stands display'd ;
While on our heads the sun so hotly shines,
That not the Indian, or the Ethiop laid
On burning sands, more needs refreshment, showers, and shade!

66. "Thinks he it then a thing of no concern,
That we, a worthless and neglected train,
Vile, useless myrmidons, to death should burn,
That he his kingly scepter may maintain?
And seems it then so great a bliss to reign,
That man should guard it at a price so high?
That he should seek his empire to retain
With soul so greedy, when, before his eye,
Of his own subjects thus such numbers faint or die?

67. "Mark the said pious Prince, his insight deep,
Humane to aid, prophetic to purvey!
Our good he quite forgets, so he can keep
His hurtful honor and vain-glorious sway:
He sees both streams and fountains waste away
From us, yet for himself cool waters sweet
Brings from far Jordan ; and at banquets gay,
With a few Magnates, shaded from the heat,
Mingles the fresh clear wave with costly wines from Crete!"

68. Thus the Franks murmur'd ; but the Grecian guide,
Long weary of the war, aloud repined :
"And why should I or my brave troops," he cried,
"Stay to be stifled by this scorching wind?
If Godfrey will be so insanely blind,
Let him and his obsequious people look
To the result! are we to be combined
In their destruction?"—no farewell he took ;
But in the silent night, silent the camp forsook.

69. This base desertion with the morning star
Was clearly seen, and wide th' infection spread;
Those who the pastoral voice of Ademar
Lately obey'd, the troops Clotharius led,
And other chiefs now number'd with the dead,
Freed from their oaths of duty by the Power
That of all human ties dissolves the thread,
Already treat of flight ; and some, the flower
Thereof, at once depart, at midnight's shadowy hour.

70. This Godfrey saw, and had been swift to take
Judgment's just dues, but such his soul abhorr'd ;
And, full of living faith, faith which can make
Hills move, and floods stand steadfast, he implored
In deep devotion earth's almighty Lord,
That he his ancient mercies would reveal,
And shed the fountains of his grace abroad ;
His hands he clasp'd, and, full of sacred zeal,
Thus with eyes raised to Heaven, to Heaven he made appeal.

71. "Father and Lord ! if in a thirsty land
Thou on thy hosts e'er rain'd ambrosial dew,
E'er with thy power indued a mortal hand,
To smite the flinty rocks, till, cleft in two,
They gush'd with living streams, O now renew
On these the like sure mercies ! and if we
Seem less deserving in thy holy view,
Thy grace that want supply ! that all may see
They are thy warriors still, and call'd, O Lord, by thee!"

72. These prayers sincere, derived from a desire
Upright and humble, were not slow, but light
And swift as winged turtles, to the Sire
Of men and seraphs took their instant flight :
Th' Eternal heard, and from his holy height,
On his faint hosts, as o'er his suff'ring child
A sympathizing parent, cast his sight,
In looks where pity beam'd, where mercy smiled,
And thus in gracious words, benevolent and mild :

73. "Till now these dear and faithful hosts of mine
Have suffer'd peril, pain, fatigue, and woe ;
'Gainst them, with arms and secret arts malign,
The world around and powers of hell below
Have both conspired to work their overthrow ;
Now a new series of events shall run ;
Smooth to the end shall their adventure flow :

Let rains descend, return Bertoldo's son,
And Egypt's hosts arrive, to grace his laurels won!"

74. He bow'd his head: the Heavens with all their hosts,
The fix'd, the wand'ring stars in their bright stations,
Shook at the sign; shook hills, and seas, and coasts,
And Orcus trembled to its deep foundations.
Instant from north to east swift coruscations
Flash'd through the skies, and with a golden sound
Roll'd the clear thunder; with glad shouts the nations
Hail the bright shining, hail'd the roll profound,
And wonder, hope, and joy in every heart abound.

75. Lo! sudden clouds, not those exhaled from earth
By the sun's rays, but from the Heavens—that rend,
And all their secret springs unlock, take birth,
Collect, combine, and fast to earth descend:
The glooms of night, ere noon is at an end,
Surprise the day; and, spreading quickly o'er
Th' encompass'd world, all things in shadow blend;
Then swell the winds, the rains impetuous pour,
And, o'er their banks escaped, the brooks and fountains roar.

76. As in the burning heats of summer, when
At length the long-wish'd rains of Heaven descend,
A flight of babbling wild-ducks in the fen,
With hoarse glad cries the coming shower attend;
Spread their dry wings to the cool moisture, bend
Their gray necks back to wet the thirsty bill,
And proyne their plumes, and as the waters blend
Into a pool, hoarse-chatt'ring, clamoring still,
Rush, duck, and flounce, and dive, and quaff the waves at will;

77. So they with glad huzzas the showers salute,
Which Heaven, in answer to their Chief's request,
Pours down in bounty; noc a voice is mute;
This one his tresses, that one soaks his vest:
From glasses some, some from their helms with zest
Quench their deep thirst; in the fresh wave profuse
Some lave their faces, some their brows; the rest,
More prudent, vases, urns, and ewers produce,
And the mellifluous streams store up for future use.

78. Nor is the drooping spirit of mankind
Alone rejoiced and eased of all its pains;
But Earth, of late afflicted, scorch'd, and pined,

A like refreshment and repose obtains :
Her chinks by virtue of the falling rains
Are closed, renew'd her vegetative powers ;
And the rich moisture through her inmost veins
Received, she ministers in plenteous showers,
To her reviving shrubs, and freshly-smelling flowers.

79. As a sick maid, when sprightly balms appease
The fever, late that scorch'd her life away,
Now disencumber'd of the long disease
That made her beauty its repast and prey,
Strengthens, revives, and flourishes as gay
As when her cheek with brightest roses bloom'd,—
So Earth, forgetful of her late decay,
The griefs and ills that had her strength consumed,
Joyful her flow'ry crowns and garlands green resumed.

80. The rains are o'er, the sun returning glows,
But with a sweet, benign, and temp'rate ray,
Yet full of virtual power, as at the close
Of show'ry April or the birth of May.
O faith divine ! the Good and Just who pray
In thy devoted strength, can dissipate
Infectious airs, malignant heats allay,
The series of the seasons change, abate
The rage of angry stars, and vanquish Time and Fate !

END OF CANTO XIII.

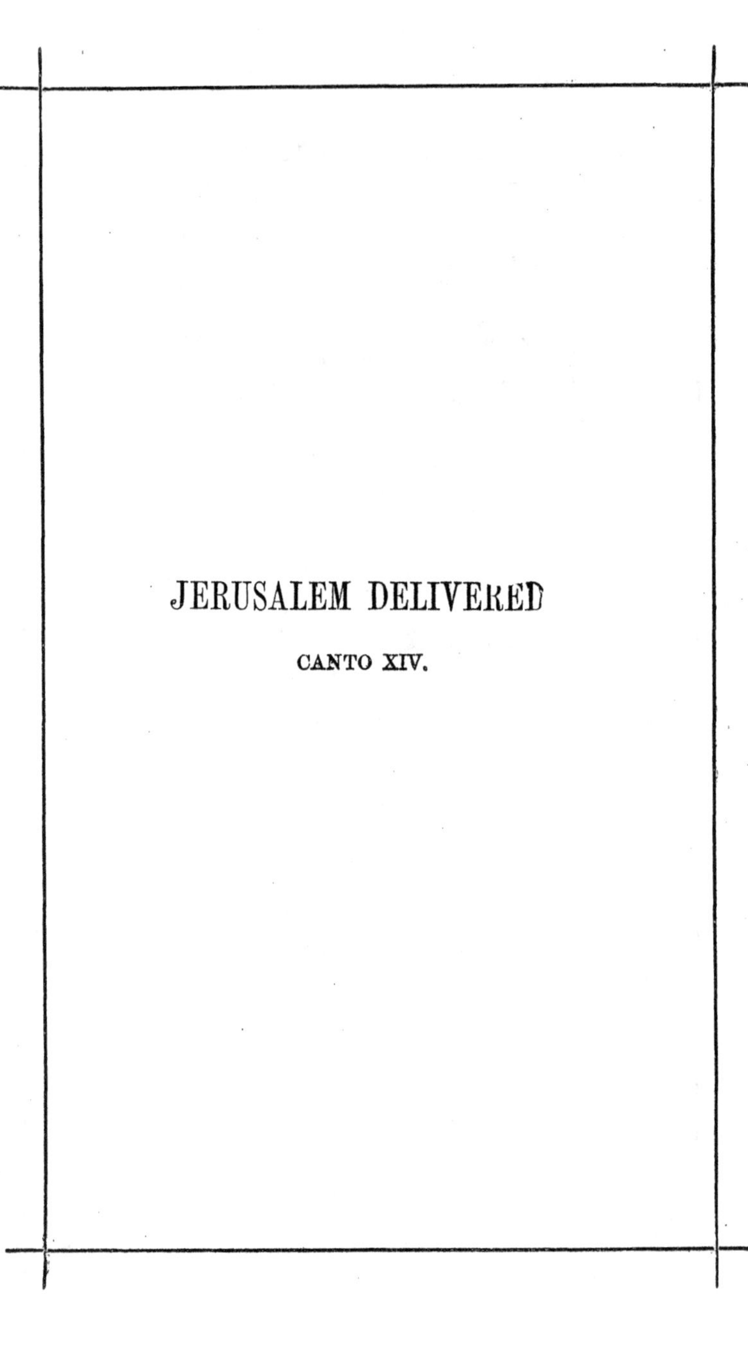

JERUSALEM DELIVERED

CANTO XIV.

ARGUMENT.

Godfrey, in vision rapt to Paradise,
Is warn'd of God to call back to the host
The good Rinaldo, wherefore he replies,
When his recall the princes have proposed,
With favor ; Peter, whom the Holy Ghost
Had previously instructed, now prepares
To send two knights where on the nigh sea-coast
A courteous wizard lives, who first declares
To them Armide's deceits, then how to 'scape her snares.

JERUSALEM DELIVERED.

CANTO XIV.

1. Now from the soft fresh lap and twilight bower
Of her still mother flew the gentle Queen
Of Shade, with light airs compass'd, and a shower
Of starlight dews, pure, precious, and serene;
And, shaking o'er the universal scene
The humid border of her veil, impearl'd
With honey-balm the flowers and forests green;
While the sweet zephyrs their still wings unfurl'd,
And fann'd to dulcet sleep and peace th' o'erwearied world.

2. Each busy thought of rude disturbing day
In sweet oblivious quietude was drown'd;
But He, whose wisdom Heaven and earth doth sway,
Yet kept his ruling watch, insphered and crown'd
With ceaseless light; and from Heaven's starry round
Casting on Godfrey the ecstatic beam
Of his mild eye, to him in sleep profound,
By silent precept of a mission'd dream,
Of his Almighty Mind reveal'd the will supreme.

3. In the rich Orient, near the valves of gold
Whence the Sun sallies, turns a crystalline
Clear gate, whose doors in harmony unfold,
Ere pale the planets, and the day-beams shine:
'Tis thence the glorious dreams which the Divine
In grace to pure and holy spirits sends,
Issuing fly forth; from that pictorial shrine
This dream to pious Godfrey now descends,
And o'er his placid face its radiant wings extends.

4. Nor dream nor gifted vision e'er portray'd
Such beautiful or lively forms, as here

To Godfrey's fancy this, which now display'd
Of Heaven and of its stars the secrets clear;
As in the mirror of a glassy sphere,
All was at once presented to his sight
That in them is, he seem'd, in swift career,
Caught up to an expanse of perfect white,
Adorn'd with thousand flames that gave a golden light.

5. Here, as the moving spheres, the vast blue sky,
The lights, and the rich music he admires,
Lo, to his side a winged knight draws nigh,
With sunbeams crown'd, and circumfused with fires!
And in a voice to which the clearest choirs
And perfect marriage of sweet sounds below,
Breathed out from beauteous lips or golden wires,
Would be but discord, said: "Canst thou bestow
No smile, or dost thou not thy once-loved Hugo know?"

6. To which the Duke replied: "That aspect new,
Which like the glowing sun so brightly shines,
Has dazzled so my intellectual view,
That it can ill recall its ancient lines:"
And saying this, to greet him he inclines;
Thrice with a fond affectionate embrace
Around his neck his loving arms he twines;
And thrice th' encircled form and radiant face
Fly like a summer cloud, or shade the sunbeams chase.

7. Prince Hugo smiled; "And think not, as of old,"
He said, "that earthly robes my limbs invest;
My naked spirit here dost thou behold,
A simple shape; I dwell, a glorious guest,
In this th' illumined City of the Bless'd:
This is the temple of our God, th' abode
Of his true knights; and here thou too shalt rest:"
"Ah, when?" he cried; "if aught in me this mode
Of bliss obstruct, loose now, O loose th' encumb'ring load!"

8. "Soon!" replied Hugo; "soon in glory thou
Shalt gather'd be to our triumphant band;
But many a laurel first must grace thy brow,
Much blood be shed by thy victorious hand;
The Pagan armies yet thou must withstand,
And from their grasp by many a toilsome deed
Wresting the scepter of the Holy Land,
Fix the Frank empire; then it is decreed,
That to thy gentle rule thy brother shall succeed.

9. "But now look round more fixedly ; behold—
To quicken for the skies thy pure desires,
These lucid halls and starry orbs of gold,
Which, whirling round, th' Eternal Mind inspires!
Observe the beauty of those siren choirs
Of seraphs ; hear th' angelical sweet strains,
In concord sung to their celestial lyres ;
Next view," he said, and pointed to the plains
Of earth, below, "what yon terrestrial globe contains.

10. "Think of your earthly titles and designs ;
With what a vile reward is virtue crown'd!
Mark what a little ring your pride confines!
What naked deserts your vain glories bound!
Earth like an island the blue sea flows round.
Now, call'd the Mighty Deep from coast to coast,
Now, the vast Ocean ; to that pompous sound
Naught corresponds, to auth'rize such a boast—
'Tis but a shallow pool, a narrow marsh at most."

11. The Spirit said : and he his sight let fall
On earth, and smiled with a serene disdain ;
Shrunk to a point, seas, streams, and mountains tall
He sees, remote, but here distinguish'd plain ;
And much he wonder'd that weak man should strain
At shades and mists, that swim before his eyes,
And chase those radiant bubbles of the brain—
Capricious Fame, and Power, that, follow'd, flies,
Nor heed th' inviting voice that calls him to the skies.

12. Wherefore he answer'd : "Since not yet thy God
Is pleased to call me from this cage of clay,
Which path of life is safest to be trod
Mid Earth's erroneous windings, deign to say."
Hugo replied : "The least fallacious way
To happiness, indeed th' alone sure track
Is that thou walkest ; turn not then astray ;
Alone I would advise thee, be not slack
From his far exile now to call Rinaldo back.

13. "For, as by Providence divine to thee
The golden scepter, the supreme command
Of that adventure is consign'd, so he
As sov'reign agent of thy schemes, must stand
Assistant to the task : the first and grand
Office is thine ; the second the Most High
Concedes to him ; he is the army's hand,
And thou the head,—none other can supply
His place, not e'en thyself, thy state does this deny.

14. "He, he alone has license to cut down
The forest guarded by such magic art;
From him thy troops, despairing of the town
From the deserters they have seen depart,
On flight themselves debating, shall take heart,
And, nerved with livelier strength by the mere sight
Of one so valiant, fresh for conquest start;
The bulwarks he shall shatter, scale their height,
And the vast Memphian hosts o'erpower in mortal fight."

15. He ceased, and Godfrey answer'd; "His return
Would be most grateful to my feelings: thou,
Who every secret purpose dost discern,
Know'st if I love him, as I here avow;
But say, what offers must I make him? how
Sooth his vex'd spirit? where my heralds send?
Wilt thou that I for his recall allow
Courtship, or use command? declare, blest friend,
How I to make this suit may fitly condescend."

16. "God," in reply th' angelic spirit said,
"Who with such high regards thy rank has graced,
Wills, that to thee all reverence yet be paid
By those who under thy command are placed;
Show thou not then facility nor haste;
Make no request; for, haply, this would lead
To scorn, and thus thy dignity, debased,
Might fall into contempt; but ask'd, concede
And yield, when first thy knights shall for forgiveness plead.

17. "Guelph shall petition thee (by God inspired)
T' absolve the headstrong youth of that offense,
To which intemp'rate wrath his spirit fired,
That he to honor may return; dispense
Thy grace; and though in loosest indolence
And love intoxicate, he now reclines
On a far foreign shore, doubt not but thence
He will return, ere many a morning shines,
Apt for thy pressing needs and difficult designs.

18. "Your Hermit Peter, to whose piercing sight
Heaven of its secrets gives perception clear,
Shall thy sent messengers direct aright,
Where certain tidings they of him shall hear;
The sage to whose abode their ship must steer,
Will show the arts and methods they must use
To free, and home conduct the wand'ring peer;

Thus Heaven at length shall, partial to thy views,
Beneath the sacred Cross each errant chief reduce.

19. "Farewell! yet ere I end, hear one brief thing,
Which will, I know, delight thy noble mind;
Your blood shall mix, and from that union spring
A glorious issue, dear to all mankind!"[10]
He said; and like a cloud before the wind,
Or azure mist upon the mountain's crest
By the hot shining of the sun refined,
Vanish'd away; sleep fled, and left his breast
With wonder and deep joy confusedly possess'd.

20. His eyes he opes, and sees the Orient blaze
With the high-risen Aurora; from repose
He starts, in iron robes his limbs arrays,
And o'er his back the purple mantle throws;
Then takes his seat; for, soon as morning glows,
To his pavilion throng the knights of state,
In customary council to expose
Their sentiments, and of the war debate;
Thither they all were met, and round in silence sate.

21. Then Guelph arose, full of the new design
Which had his mind inspired, and drawing near,
To Godfrey thus made suit: "O, Prince benign,
What I propose receive with favoring ear!
I come to ask, with all thy nobles here,
Grace for a crime, and, if it must be said,
A crime yet recent; whence it may appear,
Perchance, that my request is hasty made,
In an untimely hour, ere yet maturely weigh'd.

22. "But when I think that to a Prince so mild
My suit is proffer'd, and for whose brave sake,
That, too, the intercessor is not viled
Nor mean of rank, I cannot choose but take
The prayer for granted, which will surely make
All happy, and obtain deserved applause;
Recall Rinaldo! I my honor stake
That he his blood will, in the common cause,
Shed to redeem his fault, and satisfy the laws.

23. "What daring hand but his those haunted bowers,
So fear'd, shall e'er successfully assail?
Who, of a firmer heart, more vig'rous powers,
May hope the risks of death to countervail?
Thou shalt behold him o'er yon towers prevail,

Shatter the wall, beat down the brazen door,
And singly, before all, the rampart scale;
Restore him to the camp, kind Sire, restore!
Its hope, its heart, its hand! by Jesu I implore!

24. "To me a nephew, to thyself restore
An agent, prompt for each sublime attack;
Leave him not sunk in slumber, I implore,—
To glory, to himself, invite him back;
Let him but follow the triumphal track
Of thy bless'd flag, the world shall witness be
Of his improvement: he shall not be slack
To do illustrious deeds, beholding thee,
Rank'd beneath thy command, fulfilling thy decree!"

25. Thus sued the high-born Guelpho, and the rest
With partial murmurs the request improved;
Godfrey, as though revolving in his breast
A thing before unthought of, as behooved,
Paused, and made answer: "Can I but be moved
To grace and mercy, when you all are bent
To press me? your petition stands approved;
Let rigor yield,—what you with one consent
Desire, shall be my law: I yield, and am content.

26. "Let the brave youth return, but let him rein
Henceforth his rage more wisely; and take heed,
That the high hopes our armies entertain
Of his maturing years, be match'd indeed
By equal actions;—now, my lord, proceed,—
'Tis fit the wand'rer be recall'd by thee;
Return he will, I trust, with willing speed;
Choose then the messengers, and o'er the sea
Or sands, direct them where you judge the knight to be."

27. He ceased, and thus the warrior Dane: "I pray
To be the man commission'd; I shall slight
All danger, doubt, or distance of the way,
So I may give this sword to whom of right
It henceforth must belong:" the Danish knight
Was resolute of heart, and brave of hand;
The offer thus gave Guelpho much delight:
"Thy wish," said he, "is mine; and with thee bland
Ubaldo, sage and sure, the mission will demand."

28. Ubald in early lifetime had survey'd
Much of the world, in various realms had been;

From frozen zones to where palmettoes shade
The sultry Ethiop, had most nations seen;
Their rites observed, and with perception keen
Learn'd at whatever port his bark might touch,
To imitate the language, mode, and mien
Of the rude native; thus, his parts were such,
That, in his court retain'd, Lord Guelpho loved him much.

29. These were the knights appointed to recall
The noble fugitive; and Guelph ordain'd,
That they should shape their journey to the hall
Where Bohemond in kingly splendor reign'd;
For that the warrior there was entertain'd,
By public fame had through the host been spread,
And as a certain fact was still maintain'd:
The Hermit, knowing they were much misled,
Amidst them enter'd now, and interposing said:

30. "In following, Signior, the fallacious breath
Of public rumor, you pursue a guide
Headstrong and treacherous, which, if not to death,
From the right path will lead your steps aside:
No! give your pinnace o'er the sea to glide;
To Ascalon's near shores your sails commend;
Where a swift stream rebuts the salt sea-tide,
A hermit you will meet, my trusty friend,
Of your intent forewarn'd,—to all his words attend.

31. "Much from the foresight of his own clear mind,
Much of your voyage has he learn'd from me;
Wise as he is, the Senior you will find
As much distinguish'd for his courtesy,
His affable discourse, and manners free."
Instructed thus, no more did Charles inquire,
Nor Ubald more; but, as a fix'd decree,
Obey'd those accents, which celestial fire
Was, as they surely knew, accustom'd to inspire.

32. They bid adieu; impatience spurs them on,—
Without delay they launch, and drive before
The willing wind direct for Ascalon,
Where the blue ocean breaks against the shore;
Scarce had they caught the hoarse and hollow roar
Of breakers on the coast, than they beheld
Th' anticipated stream its waters pour
Into the sea, by recent torrents swell'd,
And o'er its rocky banks with headlong force impell'd.

33. High o'er its banks the unrestricted flood,
Swift as a flying shaft, its waters roll'd;
While in confusion and suspense they stood.
A Sire appear'd, right venerably old,
Crown'd with beach-leaves; long robes his limbs infold
Of whitest grain,—he shook a charming-rod—
The surge grew calm; and, curious to behold,
With unwet feet, in only sandals shod,
He on the waters walk'd, and tow'rd the vessel trod.

34. As o'er the Rhine when winter its broad tide
Has in smooth chains of solid silver bound,
The village girls in crowds securely glide,
With long swift strokes, in many a playful round;
So on these orient waves, though neither sound,
Nor crystallized to ice, this ancient man.
Walk'd to the deck on which in awe profound
The knights stood fix'd, stood stupefied to scan
This singular, strange sight; he came, and thus began:

35. "O friends, a perilous and painful quest
You urge, and much in need of guidance stand!
The knight you seek, far in the golden West
Lies on a wild, unknown, and Gentile strand:
Much, O how much for you remains on hand
To dare and do! what coasts must you not clear,
What spacious seas, and what long tracts of land!
Beyond the limits of our Eastern sphere,
You must your search extend, your winged pinnace steer!

36. "Yet scorn not first to view the hidden cell
Which I my secret hermitage have made;
Momentous things you there shall hear me tell,
Most requisite for you to know;"—he said,
And made the waves yield passage; they obey'd—
Murmuring sweet music, they receded swift;
And, here and there dividing, high o'erhead
Hung curling, like some proud and beetling clift,
That o'er the mining deep is seen its brows to lift.

37. He took them by the hand, and led them down
The river's depth beneath the roaring main,
By such pale light, as through some forest brown
Streams from the yellow moon, when in her wane:
They see the spacious caverns that contain
The weight of waters which above-ground break

So freely forth ; that in one lucid vein
Burst in clear springs, or, more expansive, make
The broad smooth-sliding stream, slight pool, or sheeted lake.

38. The cisterns there whence Ganges takes his course,
Po, and renown'd Hydaspes, strike their eye ;
Don, Eúphrates, and Tanais ; nor its source
Mysterious does the Nile to them deny ;
More deep, a river flowing brightly by
O'er beds of living sulphur they behold,
Brimm'd with quicksilver ; these the sun on high
Ripens, refines, and in their secret mold
Binds in resplendent veins of silver, zinc, or gold.

39. And the rich flood did all its banks instar
With precious stones, enchanting to the sight ;
Which, like bright lamps, illumined wide and far
The den's black gloom with luxury of light :
There, in blue luster, shone the sapphire bright,
Heaven's native tint ; the jacinth glister'd mild ;
Flamed the fine ruby, flash'd the diamond white,
In virgin state, on sparkling opals piled,
And, gay with cheerful green, the lovely emerald smiled.

40. In dumb amazement the two warriors pass'd,
And all their thoughts to these strange scenes applied,
Said not a word ! Ubaldo spake at last,
And thus in falt'ring speech address'd his guide :
"O Father, say where now we are ! this tide—
Where does it flow ? thine own estate explain ;
Do I behold aright ? or is this pride
And prodigality of wealth a vain
Illusion ? scarce I know, such wonder wraps my brain."

41. "You," he replied, "are in the spacious womb
Of earth, the general mother ! not e'en ye
Could ever thus have pierced into the gloom
Of her rich bowels, unless brought by me :
I lead you to my home, which you will see
Illumed with curious light, a splendid place—
I was by birth a Pagan ; but, set free
From Pagan sin, regenerate grown by grace,
I was baptized, and now Christ's holy rule embrace.

42. "Think not my magic wonders wrought by aid
Of Stygian angels summon'd up from hell ;
Scorn'd and accursed by those who have essay'd

Her gloomy Dives and Afrits to compel,[11]
By fumes or voices, talisman or spell !—
But my perception of the secret powers
Of mineral springs, in Nature's inmost cell,
Of herbs, in curtain of her greenwood bowers,
And of the moving stars, on mountain-tops and towers.

43. " For in these caves mid glooms and shadows brown,
Far from the sun, not always I abide ;
But oft on sacred Carmel's flow'ry crown,
And oft on odorous Lebanon reside ;
There without veil I see the planets glide ;
Notice each aspect ; chronicle each phase
Of Mars and Venus ; every star beside,
That, swift or slow, of kind and froward rays,
Revolves and shines in Heaven, is naked to my gaze.

44. "Beneath my feet I view, or rare or dense,
The clouds, now dark, now beautiful in show ;
Of rains and dews the generation ; whence,
Thwart or direct, the winds and tempests blow ;
How lightnings kindle, why they dart below
In orb'd or writhen rays ; so near I scan
The fireball, comet, and the show'ry bow
Wove in Heaven's loom, that I at length began,
Puff'd up with pride, myself to fancy more than man.

45. "So overweening of myself, that now
I thought my powers could compass or command
Knowledge of all above, around, below,
That sprang to birth from God's creative hand !
But when your Hermit, visiting this strand,
From sin my soul, from error purged my mind,
He taught my thoughts to soar, my views t' expand,
And I perceived how little and confined
They of themselves had been, how vain, how weak, how blind !

46. "I saw how, like night-owls at rise of sun,
Our minds with Truth's first rays are stupefied ;
Smiled at the futile webs my folly spun ;
Scorn'd my vain-glory, and renounced my pride ;
But still my genius, as he wish'd, applied
To the deep arts and philosophic quest
In which I joy'd before, but, purified
And changed from what I was, with nobler zest
Ruled by the Seer on whom implicitly I rest ;—

47. "My guide and lord! what his sagacious wit
Points out, I execute; he not disdains
Now to my poor direction to commit
Works that might grace himself,—from servile chains
To free th' unconquer'd knight whom sloth detains
By strong enchantment in a witch's hold,
Where amorous Revel high misrule maintains;
Long for your coming have I look'd, of old
By the prophetic Seer in signs to me foretold."

48. While with this tale the knights he entertain'd,
They reach'd his dwelling; large it was and fair;
Shaped like a grot, and in itself contain'd
Galleries, and rooms, and spacious halls, whate'er
Of wild or precious, beautiful or rare,
Earth breeds in her rich veins, shone forth to view;
Nor one romantic ornament was there,
That from arranging art its glory drew,
But, form'd in Nature's freaks, in native wildness grew.

49. Nor fail'd there pages, numberless, untold,
To serve the guests with ready active haste;
Nor fail'd there urns of crystal, pearl, and gold,
On stands magnificent of silver placed,
Heap'd high with whatsoe'er might please the taste:
And when with meats and wines their appetite
Was satisfied, rich fruits the table graced;
And the sage spoke; "'Tis time that I invite
To what will be, methinks, of more refined delight.

50. "Armida's deeds, her purposes, her guile,
And secret snares in part to you are known;
How to your camp she came, and by what wile
She charm'd and led your warriors to her lone
Enchanted fortress; how they then were thrown
By their false hostess into chains, and lay
Long time, their am'rous follies to atone;
Till, sent with thousand guards to Gaza, they
Were by Rinaldo freed;—mark well what now I say.

51. "Things yet unknown to you do I declare,
Strange, but most true; when the fair witch perceived
That the rich prey it took such toil to snare,
Was rescued from her grasp, she storm'd, she grieved
Stamp'd, and in anger scarce to be conceived,
That her designs should be so clearly cross'd,
Burst forth; 'Let not the wretch be so deceived,
As to suppose the pris'ners I have lost,
Are to be repossess'd without revenge or cost!

52. "'If he has set them free, he in their place
Shall suffer ling'ring misery, hopeless thrall:
Nor shall this serve; the dues of my disgrace
Shall on the whole cursed Camp in vengeance fall!'
And, raving thus, she in her heart of gall
Framed what I now disclose to you, a sleight
The most malignant and refined of all;
She came where young Rinaldo had in fight
Her warriors late subdued, or massacred outright.

53. "Rinaldo there had thrown his arms aside,
And in a Turkish suit himself disguised;
Thinking perchance that he should safer ride,
In an array less known and signalized:
Th' Enchantress came; his arms she recognized;
A headless figure in them cased, and threw
Upon a brook's green banks, where, she surmised,
It would be sure to meet the Christians' view,
When to the shaded stream for waters fresh they drew:

54. "Nor was their coming hard to be foreseen;
For she a thousand spies on all sides sent,
Who every day brought tidings to their queen
Of the far Camp, who came, return'd, or went:
Oft too her dex'trous spirits would present,
After long talk with them in hall or grot,
Familiar picturings of each fresh event;
And thus the corse she cast in such a spot,
As best subserved her aim, and deep insidious plot.

55. "Near, the most shrewd of her deceitful train
She slyly placed, in shepherd's weeds array'd;
And, what he was to do, to say, to feign,
Taught in all points, and was in all obey'd;
He, seized while hurrying from the forest shade,
Spoke with your soldiers, and among them sow'd
Seeds of suspicion; which, maturing, sway'd
The Camp to discord; till rebellion show'd
Fearless her face abroad, and fires intestine glow'd.

56. "For, as she plann'd, all thought Rinaldo dead,
By Godfrey slain, his error to atone;
Albeit indeed their vague suspicions fled,
When the first beams of truth prevailing shone.
Thus with a craft peculiarly her own,
Armida wove her wiles; the second well
Chimed with the first, as will be seen anon;
The sequel of her scheme I now shall tell,
How she Rinaldo chased, and what from thence befell.

57. " O'er hill and dale Armida watch'd the youth,
Till now his steps the swift Orontes stay'd,
Where the clear stream its waters parting smooth,
Soon to rejoin, a flowery island made :
Here on the banks, under the greenwood shade,
A sculptured column might the Prince behold,
Near which a little shallop floating play'd ;
The marble white, its workmanship, and mold,
As he admired, he read in words engraved of gold :—

58. " 'O thou, whoe'er thou art, whom sweet self-will,
Or chance, or idlesse to this region guides !
No greater wonder in design or skill
Can the world show, than that this islet hides ;
Pass o'er and see !' Enticed, he soon divides
The boat's gilt chain, and, so divinely smile
Those summer waters, o'er them tilting rides ;
But as the skiff was slight, he leaves the while
His knights ashore, and seeks alone th' inviting isle.

59. " Landing, he looks around : yet nothing sees
To claim his curious sight but waters sheen,
Rocks, mossy grots, dells, fountains, flowers, and trees,
So that he deems his fancy to have been
Mock'd by the marble ; yet the place, the scene,
Were such as might enchant the rudest minds ;
So down he sits on banks of pleasant green,
Disarms his face, and sweet refreshment finds
In the cool fanning breath of odoriferous winds.

60. " Meanwhile the river gurgles with a sound
New to his ear, and thither calls his sight ;
One placid billow in the midst whirl'd round,
And sudden sank, then rose to greater height ;
From which peep'd forth, with golden tresses bright,
A virgin's beauteous face—her neck—her breast—
Then her two lily paps of purest white,
Their budded nipples rosily express'd ;—
While whisp'ring billows flung their silver round the rest.

61. " So on the midnight stage some water-maid,
Or fairy-queen slow rises from the floor ;
And though no Siren, but a painted shade,
Yet all the fascinating grace she bore
Of those same treach'rous Sisters, that of yore
Haunted the smooth sunshiny waters nigh
The Tuscan coast ; as bright a bloom she wore ;

As musical her voice, her smile as shy;
And thus aloud she sang, enchanting air and sky.

62. "'O happy youths, whom Spring with roses sweet
Robes and adorns! let not false glory's ray,
Nor virtue's smooth insidious beauty cheat
Your tender minds, and lead your steps astray;
Who crops the lily ere it fades away,
Who follows pleasure, he alone is sage!
Press then the purple grape of life—be gay—
This Nature bids, and will you warfare wage
With her divine decrees, nor fear the frowns of age?

63. "'Fools! to fling from you, without taste or care,
The brief enjoyments of your passing prime;
Names without object, idols all of air,
Are the vain toys to which you warriors climb:
The fame which charms with such a golden chime
Proud heroes' hearts, the glories that persuade,
Are but an echo in the ear of Time,—
A dream, a shade, the shadow of a shade;
With the bright rainbow born, they swift as rainbows fade.

64. "'But let your tranquil souls with all sweet things
Your happy senses cheer, while fresh and fair;
Past woes forget; nor with the anxious wings
Of expectation speed the steps of care:
Heed not if thunders roll, or lightnings glare;
Let the storm threaten as it will, rejoice!
With languor rest, with rest enjoyment share,
This is Elysium, this true Wisdom's choice,
This Nature's self requires,—slight not her charming voice!'

65. "So sings the Phantom, and her soft sweet tune
To settling sleep allures his heavy eyes;
Sense after sense dissolves in gentle swoon;
From limb to limb lethargic sweetness flies;
Till he of death the passive picture lies,
Nor e'en the bellowing thunder now could break
The magic trance; when this Armida spies,
She, issuing swift and silent as the snake,
From her close ambush runs, her sworn revenge to take.

66. "But on his face when she had gazed awhile,
And saw how placidly he breathed, how sweet
A light seem'd e'en in his closed eyes to smile,

(Ah, were they open, what were her conceit !)
She paused in doubt, and near him took her seat ;
The more she gazed, the more fond pity sprung
To her stern heart ; till, of all angry heat
Charm'd, o'er the boy, those greens and flowers among
With loving, lovely eyes, Narcissus-like she hung.

67. " The living heat-dews that impearl'd his face,
She with her veil wiped tenderly away ;
And, to cool more the fervors of the place,
Her turban took, and fann'd him as he lay ;
And call'd the mild winds of the West, to play
Round the rich cheeks that so divinely glow ;
Mark but the change ! Love's intellectual ray
Has from her savage bosom thaw'd the snow,
And to the kindest friend transform'd the sternest foe.

68. " With bluebells, lilies, woodbines, and wild roses,
That flower'd in thousands through those pleasant plains,
She next with admirable skill composes
Garlands, festoons, and odoriferous chains,
Which round his neck, and arms, and feet she strains
Tightly yet tenderly ; and o'er his eyes
While Sleep her shadowy government maintains,
Bears upon tiptoe the imprison'd prize
To her enchanted car, and, mounting, cuts the skies.

69. " Not now to rich Damascus does she fly,
Nor where her castle crests th' Asphaltine tide ;
But, jealous of a pledge so dear, and shy
Of her new passion, betwixt shame and pride,
In the Atlantic sea resolves to hide,
Where rarely mortal oar was known to comb,
Or ne'er, green Neptune's curling waves ; there, wide
Of all mankind, she singles for her home
A little Isle, round which the billows loneliest foam.

70. " One of a cluster to which Fortune lends
Her name, th' Elysian fields of old renown ;
There she a mountain's lofty peak ascends,
Unpeopled, shady, shagg'd with forests brown ;
Whose sides, by power of magic, half way down
She heaps with slippery ice, and frost, and snow,
But sunshiny and verdant leaves the crown
With orange woods and myrtles,—speaks—and lo !
Rich from the bordering lake a palace rises slow.

71. "Here in perpetual May her virgin sweets
She yields him, lapp'd in amorous wild delight;
From that far palace, from those secret seats,
Your tasks must be to disenthrall the knight;
To brave, encounter with, and put to flight
The guards her tim'rous jealousy has set,
To keep the marble hall and shaded height;
Nor shall you need or guide or gondolet,
Nor added arms divine, th' adventure to abet.

72. "A damsel, old in years though young in show,
When from the stream we issue, you will find,
With long rich tresses curling round her brow,
And garments beauteous as the bird of Ind;
She, through the ocean, swifter than the wind
Or wing of eagles, shall direct your track,
And leave the lightning in her flight behind;
Nor will you find her as a guide less slack,
Or less secure of trust, to speed you safely back.

73. "At the hill's foot whereon the Sorceress reigns,
Bulls bellow, hydras roar, and serpents hiss,
Revengeful lions rear their frightful manes,
And bears and panthers ope the grim abyss
Of their devouring jaws; shake then but this
My fascinating wand, and at the sound
They will recede, or crouch your feet to kiss:
But on the summit of that guarded ground
More fearful perils lurk,—and subtler charms abound.

74. "For there a fountain plays, whose dancing, pure,
And smiling rills the gazer's thirst excite,
Yet the cool crystals but to harm allure,—
Strange poison lurks within its waves of light;
One little draught the soul inebriates quite,
Mounts to the brain, and to the wit supplies
A host of gay ideas; till delight
Starts into voice, shrill peals of laughter rise,
Mirth overpowers the man, he laughs, and laughing dies.[12]

75. "Turn then, O turn your lips away with dread;
Scorn the false wave that to such ills persuades;
Be not allured by wines or viands spread
By fountain sides, or under green alcades;
Let no fond gestures of lascivious maids—
The smile that flatters, or the tune that calls
To amorous blandishments in myrtle shades,

Move the fine pulse ; each glance, each word that falls,
Leave for the ivory gates, and tread th' interior halls.

76. "Within, a maze of circling corridors
Verge and diverge a thousand winding ways ;
But of its various galleries, walks, and doors,
A lucid plan this little chart displays,
To guide your steps : in center of the maze,
A spacious garden flings its fragrance round,
Where not a light leaf shakes, or zephyr strays,
But breathes out love ; here, on the fresh green ground,
In his fair lady's lap the warrior will be found.

77. "But when th' Enchantress quits her darling's side,
And elsewhere turns her footsteps from the place,
Then, with the diamond shield which I provide,
Step forth, and so present it for a space,
That he may start at his reflected face,
His wanton weeds and ornaments survey ;
The sight whereof, and sense of his disgrace,
Shall make him blush, and without vain delay
From his unworthy love indignant break away.

78. "Enough ! it were superfluous to say more,
Than that to-morrow you may hence proceed ;
And when your pleasant voyage ends, explore
The secret paths that to the lovers lead,
With safe success and all convenient speed ;
For neither shall the powers of sorcery
Your voyage hinder or your plans impede ;
Nor, (so superior will your guidance be,)
Shall the fair witch have skill your coming to foresee.

79. "Nor less securely from her fairy halls
Shall you depart and wend your homeward way ;
But now the midnight hour to slumber calls,
And we must be abroad by break of day."
This said, he rose ; and, ushering them the way,
His wond'ring guests to their apartments brought ;
And leaving them to slumber's peaceful sway,
In reveries of glad and solemn thought,
His own nocturnal couch the good old Hermit sought.

END OF CANTO XIV.

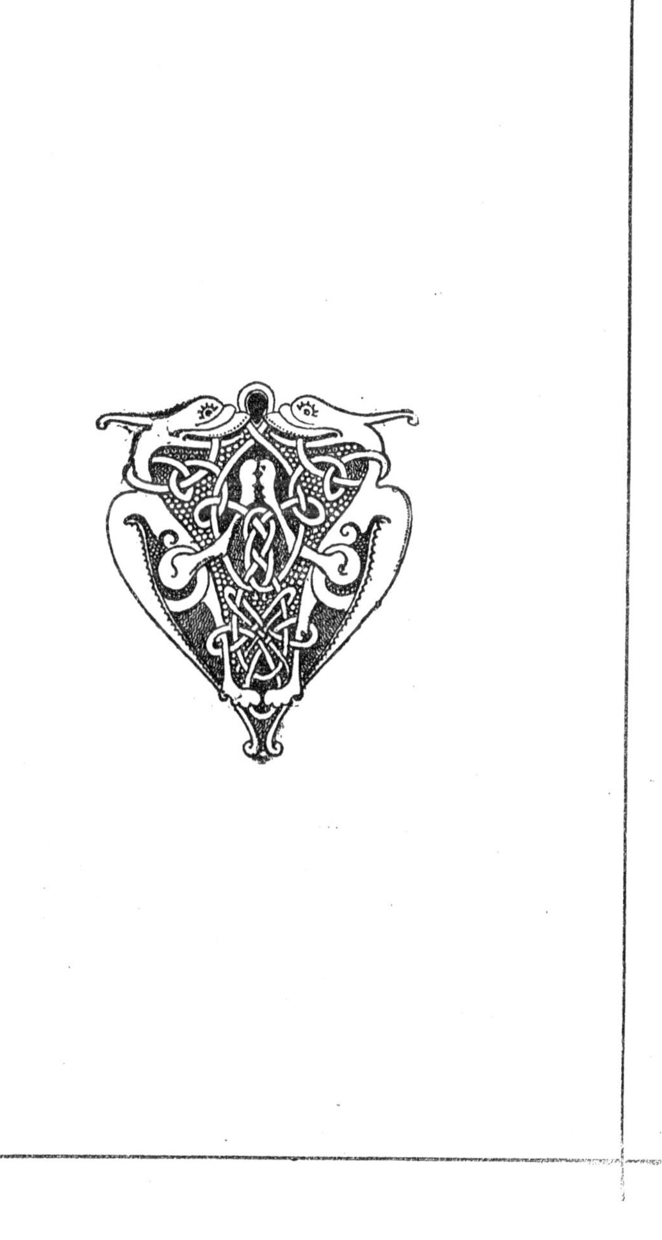

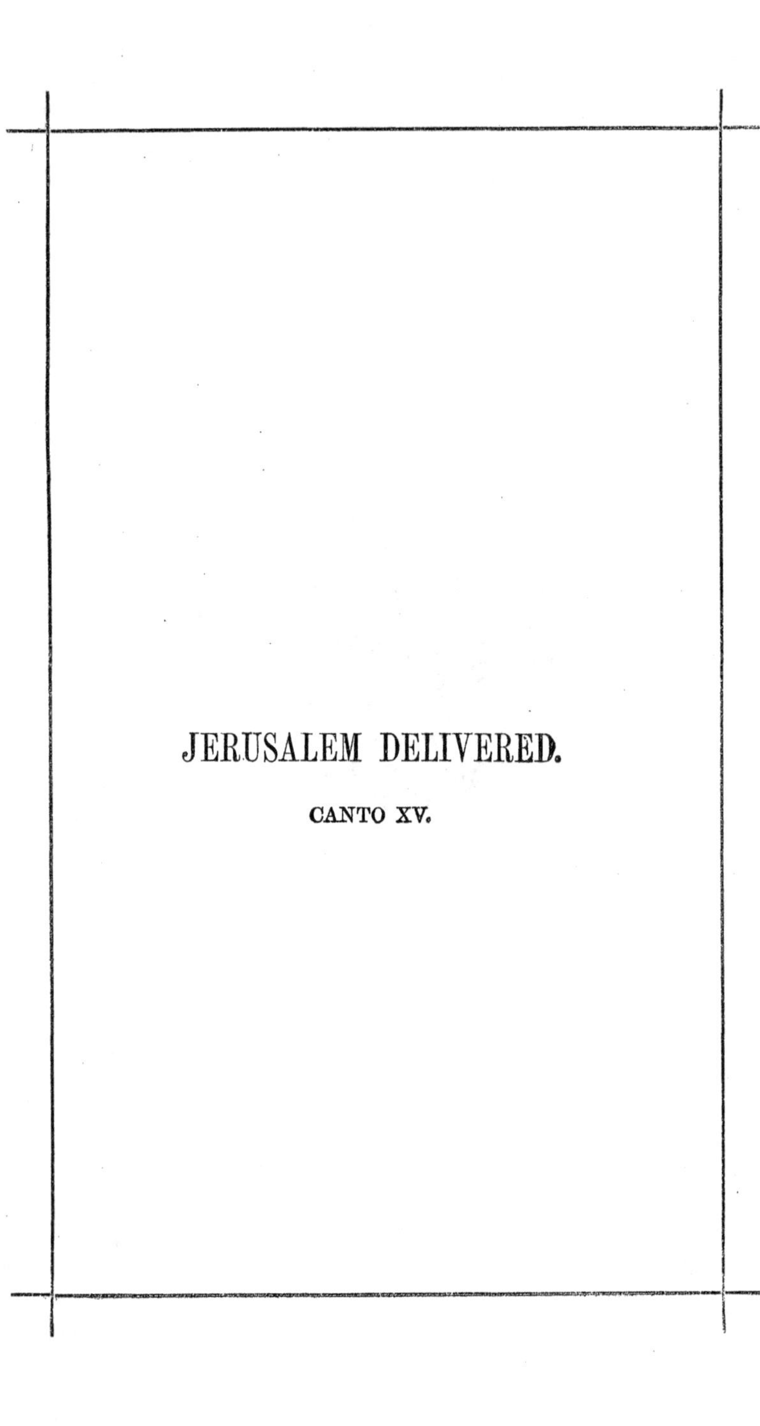

JERUSALEM DELIVERED.

CANTO XV.

ARGUMENT.

THE Seer's instructions the two knights pursue:
They reach the ready ship that rides in port,
Embark, set sail, and in the distance view
The fleet and army of th' Egyptian court.
Propitious winds within the canvas sport,
Fast bounds the vessel to the pilot's hand
O'er the blue ocean, making long seem short;
On a lone isle remote at last they land,
And every tempting sound and spectacle withstand.

JERUSALEM DELIVERED.

CANTO XV.

1. SCARCE had Aurora risen with grateful ray,
Or Syrian shepherd led his flocks from fold,
Than the Sage coming where the warriors lay,
Produced the chart, the shield, and wand of gold;
And "Rise!" he said, "ere yet the sun has told
His rosary on the hills,—soft breezes swell
To waft you on your voyage; here behold
The promised gifts that will have power to quell
Armida's witchcrafts all, and thaw each murmur'd spell."

2. But they th' expected summons had forerun,
Were up, and robed in arms from head to feet,
And straight, by paths ne'er gazed on by the sun,
Following their host, returning they repeat
The steps they took to his romantic seat
The previous day; but to the river side
When they were come, the Senior stay'd to greet
His parting guests: "Farewell, my friends!" he cried;
"Here must I leave you; go, good-fortune be your guide!"

3. Embark'd, the river with harmonious flow
The stranded vessel buoyantly upbore,
As, toss'd into the stream, a leafy bough
Is wont to rise, and, without sail or oar,
Floated them gently to the verdant shore;
There, as the spacious ocean they survey'd—
A little vessel with vermilion prore
Steer'd nigh, wherein was seen the destined maid,
And well the bounding bark her guiding hand obey'd.

4 Her locks hung curl'd around her brow ; her eyes
Were like the dove's, kind, tender, calm, and true ;
Her face an angel's, bright, and Paradise
Was in each radiant smile and look she threw ;
Her robe from white to red, from red to blue,
Lilac, green, purple, fleetingly and fast,
Long as you look'd, diversified its hue ;
You gaze again, the precious purple's past,
And a fresh tint appears, diviner than the last.

5. The feathers thus which on the neck genteel
Of the impassion'd dove their circles spread,
Not for one moment the same tint reveal,
But in the sun ten thousand colors shed ;
Now they a necklace seem of rubies red,
Of em'ralds now they imitate the light,
Then—let the gentle bird but turn its head—
They shift from green to black, from black to bright,
Then take the tints of all, still more to charm the sight.

6. "Enter," she said, "O happy youths ! the bark,
Wherein from sea to sea I safely ply ;
In which the heaviest weights grow light, the dark
Rough billows smooth, and calm the stormiest sky;
Me in his love and favor, the Most High
Sends as your guide :" the Lady spake, and now
Guilding her painted gondola more nigh,
O'er the glad waves that round in homage bow,
The green saluted shore strikes lightly with her prow.

7. Her charge received, the cable she upcurls,
Frees the fix'd keel, and launches from the land ;
Loose to the wind the silken sail unfurls,
And rules the rudder with a dext'rous hand :
Swell the full sails, as glorying to be fann'd :
Heaves the swolen stream, so deep with recent rain,
It might have borne a fleet well gunn'd and mann'd ;
But her light frigate it would well sustain,
Though to its usual state the waters were to wane.

8. Shrill airs unusual sing within the sails,
And swiftly speed them from the verdant shore ;
The waters whiten to the active gales,
And round the vessel murmur, foam, and roar.
But now they reach to where its loud waves hoar,
The river quiets in a broader bed ;
There, by the greedy sea embraced, its store

Melts into naught, or naught apparent, wed
With the vast world of waves before them greenly spread.

9. The sounding margin of the rough rude main
Is scarcely touch'd by the enchanted pine,
Than the black clouds that lower'd, presaging rain,
Clear off at once, and leave the morning fine;
The mountain-waves, smooth'd by a charm divine
Fall flat, or if a zephyr intervene,
It does but curl the clear blue hyaline;
And ne'er in Heaven's benignant face was seen
A smile so sweet as now, a purple so serene.

10. She sails past Ascalon, and cheerly drives
Her beauteous bark betwixt the south and west;
And near to stately Gaza soon arrives,
Once but a haven held in slight request,
But year by year increasing as the rest
Went to decay, a city now it stands,
Of power, and strength, and merchandise possess'd;
And at this instant, countless as its sands,
Myriads of armed men o'erspread the bord'ring lands.

11. To land the warriors look, and see the plains
With countless rich pavilions whiten'd o'er,
And knights, and squires, and steeds with glist'ning reins
Pass to and fro betwixt the town and shore;
Camels and burden'd elephants, whose roar
Comes mellow'd o'er the main, pace side by side,
And stamp the sands to dust; with many an oar
Flash the vex'd waves, and in the harbor wide,
Galleys, and light caiques, and ships at anchor ride.

12. Some with strong rowers brush'd the buxom wave;
Some spread their wings out to the winds, and flew;
Their sharp swift beaks the liquid seas engrave,
Foam the raised billows as the keels glide through.
"Though," said the Lady then, "the ocean blue
And yellow plains are fill'd, as you behold,
With hosts and navies of the trustless crew,
Fresh bands on bands, beneath his moon of gold,
By the strong tyrant yet remain to be enroll'd.

13. "Sole from his own or neighboring realms are drawn
These troops; more distant aid he yet awaits;
For to the regions of the noon and morn

Extends his influence with barbaric states ;
So that I hope we shall, with prosp'rous fates,
Have made return, ere from this subject-coast
He to Jerusalem his camp translates ;
He, or whatever Captain in his post
May o'er his other chiefs be raised to rule the host."

14. Then as an eagle passes one by one
All lesser birds, and soars to such a height,
That she appears confounded with the sun,
Her form unfix'd by the acutest sight ;—
So, betwixt ship and ship, her rapid flight
The gay and graceful Gondola holds on,
Without a fear or care, however slight,
Who may arrest or chase her, and anon
Is from the sailors flit, and out of prospect gone.

15. Past Raffia town she in a moment flew,
The first in Syria seen by those who steer
From fruitful Egypt, and had soon in view
The barren isle of lonely Rhinocere ;
Not distant, trees o'er waving trees appear
To clothe a hill embrowning all the deep
That bathes its base ;[13] not unremember'd here,
Urn'd in its heart, the bones of Pompey sleep ;
Round sigh the winds and woods ; beneath, the waters weep.

16. They next behold, by Damietta driven,
How to the sea proud Nile the tribute pays
Of his celestial treasures, by his seven
Famed mouths, and by a hundred minor ways .
Then past the city built in ancient days
By the brave youth of Macedon who bore
Palms from all lands, she sails, and soon surveys
The Pharian isle, an isle at least of yore,
But by an isthmus now connected with the shore.

17. She leaves to starboard Rhodes and Crete unseen.
And to th' adjacent shore of Libya stands ;
Along the sea productive, till'd, and green,
But inly throng'd with snakes and barren sands :
Barca she passes, passes by the lands
Where stood Cyrene, who no more presides,
Queen of the silent waste ! and soon commands
With Ptolomet the Cypress wood, whence guides
Lethe the fabled flow of his oblivious tides.

18. Syrtes, the seaman's curse, before the wind
She flies aloof, and far to seaward steers;
And, doubling Cape Judeca, leaves behind
Swift Magra's stream, till Tripoli appears,
Crowning the coast; due north, low Malta rears
Her cliffs, but Malta they not now behold;
To shun the lesser Syrtes, which she fears,
She tacks; but past Alzerbo, coasts more bold
The land where dwelt the mild Lotophagi of old

19. Next on the crooked shore they Tunis see,
Whose bay a hill on either side embrowns,—
Tunis, rich, stately, hon'rable, and free,
Beyond all Mauritanian towns;
Right opposite to which Sicilia crowns
The sea, and, roughly rising o'er the flood,
In somber shade Cape Lilybæum frowns,
Here now the damsel points where Carthage stood,
Rival so long with Rome, and drunk with Roman blood

20. Low lie her towers; sole relics of her sway,
Her desert shores a few sad fragments keep;
Shrines, temples, cities, kingdoms, states decay;
O'er urns and arcs triumphal deserts sweep
Their sands, or lions roar, or ivies creep;
Yet man, proud worm, resents that coming Night
Should shroud his eyes, in no perpetual sleep:
Biserta now they reach in silent flight
Sardinia's distant isle receding on the right.

21. Then scudding by the vast Numidian plains,
Where wand'ring shepherds wont their flocks to feed
Bugia and Algiers, the accursed dens
Of corsairs, rise, approach, and retrocede;
By Oran's towers they pass with equal speed,
And, coasting the steep cliffs of Tingitan,
Now named Morocco, famous for its breed
Of elephants and lions, they began
Granada's adverse shores through azure mists to scan.

22. And now Al Tarik's Straits they intersect,
Alcides' work, as gray traditions feign;
Haply an isthmus did the shores connect,
Till some concussion rent its rocks in twain;
And, by irruption of the horned main,
Abyla here and Calpe there was placed;
And Libya, sunder'd from romantic Spain,

No more as friends, but foes each other faced,—
Such power Time hath to change, and lay strong bulwarks waste.

23. Four times the morn has tinted Ocean's cheek,
Since the gay bark its voyage first begun ;
Nor has it enter'd once or port or creek,
For rest or stores,—well furnish'd, need was none ;
It now the entrance of the strait has won,
Shoots the slight pass, and, far as sight can flee,
Into the pathless infinite is run :
If, land-lock'd, here so spacious seems the sea,
There, where it rolls round earth, what must th' appearance be !

24. No longer now each city that succeeds
Rich Cadiz, o'er the billows they descry ;
Fast wealthy Cadiz, fast all land recedes,
Sky girds the Ocean, Ocean bounds the sky :
Said Ubald then : "Fair pilot ! make reply,
If on the boundless sea through which we glide
So swift, bark ere before was known to ply,—
And if beyond this world of waves reside
Men of like modes with ours ?" The Gondolier replied.

25. "When Hercules the monsters had subdued
That haunted Libya and the realms of Spain,
Through all your coasts his conquests he pursued,
Yet durst not tempt th' unfathomable main ;
Here then he raised his Pillars, to restrain
In too close bounds the daring of mankind ;
But these his marks Ulysses did disdain,
And, fond of knowledge still, his curious mind
E'en by Alcides' laws refused to be confined.

26. "The straits he pass'd, and on th' Atlantic sail'd,
Bold as the Sea-God in his fish-drawn shell ;
But naught, alas, his naval skill avail'd,
The roaring billows rang his funeral knell !
The secrets of his fate no records tell,
Where bleach'd his bones, or whither drove his sail :
If any since were driv'n out by the swell
Of wave or wind, they perish'd in the gale,
Or came not back, at least, to tell th' adventurous tale.

27. "Thus still this sea rests unexplored ; it boasts
A thousand isles, a thousand states unknown ;
Not void of men, nor barren are the coasts,

But fertile, rich, and peopled as your own;
Nor can the sun which cheers your milder zone,
Be in its quick'ning virtues lifeless there,
But earth is heap'd with fruits and blossoms blown;"
Said Ubald then: "Of this new world so fair,
Be pleased the worship, laws, and customs to declare."

28. "As various as the tribes," she made reply,
"Their rites, and languages, and customs are;
Some Earth, the general mother, glorify,
Some worship beasts, the sun, and morning star;
While some in woods and wildernesses far
Spare not to deify the Prince of Hell,
And heap their boards with captives slain in war;
In short, most impious are their rites, and fell
The faith of all the tribes that west of Calpe dwell."

29. "Will then," the knight rejoin'd, "that God who came
From Heaven t' illuminate the human heart,
Shut ev'ry ray of Truth's celestial flame
From that, which of earth so large a part?"
"No," she replied, "each humanizing art
Shall yet be theirs; e'en kings shall coincide
The holy Faith and Gospels to impart;
Nor think indeed that this extent of tide
Shall from your world these tribes forever thus divide.

30. "The time shall come, when ship-boys e'en shall scorn
To have Alcides' fable on their lips,
Seas yet unnamed, and realms unknown adorn
Your charts, and with their fame your pride eclipse;
Then the bold Argo of all future ships
Shall circumnavigate and circle sheer
Whate'er blue Tethys in her girdle clips,
Victorious rival of the Sun's career,—
And measure e'en of Earth the whole stupendous sphere.

31. "A Genoese knight shall first th' idea seize,
And, full of faith, the trackless deep explore;
No raving winds, inhospitable seas,
Thwart planets, dubious calms, or billows' roar,
Nor whatso'er of risk or toil may more
Terrific show, or furiously assail,
Shall make that mighty mind of his give o'er
The wonderful adventure, or avail
In close Abyla's bounds his spirit to impale.

32. "'Tis thou, Columbus, in new zones and skies,
That to the wind thy happy sails must raise,
Till fame shall scarce pursue thee with her eyes,
Though she a thousand eyes and wings displays.
Let her of Bacchus and Alcides praise
The savage feats, and do thy glory wrong,
With a few whispers toss'd to after days;
These shall suffice to make thy mem'ry long
In history's page endure, or some divinest song."[14]

33. She said, and sliced through foam toward the West
Her course awhile, then to the South inclined,
And saw—now Titan rolling down to rest,
And now the youthful Morning rise behind;
And when with rosy light and dews refined
Aurora cheers the world, more sail she crowds;
Till, in blue distance breaking, as the wind
Curls off the mist that all th' horizon shrouds,
They see a mountain rise, whose summits reach the clouds.

34. As they advance the vapors melt, nor more
Their wish'd inspection of the isle prevent;
Like the vast pyramids 'twas seen to soar,
Sharp in its peak, and widening in extent
Down to its base; it seem'd to represent
The burning hill 'neath which the Giant lies
That warr'd on Jove, for with like sulph'rous scent
It smokes by day, and still, as daylight dies,
With ruddy fires lights up the circumambient skies.

35. Then other islands, other mountains mild,
Less steep and lofty, their regards engage;
The Happy Isles, the Fortunate! so styled
By the fond lyrists of the antique age;
Which warrior, sophist, priest, and gifted sage
Believed so favor'd by the Heavens benign,
As to produce, untill'd, in every stage
Of growth, its fruits; unpruned the fancied vine
At once flower'd, fruited, fill'd, and gush'd with gen'rous wine.

36. Here the fat olive ever buds and blooms,
And golden honeys from old oaks distill,
And rivers slide from mountain-greens and glooms,
In silver streams, with murmurs sweet or shrill;
And here cool winds and dews all summer chill
The heats, and the calm halcyon builds her nest,

With every beauteous bird of tuneful bill;
And here are placed th' Elysian Fields, where rest,
In fair unfading youth, the spirits of the blest.

37. To these the Lady made: "And now," said she,
"The destined haven of your hopes is near;
The promised isles of Fortune now you see,
Whose fame has reach'd, if not fatigued your ear
With its uncertain echoes; Fiction here
Has not been idle; rich they are, and gay,
And pleasant, but not quite what they appear
In poesy:" she said, and in her way,
Pass'd the first isle of ten that clear in prospect lay.

38. Then Charles: "If, Lady, with our enterprise
Th' excursion suits, now let us leap ashore,
And mark what yet no European eyes
Have view'd—the people see, the place explore,
The rites they use, the Genius they adore,
And whatsoe'er may prompt th' inquiry keen
Of envying sages; that, recounting o'er
The perils braved, the strange new objects seen,
I may with honest pride exclaim, 'Yes! there I've been!'"

39. "Worthy," the Gondolier replied, "of thee,
Th' entreaty surely is; but what can I,
If Heaven's severe, inviolable decree
The least compliance with thy wish deny?
The perfect period fix'd by God on high
To give this great discov'ry to the day,
Is not yet come; and thus for you to eye
The Secrets of the Deep, and back convey
Th' authentic news, would be his will to disobey.

40. "To you 'tis granted, by peculiar grace
And superhuman skill, the fame t' acquire
Of rescuing to your world from thraldom base,
A youth whom nations ardently desire;
Let this suffice, for farther to aspire,
Would be to war with fate:" while she replies,
The first green isle seems less'ning to retire
From notice, and the next sublime to rise,
So blithely o'er the wave the charmed pinnace flies.

41. They now behold, how in the same degree
All in long order shun the realms of morn,
And by what equal distances of sea

The happy isles are each from each withdrawn :
Huts, curling smoke, white flocks, and ripening corn
Spoke seven of them inhabited ; the rest
Were waste, o'errun with heath and shagg'd with thorn ;
Where, fix'd in long hereditary rest,
Secure the lion prowls, the vulture builds her nest.

42. In one they find a lone sequester'd place,
Where, to a crescent curved, the shore extends
Two moony horns, that in their sweep embrace
A spacious bay,—a rock the port defends ;
Inward it fronts, and broad to ocean bends
Its back, whereon each dashing billow dies,
When the wind rises and the storm descends ;
While here and there two lofty crags arise,
Whose towers, far out at sea, salute the sailor's eyes.

43. Safe sleep the silent seas beneath ; above,
Black arching woods o'ershade the circled scene :
Within, a grotto opens in the grove,
Pleasant with flowers, with moss, with ivies green,
And waters warbling in the depth unseen ;
Needed nor twisted rope nor anchor there
For weary ships : into that so serene
And shelter'd hermitage, the maiden fair
Enter'd, her slender sails unfurling from the air.

44. "Behold," she said, "the cupolas and towers
That on yon mountain's lofty summit shine !
There Christ's lethargic champion wastes his hours
In dalliance, idlesse, folly, feast, and wine :
That slipp'ry, steep ascent of palm and pine
Mount with the rising sun ; nor let delay
Seem to you grievous ; influences malign
Th' important scheme to ruin will betray,
If any hour but that be fix'd for the essay.

45. "You yet with easy speed may reach the foot
Of the seen mountain, ere the day's expired ;"
Their lovely guide in parting they salute,
And lightly pace at length the shore desired.
They found the way so much to be admired,
So full of goodly prospects, cool with shade,
And smooth withal to tread, that nothing tired ;
And when they issued from the last green glade,
High o'er the landscape yet the evening's sunbeams play'd.

46. They see that to the mountain's stately head
O'er nodding crags and ruins they must climb;
Below, with snows and frosts each path was spread,
For bloomy heath exchanged and odorous thyme;
Cedar, and pine, and cypress more sublime
Round its white shoulders toss'd their verdant locks,
Sweet lilies peep'd from forth the hoary rime,
While (force of magic!) pinks, geraniums, stocks,
And roses, fully flower'd, hung clust'ring round the rocks.

47. Within a savage cave beneath the mount,
Closed in with shades, the warriors pass'd the night;
But when the Sun from Heaven's eternal fount
Through the brown forest shed his golden light,
"Up, up!" at once they cried; and either knight
With rival zeal along the track of frost
Began th' ascent; when, on their startled sight,
Whence they knew not, in various colors gloss'd,
Their onward path a fierce and frightful serpent cross'd.

48. Her head and scaly crest of pallid gold
She raised erect, and swelled her neck with ire;
Lighten'd her eyes; and, hiding as she roll'd
A length of way, she poison breathed and fire;
Now she recoil'd into herself, now nigher
Her tangled rings distending many a yard,
She slid along with mischievous desire,
Presenting all her stings the pass to guard,—
Much she the knights amazed, but did not much retard.

49. Already Charles, the monster to assail,
Had drawn his sword, when out Ubaldo spake:
"Soft! what is it you do? by arms so frail
How can you hope to quell th' enchanted snake?"
His golden wand of an immortal make
He shook, so that the demon, smit with fear,
No longer hissing, sought the tangled brake;
Needed no second sound to warn its ear;
Instant it slipp'd away, and left the passage clear.

50. A little further on, with sour disdain
A roaring lion the strict pass denied;
Tossing aloft the terrors of his mane,
And his voracious jaws expanding wide,
He with redoubling fury lash'd his side,
And to the knights advanced with hasty tread;
But when the wand immortal he espied,

A secret instinct chill'd his heart with dread,
And quell'd his native fire ; he howl'd, and howling fled.

51. Their track the venturous couple follow fast,
But numerous legions yet before them rise
Of savage beasts, terrific as the past,
Differing in voice, in movement, and in guise ;
All monstrous forms, all wild enormities,
All the grim creatures in their sternest moods
That betwixt Nile and Atlas, Titan eyes,
Seem'd gather'd there, with all the raging broods
That haunt th' Ercynian caves or old Hyrcanian woods.

52. But e'en this phalanx, massy, fierce, and bold
As it appear'd, could not the pair affright,
Much less repel ; for of the wand of gold
A single motion put them all to flight.
And now they climb victorious to the height
Of the rude precipice, without delay ;
Save that the Alpine cliffs and glaciers, white
With drifted snows that round austerely lay,
Of their sublime ascent more tedious make the way.

53. But when at length the steep acclivity
Is scaled, and pass'd the snows and breezes keen,
Beneath the sunshine of a summer sky
They find an even, smooth, and spacious green.
Here in a clime delightfully serene
His wings the everlasting Zephyr shakes,
And breathes a ceaseless sweetness o'er the scene ;
For here the sun one golden measure makes,
Nor ever charms asleep, nor e'er the wind awakes.

54. Not as elsewhere with fervors frosts severe,
Or clouds with calms divide the happy hours ;
But Heaven, than whitest crystal e'en more clear,
A flood of sunshine in all seasons showers ;
Nursing to fields their herbs, to herbs their flowers,
To flowers their smell, to leaves the immortal trees,
Here by its lake, the splendid palace towers
On marble columns rich with golden frieze,
For leagues and leagues around o'ergazing hills and seas.

55. The warriors weary found themselves and faint,
From their long travel up the steep rough hill ;
And loitering through the pleasant gardens went,
Walking or resting at their own sweet will ;
When lo, a fountain whose light music shrill

Allures the thirsty pilgrim, gleam'd in view!
In one tall column it descended chill,
And in a thousand crystal fragments flew,
Sprinkling with orient pearl the plants that round it blew.

56. But through the grass these delicate cascades
The same deep channel in conclusion found,
And under curtain of perpetual shades
Ran warbling by, cool, tranquil, and embrown'd;
Yet still so clear, that in its depth profound
Each glist'ning wave amid the sands was seen,
With all its curls of beauty; while around,
The mossy banks form'd couches soft and green,
Inlaid with odorous herbs, and violets strown between.

57. "See here the fount of laughter! see the stream
To which such fatal qualities belong!
Now," they exclaim'd, "let us avoid the dream
Of warm desire, and in resolve be strong;
Now shut our ears to the fair Siren's song,
And to each smile of feminine deceit
Close the fond eye!" thus warn'd, they pass along,
Until they reach to where the waters sweet
Break out a broader bed, and form a spacious sheet.

58. Here, served on ivory, stood all sumptuous food
That Taste could wish, or Luxury purvey,
And, chatt'ring, laughing, in the crystal flood
Two naked virgins, full of wanton play;
Now kissing, wrestling, breaking now away,
Now striving which the other should outswim:
Now diving, floating, as the waters sway,
Sometimes above, sometimes below the brim,
Marking their course conceal'd by some voluptuous limb.

59. These swimming damsels, beautiful and bare,
The warriors' bosoms somewhat did subdue;
So that they stay'd to watch them, while the pair
Seem'd all intent their pastimes to pursue:
One meanwhile, starting upward, full to view
Of the clear Heavens her swelling breasts display'd,
And all that might with rapture more indue
The eye, to the white waist; the waves that play'd
Round her, each limb beneath pellucidly array'd.

60. As from the waves the glitt'ring Star of morn
Comes, dropping nectar; or as rising slow
From Ocean's fruitful foam when newly born,

The Queen of Love and Beauty seem'd in show,
So she appear'd, so charm'd ; her tresses so
From all their golden rings bright humor rain'd,
Rich with the colors of the show'ry bow ;
While looking round, the knights but then she feign'd
To see, and back recoil'd offended, shock'd, and pain'd.

61. Her tresses knotted in a single braid,
She in an instant loosen'd and shook down ;
Which, thickly flowing to her feet, array'd
Her polish'd limbs as with a golden gown :
But O ! when fell the curtain from her crown,
What an enchanting spectacle was fled !
Yet 'twas enchantment, so to find it flown :
Thus gloriously with locks and waves o'erspread,
She from them turn'd askance, rejoicing, rosy red.

62. She smiled, she crimson'd deep, and all the while
Her smile the sweeter show'd the more she blush'd,
And the sweet crimson sweeter for the smile
That o'er her tender face in sunshine rush'd ;
Then with a voice so mild it might have hush'd
The nightingale, and taken an angel prey,
Rich from her warbling lips these accents gush'd :
"O happy pilgrims ! favor'd to survey
Regions so full of peace, a Paradise so gay !

63. "This is the haven of the world ; here Rest
Dwells with Composure, and that perfect bliss,
Which in the Golden Age fond men possess'd,
In liberty and love unknown to this ;
You now may lay aside th' incumbrances
Of arms, and safely hang them on the trees,
Sacred to Peace ; all else but folly is ;
Seek then soft quiet, seek indulgent ease,
Love's the sole captain here, young Love's the lord to please.

64. "The fields of battle here are mosses green
And beds of roses, where—you dream the rest ;
We will conduct you to our fairy queen,
The queen whose bounty makes her servants blest.
You of that happy band shall be impress'd,
Whom she has destined for her joys ; but first,
Your weary limbs of those rude arms divest,
In these cool waters be your dust dispersed,
And at yon board indulge your hunger, taste, and thirst."

65. Thus sang the one ; her sister play'd the mime,
In act and glance outpleading her appeal,
As swift or slow to the melodious chime
Of lutes and viols the blithe dancers wheel ;
But to these wiles the knights in triple steel
Of stern resolve had shut their souls : and hence,
The tunes they sing, the beauties they reveal,
Their angel looks and Heavenly eloquence,
But circle round and round, nor reach the seat of sense.

66. Or if of such sweet airs and glowing charms
Aught stirs the soil where buds unchaste Desire,
The heart soon Reason fills with her alarms,
And with strong hand roots up each rising brier :
Vanquish'd the nymph's remain ; the knights retire,
And, without bidding them adieu, pass on ;
These reach the palace, those with fruitless ire
Crimsoning afresh at the repulse anon
Dive in the waves, and deep beyond all sight are gone.

END OF CANTO XV.

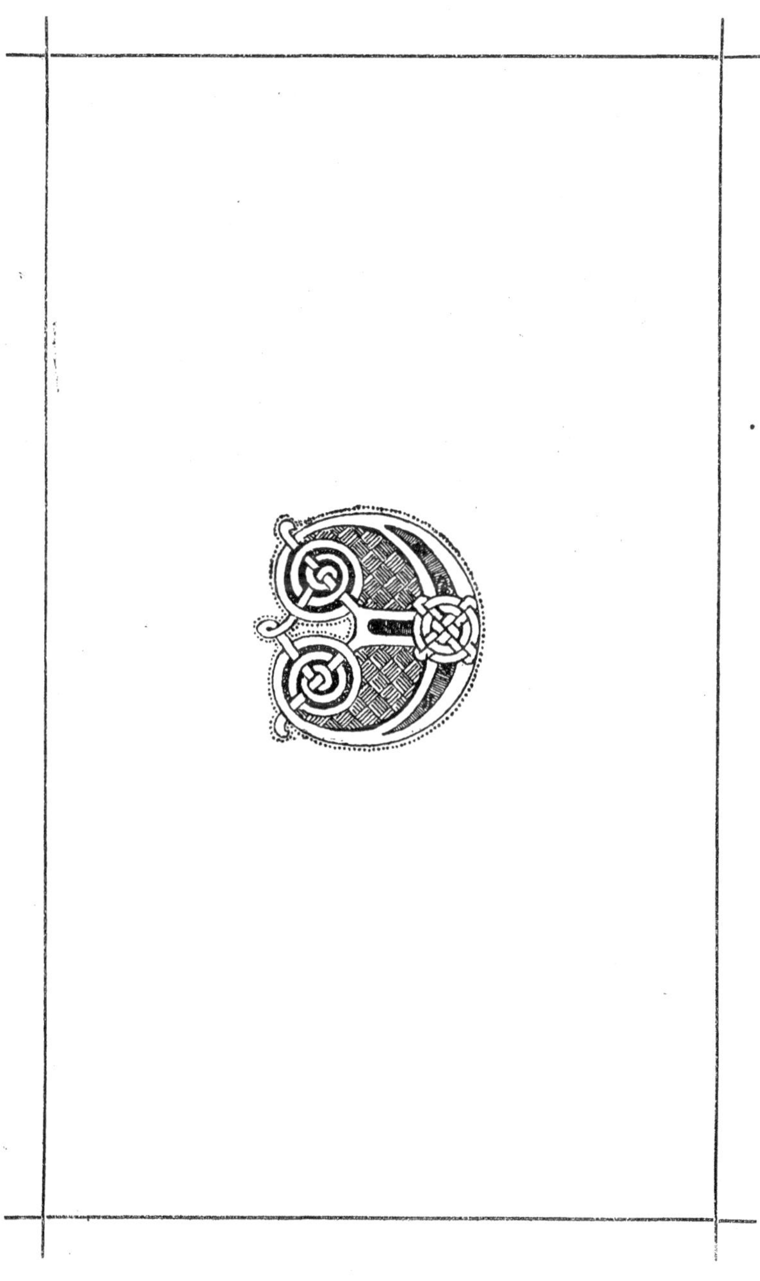

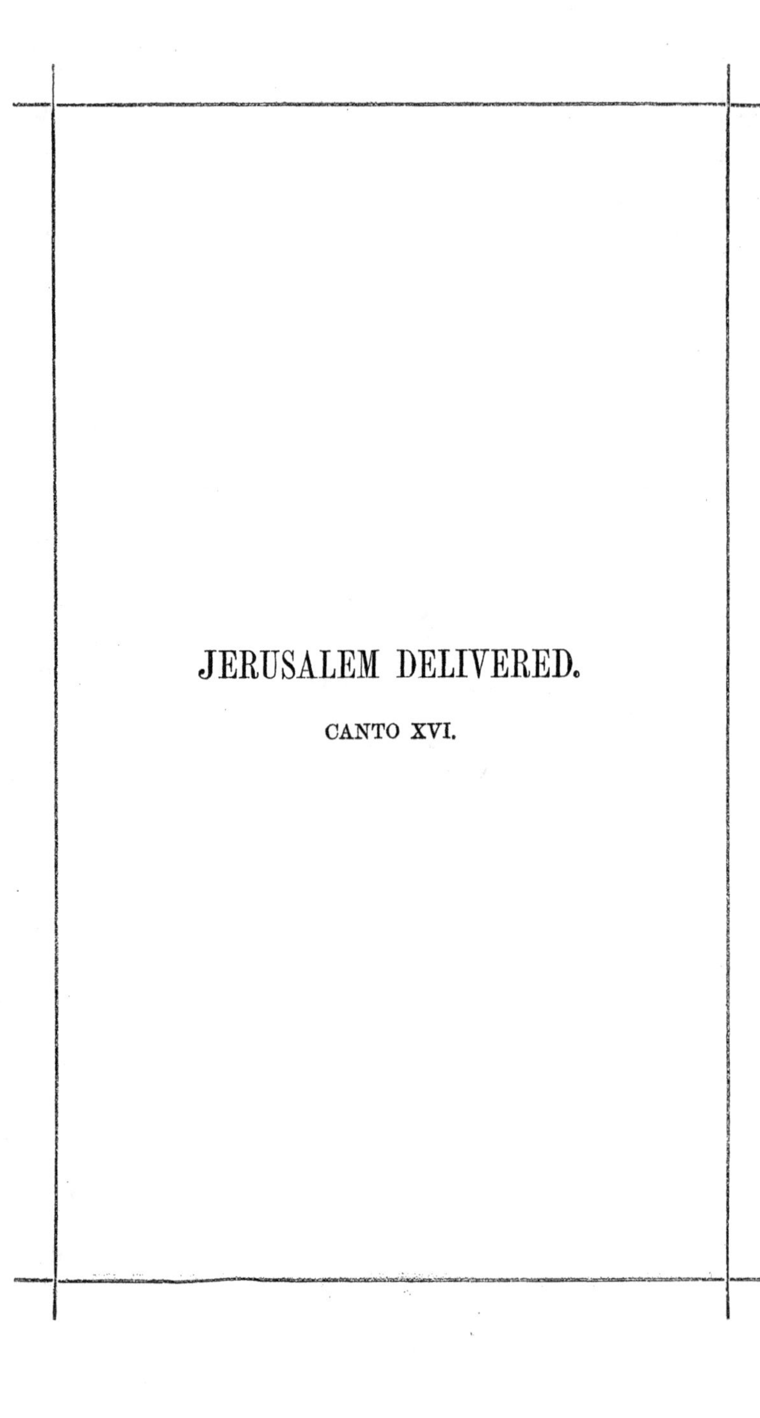

JERUSALEM DELIVERED.

CANTO XVI.

ARGUMENT.

THE spacious palace of th' enchanting Dame
The warriors tread, where lost Rinaldo lies ;
And speed so well, that, full of wrath and shame,
He bursts his bonds, and with them quickly flies :
She, to retain her loved deserter, tries
All powers of language and of tears—in vain,—
He parts ; t' avenge her wrongs, on Dis she cries,
Destroys her palace, and, in high disdain,
Flies through the stormy skies in her aërial wain.

JERUSALEM DELIVERED.

CANTO XVI.

1. Round is the spacious pile ; and in its heart,
Set like a gem, a garden is insphered,
More deck'd by nature and enrich'd by art,
Than the most beautiful that e'er appear'd
To flower in old romance ; and round it, rear'd
The Stygian sprites unnumber'd galleries,
Harmonious, seen at distance, but, when near'd,
A trackless maze discordant to the eyes,—
Through all these tortuous coils their secret passage lies.

2. Through the chief gate they tread the marble floors,
For full a hundred grace the spacious hold ;
Of fine and figured silver here the doors
On their smooth hinges sing, of shining gold :
Awhile they pause the figures to behold
Cast on the squares ; for, with extreme surprise,
They see the metal rival'd by the mold ;
Speech fails alone, but, to the trusting eyes,
The sprightly shapes e'en speak, and limb'd with life arise.

3. Here midst Mæonian girls the Grecian Mars
Sits, telling fond romantic tales : and he
Who storm'd black Orcus, and upheld the stars
Now twirls the spindle with a maiden's glee ;
Young Love looks on and laughs ; while Iole
In her unwarlike hands is seen to bear
His murd'rous arms with proud mock-majesty,
And on her back the lion's hide to wear,
Too rough a vest for limbs so finely turn'd and fair !

4. Near heaved a sea whose azure surface changed,
As close you look'd, and into silver splash'd ;

Two adverse navies in the midst were ranged
For war—blue lightnings from the armor flash'd;
In gold the bright and burning billows dash'd,
And all Leucate did on fire appear,
Ere the beaks grappled, and the falchions clash'd;
Augustus there all Rome, Antonious here,
Brought up his Eastern kings, and couch'd his Memphian spear.

5. You would declare the rifted Cyclades
Concurr'd, and mountains did with mountains jar,
When with their tower-like vessels those and these
Rush'd o'er the brine, and shock'd in mortal war;
Here, like the sparkles of a glancing star,
Darts fly, and fire-balls blaze; there, bloody dyes
The virgin whiteness of the waters mar:
While neither wins, lo where, with heavy eyes,
O'er the vex'd waves, alarm'd, th' Egyptian beauty flies.

6 And flies her Chief? can he relinguish here
The glorious world to which his hopes aspire?
He flies not, no, nor fears; he does not fear,
But follows her, drawn on by fond desire:
You see him, (like a man whom now the fire
Of love torments, and now, as shame prevails,
Disdain,) alternately regard, as ire
And tenderness were cast in equal scales,
Now the still dubious fight, and now her less'ning sails.

7 Then in the secret creeks of fruitful Nile
He in her lap appears for death to wait,
And with the pleasure of her lovely smile
Sweetens the bitter stroke of hasting fate.—
With such like arguments of various date
And issue in Love's story, were emboss'd
The glitt'ring metals of that princely gate;
The figured tales long time the knights engross'd;
At length the charm they broke, and o'er the threshold cross'd.

8. As 'twixt its crooked banks Meander plays,
Curls and uncurls in its uncertain course,
Now to its spring, now to the Ocean strays,
Now meets itself returning to its source:
Such, only intertangled with a force
Yet more mysterious, of this mazy spot
The paths appear; but now they have recourse
To the clear chart, which, pointing out both what
To shun, and what pursue, resolves th' enchanted knot.

9. These windings pass'd, the garden-gates unfold,
And the fair Eden meets their glad survey,—
Still waters, moving crystals, sands of gold,
Herbs, thousand flowers, rare shrubs, and mosses gray,
Sunshiny hillocks, shady vales; woods gay
And grottoes gloomy, in one view combined,
Presented were; and what increased their play
Of pleasure at the prospect, was, to find
Nowhere the happy Art that had the whole design'd.

10. So natural seem'd each ornament and site,
So well was neatness mingled with neglect,
As though boon Nature for her own delight
Her mocker mock'd, till fancy's self was check'd;
The air, if nothing else there, is th' effect
Of magic, to the sound of whose soft flute
The blooms are born with which the trees are deck'd;
By flowers eternal lives th' eternal fruit,
This running richly ripe, while those but greenly shoot.

11. Midst the same leaves and on the self-same twig
The rosy apple with th' unripe is seen;
Hung on one bough the old and youthful fig,
The golden orange glows beside the green;
And aye, where sunniest stations intervene,
Creeps the curl'd vine luxuriant high o'erhead;
Here the sour grape just springs the flowers between,
Here yellowing, purpling, blushing ruby red,
Here black the clusters burst, and heavenly nectar shed.

12. The joyful birds sing sweet in the green bowers;
Murmur the winds; and in their fall and rise,
Strike from the fruits, leaves, fountains, brooks, and flowers,
A thousand strange celestial harmonies;
When cease the birds, the zephyr loud replies;
When sing the birds, it faints amidst the trees
To whispers soft as lovers' farewell sighs;
Thus, whether loud or low, the bird the breeze,
The breeze obeys the bird, and each with each agrees.

13. One bird there flew, renown'd above the rest,
With party-color'd plumes and purple bill,
That in a language like our own express'd
Her joys, but with such sweetness, sense, and skill,
As did the hearer with amazement fill;
So far her fellows she outsang, that they
Worship'd the wonder; ev'ry one grew still

At her rich voice, and listen'd to the lay :
Dumb were the woods,—the winds and whispers died away.

14\. "Ah see," thus she sang, "the rose spread to the morning
Her red virgin leaves, the coy pride of all plants !
Yet half open, half shut midst the moss she was born in,
The less shows her beauty, the more she enchants;
Lo, soon after, her sweet naked bosom more cheaply
She shows ! lo, soon after she sickens and fades,
Nor seems the same flower late desired so deeply
By thousands of lovers and thousands of maids !

15\. "So fleets with the day's passing footsteps of fleetness
The flower and the verdure of life's smiling scene :
Nor, though April returns with its sunshine and sweetness,
Again will it ever look blooming or green ;
Then gather the rose in its fresh morning beauty,
The rose of a day too soon dimm'd from above ;
While, beloved, we may love, let—to love, be our duty;
Now, now, while 'tis youth, pluck the roses of love !"[15]

16\. She ceased ; and, as approving all they heard,
That tender tune the choirs of birds renew ;
The turtles bill'd, and ev'ry brute and bird
In happy pairs to unseen glooms withdrew.
It seem'd that the hard oak, the grieving yew,
The chaste sad laurel, and the whole green grove,—
It seem'd each fruit that blush'd, each bud that blew
The earth, air, sea, and rosy heavens above,
All felt divine desire, and sigh'd out sweetest love.

17\. Midst melody so tender, midst delights
So passing sweet, and midst such tempting snares,
Cautious, serene, and serious go the knights,
And steel their souls to the loose Lydian airs.
Lo, betwixt leaves and leaves, at unawares
Advancing slow, they see, or seem to see,—
They see most surely, crown of all their cares !
The lover and his darling lady ; he
In the fair lady's lap, on herbs and violets she.

18\. Her veil, flung open, shows her breast ; in curls
Her wild hair woos the summer wind ; she dies

Of the sweet passion, and the heat that pearls,
Yet more her ardent aspect beautifies :
A fiery smile within her humid eyes,
Trembling and tender, sparkles like a streak
Of sunshine in blue fountains ; as she sighs,
She o'er him hangs ; he on her white breast sleek
Pillowing his head reclines, cheek blushing turn'd to cheek.

19 His hungry eyeballs, fix'd upon her face,
For her dear beauty pine themselves away ;
She bows her head, and in a fond embrace,
Sweet kisses snatches, betwixt war and play,
Now of his just touch'd eyes, in wilder prey
Now of his coral lips ; therewith he heaves
Sighs deep as though his spirit wing'd its way
To transmigrate in her : amidst the leaves,
This am'rous dalliance all each watchful knight perceives.

20. A polish'd glass, whose sheen the stars excell'd,
Strange arms ! hung pendent at Rinaldo's thigh ;
He rose, and to the fair the crystal held,
Her chosen page in each love-mystery :
Both—she with smiling, he with glowing eye,
Mark but one scene of all the scenes they view ;
Her angel form and aspect they descry,
She in the glass, he, fond enthusiast ! through
A sweeter medium fan—her eyes of heavenly blue.

21. She in herself, he glories but in her ,
He proud of bondage, of her empire she ;
" And why," he murmurs, " so to this recur ?
Turn, my beloved, turn thine eyes on me,—
Those smiling eyes, that no less blessed be,
Than blessed make ; ah, know'st thou not, that best
They in mine eyeballs must thy beauty see ?
And know'st thou not thy graces are express'd
Less clear in this gay glass than in my faithful breast ?

22. "Though me thou scorn, thou might'st at least consent
To mark thine own most interesting face ;
Those looks, else unrepaid, must rest content
With joy, if on themselves themselves they place ;
So rare an image can no crystal trace,
No glass a perfect Eden can comprise
In its small round ; to see aright thy grace
Thou must consult the mirror of the skies ;
Heaven is thy glass, the stars reflect thy sparkling eyes."

23. Armida smiled at this, yet not the less
Kept to her toilet, gath'ring up behind
Her hair, restricting each resplendent tress
That in loose tangles wanton'd in the wind ;
The less she curl'd in rings, and with them twined
Flowers that, like lazuli in gold, impress'd
A deeper charm on the beholder's mind ;
Then to the native lilies of her breast
She join'd the foreign rose, and smooth'd her veil and vest.

24. Not Juno's bird such beauty spreads to show
In her eyed plumes so ravishingly bright,
Nor Iris such, when her celestial bow
Spans the dark cloud with gold and purple light ;
But rich beyond all richness shines to sight
The glorious cest which 'tis her wont to wear
At all times, e'en though naked, and at night ;
A local shape she gave to things of air,
And in it blended all of lovely, sweet and rare :—

25. Tender disdains, repulses mild, feign'd fears,
Kind looks, sweet reconcilements, blissful stings,
Smiles, little love-words, sighs, delicious tears,
Hopes, turtle kisses, music, marriage rings ;
Embraces dear, and all ambrosial things
She fused, commingled slowly in the chaste
Bright fire, attemper'd in cool Lydian springs,
And fashion'd thus this talisman of Taste,
Which, in itself a charm, clasps round her charming waist.

26. At length, their courtship o'er, she farewell took,
Gave him a kiss, sigh'd, smiled, and went her way ;
For o'er the pages of her magic book,
Murm'ring her charms, she spent some hours each day ;
He, by a kind of charm compell'd to stay,
Remain'd ; for not one moment from these groves
Her jealous fear allow'd his steps to stray :
Alone mid bees, birds, fountains, flowers, alcoves,
And grots, save when with her, the hermit lover roves.

27. But when the soft and silent shade recalls
The ready lovers to their stolen delights,
Under one roof within the palace walls
They meet, and happy pass harmonious nights.
Now when Armida for severer rites

Had left her hermit love, her pleasant play,
And variegated garden, the two knights,
From the green bushes where conceal'd they lay,
Rush'd forth in radiant arms whose light enrich'd the day.

28. As the fierce steed, from busy war withdrawn
Awhile to riot in voluptuous ease,
Midst his loved mares loose wantons o'er the lawn,
If chance he hears once more upon the breeze
The spirit-stirring trumpet sound, or sees
The flash of armor, thither, far or near,
He bounds, he neighs, he prances o'er the leas,
Burning to whirl to war the charioteer,
Clash with the rattling car, and knap the sparkling spear.

29. So fared Rinaldo, when the sudden rays
Of their bright armor on his eyeballs beat;
At once those lightnings set his soul ablaze,
His ardor mounts to all its ancient heat;
Their vivid beam his sparkling eyes repeat,
Drown'd though he was, and drunken with the wine
Of siren wantonness: on footsteps fleet,
Ubald meanwhile to where he lay supine
Came, and the diamond shield turn'd to him, pure and fine.

30. Upon the lucid glass his eyes he roll'd,
And all his delicacy saw; his dress,
Breathing rich odors, how it gleam'd with gold!
How trimly curl'd was each lascivious tress!
And with what lady-like luxuriousness
His ornamented sword address'd his side!
So wrapp'd with flowers it swung, that none could guess
If 'twas a wounding weapon, or applied
As a fantastic toy, voluptuous eyes to pride

31. As one by heavy sleep in bondage held,
Comes to himself when the long dream takes flight,
So woke the youth when he himself beheld,
Nor could endure the satire of the sight:
Down fell his looks; and instantly, in spite
Of recollected pride, the color came
Across his face;—in this embarrass'd plight,
A thousand times he wish'd himself in flame,
Ocean, in earth, th' abyss, to shun the glowing shame.

32. Then spake Ubaldo ; "Hearken and give ear ;
Asia and Europe to the battle crowd ;
Whoever counts or faith or glory dear,
Stands to the strife for Christ against Mahmoud.
Thee, son of Berthold, thee alone, the vow'd
To honor and renown, loose idlesse charms
To a small angle of the world, more proud
To play the lover in a lady's arms,
Than champion deathless deeds,—thee only naught alarms !

33. "What sleep, what lethargy, what base delights
Have melted down thy manhood, quench'd thy zeal ?
Up ! up ! thee Godfrey, thee the camp invites ;
For thee bright Vict'ry stays her chariot wheel.
Come, fated warrior, set the final seal
To our emprise ! thy coming all expect ;
Let the false Saracens confounded feel
That sword from which no armor can protect ,
Haste, and in total death destroy the impious sect !"

34. He ceased ; the noble Infant for a space
Stood stupefied, attempting no defense ;
But soon as bashfulness to scorn gave place,
Scorn, the fine champion of indignant sense,
Then, with a yet diviner eloquence,
Another redness than of shame rush'd o'er
His cheeks, almost atoning his offense ;
The rich embroider'd ornaments he wore,
Away with hasty hand indignantly he tore.

35. Begone he would, and through the intricate
Labyrinth of galleries from the garden fled ;
Meanwhile Armida, by the regal gate
Starts to behold her savage keeper dead.[16]
At first a vague suspicion, a blind dread,
Then a quick feeling of the fatal truth
Instinctive flash'd across her mind ; her head
She turn'd, and saw (too cruel sight !) the youth
Haste from her bless'd abode, without concern or ruth.

36. "Oh cruel ! leav'st thou then Armida spurn'd ?"
She would have said, but choking sorrow drown'd
The issuing cry, and the faint words return'd,
With bitter echo in her heart to sound :
Poor wretch ! her happiness its term has found ;
A power and wisdom above hers constrain
Thy youth to hurry from th' enchanted ground

With so much speed ; she sees it, and in vain
Tries all her wonted arts, the recreant to retain.

37. All dreadful strains that o'er Thessalian lips
Spoke to lost spirits, every potent spell
That could arrest the planets, or eclipse,
And call up demons disenchain'd from hell,
She knew, she tried, yet could not now compel
One gibb'ring ghost to answer to her cry;
Thus she gave o'er her incantations fell,
And would essay if stronger sorcery
Dwelt in pale Beauty's tear and supplicating eye.

38. Careless of honor, off she ran, she flew ;
Where are her vaunts, ah, where her triumphs now?
She who the total sway of Love o'erthrew,
And judgment gave but by her bending brow ;
And like her pride was her disdain ! O how,
Loving their love, did she her slaves despise !
Herself alone could she at all allow
To pleasure her, nor aught in man could prize,
Beyond th' effect produced by her two radiant eyes.

39. Left and neglected now, she follows swift
Him who forsakes her in his careless scorn ;
And summons all her tears up, the poor gift
Of her rejected beauty to adorn ·
Headlong she runs, uncheck'd by brier or thorn ;
O'er rugged Alpine rocks and glaciers hoar
Her tender feet adventure to be torn ;
Lord cries, as messengers, she sends before,
Which reach not him, till he has reach'd the winding shore.

40. Madly she cries ; "O cruel fugitive !
That bear'st with thee my dearer half away,
Either take this, or that restore, or give
Death to them both together ; stay, O stay !
Let my last words to thee at least find way,
I say not kisses ; these sweet gifts from thee
Some worthier favorite may receive,—delay
Thy flight, unkind ! what dost thou fear from me ?
Thou canst as well refuse, when thou hast ceased to flee."

41. "Signior," said then Ubaldo, "to refuse
Her wish, would be unkindness too severe :
Most sweetly bathed in sorrow's briny dews,

Arm'd with fond prayers and beauty she draws near.
Thy tempted virtue will shine forth more clear,
If, list'ning to the siren, thou remain
Proof to her winning voice and starting tear ;
So Reason shall resume her peaceful reign
O'er sense, and thus refined, her native light regain."

42. At this he stay'd until she reach'd the shore ;
Pale she came up, faint, breathless, all in tears,
And mournful past expression ; but the more
She mourns, her beauty more divine appears :
Eager she eyes him ; but mistrustful fears,
Disdain, amazement, or excess of woe
Keeps her quite mute ; Rinaldo volunteers
No look, no glance at her, at least in show,
But stands with bashful eyes at stealth unclosing slow.

43. As skillful singers, ere they strain on high
Their voice in the loud song's symphonious flow,
Prepare the mind for the full harmony,
By sweetest preludes, warbled soft and low :
Thus she, who had not, e'en in deepest woe,
Wholly lost memory of her fraudful art,
First breathed a symphony of sighs forth, so
By just degrees to predispose the heart,
To which her words the print of pity would impart.

44. Then thus : "Expect not I shall fondly bow,
Cruel ! to thee, as loves to lovers should ;
Such once we were,—if such no longer now,
If e'en the thought of thine impassion'd mood
Move thy displeasure, as I judge, be woo'd,
At least, my mournful plea to entertain,
As foemen the proud prayers of foes subdued ;
My suit is such, as thou with little pain
Mayst grant, and yet keep all thy harshness and disdain

45. "If me thou hate, and in it tak'st delight,
Hate on, I come not to disturb thy joy ;
Just it may seem, just be it, for with spite
Thy sect, thyself I labor'd to destroy !
What fierce expedients did I not employ,
A Pagan born, to sap your power ! nay, more,
Thee did I hate, thee chase, and thee decoy
To the strange borders of an unknown shore,
Far from the din of arms, where only sea-waves roar.

46. "And, which seems most to move thy grief and
shame,
Add with how much of tender, kind, and sweet,
Thy frozen heart I fondled into flame,
An impious fondness, sure, a vile deceit!
To let my virgin fruit be pluck'd and eat;
My blooms be spoil'd; my tamelessness subdued,
And cast my beauties at the tyrant's feet!
Those youthful charms for which a thousand sued,
To a mere stranger given, uuhoped, unwish'd, unwoo'd!

47. "Yes! number them amongst my sins, and let
These many crimes against thee hasten more
Thy prompt departure; heed not, but forget
This thy fair mansion, so beloved before!
Go, pass the seas; fight, glut thyself with gore;
Quick to the task! I bid thee o'er the brine;
Destroy our faith—'twill be but what you swore;
What say I? ours? ah no! not mine! not mine!
I, cruel idol! seek alone thy reverenced shrine!

48. "Let me but follow thee! 'tis all I crave;
This mightst thou grant, though I had proved unkind.
Seldom the conqu'ror parts without his slave,
The robber rarely leaves his prey behind:
Me with thy other hapless prisoners bind
For exhibition; to each other aim
At praiseful acts, let this, I pray, be join'd,—
That all may point the finger, and exclaim,
'There the proud scorner goes, now scorn'd with equal
shame!'

49. "A bondslave spurn'd, why longer do I keep
My locks unshorn, by thee now render'd vile?
Cut them clean off! the ground they shall not sweep,
To mock the misery of my servile style.
Thee will I follow from this hated isle;
Thee, when most fervent glows the fight, pursue
Through hostile crowds; I shall not want the while
Spirit or strength a thousand things to do,— [yew.
Bear darts, guide steeds, and strain myself the bending

50. "Either thy shield or shield-bearer, which best
May please thee, I in thy defense will be;
Nor spare my person,—through this throat and breast
The sword shall pass, before it injures thee:
The foe will scarce have so much cruelty
As to strike then, but will perhaps direct

Their darts elsewhere, not to endanger me ;
And smother their fierce vengeance, in respect
Of these poor charms, to which thou dost such strange
neglect.

51. "Wretch ! do I still presume, still place my worth
In these scorn'd charms, which nothing can obtain !"
More would she say, but bitter tears gush forth,
Like springs from Alpine rocks, or falling rain :
She sought to grasp his hand ; she sought to strain,
In suppliant attitude, his robes ; but no—
Himself he curb'd, his tenderness restrain'd,
And started back ; love found no entrance, though
The swelling tears rose high, and stood prepared to flow.

52. Love enter'd not, to fan within his breast
The ancient flame which reason had congeal'd ;
But Pity enter'd in its place at least,
Love's chaste companion, ever prone to yield ;
And touch'd him so, that scarcely he conceal'd,
Scarce, with much pain, the yearning tears repress'd ;
Yet, though she loudly to his heart appeal'd,
The fond emotion he within compress'd,
And when he could, the fair thus tranquilly address'd :

53. "I feel for thee, Armida ! if my powers
Were such, how gladly would I cure the pain
Of the ill-starr'd warm passion that devours
Thy soul,—I have no hatred, no disdain ;
No wish for vengeance moves me ; peace I fain
Would give thee ; wrongs I know not of, much less
Thee as a slave or foe would I retain ;
True, thou hast err'd ; and now all tenderness,
Now all dislike, hast loved and hated to excess :

54. "But these are frailties shared by all, and them
Thy native laws, thy sex, and youth excuse ;
I too have sinn'd, nor thee can I condemn,
If thou to pardon me dost not refuse.
'Midst the dear images I ne'er can lose,
Thine shall be dearest still ; on thee, sweet maid,
In joy and woe 'twill be my bliss to muse ;
Thy champion still—thou still shalt be obey'd,
Far as with honor suits, and our divine crusade.

55. "Let now our mutual faults and follies cease,
And with our faults our shame too have an end ;
And in this lonely island sleep in peace

Their sad sweet memories, let them here descend
As to the silent grave; where'er I wend,
This only act of mine let no one trace,
None whisper to the wind; nor thou, dear friend,
Do, I implore thee, aught that would debase
Thy name, thy worth, thy charms, or shame thy princely race!

56. "Farewell! I go; thy wishes must be vain,
Fate grants them not; Armida, thou art wise!
Or go some happier way, or here remain,
And calm the thoughts that to such wildness rise."
She, while the pensive warrier thus replies,
Restless, disturb'd, could scarce her passion stay;
Long time she roll'd on him her angry eyes,
Nor knew in what fierce terms her scorn to say;
At length the storm broke loose, and these mad words found way.

57. "Thee no Sophia bore, no Azzo gave
Blood for thy being! thy fierce parents were
The icy Caucasus, the mad sea-wave,
Some Indian tiger or Hyrcanian bear!
Why should I longer fawn? did the man e'er
Show but one sign of warm humanity?
Changed he his color at my sharp despair?
Did he but dash one tear-drop from his eye?
Or breathe for all my pangs a single suffering sigh?

58. "What things shall I pass over, what repeat?
He swears he's mine, yet with the whirlwind flies;
Good, merciful, kind victor! to forget,
And pardon your fond foe's indignities.
Hear how he counsels! hark but to his wise
And modest words! this coy Xenocrates,
Hear how he talks of love! O Gods! O skies!
And can you suffer holy men like these,
To burn your towers and towns, and act what sins they please?

59. "Begone, false wretch, with all that peace of mind
Thy treason leaves to me! begone, I say!
Soon shall my ghost, a haunting shade behind,
From which thou canst not tear thyself away,
Dog all thy thoughts by night, thy steps by day;
With snakes and torches, a new Fury, I,
Much as I loved thee, so much will dismay;

And if it be thy fate the strife to try,
Scaped from the roaring waves and tempests of the sky,—

60. "There, midst the dead and dying, thou shalt fall,
And pay for all my wrongs, false chevalier!
Oft on Armida's name distracted call,
In thy last groans, which soon I hope to hear!"
But there the mourner's spirit fail'd, nor clear
Were the last accents; her sweet color flies,
She faints, she falls, her speaking lips adhere,
An icy sweat on her cold forehead lies,
Droops her dejected head, and close her radiant eyes.

61. Thine eyes are closed, Armida; the stern powers
Of fate deny all solace to thy woe;
Look up, poor girl, and see what bitter showers
Stream from the eyes of thine imagined foe!
Couldst thou but hear his sighs, couldst thou but know
The pain he feels, it must thy love renew,
And in thy bitter cup fresh sweetness throw;
All that he can, he gives to thee, still true,
And takes (thou think'st it not) a last—a fond adieu.

62. What should he do? leave on the naked sands
The lady thus, betwixt alive and dead?
Pity forbids, and courtesy withstands,
But hard necessity compels,—'tis sped;
One farewell kiss,—he parts; the grot they tread,
And launch from land; mild blow the western gales
Midst the rich tresses of the pilot's head;
Fast o'er green ocean glide the golden sails;
To land he looks, till land his grieving vision fails.

63. Waked from her trance, Armida, with a start,
Look'd round her,—all was silence; all was shade;
"And *is* he gone?" she said, "and *had* he heart
To leave me thus, nor for a moment stay'd,
In doubt of life or death, a little aid
To lend? nor for one moment linger'd o'er,
To watch the pale, mute ruin he had made?
And do I love him still, and on this shore
With folded arms still sit, still unrevenged deplore?

64. "Why weep I longer? other arms and arts
Command I not? I will the wretch pursue;
Nor shall the deep o'er which his bark departs,
Nor heaven's high vault secure him from his due!

I will o'ertake him; cleave his heart in two;
And hang his sever'd head upon a spot,
Where all like traitors may the monster view;
Versed as he is in guile, I will outplot
His brain,—alas, I rave! I talk I know not what!

65. "Then, wretched girl! thou shouldst have wreak'd thy hate,
When he lay safely curling in thy chain;
That had been something worth! now all too late
Come thy hot wrath, and thy incensed disdain!
But, if my beauty and ingenious brain
Can nothing here, not fruitless shall this strong
And passionate desire of mine remain;
O my scorn'd charms! yours, yours was all the wrong;
To you shall the dear task of vengeance now belong.

66. "These charms of mine shall be the fix'd reward
Of him who slays the man! your swords prepare,
O my famed lovers! though the task seem hard,
Yet great and glorious is the deed you dare:
I, who in independent state shall wear
The crown of rich Damascus, will be nigh,
In guerdon of the victim; if this rare
Reward appear too poor, revenge to buy,
Nature! I thank thee not for charms ill praised so high.

67. "False, fatal gifts! I spurn you back! I scorn
The hated kingdom which I have to give;
I hate my life, the hour when I was born,
Alone in hope of sweet revenge I live!"
In broken words, enraged, thus does she grieve,
Thus rave; then turns with a distracted pace
From the lone shore, the moments to retrieve;
Showing what fury in her heart found place,
By her dishevel'd hair, fierce eyes, and crims'ning face.

68. Reach'd her abode, with foaming lips she call'd
Three hundred ghosts from Tartarus the dun;
Black clouds the tranquil face of heaven appall'd,
Pale in a moment grew th' eternal sun;
The whirlwinds bluster'd on the hills, air spun,
Hell bellow'd at her feet; then might you hear
Through the enchanted halls the damned run,
Unchain'd and raging, now far-off, now near,—
Shrieks, hissings, yells, drear groans, and whisp'rings yet more drear.

69. A raven shade, more dark than darkest night,
Cloak'd all the hill, enliven'd by no ray,
Save now and then dull flashes of blue light,
That made the following gloom yet more dismay.
Slowly at length the blackness clear'd away;
The round pale sun shone out, but nothing clear;
Gloomy the earth, the air was aught but gay,
Nor of the palace did one trace appear,
Nor would you venture now, e'en to exclaim, 'twas here.

70. As when the clouds at summer eve have drawn
In air huge towers and temples, they remain
Till wind or sunshine comes, and straight they're gone,
Like a dream figured in the sick man's brain:
So melt th' enchanted towers, with all their train
Of rich delights, and leave but for the eye
The hoary face of nature,—the still main,
Brown hills, and frowning woods. Her chariot nigh
She as is usual mounts, and fast away doth fly.

71. The clouds she cleaves, and round her doth enroll
Thunders and tempests, lightnings, wave, and wind;
The regions subject to the Southern pole,
And all their unknown natives left behind,
Calpe she cross'd; nor, in her fretful mind,
Stoop'd to the Spaniard, or the Moor, but o'er
The Midland Sea her winged car inclined;
Nor to the right, nor to the left hand bore,
Till in mid air she reach'd the known Assyrian shore.

72. Not now to fair Damascus does she post,
But shuns the aspect of her once dear land,
And guides her chariot to the Dead-Sea coast,
Where the strong-holds of the Enchantress stand.
Alighting here, she from her duteous band
Of damsels and of pages hides her face,
And, wand'ring lonely on the sea-beat strand,
Fluctuates from scheme to scheme in doubtful case;
But soon all shame to rage and wish'd revenge takes place.

73. "Yes, hence I will," she cried, "before his swarms
Th' Egyptian king shall move in Sion's aid;
Each art react, remuster all my charms,
To ev'ry uncouth thing my sex degrade,
That may assist my purpose;—undismay'd,
Handle the brand and bow, become the flame

Of the most potent, and direct his blade ;
Let me but have the just revenge I claim,
Farewell, vain self-respect ! farewell, fond maiden shame !

74. " And for the faults I shall hereby commit,
Let my sage guardian blame himself, not me ;
He first to thoughts and offices unfit
Set my frail sex and daring spirit free ;
He made me first a gadding damsel, he
Spurr'd on my ardor, loosed me from the rein
Of timorous awe and shame-faced modesty ;
His be the guilt of all then that may stain,—
All I have done through love, or may do through disdain."

75. Thus fix'd, she gather'd in, on Arab steeds,
Damsels, and knights, and servitors in haste ;
And in their sumptuous arms and woman's weeds,
Display'd at once her fortune and fine taste.
Forward she set ; and, journeying the wild waste,
Took nor repose by night, nor rest by day,
Till her keen eye along th' horizon traced
Th' Egyptian hosts, that in their mail'd array
Wide o'er the sunbright sands of antique Gaza lay.

END OF CANTO XVI.

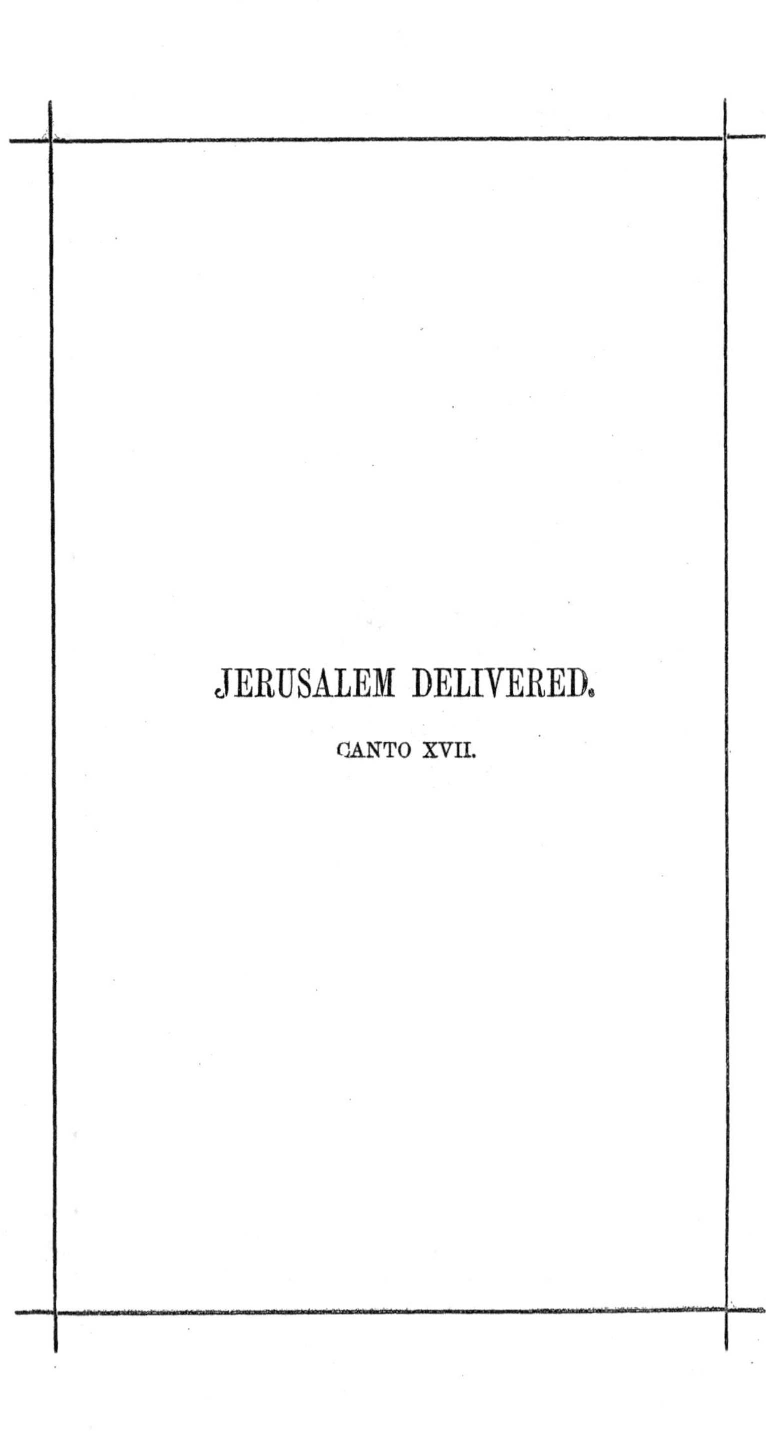

JERUSALEM DELIVERED.

CANTO XVII.

ARGUMENT.

His countless swarms th' Egyptian Prince reviews,
And 'gainst the Croises sends them forth ; Armide,
Who, still incensed, Rinaldo's death pursues,
Joins with her train the hosts ere they proceed,
And, with the surer certainty and speed
To wreak her will, presents her charms divine,
In guerdon of revenge ; the Hero, freed,
Puts on invulnerable arms, where shine
In bold relief the deeds of his illustrious line.

JERUSALEM DELIVERED.

CANTO XVII.

1 UPON Judea's confines, on the way
That leads to old Pelusium, Gaza stands;
Built on the shore, it overlooks the bay,
And on the east the bordering tract commands,—
A fruitless waste, a solitude of sands,
Which, like the waters of the tossing main,
The breathing whirlwind spreads o'er all the lands,
And scarce the pilgrim can his course maintain,
Against the frequent storm that sweeps th' unstable plain.

2. The Caliph's frontier city, it had been
Won from the Turk, the fruit of old debates;
And being situate nearest to the scene
Of the vast enterprise he meditates,
The seat of empire hither he translates
From Cairo, bord'ring on the Red Sea coasts,
His sumptuous Capital: from all his States
The flower of warriors which each province boasts,
He has assembled here, and musters now his hosts.

3. Muse! to my mind recall those bygone times;
Say what was then the standing state of things;
What powers the Caliph moved, from what far climes,
What troops of vassals, and what trains of kings;
The hosts, the leaders and the arms he brings
From the wide Orient to the South, rehearse!
Thou, only thou hast power t' unlock the springs
Of antique story, and assist my verse
In arms to venture half the banded universe!

4. When from the Grecian Cæsar Egypt first
Rebell'd, a warrior from th' Arabian Seer

Sprung, in the same fierce superstition nursed,
Tyrant became, and fix'd his kingdom here ;
Califfe the chief was call'd, a name of fear,
And those who after him the scepter held,
Took the same term, as Nile, from year to year,
Her Pharaohs first, then Ptolemies beheld,
Renew'd from sire to son, till both this third expell'd.

5. Long years their empire had confirm'd, and now
Behold its spacious bounds ! it comprehends
Libya, from where the palms of Barca bow,
Cyrene towers, and Marmarica bends ;
Thence, passing southward up the Nile, extends
To where in lonely state Syene stands ;
And, compassing unpeopled countries, ends
In spicy sweet Sabæa's happy lands,
And where Euphrates winds his way through silent sands.

6. To right and left in its embrace it boasts
The rich Red Sea and all its incensed shore,
On to the regions of those Eastern coasts,
Whose suns the Persian did whilere adore ;
Much is the kingdom in itself ; but more,
Ruled by a king resolving to assert
The ancient honors and renown it bore,—
A prince by blood, but more so by desert,
In ev'ry warlike art and policy expert.

7. Oft 'gainst the Persians, 'gainst the Turks he rear'd
His flag, assailing or assail'd ; the same,
Conqu'ring or conquer'd, save that he appear'd
Greater, o'ercome, than when he overcame :
Now, gray with age, he left the toilsome game,
The soldier's hauberk for the caliph's gown,
And sheath'd his saber ; but the warrior's flame
Still warm'd his heart, nor did he yet lay down
Th' ambitious will that grasp'd at limitless renown.

8. Still through his ministers he wars, and yet
So full of vigorous intellect appears,
That the vast frame of empire seems a weight
Too slight to cumber much his wintry years.
Libya through all her petty kingdoms fears
His nod, and trembles at his naked blade ;
Remotest India his decree reveres ;
And one and all send tributary aid,
Either in troops, or gold, with prompt submission paid.

9. Such was the king who from each Orient realm
Had summon'd forth, and now impels the flower
Of his vast forces northward, to o'erwhelm
The conqu'ring Franks, and crush their rising power;
Last comes Armida, in the very hour
Fix'd by the king his armies to survey,
Apt for review : apart from tent and tower,
On the vast plain the hosts, at break of day,
Proudly before him pass in orderly array.

10. High on a sumptuous throne he takes his seat,
Climb'd by a hundred ivory steps ; his tread
Is upon gold and purple ; from the heat,
A spacious sky of silver shades his head ;
In glitt'ring interchange of white and red,
Diamond and rubies grace his robes, not spare
Of more barbaric ornaments ; instead
Of the gemm'd diadem, white linen fair,
Wrapp'd round in thousand folds, crowns high his rev
erend hair.

11. His right hand holds the scepter,—white as snow
Descends his venerable beard ; serene
With some severity, his eyes yet glow
With their first fires, intelligent and keen :
In all his acts the majesty was seen
Of age and empire, majesty that knew
No change of state ; perchance with such a mien
Great Phidias sculptured, and Apelles drew
Jove the divine, but Jove as he his thunders threw !

12. Near him to right and left two Satraps stand,
Pre-eminent,—the one of most renown
Sustains the sword of justice in his hand,
Unsheath'd ; the other bears beneath his gown
Th' imperial seal, and, counsel to the crown,
Transacts the civil business of the state ;
But he who wears a more habitual frown,
Has powers more terrible—high magistrate,
Prince of the hosts, and sworn executor of fate.

13. Below, a standing guard around the throne,
His Mamalukes plant their lances, thick and wide,
Arm'd not with spears and cuirasses alone,
But long curved sabers pendent at their side.
Thus sate the Tyrant ; and at leisure eyed,
From his high station, the collected cloud
Of nations pass : ministrant to his pride,

Low at his feet, in passing, the mute crowd
Their ensigns, arms, and plumes in meek devotion bow'd.

14. First march th' Egyptian troops, four squadrons, led
Each by a chief ; two in her Upper plain
Where heavenly Nile uprises, and two bred
Amidst her Lower regions, a domain
Won by his waters from the salt-sea main,—
Their rich alluvial slime outstretch'd the shore,
And, settling, form'd a fruitful soil for grain ;
Thus Egypt grew, and what was sea before,
Is now far inland ground, obnoxious to the oar.

15. In the first troop appear the dusky race
Whom the rich plain of Alexandria breeds ;
With those who dwell along the coasts that face
The glowing West, a region that succeeds
The Libyan Isthmus ; these Araspes leads,
A proud and potent Chief, but less renown'd
For hardy valor than for crafty deeds,
In every art of Moorish war profound,
Skill'd in false flights t' attack, in ambuscades to wound

16. Next come the tribes that front the morning star
And Asian coasts ; they rank beneath the crest
Of soft Arontes, whom no deeds of war,
But rank and titles raise to some request.
Ne'er has the helm till now his temples press'd ;
Nor e'er till now have the shrill serenades
Of morning trumpets broke his present rest ;
But fond ambition him at last persuades,
To try the soldier's life and leave his native shades.

17. The third that follows seems no single band,
But a vast host ; it fills the fields and shore ;
You'd think that all the harvests of the land
Were, for such swarms, an insufficient store :
Yet them a single City, rank'd before
Whole provinces in strength, wherein reside
Myriads of men—Grand Cairo sends ; thence pour
The mighty swarms that pass, troops yet untried
In the debates of war, and Campson is their guide.

18. Next under Gazel march the men who reap
The grain that in the bord'ring garden grows
Far up the River, to the lofty steep
O'er which its second cataract foaming flows.
All these Egyptians have but swords and bows ;

No helm their heads, no cuirass fortifies
Their breasts, but passing rich their vesture shows,
Which leads the foe in battle to despise
Chance of impending death, in passion for the prize.

19. Next come, half naked and unarmed, the hordes
Of Barca, rank'd beneath Alarcon's sway,
Who for long ages with voracious swords
Have ranged the deserts, and sustain'd by prey
Their famish'd lives ; more civilized than they,
But inexpert in marshal'd war, succeed
Those who Zumara's turban'd king obey,
And them from Tripoli ; they both exceed
In flying fights, and wound with all a Parthian's speed.

20. Then follow those who in Arabia dwell,
The Stony, and the Happy land, which knows
Neither (if true the tales that pilgrims tell)
Th' excess of summer heats, or winter snows.
Where flourishes the balm, the spikenard blows ;
Where dies the immortal Phœnix to assume
Fresh life, with leaves of myrtle and of rose,
And each diviner plant of sweet perfume,
Building at once her bower, her cradle, and her tomb.

21. With bow and cimeter resembling those
Th' Egyptians bear, less dainty is their dress ;
Their dark array the Bedouin Arabs close,
Who no fix'd region or abodes possess ;
But o'er the wild unstable wilderness
Their migratory tents and cities bear,
Perpetual pilgrims ; womanlike, not less
Shrill are their voices, short their forms and spare,
Long their wild raven locks, their faces just as fair.

22. Long Indian canes, with iron tipp'd, they bear,
And upon steeds so nimble sweep along,
You'd say a whirlwind blew them past, if e'er
The wings of whirlwinds had a speed so strong.
Syphax the first undisciplined rude throng
Commands ; the next Aldino trains for fight ;
The rest to fierce Albiazar belong,
Whom rapine, wounds, and blood alone delight,
A sort of kingly thief—a murderer, not a knight.

23. Then pass the Islanders with fleecy curls,
Whose homes are compass'd by th' Arabian waves,
By whom those shells which breed the Persian pearls

Are dived and fish'd for, in their Green-Sea caves.
With them are join'd a host of sable slaves,
Negroes, along the coasts of Nubia born ;
Foremost of those kings Agricalt outbraves
The best, while these obey Osmida's horn,
A wretch that mocks at faith, and laughs all laws to scorn.

24. The Isle of Meröe next its Ethiops sends,
Which Nilus there, and Astrabora here,
Gird with their waves ; three realms comprehends
And two religions in its spacious sphere :
Them young Canario leads, and Asimire,
Both monarchs, both Mahometans, and both
The Caliph's tributary friends; but here
The third comes not,—the Caliph would be loath
Or to employ his arms, or trust his Christian oath.

25. Two other subject kings, in brave array,
Bring up their archers next, a goodly band ;
The first from Ormus, which the Persian bay
Encompasses, a rich luxurious land,—
The last from Böecan, whose banks of sand
Th' embracing ocean at high tide sweeps o'er,
And forms an isle ; but shortly, from its strand,
When the tide ebbs, men scorn the billows' roar,
And with unmoisten'd feet pass safe from shore to shore.

26. Nor could a much-loved wife, great Altamore,
Thee in her happy bridal bed detain ;
Her breast she beat, her golden tresses tore,
To stay thy fatal voyage, but in vain.
"Cruel !" she said, "has then the frightful main
A face than mine more lovely or more mild?
And can it seem more pleasant to sustain
The sword and shield with bloody dust defiled,
Than kiss thy consort's cheek, and dance thine infant child?"

27. He is the king of Samarcand ; his crown
Is free, but not in this his glories dwell ;
Well versed in arms, his courage and renown
All others' courage and renown excel ;
Th' unconscious Franks shall know it but too well,
Already have they cause to fear his face :
His soldiers, each rude weapon to repel,
Wear coats of mail, fine helms their temples grace,
Their thighs the sword display, their saddle-bows the mace.

28. Lo, next, where fierce Adrastus from far Ind,
Aurora's land, comes frowning! he nor bears
Breastplate nor helm, but for a charm, behind,
A rich green snake-skin streak'd with sable wears:
Thus arm'd, all dangers of the fight he dares;
Upon a monstrous elephant he rides,
His constant wont when he for war prepares;
From this side Ganges he the people guides,
That live where Indus rolls to sea his mighty tides.

29. Next come the king's own troops, choice warriors, class'd
The flower of Memphian chivalry; all those
Who with most honor and renown had pass'd
Through peace and war, this body-guard compose;
Arm'd for security and fear, each shows
A barb obedient to his armed heel;
And heaven itself smiles, sparkles, shines, and glows
From their array—as round the field they wheel,—
Helm, cuirass, mantle, plume; gems, crimson, gold, and steel.

30. Here rides Alarco fierce, and Odemar,
Marshaler of armies; Idraote, Rimedon,
For proud audacity renown'd afar,
Who laughs at death, and veils his plume to none;
Rapoldo, glorious for his murders done,
Corsair and tyrant of the sea; inflamed
Tigranes, Ormond, whom the mighty shun,
And Marlabust Arabicus, surnamed
From the rebellious hordes his sword so oft has tamed.

31. Orindo, Pirga, Arimon, Brimarte,
Scaler of towns, are here with swift Siphante,
Tamer of steeds; and, of the wrestler's art
Thou the great master, strong Aridamante!
And, foremost upon tower and crag to plant
His standard, thunderbolt of war, severe
Young Tisaphernes! with whom none can vaunt
Like skill, in tilt or tournay to career,
On foot the sword to wave, in selle to toss the spear.

32. A brave Armenian guides them, who in youth,
Unfix'd in Christ, Mahometan became;
Then Clement he was call'd, but from the truth
Departing, Emirene is now his name;
In all besides a man of noble fame,
Dear to the Caliph above all his band

Of Satraps,—equal honor may he claim,
Soldier or chief, in action or command,
For wisdom, dauntless heart, and valiant strength of hand.

33. All were now pass'd; when lo! in splendid state
Appears Armida, and her troop displays;
With robes succinct, high on her car she sate,
Arm'd like the quiver'd Goddess of the chase.
The new displeasure in her angel face
Mix'd with the native sweetness which it wore,
To its fine features gave but sharper grace;
Wounded herself, deep wounds and torments sore
She seems, incensed, to threat, and threat'ning charms the more.

34. Her car, that glorious as Aurora's roll'd,
With rubies, pearls, and hyacinths glister'd clear;
Four pairs of unicorns, with yokes of gold,
Pass to the rich reins of the charioteer.
A hundred pages and fair girls appear
Near her, whose quivers at their backs resound;
Smart archers all, they o'er the plain career
On milk-white steeds, well practiced to wheel round
And swift with horny hoofs spurn back the dinted ground.

35. Her army follows, from Damascus sent
By Idraote, and led by Aradine:—
As when the new-born Phœnix makes ascent
To visit her warm realms beneath the Line,
With golden crown, starr'd wings, and necklace fine
Of all rich feathers—purple, crimson, green,
A sparkling carcanet,—her state divine
The world beholds amazed, and round their queen
A crowd of awestruck birds fly, glorying in her sheen.

36. So pass'd Armida, so Armida shined
In habit, gesture, and commanding grace!
Nor was there one so stern and uninclined
To love, but glow'd those beauties to embrace.
If she can charm in this her sullen case
Nations so various, in so short a while,
What will she do when with a happy face
She pays court to them in her sweetest style,
Woos with her radiant eyes, and thrills with her fond smile!

37. But when she too in her admired costume
Had pass'd applauded, and the pageant closed,
The king for Emerino sent, to whom,
Preferr'd to all his captains, he proposed
To give the sole direction of the host;
Divining his intent the Chief attends,
And with an air that shows him for the post
Well worthy, comes—the guard asunder rends,
Leaving a midway path, and he the throne ascends.

38. He bows his head, he bends his knee, his hand
Lays on his heart, and thus the king: "To thee
This scepter, Emirene, to thy command,
I yield these hosts,—rule thou in lieu of me;
Setting the subject king of Judah free,
Bear not the sword of my revenge in vain;
Go, see, and conquer! let no Christian be
Saved from the slaughter, or, if some remain,
Let them to me be brought, and fill no gentle chain."

39. Thus spoke the Tyrant; and the turban'd Peer
The sov'reign rule accepting, thus replied:
"From thy unconquer'd hand, blest Sire, I here
The scepter take, with fortune for my guide!
Strong in thy strength, thy captain, I confide
Herein t' avenge upon the Latin race
All Asia's wrongs; but this let strokes decide;
Ne'er but as victor will I see thy face;
The war our death may bring,—it shall not bring disgrace.

40. "Heaven grant, if all (though none indeed I dread)
Should be ordain'd to trouble our success,
The whole black storm may burst upon my head!
Safe be the host, and its dead leader less
In funeral sorrow than the happiness
Of pomp triumphal home be borne along!"
Thus spake the Chief; and closing his address,
Loud shouts arose from all that mighty throng,
With harsh barbaric sounds from atabal and gong.

41. Midst this wild music and these shouts, the king,
Girt by his brave Circassians, left the throne
For the gay tent, and to rich banqueting
The Chiefs inviting, took his seat alone;
Whence, now rich dainties, now in pleasant tone
He graceful compliments to each address'd,
Not one neglecting; here when all were flown

With mirth, the wine-cup circling with the jest,
Fit space Armida found, her project to digest.

42. But, the feast finish'd, and all eyes intent
On her fair aspect, she, who clearly read
By well-known signs that to her heart's content
Her pleasing poison in all minds was shed,
Rose, turn'd toward the king her graceful head,
And, in an attitude 'twixt grief and cheer,
Rev'rence and inborn haughtiness, thus said :
Studying in voice and gesture to appear,
Much as she could, serene, fierce, gen'rous, and severe.

43. "I too am come, great king ! to dare the worst,
Firm for our faith, our country, and our right ;
A Lady, true, but in a palace nursed,—
A Princess sure may well become the fight.
Who hopes to rule an empire, should not slight
One brave accomplishment,—the self-same hand
Should poise the spear as scepter ; mine shall smite,
(Nor slow, nor torpid to the bow or brand,)
And learn with foeman's blood to fertilize the land.

44. "Think not that now for the first time the star
Of glory lights me to this noble aim ;
That only now I have been prompt by war
T' uphold our laws, and fortify the frame
Of thy vast empire ! whether what I name
Be true, or utter'd out of vain parade,
Thou shouldst thyself remember,—thou my fame
Hast heard—what troops of those who bear display'd
The Redcross, Nobles all, my captive slaves I made :—

45. "They in my snares were taken, were secured,
And as a noble gift to thee were sent,
And might have lain perpetually immured
In thy dark dungeons,—such was mine intent,—
So hadst thou now gone forth more confident
Of ending, by a glorious victory,
The desp'rate conflict upon which we're bent,
Had not Rinaldo, doom'd our curse to be,
Slain my appointed guards, and set the prisoners free.

46. "Who this Rinaldo is, is not unknown ;
The world's but too much pester'd with his name ;
This is the savage who has overthrown
Our hopes, nor have I yet avenged the shame.
Hence does fierce anger, with just cause, inflame

My rising spirit; hence does it inspire
This my resolve to arms; I am all flame:
For other wrongs I have, but they would tire,
Let what is said suffice; revenge is my desire.

47. "And I revenge will have! all shafts the skies
Cut not in vain, some work the shooter's will;
And Allah oft his red right hand applies
To dart his bolts against triumphant ill.
But lo! if any will the ruffian kill,
Cut off the head I so much hate to see,
And cast it reeking at my feet, his skill
Shall have my thanks; the vengeance sweet will be,
But O, ten times more sweet, if wrought indeed by me.

48. "Yes, 'twill be sweet; so sweet, I will resign
What most I prize, what numbers vainly sued,
My crown, my marriage portion, and, in fine,
Myself, if that be the reward he would.
All these I vow, and make my promise good
By the firm oath; all solemnly I swear
Inviolable faith and gratitude
Through life; if any think the proffer fair,
Let him in terms as frank the rising thought declare!"

49. When thus the Lady had proclaim'd her mind,
Adrastus, greedy of her charms, replied:
"Now Heaven forbid thy shafts should be so kind
As to destroy the barbarous homicide!
So base a heart—does it deserve," he cried,
"That thou, fair Amazon, its blood should shed?
Forego the thought! and in my arm confide
To gratify thy wrath, revenge the dead,
And at thy saintly feet to roll his odious head!

50. "I'll pluck his heart out; to the vultures I
Will, joint by joint, his carcass cast!" thus spoke
The swarthy Indian; but his vaunting high
The gallant Tisaphernes ill could brook:
"And who," he cried, with anger in his look,
"Art thou, who giv'st thyself such gorgeous airs
Before the king, nor fear'st our fierce rebuke?
Look round! here's one perchance at least that dares
Outact thy mighty vaunts, though more his words he spares."

51. Quick the fierce Indian answer'd; "I am one
Whose deeds were never by his words surpass'd;

But if elsewhere thy insolence had run
To such excess, the insult were thy last."
And here from threats to blows they soon had pass'd;
But all repress'd the quarrel, and between
Both chiefs the monarch his dread scepter cast:
Then to Armida said: "Illustrious queen!
Thy soul indeed is great, thy manly courage keen.

52. "Worthy thou art that these abase their pride
To thee, and in the sweet abasement joy;
That thou hereafter mayst their sabers guide
With surer aim, that felon to destroy;
There let both chiefs their chivalry employ,
And in a happier field their worth contest:"
This said, the monarch ceased; they, nothing coy,
Offer again on scorn'd Rinaldo's crest
To prove whose sworded arm shall wreak her vengeance best.

53. Nor these alone; but all the heroes there,
Renown'd in war, ambitious of her bed,
Offer with vaunts their services,—all swear
To take revenge on his accursed head.
So many arms she moved! such hatreds bred
Against the knight whom late her tender love
Woo'd with all sweets! but he, since first he fled
Th' enchanted isle, and the blue ocean clove,
Swiftly before the wind with all good omens drove.

54. In the same track that it before had plough'd,
The charmed gondola is homeward borne;
And ev'ry air that sings in sail and shroud,
With equal kindness speeds its gay return:
The youth now marks, stretch'd pensive at the stern,
The Pleiads smile, the misty Hyads weep;
Now round the Pole the Bears slow wheeling turn;
And now, as twilight tints cascade and steep,
The rocks whose umber woods o'erhang the shaded deep.

55. Now of the Camp, of foreign nations now,
The various customs he inquires, and weighs;
And thus the briny seas they ceaseless plough,
Three starry nights, and three sunshiny days.
But when the fourth calm sun with farewell rays
Far o'er the waters of the west descends,
The grounding vessel its swift motion stays;
Then spoke the damsel; "Palestine, my friends,
Is won! your voyage here, and here my duty ends."

56. She set the knights ashore, and disappear'd,
Ere they could take farewell, or say, she's gone ;
Meanwhile the Night her sable standard rear'd,
All hues and objects mingling into one.
Long o'er those waste sands, through the twilight dun,
The knights gazed anxious to discern some ray
From tower or cottage-shed, but light was none ;
Nor step of man, nor tract of beast astray,
Nor aught besides was seen that might direct their way.

57. Forward at length they move, and when the dash
Of breaking billows, on the shingles roll'd,
Melts from their ear, far off a sudden flash
Of something radiant may their eyes behold ;
Which, with mild silver rays and gleams of gold
Making the lone night beautiful, withdraws
The shadowy screen that had before controll'd
Their confidence and cheer ; they make no pause,
But to the light advance, and soon perceive the cause.

58. Arms newly forged they see, to a tall elm
Against the rising moon suspended high,
Whence sparkling gems, upon the gilded helm
And mail, shed fire as from a starlight sky :
Near as they draw, much rich-wrought imagery,
Footmen, and knights that on war-horses ride,
On the vast shield emblazon'd they descry ;
An aged watchman sat the arms beside,
Who to receive them rose, when their approach he spied.

59. Well the two warriors knew the ancient face
For that of their wise host and courteous friend ;
He straight received them with a warm embrace,
And when their mutual courtesies had end,
Turn'd to the Youth, who silent seem'd to send
To the tall form he reverenced and admired,
An asking eye, and greeting said : "Attend,
My son ! thee solely in this place retired
I wait, and much to see thy aspect have desired.

60. "For know, I am thy friend, and for thy good
How truly I have cared, inquire of these ;
Who, taught by me, th' enchantments have subdued,
That bound thy life up in voluptuous ease.
Mark now my heavenly precept, which agrees
With perfect bliss, though adverse to the smooth
Seducing siren's ; let it not displease,
But keep it well in mind, till in the truth
A wiser, holier tongue instruct thine erring youth.

61. "Not underneath green shades, by fountains shrill,
Amidst the nymphs and sirens, fruits and flowers,
Is placed our bliss, but on the steep rough hill
Of virtue, climb'd through sunshine, snow, and showers.
He that, embosom'd in Idalian bowers,
Treads but gay Pleasure's primrose path, will ne'er
Reach the high crown ; the royal eagle towers
Round the steep cliff, and thou, wilt thou forbear
To spurn the lowly vale, and fix thine eyrie there?

62. "Nature has given thee elevated thought,
Nature has raised thy face toward the skies,
That thou shouldst look erect, and by well-wrought
Heroic deeds to loftiest glory rise :
Nature has given thee ardent sympathies,
And a brisk wrath, not on each slight pretence
To waste in civil broils, nor yet, unwise,
To be the ministers of appetence,
And ev'ry loose delight discordant to good sense :

63. "But that thy valor, by these passions arm'd,
With more success thy outward foes may quell ;
And check the lusts with which the heart is charm'd
When the strong demons in the blood rebel :
The wise man governs and applies them well
Each to the proper end for which 'tis plain
They were assign'd,—now bids them sink, now swell
As intellectual Reason does ordain,
Prompt to impel them now, now cautious to restrain."

64. Thus spake the Senior ; the hush'd youth, intent,
Stored in his grateful memory all he said,
And, conscious of his errors, meekly bent
His eyes to earth, with cheeks all rosy red.
Well mark'd the Sage the sweet confusion spread,
Well guess'd the secret sentiments that roll'd
Across his mind, and added ; "Raise thy head ;
And in this sculptured shield, my son, behold
What thy illustrious sires achieved in days of old.

65. "Of thy dead ancestors the long bright track
Shall be reveal'd thee in this desert place,
While thou, degen'rate loiterer, hangest back,
Nor stirr'st a step in glory's ardent race !
Arouse thyself ; up ! up ! thy spirit brace ;
Let what I here point out to thee, incite
Thy slumb'ring valor their renown to grace."

Thus spoke the Sage; and, as he spoke, the knight
Fix'd on the pictured shield his keen perusing sight.

66. The learned sculptor, with a master's hand,
In narrow field unnumber'd forms had done;
Here all the race of glorious Azzo stand,
In long unbroken order, sire and son.
The pure unspotted streams were seen to run
From the old Roman source in ancient days;
The Lords stand crown'd with laurel; one by one,
The hoary Sage selects them, and displays
Their wars and glorious deeds, and points his speech with praise.

67. He show'd him Caius, when to foreign foes
The nodding Empire first became a prey,
As the first Prince of Esté, fairly chose
By a glad people, proud his will t' obey;
And how the weaker neighboring states each day
Flock'd to his wing for safety; how he bore
O'er them free rule; and, when by his weak sway
Honorius call'd the Goths, to make once more
The bold and bloody march which they had made before;—

68. And when all Italy appear'd in flame
From their barbaric torch, and weeping Rome,
A slave and prisoner, mourn'd her perish'd fame,
And fear'd the dreadful trumpet of her doom,
How well Aurelius, in that hour of gloom,
Preserved his vassals wholly unenslaved;
Then how, distinguish'd by his lofty plume,
The bold Foresto resolutely braved
The Hun whose barbarous flag Italian breezes waved.

69. By his grim aspect Attila was known,
His eyes like dragons' flashing through the dark;
With his dog's visage who beheld him frown,
Would soothly swear they heard him snarl and bark.
Then, foil'd in duel, you the man might mark
Steal off amidst his train in shame and rage,—
And how from Aquileia's towers, the ark
Of Roman liberty, Foresto sage
Roll'd back the storm of war, the Hector of his age.

70. He fell, and half the fabric with him fell
Of his loved country, Acarine, his son,
Built up the breaches, and defended well

Th' Italian bulwarks, as his sire had done ;
To the strong Fates, not to the savage Hun,
He yielded up Altino, soon renew'd
Upon a safer site,—he join'd in one
A thousand scatter'd seats and hamlets rude,
Where through a fruitful vale his course the Po pur
sued.

71. With walls he bank'd it, in all points complete,
Strong to withstand th' o'erflowing river's rage ;
Thus rose the city doom'd to be the seat
Of Esté's princes in a later age :
Drawn is he driving from his heritage
The savage Alans ; next, with crimson glave,
Venturing with Odoacer to engage,
He dies for Italy ; what fate more brave,
Than thus to share at once his sire's renown and grave !

72. With him fell Alphorisio ; Azzo sad
With his dear brother into exile goes,
Soon to return with arms and counsel, glad
The tyrant's power hath found a timely close ;
Near him, an arrow in his eyeball, shows
Esté's Epaminondas, he who seal'd
With blood his patriot vows ! he in the throes
Of doom dies happy, since from the red field
Fierce Totila is fled, and saved his darling shield.

73. Of Boniface I sing : his boyish son,
Valerian, follows in his steps ; his brand,
And his already manly arm, not one
Of all the Gothic squadrons dare withstand.
Near, of ferocious aspect, sword in hand,
Sculptured is bold Ernesto, cap-a-pee,
Smiting the wild Sclavonians from the land ;
Then comes th' intrepid Aldoardo, he
Who shut the Lombard king from fair Montselice.

74. Henry was there, with Berenger, whose might,
When Charlemagne his flag angust display'd,
Was seen still foremost in the ranks of fight,
Whether he ruled the squandon, or obey'd.
Him Lewis followed,—he from friendly made
Adverse, against that nephew who the throne
Of Italy possess'd, bold battle weigh'd,—
Conquer'd, and took him captive ; next was shown
Otho, by his five sons indisputably known.

75. Here shines Almerico, first Marquis styled
Of that fair City, Princess of the Po;
His musing attitude, and glances mild
To heaven upraised, his pious spirit show,
Founder of churches and of shrines; but lo,
In other mood the second Azzo wars
With Berengarius, his immortal foe!
Who, after various turns of fate, withdraws,
O'ercome, and Azzo gives th' Italian cities laws.

76. Albert, his son, in Germany maintains
His fame; his chivalry is voiced so wide,
From warring, conqu'ring, tilting with the Danes,
That Otho wöos his daughter for a bride,
With a large dowry; next him, is descried
The gallant Ugo with his waving crest,
Whose valor tamed the horns of Roman pride;
He, Marquis now of Italy address'd,
Beneath his guardian care all Tuscany possess'd.

77. The eye Tebaldo, next, and Boniface
Close by his Beatrice's side, engage;
Then no male heir of the illustrious race
Lives to enjoy the extensive heritage.
Matilda follows, who in sex and age
Well that defect supplied by her renown
And hardy deeds; fair, brave, discreet, and sage,
Beyond the golden specter, throne, and crown,
She had the power t' advance the wimple, coif, and gown.

78. A manlike spirit sparkled in her eye,
A more than manlike courage arm'd her look;
The Normans beat, she forced their chief to fly,
Guiscard, who ne'er before the field forsook;
Here the fourth Henry broke, his standard took,
And with the spoil the solemn temple graced;
And there the Pontiff who the thunders shook
Of the dread Vatican, his pride abased,
In high Saint Peter's chair with dignity replaced.

79. Now at her side, now seconding her views,
With looks of reverence and of love, is seen
Azzo the Fifth; but, blest with all kind dews,
From the Fourth Azzo's stock upshooting green,
Yet happier branches beautify the scene;
Lo, where to Germany Lord Guelpho goes!
(Guelpho, his son, by Cunigond his queen;)

Thus in Bavarian fields, transplanted, grows
The good old Roman graft that in Ferrara rose.

80. There with this Estéan branch the Guelphic tree
Engraft, revives, as it was waxing old ;
Now in its scions you the Guelphs might see
Renew their scepters, stars, and crowns of gold,
Brighter than ever ; while each orb that roll'd
In heaven, its fairest rays and aspects shed ;
So that it flourish'd still, and, uncontroll'd,
Tower'd till the heavens themselves confined its head,
Which half the spacious land with fruit and shade o'erspread.

81. Nor less luxuriantly the royal stem
Flower'd in th' Italian boughs ; Bertoldo here
Shot forth, confronting Guelpho, and with them
Azzo the Sixth renew'd the glories clear
Of his great sires :—thus animate appear
Upon the breathing shield, in long array,
These forms, to Fame and to Rinaldo dear ;
A thousand sparks of pride that fond survey
Struck forth, that in the wreck of honor latent lay ;

82. And, for the like divine renown ablaze,
Their gallant actions so transport his brain,
That he already in his mind portrays
The city conquer'd, and the people slain ;
All seems presented, palpably and plain,
Before him,—the storm'd towers, the rending walls ;
He snatches up the arms in ardent vein,
And, almost fancying that the trumpet calls,
With wing'd aspiring hopes the vict'ry far forestalls.

83. Then Charles, who had related long before
The Danish Prince's death, with frank address
The sword presented which Prince Sweno wore,—
"Take it," he said, "and with it good success !
With just and pious sentiments, no less
Than a brave hand employ it, sound and strong,
In Christ's good cause ; may he thine efforts bless !
And thou avenge its former master's wrong,
Who waits it at thy hands, who loved thy virtues long !"

84. "God grant," the knight replied, "for his dear sake,
Since of his sword thus happily possess'd,
That I indeed may full requital take,
And duly thus fulfill his last request !"

Charles, overjoy'd, in brief his thanks express'd,
And added tributes of affection paid;
But here the Sage, with the desire impress'd
To expedite their course, stepp'd in, and pray'd
That their return might now no longer be delay'd.

85. "High time it is," he said, "that you prepare
To reach the army; you will not arrive
Unlook'd-for,—come then, through the dusky air;
Trust to my guidance, safely will I drive."
He said: his words their eagerness revive;
They climb the car, and take their seats; this done,
He cheers his coursers to the lash, which strive,
Curving their necks, each other to outrun,
And shapes their rapid course to meet the morning sun.

86. Through the brown darkness of the night serene
Thus they rode on, with deep reflection mute;
When the Sage spoke: "Thou of thy race hast seen
The various boughs, and traced them to their root;
Yet fancy not, because that ancient shoot
Has thriven so fully in its morn of May,
The fruitful mother of heroic fruit,
That through old age it ever will decay,
And want or fruit or flower, to grace a verdant spray.

87. "O that, as I thy elder sires have drawn
Forth from the Gothic gloom of antique night,
I could the figures of thy sons unborn
Paint on the shield, with hues as clear and bright!
That, ere they ope their eyelids to the light,
I could their triumphs to the world resound!
Then shouldst thou see, with all a sire's delight,
A host of future heroes crowd around,
Their series no less long, their deeds no less renown'd.

88. "But my skill serves not of itself to mark
A ray of truth from out the future shine,
Other than dim and dubious, as the spark
Of a far taper in a misty mine:
Yet, if some tidings of thy future line
In certainty I give, without disguise,
Call it not bold; for what I thus divine,
Is learn'd from One before whose vision lies,
Clear and unveil'd, the scenes and secrets of the skies.

89. "What God's pure light to him, and he to me
Has shown, as freely I to thee relate;

Nor Gentile, Greek, or Latin progeny,
Or in these times, or those of elder date,
E'er teem'd with heroes of such noble state
As Heaven, in its high favor, does foredoom
To thee and thine ; nor may the good and great
In Sparta, Carthage, Macedon, or Rome
To match their glorious fame or majesty presume.

90. "But far o'er others shall Alphonso shine,
In title second, but the first in worth ;
When for illustrious men the world shall pine,
Old and corrupted, shall this prince have birth :
None, in those days of darkness and of dearth,
Shall better sway the sword or scepter bright ;
None with his wisdom so enlighten earth,
Charm in the Court, or fulmine in the fight ;
Thy seed's ascendant pride, his age's guiding light !

91. "While yet a youth, he shall give pregnant signs
Of manhood,—prince in each gymnastic play ;
Scourge of wild beasts mid mountain peaks and pines,
Graced, at all solemn tilts and tournays gay,
With the first shouts and favors of the day ;
And when to actual warfare he shall pass,
Rich spoils and palms victorious bear away ;
And for brave deeds, writ down in breathing brass,
Wear many a votive crown of laurel, oak, and grass.

92. "The equal glory of his riper age
Shall be to stablish peace and calm repose ;
To keep his cities tranquil, from the rage
And powerful influence of surrounding foes ;
To foster genius, ignorance to depose,
The arts encourage, his fond Court present
With joyous pageants, plays, and splendid shows ;
Deal with just hand reward and punishment,
Evils uncome foresee, and seen, with ease prevent.

93. "And O, if e'er against the race whose crimes
Th' infested seas and ravaged shores pollute,—
Tyrants that force in those unhappy times
Illumined nations humbly to make suit
To them for peace,—he march to execute
Justice for fanes down-tumbled, treasure wreck'd,
And violated shrines, in that dispute
What heavy vengeance may they not expect
On the barbarian king and his accursed sect !

94. "In vain the Turk against his marshal'd ranks,
In vain the Moor might muster band on band ;
For far beyond Euphrates' willow'd banks,
The snows of Taurus, and the happy land
Where dwells perpetual sunshine, would his hand
Advance the Golden Lilies, loose the wing
Of the White Eagle, the furl'd Cross expand,
And, by due baptism of each Negro king,
Compel imperial Nile to show his secret spring !"

95. Thus spoke the Senior ; the rapt youth took heed
Of all he utter'd, and with transport fed
On the fair promise of his future seed,
Which o'er his mind a sweet sereneness shed.
Meanwhile before the break of morn fast fled
The twilight hours ; Aurora, dropping dew,
Advanced, and touch'd the heavens with rosy red .
And now the trembling of the flags that flew
On the high tents far off, distinctly met their view.

96. Then thus again the Sage : "These shadows brown
See how the sun disperses ! and displays,
The tents, the plain, the mountains and the town,
With the kind comment of his grateful rays !
O'er unknown tracks, by unobstructed ways,
Safe, without danger or delay, nor slow,
Here have I brought you ; you yourselves may trace
Your onward way, nor fear a single foe ;
Thus then we part ; farewell ! no farther must I go."

97. Embracing, they depart ; and straight pursue
On foot their journey with the crimson cloud
That, floating eastward, a rich radiance threw
On tent, and silent crag, and rampart proud.
Fame flew before them, and divulged aloud
The Baron's wish'd arrival ; wide and fleet
Tho news was borne amidst the cheering crowd ;
Godfrey, thus advertised, his ducal seat
Left, and with stately step went forth the youth to meet.

END OF CANTO XVII.

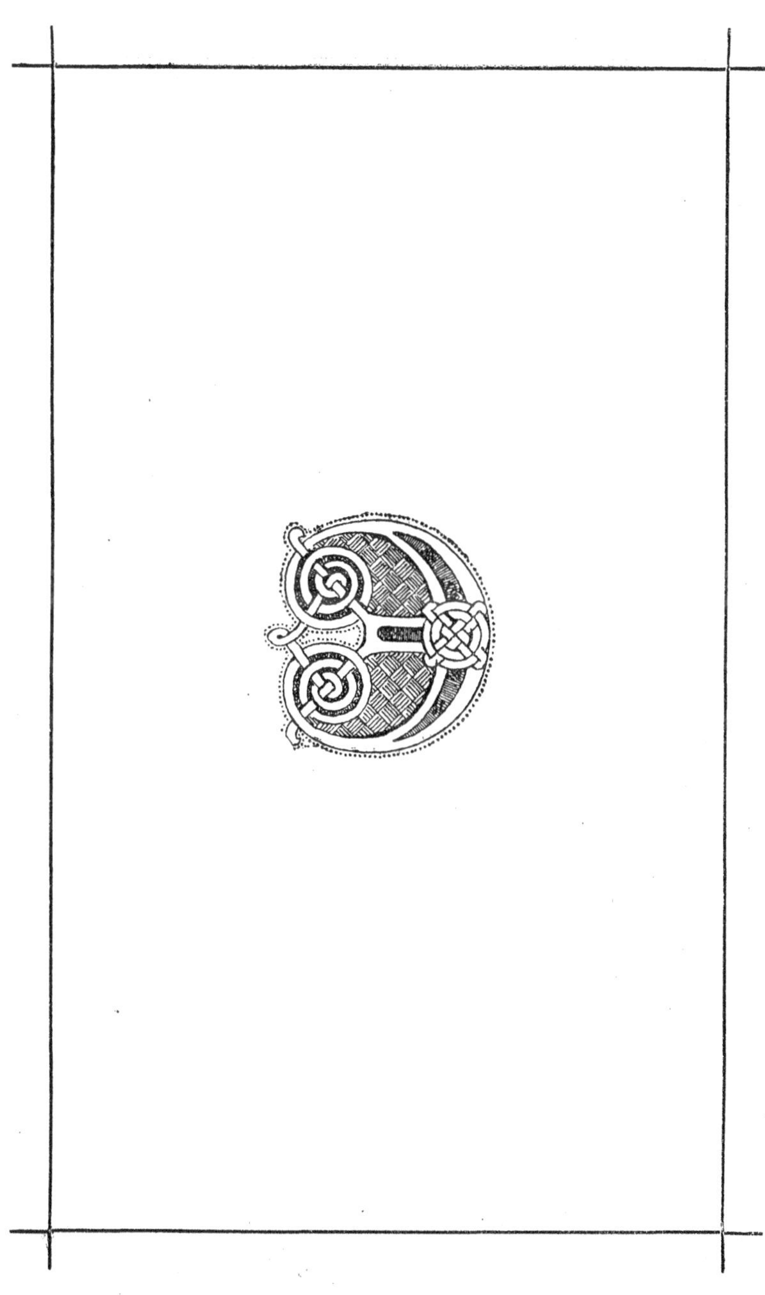

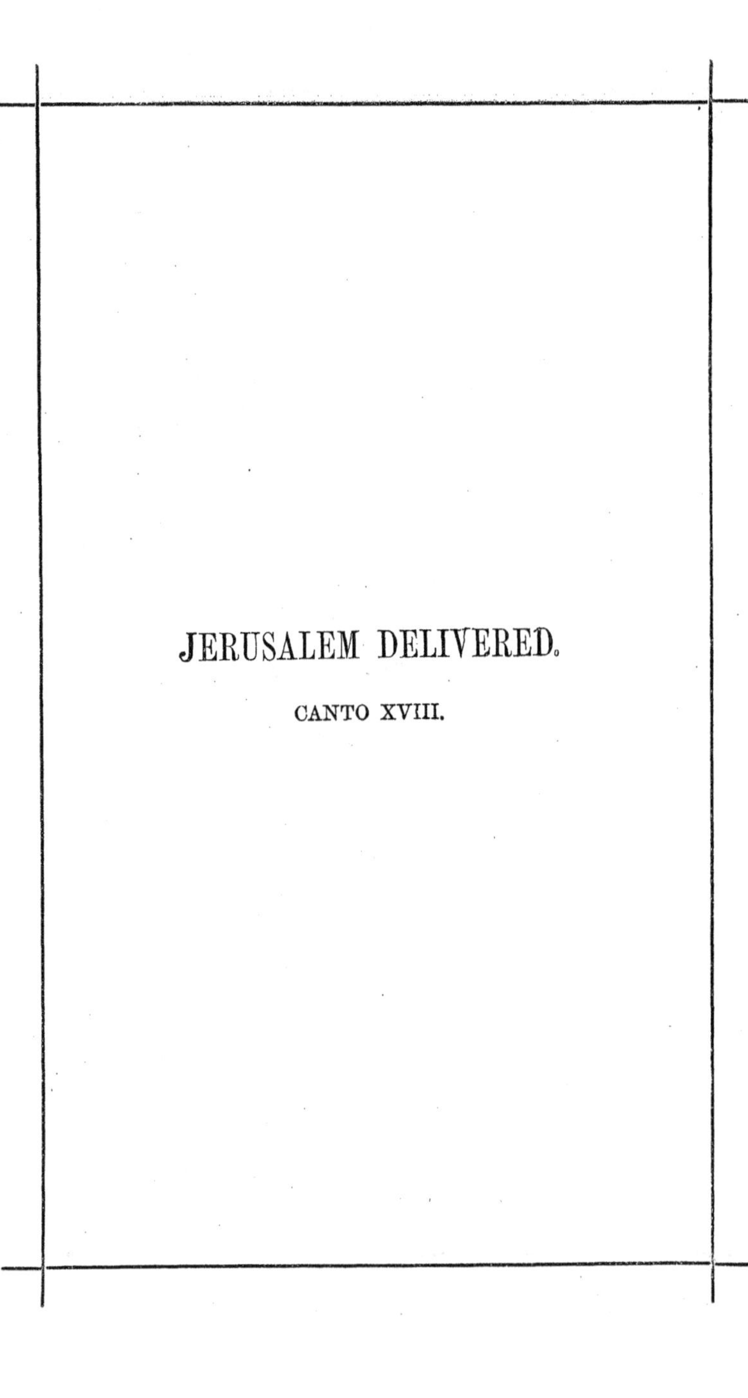

JERUSALEM DELIVERED.

CANTO XVIII.

ARGUMENT.

His errors first the good Rinaldo mourns,
Then seeks th' enchanted wood,—the spirits fly
Before him ; Godfrey by a courier learns
Of the Egyptian host, which now draws nigh,
Important tidings ; yet the dext'rous spy,
Vafrino, goes t' inspect it ; sharp the fight
Waxes round Sion, but the hierarchy
Of Heaven so aids the flush'd Crusaders' might,
That soon their banners float on each bombarded height.

JERUSALEM DELIVERED.

CANTO XVIII.

1. Arrived where Godfrey to salute him stood,
Rinaldo spoke: "Revengeful discontent
And jealous honor spurr'd me to my feud
With dead Gernando, which I much repent;
And 'tis with sorrow still for that event
And thy displeasure that I seek thy face;
Now at the instance of thine envoys sent
For my recall, I come, the stain t' efface
By whatsoe'er good deeds may win me back thy grace."

2. Low as he kneel'd before him Godfrey cast
His arms around his neck, and kindly said:
"No more revive the melancholy past;
In peace repose the memory of the dead!
And no amends I seek for frenzy fled,
Than that thy wonted valor be renew'd,—
That, for the ruin of the foe, thou tread
Enchanted ground, and, for the general good,
From spells and monsters free th' inviolable wood.

3. "That immemorial forest whence of late
We drew our timbers, is defended now,
I know not from what cause, by charms innate,
Deep, strong, and dreadful to the boldest brow;
Nor is there one that dares disturb a bough,
Much less a single sapling of the grove
Touch with the axe; yet without engines, how
Can we the city take? yea! risks which move
To fear our stoutest hearts, will now thy courage prove."

4. The youth accepts the risk and toil, without
Much protestation, but with an address

So full of dignity, that none can doubt
From his laconic speech his sure success.
Then to his other noble friends that press
Affectionately near him, he bestows
His courteous hand ; and now with cheerfulness
Embraces Guelpho, Tancred now, and throws
Kind nods to all the chiefs that round his person close.

5. When many a welcome, many a dear embrace
He to the sov'reign princes had bestow'd,
With like familiar love and gentle grace
He took the greetings of th' inferior crowd :
With martial shouts these testified aloud
Their joy, and throng'd as thickly to his side,
As if, by elephants or leopards proud
Drawn in high triumph, he had tamed the pride
Of all the realms through which the Nile and Ganges glide.

6. Thus hail'd, to his pavilion he retires,
And entertains his dearest friends around ;
And much to them replies, and much inquires
Both of the war and of the charmed ground.
But when, all leaving him, the Hermit found
Leisure for serious talk, he spoke, and said :
"Great things are those, young Voyager renown'd,
Which to thy pilgrim eyes have been display'd,
And long the wondrous tract o'er which thy steps have stray'd !

7. "How great thy debt to the Celestial King,
Who thus redeems thee from the charmer's den !
Nor spares, with all a shepherd's love, to bring
Back the lost lamb into his holy pen ;
That now, by Godfrey's voice, he makes again
Thee second agent in his high design !
Yet art thou changed ; not pure of heart, as when
Thou last waged war, and, lain so long supine,
Thou mayst not yet engage in service so divine.

8. "Darkness, the world, the flesh, spiritual sin
With such infectious stains thy soul defile,
No earthly spring can wash thy conscience clean,
The streams of Ganges, or the floods of Nile,
The secret source of what in thee is vile
Heaven's grace alone can fitly purge away ;
Turn to thy Saviour then, in lowly style

Ask for forgiveness, all thy sins display,
Cling to the Cross in faith, weep, tremble, praise, and pray."

9. He said ; and first the youth bewail'd his fall,
His amorous follies, and fierce wrath ; then kneel'd
Contritely at the Hermit's feet, and all
His youthful crimes and levities reveal'd.
This done, the minister of Heaven repeal'd
His sins, and absolution gave ; then said,—
"Seek now, by prayer to have thy pardon seal'd,
When next the morning o'er the world is spread,
The hill that on the East rears high its reverend head.

10. "Then to the haunted Forest march, where dwell
Such frightful phantoms and gigantic things ;
Thou wilt, I know, those fiends and furies quell,
If no fresh error thy tuned soul unstrings.
Let no strange voice that mourns, or sweetly sings,
No smile of ruby lips or radiant eyes
Steal to thy heart and touch fond pity's springs
With their bewitching beauty, but despise
All their fond aspects feign'd, false tears, and fancied cries."

11. Thus the Sage counsels, and the ardent knight
Prepares with hope for the sublime emprise ;
Thoughtful he spends the day, and sad the night,
And ere the breaking morn begins to rise,
Girds on his beautiful bright arms ; applies
The falchion to his side, and o'er his mail
Throws a new mantle prank'd with rarest dyes ;
Leaves the warm friends that, as he passes, veil
Their plumes, and all alone treads slow the silent dale.

12. It was the hour when, grieving to be gone,
Night on the confines of the day still slept ;
The East grew rosy with the flame of morn,
Yet still some stars her radiant portal kept.
When, as to Olivet the sward he swept,
And as his serious eyes, to heaven inclined,
Mark'd, with the spangling tears which Night had wept,
The incorruptible pure lights that shined
On high,—to solemn thoughts he gave his musing mind.

13. "O," to himself he thought, "how many bright
And glorious fires heaven's vaulted temple fret !

Day has his car, her golden stars the Night,
And the round silver moon, more radiant yet;
But we, nor these nor those revering, set
On the pale meteors with a flashing eye,
A brilliant smile, or glowing canzonet,
Strike from the twilight of our transient sky,
Our inconsiderate hearts,—gaze, grieve, admire, and die!"

14. And musing thus, awed, melted, and abased,
He reach'd the summit clothed with mountain thyme;
Above the heaven of heavens his thoughts were raised,
And thus, his face turn'd to the Orient clime,
Kneeling, he pray'd: "The errors of my prime,
O holy Father! in thy mercy, view
With the mild eye of clemency; sublime
My low desires; the evil seed subdue;
And in my soul be pleased thine image to renew!"

15. Thus as he pray'd, with blushing roses crown'd
The radiant Morn appears; which with its sheen
His helm, his arms, and all the mountain round
At once illumed, and golden turn'd the green.
Fresh on his bosom and bent brow serene,
He felt the spirit of that peaceful hour,
Fann'd with its wing; while o'er his head unseen,
Shook from Aurora's lap, distill'd a shower
Of dew more pure than e'er bespangled blade or bower.

16. The dew celestial on his garments fell,
Which show'd as ashes to a tint so bright;
Illumined so, they look no longer pale,
But change their color to a shining white.
So the scorch'd summer flowers, at morning light
Steep'd in fresh dews, their wither'd bells unfold,
With added beauty; so, to the delight
Of a new youth return'd, after long cold,
The joyful snake shines out, new flourish'd o'er with gold.

17. The lively whiteness of his alter'd vest,
Seen by himself, he ceased not to admire;
Then to the old gray forest swift he press'd,
With a firm boldness and sublime desire.
He reach'd that bosky wilderness of brier
And bough, the sight alone whereof dismay'd,
And forced less valiant champions to retire;

Yet saw he nothing in the wood, that made
So much a frightful gloom, as a delightful shade.

18. He passes onward—the charm works; a sound
Sweet as the air of Paradise upsprings;
Hoarse roars the shallow brook; the leaves around
Sigh to the flutt'ring of the light wind's wings;
Her ravishing sweet dirge the cygnet sings,
Loud mourn the answering nightingales; sad shells,
Flutes, human voices tuned to golden strings,
And the loud surging organ's glorious swells,—
Such and so various sounds one single sound expels.

19. He was expecting, like the rest, to meet
The strange wild groans and thunders of dismay,
And lo, a symphony of sirens sweet,
Birds, winds, and waters, for his pleasure play!
Wond'ring he checks his steps,—they melt away,
And on he walks, but circumspect and slow;
And naught occurs to interrupt his way,
But a transparent flood, whose waters go
Through the green wood, serene, and silent in their flow.

20. Flowers and choice odors richly smiled and smell'd,
On either side of the calm stream, which wound
In a so spacious circle, that it held
The whole vast forest in its charming round;
Nor only with green bowers and garlands crown'd
The compass in its keep,—a streamlet stray'd
Through this sweet isle, enlivening all the ground;
A most delightful interchange they made;
The mild wave bathes the woods, the woods the wave o'ershade.

21. While he roved round to find a ford, behold,
A wondrous passage to his wish appear'd!
An exquisite rich bridge of shining gold
Spann'd the pure waves, on stable arches rear'd;
The golden bridge he pass'd, the water clear'd,
But had no sooner touch'd the farther shore,
Than the whole glorious fabric disappear'd;
And the sweet river, so serene before,
To a vast torrent swell'd, that stunn'd him with its roar.

22. He turns his face, and sees it swoln and spread,
Like a strong flood increased by melting snows;
And, whirling round as to its fountain head,
A thousand rapid curls and gulfs it shows;

But, curious of new objects, on he goes
Through the brown arches thick of aged trees,
That now on every side his steps inclose ;
And in these savage glooms, to strike or please
At every strange new turn, some strange new wonder sees.

23. Where'er he plants his foot some charm springs out,
The wild brook warbles, or the sweet turf flowers ;
There lilies open, here young roses sprout,
There the shrill fountain falls in silver showers,
And round, o'erhead, th' austere and aged bowers
Renew their youth,—the hoary bark is seen
To soften, the moss falls, the gray trunk towers,
Each bough its buds, each leaf renews its green,—
Mild shines the summer sun, and decks th' enchanted scene.

24. Impearl'd with manna was each fresh leaf nigh ;
Honey and golden gums the rude trunks weep ;
Again is heard that strange wild harmony
Of songs and sorrows, plaintive, mild, and deep ;
But the sweet choirs that still such tenor keep
With the swans, winds, and waves, no ear can trace
To their conceal'd abode in shade or steep ;
Nor harp, nor horn, nor form of human face,
Look where he would, was seen in all the shady place.

25. While his eye wanders, and his mind denies
Trust to the truths his charm'd ear recommends,
He sees far off a wondrous myrtle rise,
Where in a spacious plain the pathway ends ;
To this he walks ; its boughs the plant extends
Wide as the choice tree of Dodonian Jove,—
O'er pine, and palm, and cypress it ascends ;
And, towering thus all other trees above,
Looks like th' elected queen and genius of the grove.

26. Scarce had the hero reach'd the spacious field
Than stranger novelties his eye arrest ;
He sees an oak, self-aided, cleave, and yield
Spontaneous offspring from its fruitful breast :
A full-grown nymph, in gown and turban dress'd,
On whose ripe cheek celestial beauty blooms,
O wonder ! issues from that hoary chest ;
A hundred other girls from sylvan wombs
A hundred others child, amidst the circling glooms.

27. As the stage shows, or as we painted see
The sylvan Goddess, with her white arms bare,
With hunting weeds tuck'd up above the knee,
Buskins of blue, and loose luxuriant hair,—
Just such, to all appearance, are the fair
Fictitious daughters of these wild woods old;
Save, that for horns, to wake some sprightlier air,
Quivers, and bended bows, they in their hold
Have viols, lutes, and harps, of ivory, pearl, and gold.

28. Ranging themselves into a ring, their hands
They knit together, and with joyous cheer
Dance round about Rinaldo as he stands
The willing center of this moving sphere:
The tree they compass too, and carol clear,
As in light morrice to the charm they move;
"Welcome, thrice welcome, gallant chevalier!"
They sing, "our Lady's hope, our Lady's love:
In blessed hour all hail to this delightful grove!

29. "Timely thou com'st to cure her, wounded sore
With am'rous thoughts and languishing desires;
These groves, so dark and desolate before,
Her grief's fit dwelling, choked with thorns and briers,
Lo, at thy coming what quick joy inspires
Each tree and leafy bough! how redolent
They breath, dress'd freshly in their green attires!"
Such was the song, and from the myrtle went
First a melodious sound, and then the sylvan rent.

30. A rude Silenus oft the days of old
Have seen unclose, and yield some Goddess fair,[17]
But never yet did sylvan image hold
Charms such as issued from the myrtle rare:
For forth a Lady stepp'd with golden hair,
With angel beauty, angel mien and grace;
In whom, albeit of visionary air,
Rinaldo starts Armida's form to trace,
The same expressive eye, fond smile, and radiant face.

31. Sorrow and joy into her looks she cast,
A thousand passions, which one glance betrays;
"And art thou then indeed return'd at last
To thy forsaken love," she pensive says;
"Why com'st thou hither, my beloved? to raise
My drooping soul, and with remember'd charms
Solace my widow'd nights and lonely days?

Or to wage war, and scare me with alarms?
Why hide thy lovely face? why show these threat'ning arms?

32. "Com'st thou a foe or friend? I did not rear
That glorious bridge to entertain my foe;
Unlock'd not brooks, flowers, fountains, made not clear
For him that wilderness of brambles—no!
Take now, take off this horrid helmet, show
Thy face for friendly, glad me with the shine
Of those celestial eyes; say, why so slow?
Kiss me, embrace me, oh my love! I pine;
Or press at least once more my cold, cold hand in thine."

33. Thus as she woos, her beautiful bright eyes
Rueful she rolls, and pale as death appears;
Feigning, with ev'ry tear, the sweetest sighs,
And melancholy moans, and bashful fears.
It might have moved a heart of stone to tears,
To hear how fondly she herself deplored;
But he, unmoved by all he sees and hears,
Cautious, not cruel, to the plaints she pour'd
No longer pays regard, but draws his fatal sword.

34. The myrtle he approach'd; but she with fright
The dear trunk clasping, interposed, and cried:
"Mercy, ah mercy! do me not such spite,
As to cut down my myrtle-tree, the pride
And last poor solace of forlorn Armide;
Put up thy sword, O consort most unkind!
Or sheath it, cruel, in thy lady's side;
For through this only it shall passage find,
To strike my lovely tree and hurt its hallow'd rind!"

35. Deaf to her prayers, he rears his sword, and she
Transforms herself as swift as when at night
Our dreams, ne'er constant to the thing we see,
Shift the fond object we had first in sight;
Gross grew her members, dark her face, upright
Her horrent hair; gone by are all her charms,
White breast, and rosy cheek,—enlarged in height,
A giantess, she glows with feign'd alarms,
Like fell Briareus, limb'd with full one hundred arms

36. With fifty swords she fought; on fifty shields
She clash'd defiance, bluster'd, roar'd, and bray'd;
Each other nymph the like weird weapons wields,
A frowning Cyclop, a gigantic Shade!

He fear'd them not, but with his waving blade
On the charm'd myrtle multiplied his blows,
Which at each stroke distressful moanings made;
Air seem'd a hell in hubbub, awful shows
Throng'd the black sky, and ghosts in swarms on swarms arose.

37. Thunder'd the flashing heavens above, the ground
Groan'd underneath,—that bellow'd and this shook;
While the loosed winds and tempests blust'ring round
Blew the sharp sleet and hailstones in his look;
Yet not for this the knight his post forsook,
His aim he miss'd not, changed not in his cheer,
But the more fiercely for their fury strook;—
'Tis done! the myrtle falls; th' enchantments drear
Flit with the ended spell; the phantoms disappear.

38. Air still, the heavens serene, the woods resume
Their wonted quiet and sequester'd state;
Not terrible, nor cheerful, full of gloom
From palm and cypress, but a gloom innate.
The Victor tries again if as of late
Aught yet forbade the felling of the trees,
And finding nothing check his sword, sedate
Smiles and says inly: "O vain semblances!
O fools, to be deterr'd by shadows false as these!"

39. Then to the camp he turns; meanwhile aware
Of these events, the solitary Seer
Exclaim'd: "The charm is o'er, the forest fair
Of evil spirits, and the victor near;
See where he comes!" and now distinguish'd clear
In his pure mantle from afar, the knight
Struck the spectators with a holy fear;
For the spread pinions of his eagle white
In the clear sunshine shone with unaccustom'd light.

40. With glad huzzas for victory achieved
Rang the wide hills around, and skies above;
The conqu'ring knight by Godfrey is received
With praise unmix'd by envy, and with love.
"Sire," said Rinaldo, "to the dreadful grove
As you desired, I went; the sprites impure
I saw—I saw and conquer'd them; improve
Th' occasion then, the ways are quite secure,
Send then the workmen forth, the timbers to procure."

41. Straight to the aged woods they went, and hew'd
What Art thought proper for the task in hand ;
The first artificers in skill were rude,
And little did machinery understand :
But now a noble mechanician plann'd
The important works, selected well the trees,
And every movement of the workmen scann'd,—
William—who lately with his Genoese
Roved the Levantine waves, sole Signior of the seas.

42. But, forced before th' Egyptian fleet at length
His azure kingdom of the sea to quit,
He to the Camp transferr'd his naval strength ;—
To frame such works was never man more fit ;
For an ingenious brain, a fruitful wit,
Industrious hand and scientific mind,
To him almost might Dædalus submit ;
A hundred meaner architects combined
To execute the schemes his genius now design'd.

43. He undertook to build, not vines alone,
Balistæ, rams, and catapults, of power
To batter down defended walls of stone,
And on high bulwarks rain an arrowy shower,
But, plank'd with pine and fur, a wondrous tower,
The masterpiece of art ; and, to provide
Against th' adhesive flames that might devour
The timbers else, he lined it well outside
With fire-proof skins of sheep and quilts of tough bull-hide.

44. The separate beams and timbers, mortised tight,
Are join'd ; completed is the pile ; below,
Swings the vast ram, which with its horned might
Threats at each stroke the city to o'erthrow ;
Its waist lets down a bridge, which falling slow,
Work'd by a windlass, joins th' opposing wall,
And forms an instant passage to the foe ;
While from the top a second tower less tall,
Inly conceal'd, at need shoots up o'ergazing all.

45. With little cost of toil th' enormous mass
Upon its hundred wheels volubil roll'd,
Though bearing, arm'd in brigandine of brass,
A little army in its spacious hold ;
Round stood the soldiers, marveling to behold
With what consummate ease the workmen plied
Their several tasks ; much they their skill extoll'd,

Much the vast engine ; two more towers beside,
Plann'd like the first, were built, ere yet the daylight
died.

46. But neither were their works nor their designs
From the mew'd Pagans meanwhile wholly hid ;
For on the wall that to the Camp inclines,
Keen spies were placed, to notice all they did :
These, though the distance insight clear forbid,
Saw what vast loads of cypress, pine, and hew,
Were from the sable forest drawn amid
The tents ; they mark'd the rising engines too,
But of their shape and plan no clear conception drew.

47. They too frame engines, and with equal art
The towers and bulwarks fortify again,
And raise so high the fortress on the part
Last storm'd, the brunt of battle to sustain,
That now, as fondly they suppose, no train
Of circumstance, or force of arms will e'er
Avail, th' assaulted city to obtain ;
While dark Ismeno studies to prepare
Beyond all else, fresh fires, unusual, strange, and rare.

48 With sulphur did the cursed Magician mix
Bitumen, from the lake of Sodom brought,
Brimstone, received, it strikes me, from the Styx,
And fiery spume, in hell by demons wrought ;
And thus composed a cruel fire, so fraught
With smoke and stench, that, darted in the face,
Whom once it strikes it stifles ; well, he thought,
By these revenging fireballs to efface,
For the enchanted wood cut down, his late disgrace.

49 While thus to win or to defend the wall
Both hosts their engines frame, a turtle dove
In the blue firmament is seen of all
To pass, the Christian multitude above :
With outspread wings the liquid air she clove,
And went away as lightly as the wind ;
This wand'ring, mute communicant of love,
So soon as she had left the camp behind,
Down from the lofty clouds t' accost the town inclined.

50. When lo ! they knew not whence, a falcon arm'd
With hooked beak and talons, sail'd in sight ;
Which, 'twixt the city and the camp, alarm'd
Th' opposed mild bird in her descending flight :

She waited not his truss; but, full of fright,
On instant wing to the pavilions fled,
And at the moment when the cruel kite,
Down stooping swift, just touch'd her tender head,
In Godfrey's bosom fell, betwixt alive and dead.

51. Godfrey the bird protected, and espied,
As he her plumage smooth'd, a curious thing:
For from the neck, by flax of Egypt tied,
A letter hung, conceal'd beneath her wing.
Marveling to see it, he untwines the string,
And breaks the seal; then well he comprehends
The purpose of the scroll: "To Judah's king,"
Thus spoke th' inscription, "to his first of friends,
Health, honor, joy, and peace th' Egyptian Caliph sends.

52. "Fear not, my noble lord! resist, endure,
Till the fourth day, or till the fifth at most;
For by that period thou shalt see, besure,
My slaught'ring sword devour the hostile host."
Such was the secret in the note inclosed,
In Syriac ciphers writ, and seal'd with care,
Given in commission to this flying post;
For in the East these couriers of the air,
Train'd to the trusty charge, were then by no means rare.

53. The bird he freed; she, cooing her concern
That her lord's secrets had been thus betray'd,
Durst not, though innocent of ill, return
A rebel back, but fled far thence afraid.
Godfrey the intercepted scroll display'd
Before the lords and princes that compose
His military Council; "See," he said,
"How well the goodness of our God foreshows
To us the close designs and secrets of our foes!

54. "We must no longer now protract the time,
But clear away fresh outworks; we must spare
No sweat, no labor, no fatigue to climb
The South-West walls; 'tis true, the crags are there
Steep, sharp, and high, nor apt, I am aware,
For the approach of arms and engines; still
It may be done: I have survey'd with care
The coast, and find that, strengthen'd by the hill,
Those towers have been defensed with little cost of skill.

55. "Thou, Raymond, with thy men the crags ascend,
And storm those walls, while I with all the state

And pomp preparative of battle, bend
My horned rams against the northern gate ;
So that the foe, beguiled t' anticipate
In arms our principal bombardment there,
May leave me free hereafter to translate
My tower that slides so easily, to bear
Ruin, and dread, and death, and victory elsewhere.

56. " At the same time, Camillo, thou close by,
Or not far off, the third tower must dispose :"
He said, and good Count Raymond who sate nigh,
And as he spoke weigh'd well each accent, rose
And said : " This counsel no one can oppose,
'Tis given in perfect wisdom, the event
Will surely prove it such ; I would propose
Alone that some one midst our foes be sent,
Into their plans to pry, and creep from tent to tent ;—

57. " Number their troops, and with instinctive wit
Fathom their thoughts, as far as in him lies :"
Said Tancred then, " I have a Squire most fit
For the exploit, the very prince of spies ;
Quick, subtle, dexterous, he has Argus eyes
For such concerns ; shrewd, supple, light of toe ;
Bold too, but in his boldness close and wise ;
And many tongues he talks, and varies so
His gesture, voice, and gait, that none the man can know."

58. Sent for, he came ; and soon as he had heard
Duke Godfrey's pleasure and his lord's, was won
To their desire ; he, smiling, with a word
The task embraced, and said, " My Lords, I'm gone ;
Into their unsuspicious camp anon
Enter I will, and pay implicit heed
To all their motions, recognized by none ;
E'en at midnoon through all the host proceed,
And number every man, and number every steed.

59. " Their hosts, their squadrons, and the arms they bring
I pledge myself to notice ; nay, I vow
The closest thoughts and counsels of the king
To win adroitly from him,—ask not how."
Thus with bold air Vafrino spoke ; and now
Stay'd but to bare his graceful neck, to wind
Long rolls of linen round his manly brow,
Change for a mantle his juppon, and bind
Round his broad waist a belt, a quiver hang behind.

60. And thus accoutred, in his dexter hand
A Syrian bow, with gestures nothing meek,
He seems a pure barbarian, and all stand
In absolute amaze to hear him speak
Such various tongues, so that in Greece a Greek,
In Tyre a true Phœnician, in the waste
Of marbled Tadmor an Arabian sheik
All would have thought him ; off he rides in haste,
On a swift steed that scarce disturb'd the sands it paced.

61. But ere the third day shone, the Franks had strain'd
Each nerve to smooth the rough uneven ways,
Finish'd their engines, and in fact maintain'd
One ceaseless vigil of fatigue ; the days
Alone sufficed them not ; but by the blaze
Of piny torches did they task the night
With toil, disdaining sleep : to Godfrey's gaze,
All was now ready with the morning light
To prove the last extremes and fortunes of the fight.

62. The Chief great part of the preceding day
Had spent in prayer, and had employ'd the priest
To shrive the army of their sins, that they
Might share with him the sacramental feast.
Then to the parts where he intended least
To stand the brunt of battle, he applied
His rams and mighty engines, which increased
The blinded Pagans' transport, hope, and pride,
Seeing them face the gate most strongly fortified.

63. But when the night had spread her raven pall,
The huge light tower he spirited away,
To where less strong and crooked show'd the wall,
And jutting angles less forbade the play
Of the strong ram : his armed tower ere day
Raymond too planting on the hill's tall crest,
Took the whole city in his broad survey ;
While his Camillo to that point address'd,
Where from the north the wall wheels round to front the west.

64. When now the roseate messenger of morn
Had tipp'd the eastern hills and towers with light,
The Pagans stared to see the tower withdrawn
Far from the spot where it stood overnight,
And seeing trembled ; to the left and right
New structures also, mann'd and managed well,
Till now unnoticed, burst upon their sight,

With countless fresh machines,—balistæ fell,
Cat, scorpion, crossbow, ram, war-wolf, and mangonel.

65. The Syrian people, though depressed at heart
By this deception, were by no means slack
Thither to move their engines from the part
Where first Duke Godfrey menaced the attack;
But he meanwhile, aware that at his back
Th' Egyptian army march'd, thus gave command
To Guelph and the two Roberts: "On the track
That leads to Gaza, station each a band
Of horse, and toward the south watch well, with sword in hand.

66. "And have regard, that while I storm the part
Where the gray battlements most weak appear,
No sudden squadron, with insidious art,
Bring round the rage of battle to my rear."
He said; three times the trumpet tubes blow drear;
To the three sounds, three valiant nations made
On three sides horrible assault severe,—
'Gainst each of which, the king in brave parade
Of arms long laid aside, his hostile powers array'd.

67. Cased in old arms, and with the weight of age,
Not fear of danger trembling, forth he goes,
Long lost to war, Count Raymond to engage,
The most sagacious of his numerous foes:
The Soldan strides Duke Godfrey to oppose,
Argantes good Camillo, at whose side
Stands Bohemond's brave nephew; fortune chose,
Or rather Providence, the Prince to guide
Thus to the destined foe whose blood his falchion dyed.

68. Straight the strong arches from their bows let fly
Ten thousand mortal barbs with poisonous stings;
That underneath a cloud of shafts, the sky
Grows dark, as though beneath the night's black wings;
But blows of more tremendous force from slings
And huge balistæ come, with ruder shocks;
For thence fly, every time the huge ram swings,
Stones, rugged masses of uprooted rocks,
Trees shod with pointed steel, lead, marble, logs, and blocks.

69. Each stone a thunderbolt appears, and so
Where it alights, the arms and members breaks,

Not life alone and spirit from the blow,
But form and feature e'en the man forsakes;
The long lance stays not in the wound it makes,
But onward still, still on long after hies;
Piercing the warrior's coat of mail, it takes
Its course right through him, as he fights or flies;
He feels the piercing point, and as it passes dies.

70. Yet cannot all this force and fury drive
The desperate Pagans to forsake the wall;
Still to their arms resolved they stand, and strive
Or to revenge each charge, or to forestall!
Against the strokes of the strong ram, they call
For bales of pliant wool, which from on high
They hang, and deaden thus the blows that fall;
And where the Franks show most exposed and nigh,
With thousand thousand shafts give back a proud reply.

71. Yet still the Franks, arranged in closest file,
Move on three sides the ramparts to assail,
And underneath the cat and tortoise, smile
To hear the sounding storm of arrowy hail.
To the high walls, despite the men in mail
That line their battlements, the towers are led,
And strive to launch, albeit at first they fail,
Their light pontons; while, work'd beneath its shed
Buts the bombarding ram with adamantine head.

72. Irresolute meanwhile Rinaldo stands,
This risk and that were far too poor a praise;
And 'twould be base in him with armed bands
To bear his flag by plain and beaten ways;
Debating thus, he casts around his gaze,—
That path alone at which all else would halt,
It pleases him to move in; he surveys
The loftiest walls their battlements exalt,
Warr'd on by one,—'tis there he will begin th' assault.

73. And turning to the troop—famed heroes all—
Whom Dudon lately led, he made exclaim;
"What, my compeers! shall then this old gray wall
In the grand wrack repose in peace? O shame
To generous knighthood, chivalry, and fame!
Each hazard to the Brave assurance yields,
And all steep paths are plain to those who aim
At praise,—come on then; quick! join shield to shield,
And to their cruel shafts a stubborn tortoise build.

74. Swift at the word all join with him, all cast
Their targets o'er their heads in brave disdain,
And, man thus wedged with man, compacted fast
Form a tight penthouse that defies the rain
Of stones and arrows, under which amain
They speed the rapid march no rage can stay;
For well the iron tortoise does sustain
All the huge weights that with tempestuous sway
From the throng'd walls descend, to bar their onward way.

75. The walls are reach'd; and now Rinaldo rears
Aloft a scaling ladder with a flight
Of full two hundred steps, which he appears
To move and manage with an ease as light
As winds the willow; from the rampart's height
Now rocks, now spears, now beams down thundering go;
Yet upward still ascends the dauntless knight,
By each rebuff unscared, unmoved, although
They should Olympus down, or piny Ossa throw.

76. A wood of arrows on his shield alights,
A very mount of fragments, steel and stone,
On his strong back; one arm the bulwark smites,
And one the guardian target o'er the cone
Of his bright helm suspends; the courage shown
By him excites his brave compeers no less
To deeds of daring; he mounts not alone;
Numbers besides with ladders forward press,
And climb, with various turns of valor and success.

77. One dies—another falls—he mounts sublime,
These his praise cheers, and those his threats alarm;
And to a height so lofty does he climb,
That now he grasps with his extended arm
The topmost battlements; vast numbers swarm
Round the young knight with dagger, axe, and brand,
To smite and hurl him down: but him no harm
Repels,—O wonderful! a single hand,
Hung in mid air, has power arm'd thousands to withstand.

78. Not only he withstands, but livelier grows,
And like the palm-tree when by weights oppress'd,
More strong and valiant from resistance shows,
His pulse beats brisker, loftier shoots his crest.
Some of his foes he slew, dispersed the rest,
The spars and stones that on his buckler weigh'd
Shook off, leap'd o'er the battlements, possess'd

The walls he wish'd, and with his ruling blade
Safe for his following friends the obstructed passage made.

79. And to the youngest brother of the brave
And virtuous Godfrey, just about to fall,
His kind victorious hand Rinaldo gave,
And help'd him second so to scale the wall.
Godfrey meanwhile, whom nothing could appall,
In other quarters various fortunes proved,
Nor were the perils he encounter'd small;
For there not knight alone with knight approved
His strength, but tower 'gainst tower, 'gainst engine engine moved.

80. And there the Syrians had uprear'd a pine
That once had served some admiral for a mast,
And hung thereto, by many a twisted line
To a huge transverse beam on high made fast,
A long steel-headed ram, stout, rude, and vast,
Which backward drawn by cords, tempestuous fell,
And shatter'd all at which its front was cast:
By turns the beam they pull, by turns propel,
As the snail now shrinks in, now creeps from forth its shell.

81. Beats the huge beam, and on the tower so sore
Doubles its loud percussions, as to smite
Some paces back the pile, with all it bore,
And many a mortised rafter disunite:
The tower, for ev'ry exigence of fight
Prepared, brook'd not the sounding insult long,
But from within, till now conceal'd from sight,
Launch'd out two scythes, large, crooked, sharp, and strong,
And cut the cords on which th' enormous engine swung.

82. As a huge rock, which age or stormy winds
Uproot or loosen from some mountain steep,
Rolls headlong down, and into thin dust grinds
Woods, houses, hamlets, herds, and flocks of sheep;
So fell the frightful beam with giant leap,
Hideous, enormous, bearing to the ground
Arms, men, and turrets in its stormy sweep:
Shake the firm ramparts; rocks the tower; and round,
The hills and hollow glens rebellow back the sound.

83. All sanguine now to win the wall advanced
The conqu'ring Chief ; but suddenly he sees
Thick noisome clouds of flame sulphureous lanced
Against him, favor'd by the driving breeze :
Ne'er did Mount Etna send forth flames like these,
Dispensing death from her cavernous womb ;
Nor e'er did Indian skies, when most disease
And fervent summer fill'd the air with gloom,
Rain such thick vapors down, mute Nature to consume.

84. Here globes of wild-fire, there fly burning spears ;
This flame burns black, that bloody red ; the smell
Poisons, the thunder deafens all their ears,
Smoke blinds their eyes, fires scorch them, hot as hell,
Not long can e'en the moist bull-hides repel
Their fierceness, scarcely do they now defend
The tower, already they begin to swell ;
They reek, they shrink, and with the blaze must blend,
Height'ning its ardent rage, if Heaven no succor send.

85. Still in the front of all the Duke abides,
Nor changes color, countenance, or place !
But cheers on those, who from the shriv'ling hides
With water strive th' advancing fires to chase.
Thus went the war ; thus urgent stood their case ;
Their well-used water disappearing fast,
The gath'ring flames they could no longer face ;
When on the sudden rose a friendly blast,
And the fierce wild-fire back upon its authors cast.

86. The winds fought with the flames, and backward blew
The fires ; for where the foe their sheds had rear'd,
Upon the soft materials swift it flew,
Which kindled, crackled, blazed, and disappear'd.
O glorious Captain ! to thy God endear'd,
By thy God guarded ! Heaven itself was found
Ranged on thy side ; the very winds revered
Thy will, and, summon'd by thy trumpet's sound,
Obedient rush'd to war from all their regions round.

87. But fell Ismene, who saw his sulph'rous fires
Forced back against him on the adverse gale,
By his black art, despite the winds, aspires
The laws of Nature yet to countervail ;
Betwixt two hags, his vow'd attendants, pale
In his dark mantle, on the walls he rear'd

His hideous shape ; and with his length of nail,
His squalid aspect, and dishevel'd beard,
Pluto himself between two Furies dire appear'd.

88. And now were heard those awful sounds which fill
With deepest horror hell's profoundest streams ;
The winds already roar'd on ev'ry hill,
The sun in clouds withdrew his golden beams ;
When sudden, frustrate of his impious schemes,
A stone, or rather rock, the tower robust,
As still th' accursed wretch high Heaven blasphemes,
Hurl'd from its bowels with a stroke so just,
As bray'd at once their bones and bodies into dust.

89. To bloody dust minute their heads and brains
Were widely scatter'd with a roaring sound ;
To bloody dust, minuter than the grains
Of corn to meal betwixt rough mill-stones ground ;
With groans the three foul spirits leave the round
Of the blue heavens and fine ethereal sense
Of joy and sunshine, for the shades profound
Of hell ;—learn, mortals, piety from hence,
Nor dare God's slumb'ring wrath omnipotent incense !

90. Meanwhile the engine rescued from the flame
By the kind whirlwind, to the city ran,
And, all resistance now defeated, came
So near the ramparts that its bridge began,
Launch'd, to attach ; but thither Solyman
Rush'd on the instant ; sharply did he ply
His strokes, and certainly th' audacious man
Had hew'd it down, but suddenly his eye
Another tower beheld, uprising in the sky.

91. Th' enormous pile shot up into the air
Far above spire, mosque, minaret, and tower ;
So that the Pagans in their stupor stare
To see the city subject to its power ;
But the fierce Turk still keeps his stand, though lower
The clouds of ruin round him ; he derives
Strength from the strife : and, careless of the shower
Of stones, to cut the bridge still trusts, and strives ;
And his despairing friends with glorying shouts revives.

92. Th' archangel Michael, clad in arms divine,
To Godfrey then, but visible to none
Besides, appear'd ; his face did far outshine,
When clear of ev'ry cloud, the noonday sun.

"Godfrey," he cried, "the fated sands are run;
This is the hour to cancel with thy blade
The chains of Sion; thy desire is won!
Droop not, droop not thine eyes to earth, dismay'd,
But see what num'rous hosts I bring, thine arms to aid.

93. "Lift up thine eyes, and in mid air th' immense,
Immortal army on its march survey!
For the dim veil that clouds your mortal sense,
And from the cradle to the tomb your clay
Wraps round with darkness, lo! I rend away,
That thou the angels in their shapes mayst see,
And, one short moment, the effulgent ray
Of their celestial essences, with free
Undazzled sight sustain,—long time it may not be.

94. "Observe the souls of ev'ry lord and knight,
Christ's blessed saints, who late but champions were!
With what a holy zeal they seek the fight,
The final glory with thyself to share!
Lo! what mix'd clouds of smoke and dust in air
Fluctuate aloft from the dismantled town;
And lo, that lofty heap of ruins! there,
Hugo, conspicuous by his sapphire crown,
Heaves high his golden mace, and beats the huge towers down.

95. "Dudon is he who at the Northern fort,
Which he with fire and sword assaults, prepares
Arms for the Franks, nor ceases to exhort
Fresh knights to mount the tall scalades he bears;
That surpliced Saint who in his tresses wears
The sacerdotal crown, on yonder hill,
Is the bless'd soul of Ademar,—his cares
The same as erst; observe with what good-will
He deals his pastoral signs and benedictions still.

96. "Look higher yet, and, witnessing the war
The whole hierarchy of heaven survey!"
He raised his eyes; and at one prospect saw,
In myriad numbers numberless, th' array,
Three squadrons wing'd; each radiating away
In triple phalanx from th' observer's eye,
Ring beyond ring,—a beautiful display
Of winged orbs, that, widening as they fly
Sublime, possess the whole circumference of the sky.

97. Here he his dazzled eyes declined, nor more
The glorious vision in its pomp descried;
When next he look'd, the wondrous show was o'er,
And gazing round, he saw on every side
His troops victorious; many a hero vied
After divine Rinaldo to command
The walls, leap'd up, and deep his falchion dyed;
Godfrey, this seen, aloof disdain'd to stand,
But snatch'd the Red-Cross staff from his flag-bearer's hand,

98. And passes first the bridge; but midway here
Finds the stern Soldan ready to debate
His farther passage; few their strokes, but clear
Their prowess,—a small plank the field of fate!
"Lo, here," the Soldan shouts, "I consecrate,
Here yield my gallant spirit up this day,
For Sion's good! So ho! my friends, I prate,—
Cut the ponton down at my back, and they
Shall have small cause to boast the pleasure of their prey!"

99. But when he saw far-off Rinaldo tend
Toward him, and all his friends in flight, he said:
"What now remains? if thus my life I spend,
To what advantage will my blood be shed?"
Revolving thus, with slow disdainful tread
He turn'd aside, and left the pass essay'd
Free to the Chief: who, following as he fled
The Soldan's footsteps, with his brandish'd blade,
High on the rampart walls the purple Cross display'd.

100. The glorious ensign in a thousand wreaths
And folds voluminous rejoicing twines;
It seems the wind on it more sweetly breathes;
It seems the sun on it more brightly shines;
That each toss'd javelin, each aim'd shaft declines
To strike the staff; the streets Hosannas sound;
Floods clap their hands, on mountains dance the pines;
Seems it that Sion, that her green hills crown'd,
Stoop from the clouds their crests, and bend adoring round.

101. Then raised the Christians all their long loud shout
Of Victory, joyful, resonant, and high;
Their words the towers and temples lengthen out;
To the glad sound the mountains make reply;

At the same moment, joining in the cry,
Tancred each strong obstruction overthrew
Raised by Argantes ; brought his engine nigh,
Cast out his bridge, and, without more ado,
Leap'd on the conquer'd wall, and raised his standard
too.

102. But on the hills toward the South, where fought
Raymond the hoary with the Syrian king,
The Gascon knights their engine had not brought
Yet to the walls, nor possibly could bring ;
For there the Tyrant had in aid a ring
Of soldiery, the flower of all his host,
Who stubbornly with mace, with sword, and sling,
Stood to the strife ; the walls too on that coast
Were, as less firm and high, with engines strengthen'd
most.

103. Besides, on that steep side th' enormous tower
Less steady footing for its passage found ;
Nor could their utmost industry and power
Correct the rugged nature of the ground :
But when the shout from all the quarters round
Reach'd the two hosts that here the walls contest,
Both Aladine and Raymond by the sound
Were well assured that on the North and West,
The long defended town already was possess'd.

104. Which heard, the Count shouts to the knights he led:
"Taken already is th' assaulted town ;
And does it conquer us ? shall it be said
We only share not in the day's renown ?"
But here the troubled king, quite desp'rate grown
Of the dispute, drew off his chivalry
To the strong-hold of his endanger'd Crown,
His last lorn hope, a fortress strong and high,
Where yet long time he trusts th' assailants to defy.

105. Then the whole host pours in, not o'er the walls
Alone, but through the gates, which soon unclose,
Batter'd or burnt ; and in wide ruin falls
Each strong defense that might their march oppose.
Rages the sword ; and Death, the Slaught'rer, goes
'Twixt Woe and Horror with gigantic tread,
From street to street ; the blood in torrents flows,
And settles in lagoons, on all sides fed,
And swell'd with heaps on heaps of dying and of
dead.

END OF CANTO XVIII.

JERUSALEM DELIVERED.

CANTO XIX.

ARGUMENT.

TANCRED in single combat slays his foe.
The terrible Argantes ; Aladine
Flees to the citadel, and saveth so
His host ; Erminia challenges Vafrine,
Of the leagued hosts reveals the mask'd design,
Accompanies him back, and on the sands
Finds her loved lord half dead beneath a pine ;
First mourns, then cures him ; Godfrey understands
Ormondo's plot, and acts as circumstance demands.

JERUSALEM DELIVERED.

CANTO XIX.

1. Now prudence, death, or fear, each Pagan knight
Has ravish'd from the walls; alone his mace
Argantes plies upon the battled height,
And obstinately still disputes the place;
Still with a cheerful and intrepid face
Fights on secure against the chivalry
That hems him in; and, dreading the disgrace,
Far more than death, of being forced to fly,
Sooner than seem to yield stands all resolved to die.

2. But beyond all importunate to quell
The Pagan, Tancred presses through the crowd;
The knight Argantes recognized right well
By his known arms, keen strokes, and bearing proud,
For him who fought with him before, and vow'd
Return on the sixth morning, nor the vow
Fulfill'd, made captive; whence he shouts aloud:
"Prince! is it thus you keep your faith? and now
Return you thus to war, redeem'd one scarce knows how!

3. "Late you return, and not alone, yet I
Shun not the battle, nor the issues fear;
Although, to all appearance, you draw nigh
Not as a knight, but as an engineer:
But make a shield of your Italians here,
New forms of war, strange arms invent in aid,
They shall not serve you now, false chevalier,
Foul slaught'rer of fair ladies, to evade
The death already due to my defrauded blade!"

4. The good Lord Tancred answer'd with a smile
Of some disdain, in terms of like proud glee;
"All late as is my slow return, –erewhile,

'Twill seem, I fancy, much too soon for thee ;
For thou shalt wish, on how devout a knee,
Some Alp or ocean spread its wide barrier
Of space betwixt us ; then too shalt thou see,
By fatal proof, if cowardice or fear
Has made indeed my sword so long a stranger here.

5. " But step aside, O thou whose haughty arms
Big giants only and tough knights chastise ;
Thee to a field apart from these alarms
The mighty slaught'rer of fair dames defies !"
This said, he to his followers turns, and cries ;
" Back from the warrior ! brave him not a blow !
Nay, vassals, never grudge your chief his prize ;
For mine he is more than a common foe,
Mine, both by challenge now, and promise long ago."

6. " Come down, alone or follow'd, to the feud,
E'en as you will," the Saracen replied ;
" To the throng'd field or to the lonely wood,
Whate'er the odds, I stir not from your side !"
Thus ending parle, the challenged and defied
In open concord from the walls descend,
By mortal fight their quarrel to decide ;
Hate made them one, and, e'en as friend would friend,
Each did the other's life, from pure despite, defend.

7. Great is the thirst of praise, great the desire
Which Tancred has to slay a foe so grand ;
Nor would his blood, he fancies, slake his ire,
If but a drop were shed by other's hand :
He guards the Pagan with his shield ; and, " Stand !
Strike not!" he cries to all he meets ; and so,
Safe from the rage of each encountering band,
From falchion, dagger, spear, and bended bow,
Through thousand angry friends he brings his careless foe.

8. The busy roar of war, th' invaded town,
And void pavilions far they leave behind,
Following a footpath, that o'er dale and down
In many a secret coil and tangle twined;
At length a small secluded vale they find,
Deep in the heart of woody hills embay'd,
As it for sylvan sport had been design'd,
Or Roman circus by proconsul made
For Gladiatorial show,—shut in by silent shade.

9. Here then they paused; and, full of anxious thought
Argantes turn'd, th' afflicted town to view;
Tancred, perceiving that the knight had brought
With him no shield, his own to distance threw;
And said, "What gloom does thus thy soul subdue?
Think'st thou the destined hour to terminate
Thy life at length is come? if this thou rue,
With pensive mind prophetic of thy fate,
Thy fear is useless all, thy foresight comes too late!"

10. "I think," said he, (and sigh'd,) "on that lorn town,
The pomp of realms, about to pass away,
That queen of Syria, hoary in renown,
Whose fatal ruin I have fail'd to stay:
I think how insignificant a prey
To my disdain and vengeance is the due
Which on thy head Heaven destines me to-day!"
He ceased; and each to each with caution drew,
For well each armed knight his rival's prowess knew.

11. Tancred is light of limb in hand and foot,
Swift as the wind that o'er the valley scours;
Monstrous in girth, like some terrific brute,
And taller by the head Argantes towers;
Tancred now wheels, now traverses, now cowers,
Like the coil'd snake in act at will to glide
Home to his victim, or with fiercer powers
Shoot out; still parrying stroke with stroke, he tried
All points of skill to turn th' assailing sword aside.

12. But spacious and erect, Argantes shows
Like skill, in diff'rent posture; as he can,
Straight to his mark with stretch'd-out arm he goes,
And seeks t' encounter not the steel, but man;
That tries each moment some new point or plan,
This never fails an instant to present
His saber at the face; and, swift of scan,
With threat'ning blade stands ready to prevent
The stol'n advance, quick pass, and treach'rous feign'd
intent.

13. E'en thus two gallant ships, when not a gale
Stirs the smooth surface of the silent main,
One famed for size, and one for speed of sail,
With force unequal, equal fight maintain;
This bears down lightly, goes and comes again,
Wheels round from prow to poop, and still the eye
Mocks, while the other doth unmoved remain,

And ever as the nimbler one draws nigh,
Threats with its vast machines wild ruin from on high

14. While to rush in the wily Latin strives,
Shunning the point that glitter'd at his breast,
The blade Argantes brandishes, and drives
Full at the face, which Tancred would arrest;
But the fell Pagan, as he forward press'd,
Strongly, and swift as flies a Parthian shaft,
Coil'd his strong wrist aslant,—the sword digress'd,
And plough'd his side; whereat he gayly laugh'd
And cried; "By blest Mahound, the craftsman's foil'd in craft!"

15. Prince Tancred bit his lips 'twixt scorn and shame,
Laid by all points of skill, and on his foe
Burns for revenge with such an eager aim,—
Vict'ry appears defeat, achieved so slow;
The boast he answers by his sword, and lo!
Where the barr'd vizor opens to the sight,
Dares a fierce thrust; the formidable blow
Argantes breaks, and, in the last despite
Of risk, at half-sword's length stepp'd in th' audacious knight.

16. With his left hand the Pagan's strong right arm
He seized, and with his right his falchion plied
With many a deadly gash of deepest harm,
Piercing at will the undefended side.
"To his triumphant tutor," loud he cried,
"This happy answer the foiled sciolist
Yields in reply!" with passion, pain, and pride,
Argantes groan'd, and writhing, strove to twist
From th' Italian's grasp, in vain, the prison'd wrist.

17. His sword suspended by its chain at length
He left, and griped his rival round the waist;
The same did Tancred, and with all their strength
Each grappling crush'd the other, breast to breast:
Not with more force divine Alcides press'd
Upheaved Antæus on the Libyan sands;—
In this their long and muscular caress
Of hate, they knit tenacious, knots and bands,
Flinging in various forms their brawny arms and hands.

18. Pressing, compress'd, whirl'd round, they wrestled, till
Both overpower'd, together press'd the ground;

Argantes, whether by good chance or skill,
His better arm in perfect freedom found;
But the more dexterous hand to strike and wound
Tancred had undermost, and thus restrain'd,
Himself from the fierce arm that clasped him round,
Strong with the sense of risk, he disenchain'd,
And lightly leaping up, firm footing straight regain'd.

19. Far slowlier rose th' unwieldy Saracine,
And ere he rose received a cleaving blow;
But as in blust'ring winds the mountain pine
Rears, the next moment that its head stoops low,
Its leafy forehead to the clouds, e'en so
When most oppress'd, his valor rises higher;
And now again ferocious thrusts they throw,
Fierce strokes exchange, and, in their sightless ire,
The fight, with less of skill, grows momently more dire.

20. From Tancred's wounds large drops of purple came,
But from the Pagan's flow'd a perfect flood:
And now his fury, like a wasting flame
Unfed with fuel, faints from loss of blood;
Tancred, who saw his foe, in strength subdued,
Slowly and slowlier wave his weary blade,
To noblest pity calm'd his own fell mood,
The angry passions of his soul allay'd,
Stepp'd a few paces back, and thus mild speaking, said:

21. "Yield thee, brave man! and recognize in me,
Or in strong Fate, thy victor; live, Sir Knight!
No spoil, no triumph do I seek o'er thee,
Nor to my arms reserve a victor's right!"
To this the Pagan, with a frown like Night,
More fierce than ever, kindling into flame
The slumb'ring furies of his soul, in spite
Replied; "Dost thou, dost thou th' advantage claim?
And dost thou dare to tempt Argantes to his shame!

22. "Use thy scorn'd fortune; I will yet chastise,
Presumptuous fool! the frenzy of that phrase!"
As a spent taper musters ere it dies
Its flames, to perish in the splendid blaze,
So, cherishing with rage the blood that plays
Thus feebly in his veins, he would supply
Strength to the spirit which so fast decays;
And his last hour of life, which now drew nigh,
Crown with a glorious end, and like a hero die.

23. To his left hand its fellow he applied,
And with them both impell'd his heavy blade;
Down it descended,—meeting, struck aside
The prince's sword, nor there its fury stay'd;
But, glancing from the shoulder, did invade
All his left side in its oblique career,
And many wounds at the same moment made;
If Tancred quail'd not at the stroke severe,
'Twas that his heart was form'd incapable of fear.

24. His blow the Paynim doubled, but he spent
On the void air his desperate energy,
As Tancred, conscious of his fierce intent,
The stroke prevented, slipping nimbly by.
By thine own weight o'erbalanced dost thou lie
On earth, Argantes, nor couldst shun the fall;
Thyself hast thou o'erthrown,—O fatal die,
Well cast! thrice happy, that none else can call
Himself thy conqu'ror now, or triumph in thy thrall.

25 His gaping wounds the fall made yet more wide,
And from their lips fresh purple torrents broke;
Raised by his hand upon one knee, he tried
On new defense the battle to provoke.
"Yield," cried the courteous prince, "and live!" one stroke
He struck or menaced, as he made th' appeal;
The sullen Pagan not an accent spoke,
But at swift stealth shot out his treacherous steel,
And with a shout of joy exulting pierced his heel.

26. Then rose the rage of Tancred, and he said;
"Villain! dost thou my mercy thus deride?"
Then plunged, and plunged again his fatal blade,
Where a free pass the aventayle supplied.
Thus died Argantes: as he lived, he died,
Dying, he menaced death: no lamentation
Broke from his lips, but fix'd, unbending pride,
Ferocious hate, and scorn of all salvation,
Spoke in his latest words and last gesticulation.—

27. His sword then sheathing to his guardian Saint
Prince Tancred paid his solemn thanks sincere;
But from the strife enfeebled, worn and faint,
His bloody meed has cost the victor dear;
So that he seriously began to fear
His limbs would scarcely serve him to retrace
His homeward path; yet to the pine-tree near,

Which kept the entrance of that shady place,
He step by step moved on, with slow unsteady pace.

28. Not far can the weak knight his steps command,
The more he hastes, more tired, the less his speed,
Whence he at length sits down, and on his hand,
His hand, that trembles like a shaking reed,
Propp'd on his elbow, leans his head ; fast bleed ;
His wounds, the scene spins round, his giddy brain
Grows dull, and night seems in her sable weed
To wrap the day ; at length he swoons with pain,
And undistinguish'd lies the slayer from the slain.

29. While the two lords pursue their lonely fight,
So fierce and bloody made by private hate,
The angry victors in the city smite
The guilty people wide from gate to gate :
Press'd, on all sides they rush, to shun their fate ;
Oh who can fully picture in his page
The horrors of the sack ! what tongue relate
In fitting terms the agony—the rage—
The dreadful scenes that pass'd on such a spacious stage !

30. Each place is choked with carnage, fill'd with death ;
In intertangled heaps the slaughter'd lie ;
The falling rests upon the fallen ; beneath
Th' unburied dead the buried living die ;
Here with dishevel'd locks mad mothers fly,
Straining their infants to their breasts ; and there
The savage spoiler, drunk with victory
And rifled treasure, by her golden hair
Drags off the shrieking maid to his voluptuous lair.

31. But through the streets which near the western hills,
Where he beholds the solemn Temple stand,
All moist and horrid with the blood he spills,
Rinaldo, rushing, drives the Paynim band ;
The cruel falchion in his red right hand
O'er their plumed heads in bickering circles waves ;
Its strokes nor shield nor helmet can withstand ;
He bleeds who vainly turns, he dies who braves ;
It is the want of arms, not armor here which saves.

32. On steel alone his noble steel descends,
Th' unarm'd he scorns to hurt ; the arm'd, the strong
Who dare him not, and whom no mail defends,
By frowns and dreadful shouts he drives along.

O who can tell, nor do his valor wrong,
What prodigies he wrought; how wide he spread,
How menaced, spared, spurr'd on the trembling throng;
How with unequal risk, but equal dread,
Arm'd and unarm'd alike his face affrighted fled!—

33. Already with the crowd their bravest men,
A numerous party, had the Temple gain'd;
Which, burnt and oft rebuilt as it had been,
The name of its great founder still retain'd.
Of cedar, gold, and marbles richly stain'd,
The glorious tribute of a thousand shores,
King Solomon had framed it: it remain'd.
If with less splendid roofs and plainer floors,
Strong with embattled towers, firm walls, and brazen doors.

34 Reaching this fortress, in whose spacious heart
The multitude were fled, Rinaldo found
The portals closed, and every single part
Of the high battlements with lances crown'd,
And threat'ning mangonels: he roll'd around
His flashing eyes, and twice the strong retreat
Scann'd from its topmost turret to the ground,
Some narrow pass to spy, and twice in heat
Circled the spacious pile on swift, impatient feet.

35. As the destroying wolf at midnight prowls,
With eager hungry jaws and eyes of fire,
Round the penn'd fold, and disappointed growls
With fierce instinctive hate and native ire;
So goes Rinaldo, wild with the desire
To penetrate the fabric he surveys;
In vain—it stands impassive and entire;
In the grand Court at length his steps he stays,
And they th' assault expect with fix'd, despairing gaze.

36. By chance, for some rare use reserved, there lay
A long and tapering beam the hero nigh;
The tightest argosy in Genoa's bay
Has not a mast more stately, stout, and high;
In this the noble Infant cast his eye,
And with that hand to which all weights were light,
Poising the formidable lance on high,
To his friends' wonder and his foes' affright,
Hurl'd it against the gates, with unexampled might.

37. Nor brass nor marble stone could stand before
The sudden force of that tremendous blow;
The sounding hinges from the rock it tore,
Broke the strong locks, and laid the portals low;
Nor batt'ring engine, nor balista-bow,
Nor fulmining petard, death's thunder-ball,
Could have done more: in, like a deluge, flow
Through the void pass vast numbers, at the call
Of the triumphant youth, th' inspiring soul of all.

38. Their dreadful slaughter black and mournful made
That lofty pile, once consecrate to God;
O heavenly justice! sharp, if long delay'd,
On wicked nations falls thy chast'ning rod:
Under thy secret influence, at thy nod,
Rage woke in hearts by nature soft and mild;
Till the grim Frank alone on corses trod,
And the revilers, in their turn reviled,
Wash'd with their blood the fane their sins had late defiled.

39. But Solyman meanwhile to the strong tower
Which yet the name of David bore, was sped,
And with the gather'd remnant of his power,
Block'd up each street that to the fortress led;
And thither too the feeble Tyrant fled,
Whom when the Soldan saw, he thus bespoke:
"Come, famous Prince! and shield thy noble head
On the tower'd summit of this lofty rock,
Where thou the worst assaults of battle still mayst mock.

40. "Here from the rage of hostile swords, thy crown,
Thy life, and kingdom mayst thou yet defend,"
"Woe's me!" he answer'd, "woe is me! my Town
Barbaric hands from the foundations rend;
My race is run,—my rule is at an end,—
I lived, I reigned; I live and reign no more;
For all that now is left me, O my friend,
Is to exclaim, 'We were!'—all, all is o'er!
Our final hour's at hand; pale Death is at the door!"

41. "Where then!" the angry Soldan made exclaim,
"Where is thine old heroic courage flown?
Ill-fortune take our kingdoms! are not fame,
Worth, pride, and kingly grandeur yet our own!
These with us stay, though those be overthrown:
But rest within thy weary limbs, and court

Refreshment; there are those will guard thy throne."
Thus saying, he at once unclosed the port,
And led the hoary king within th' embattled fort.

42. His iron mace he grasps with both his hands
Girds fast the trusty saber to his thigh,
And in th' attempted pass intrepid stands,
The whole Frank people singly to defy;
Quick, mortal blows fall horrid from on high,
The rash they daunt, th' heroic they abase;
Whom they kill not, they stun at least,—all fly
At length, and vacant leave th' invested place,
Where'er he cares to move with his gigantic mace—

43. But lo! well sheath'd in brigandine of brass,
Arrived, and follow'd by a hundred knights,
Earl Raymond rushes to the dang'rous pass,
And the tremendous weapon sternly slights;
He at the Soldan first, but vainly smites,
Vainly his sword descends; but not in vain
The furious Saracen his stroke requites;
Struck on the temples, with bewilder'd brain
And quiv'ring arms he lies, extended on the plain—

44. And now the vanquish'd reassume the fire
Which fear had banish'd from their hearts of late,
And the Frank victors, beaten back, retire,
Or slaughter'd fall within the portal-gate:
But the Arch-Genius of the fierce debate,
Seeing the earl, betwixt alive and dead,
Lie with the slaughter'd at his feet, elate,
Call'd to his Saracens behind, and said;
"Drag in this captive knight; what now have ye to dread?"

45. Forward they rush'd to execute the deed,
But found the task both dang'rous and severe;
For to the rescue, with like eager speed,
All Raymond's people flock, with sword and spear.
There pious duty fights, brute fury here,
In no mean cause, and with no mean intent;
The life—the freedom of so brave a peer
Hang on their blades; to seize him these are bent,—
Those bleed, th' affront at once t' avenge and to prevent.

46. Yet had the stubborn Turk at length prevail'd,
Such eager thirst for vengeance he display'd,
For 'gainst his thund'ring weapon naught avail'd

The sevenfold shield, fine helm, or temper'd blade,—
But from each side a new and powerful aid
Was suddenly perceived approaching near,
The well-contested fortress to invade ;
And both at once, from adverse points, appear—
The sov'reign Captain there, the young Rinaldo here.

47. Then as a shepherd, when the whirlwind's blast
Comes sweeping on, with lightning, hail, and rain,
Seeing the skies with thousand clouds o'ercast,
His fleecy charge drives from the open plain ;
And looks around, solicitous to gain
The shelter'd valley or o'erarching rock,
Where Heaven's hot wrath they may unhurt sustain,
With crook and cry he forward speeds the flock,
And last avoids himself the storm's infuriate shock :

48. Just so the Pagan Prince, when he descried
Th' inevitable tempest, heard the blast
That startled heaven, and saw, on either side,
The field with groves of lances overcast,
Sent back his men, well guarded by his vast
Encircling shield and adamantine mace,
Into the tower, himself retiring last ;
Last he retires, but with that haughty pace,
Which shows he neither yields in fear nor in disgrace.

49. 'Twas task enough for him the tower to gain ;
Scarce were the portals barr'd, th' escape made good,
Than both the doors and bars were rent in twain,
And on the threshold young Rinaldo stood ;
Nor linger'd there ; desire to see subdued
The knight in deeds of arms unmatch'd, disdain,
And his own oath impell'd him to the feud ;
Rememb'ring well his promise to the Dane,
Of keen revenge on him who had Prince Sweno slain.

50. And then, e'en then had his unconquer'd hand
Essay'd the stubborn citadel, nor there
Had the Turk found perchance his dauntless stand
Of much avail—the victor's blade was bare,—
But falling twilight now obscured the air,
And loud and long the warning trumpet blew,
Sounding retreat ; within the spacious square
Godfrey abode, and round his forces drew,
Prompt with the morning sun the struggle to renew.

51. "Lo!" he exclaim'd, with transport on his brow,
"The God of Sabaoth has our armies bless'd;
The tug of war is o'er; but little now
Remains, my friends, your glory to arrest,
Naught to dismay; this tower which we invest,
The last sad refuge of the Paynim, ere
To-morrow ends, we from their hands shall wrest;
Meanwhile let pity urge you with all care
To tend your comrades' wounds, and sooth the pains they bear.

52. "Go, care for those who at a price so dear
Have of these kingdoms purchased thus the sway!
This more befits the Christian chevalier,
Than base desire of vengeance, or of prey.
Too much, ah, too much cruelty this day
Hath witness'd! too much lust of treasure still—
I speak it to your shame—do some display!
But at your peril plunder more, or kill;
Heralds! your trumpets sound, and publish forth my will."

53. This said, he went where, from his swoon awoke,
Groan'd in his pain the faint Provençal Chief:
Nor with less boldness to his soldiers spoke
The dauntless Turk, and thus disguised his grief;
"Heaven, O my friends, will yet a bright relief
Bring to our gloom! be firm; in fortune's spite,
Your flower of hope yet shows a verdant leaf;
For under all this glare of false affright,
Our harm has been but small, our loss exceeding light.

54. "The City is not seized; the Christian Lords
Have gain'd the ramparts, beat the vulgar down,
But in the person of your king, your swords,
And shields, you yet comprise the glorious Town.
Safe stands your Monarch, safe you see his crown,
Safe his best knights, while round this noble host
Strong walls arise; vain trophy of renown,
Let the gay Franks th' abandon'd suburbs boast,
To them th' ambitious game may yet at last be lost.

55. "May be? it must! for, flatter'd into pride
By their so prosp'rous fortune, all their mind
Will but to ceaseless riot, homicide,
And most intemp'rate dalliance be inclined.
In this wild tumult, drunk with blood, and blind
To all but beauty, they must needs appear

But as a rolling wave before the wind,
If the Egyptian host, which now is near,
Come with the clouds of night, and take them in the rear.

56. "We with our engines may meanwhile annoy
Each street that leads to yon accursed tomb;
The loftiest structures o'er our foes destroy,
And thus our lordship in the town resume."
With these bold words he dissipates their gloom;
Exiles their fear, exiles their wild amaze,
And plants both hope and courage in their room:
While these events were passing, midst a blaze
Of arms and gorgeous tents, unawed Vafrino strays.

57. The lark was warbling sweet her evening song,
When through the shadows of declining day
Valfrino left th' encampment; all night long
He travel'd on his dark and lonely way;
High Ascalon he pass'd, ere morning gray
O'er the dim landscape shed its grateful light,
And when the sun with culminating ray
Had reach'd its hot meridian, to the right
The vast, the boundless camp burst proudly on his sight.

58. Millions of tents, o'erwaved with flags unfurl'd,
Green, purple, gold, and crimson, he espies;
And hears such strange wild tongues, and such a world
Of savage sounds from barbarous metals rise,
Trumpet, and horn, and gong, with camels' cries,
Roarings of elephants, and neighings clear
Of shrill-voiced coursers, climbing to the skies,
That to himself he says, with soul sincere,
"All Asia, Libya, all are sure transported here!"

59. He first th' encampment and its strength surveys,
The circling rampart, its extent, and height,
Then seeks no more obscure and winding ways,
But boldly issues to the public sight;
And with an air most unconcern'd and light
Enters the regal gates direct, and now
Asks, and now answers questions, with a sleight
But to be equal'd by the frank bold brow
Which makes his answers good, and greets it cares not how.

60. Through the long crowded streets, the tents and squares,
Now here, now there, solicitous he turns ;
The horses, armors, chiefs, the name each bears,
Their arts and customs he observes and learns
Nor satisfied with this, his spirit burns,
And partly manages to know the bent
Of their most secret projects and concerns
So well he speeds beneath his fair ostent,
As e'en to win access to the imperial tent.

61. Here, looking round, he mark'd a rent, through which
The voice within found egress, and whereby
The Viceroy's private cabinet, a rich
Recess, was obvious to the curious eye ;
So that whoever chose thereto t' apply
His ear without, might gather whatsoe'er
Transpired within ; at this the matchless spy
Planted himself, as with assiduous care
The tent's defective seam adroitly to repair.

62. The Chief bareheaded stood, in arms, and wore
A vest of Tyrian purple ; in the rear
Two pages his bright shield and helmet bore ;—
Thoughtful he stood, and, leaning on his spear,
Gave heed to one who with a look severe,
Tall in his stature, sinewy in his frame,
High points discuss'd : Vafrino was all ear ;
And, surely fancying that he heard the name
Of Bouillon's lord, yet more inquisitive became.

63. He heard the Chieftain question : "Art thou then
So sure of Godfrey's death ?" "So sure," said he,
"I take my oath by Allah, ne'er again
But as a matador thy face to see ;
I will outstrip all those who are with me
Sworn to the deed ; nor ask I other bliss,
Than to hang up in trophy, by decree
Of our great prince, in his metropolis,
The man's rich arms, subscribed with some such verse as this :—

64. "'These arms in war from the Frank Chief, the curse
And scourge of Asia, brave Ormondo tore,
When him he slew ; the fame whereof, this verse
And trophied marble laud for evermore !'"
"Of this," the armed Leader said, "no more ;

Think not the king will leave unglorified
A deed which both the Egypts must adore;
Thy wish, besure, he will fulfill with pride,
And grace thy conqu'ring brows with priceless gems beside.

65. "Now then the counterfeited arms prepare,
For the great day of fight approaches fast:"
"They are all ready," he replied, and there
Both ended parle, and from the chamber pass'd.
Suspense and doubt Vafrino's mind o'ercast;
Long as he weigh'd the seeming aim and end,
Of their discourse, the project to the last
Remain'd obscure,—he could not comprehend,
What by this feint of arms the traitors could intend.

66. Thence he departed, nor the livelong night
His eyes to slumber or repose resign'd;
But when that mighty camp at morning light
Unfurl'd its thousand banners to the wind,
He in their march the hostile squadrons join'd,
Like the train'd hound sequacious of its scent;
With them he halted when the day declined,
And, as before, stalk'd slow from tent to tent,
Eager to gather more of this disguised intent.

67. On a rich throne mid knights and damsels gay,
Searching around, Armida he descries;
Forlorn she sits, and inly seems to weigh
Some deep sad thought, for as she sits she sighs
On her white hand in melancholy guise
She leans her rosy cheek, and so would fain
Hide the love-darting radiance of her eyes:
Weeps she or no he knows not, but 'tis plain
The stars in heaven are dim, and lower, presaging rain.

68. In frônt of her Adrastus sits, nor heeds
Aught but her charms,—he moves not, scarce respires,
So steadfastly he hangs on her, and feeds
His pining hopes and unappeased desires.
But Tisaphernes now the dame admires,
Now eyes the savage, whom in soul he spurns
From her dear sight; the while with changeful fires
His visage dark and radiant shows by turns,
As Love's mild watchlight shines, or Wrath's hot beacon burns.

69. Then Altamore he views, where more apart
He stands, inclosed amidst her virgins bright;
He lets not loose his glances, but with art
Rules his fond fancy and his wishful sight:
His left eye marks her hand, her face, his right
Glides down voluptuous on a sweeter quest,
And secretly slips in, to its delight,
Where the too careless and indulgent vest
Reveals, at ev'ry swell, the beauty of her breast.

70. At length Armida raised her eyes, and straight
Her brow clear'd up; and through the clouds of grief
With which her pensive features gloom'd of late,
Flash'd a sweet smile in beautiful relief.
"Prince," she said, turning to the Indian Chief,
"Thy vaunts have power my sorrows to assuage;
For they confirm me in the fond belief
That I shall have quick vengeance: sweet is rage,
When willing Hope takes up Revenge's daring gage."

71. "For Allah's sake, serene," the Indian said,
"Thy mournful aspect, and thy griefs control;
For soon indeed Rinaldo's hated head
I in glad vengeance at thy feet will roll;
Or, if it more thy sorrow should console,
In chains conduct him to whatever jail
May please thee most; I swear it on my soul."
His rival, hearing thus the ruffian rail,
Deign'd not a word himself, but gnaw'd his bitter nail.

72. She, turning then on Tisapherne a smile,
Said; "What say'st thou, and how dost thou decide?"
"I, who am backward in this vaunting style,"
The noble Prince in irony replied,
"Will follow this grim champion with a stride
Less stately, and at distance:" his sharp sneer
Stung the fierce savage to the quick, who cried:
"And fit it is that he whose arm must fear
To match the king of Inde's, *should* linger far arear."

73. The Persian, nettled at the word, toss'd high
The haughty plumes upon his head, and said:
"O, were I master of my will, had I
But free permission to unsheath my blade,
Which was the ling'rer should be soon display'd!
Nor thee, nor thy big vaunts, ferocious brute!
But Heaven and unconsenting Love I dread:"
He ceased; Adrastus rush'd to the dispute;
But then Armida rose, and 'twixt them placed her foot.

74. "Why will you thus retract the oaths," said she,
"Which you so oft have given; respect my woes:
Both are my champions; let that title be
The bond your fatal discords to compose:
He that is wroth, is wroth with me; who throws
Scorn on his comrade, spares not to provoke
My just displeasure; to your cost be foes!"
Thus she exclaim'd; and thus, beneath a yoke
Stronger than steel, their hot, rebellious spirits broke.

75. Vafrine was there; and, treasuring in his mind
All he heard mention'd, from the tent retired;
Some deep dark plot he clearly saw design'd,
Some plot, that was not thus to have transpired;
But this was all; he busily inquired
The naked fact, but fruitlessly; defeat
And difficulty but the more inspired
The anxious wish his mission to complete;
Fix'd or to learn the truth, or there his death to meet.

76. A thousand tricks and subtleties of brain,
A thousand unimagined means he tried,
To worm the secret out, but still in vain,—
The plan was still unknown, the arms unspied.
Fortune at length, when wit alone could guide
His steps no farther, lent her gracious aid,
And the dark knot of all his doubts untied;
So that all points of the dire project laid
Against good Bouillon's life, before him were display'd.

77. Thither he turn'd again, where still among
Her armed lovers sat the Syrian queen,
Judging the truth would soonest find a tongue,
Where such a crowd of visitors convene.
Here now he greets a damsel with the mien
Of one in all polite enchantments versed,
As though the lady he before had seen,
And but renew'd some friendship that had erst
'Twixt them subsisted long; and frankly he conversed.

78. "Fain would I too," he sportively began,
"Become the champion of some charming maid,
And, in fulfillment of the purposed plan,
The blood of Bouillon or Rinaldo shed;
Ask then some boon, my Beauty, that may wed
My soul to your sweet service; what you please,
Or stout earl's heart or barb'rous baron's head:"
Thus he commenced, intending by degrees
To slip from gay to grave, and learn the chief's decrees.

79. But as he spake, he smiled ; and in a way
So natural and unfeign'd, that to his side
Another damsel, who had mark'd the play
Of his expressive face, drew near, and cried :
"Nay ! for thy falchion choose no other bride
Than my commands, for on its aid my heart
Is set ; nor think such love misplaced,—beside
By old consent my knight indeed thou art,
And e'en as such, we two must have some talk apart."

80. Withdrawn, she spoke : "I know thee well, Vafrine;
Me too thou needs must know ;" the subtle Spy
Felt his heart fail him, but with lively mien
Her glance return'd, and smiling made reply :
"Nay, gracious lady ! ne'er before have I,
That I remember, seen your face, although
Its beauty asks the gaze of every eye
Fitly to praise it ; this alone I know,
My name is much unlike the one which you bestow.

81. "My mother bore me on Biserta's plains,
Her name Lesbina, mine is Almanzore :"
Quick she replied : "All that to thee pertains
I long have known, dissemble it no more ;
Hold not thyself so secret, I implore ;
I am thy friend, and for thy good would dare
No little risk,—Erminia I, of yore
A Queen's bless'd daughter and a King's rich heir,
Then good Prince Tancred's thrall, and subject to thy care.

82. "Two blessed months thy captive I remain'd,
A reverenced nun in a delightful cell,
And in all courteous modes was entertain'd,—
The same, the same I am ; behold me well !"
The squire fail'd not, when on her beauty fell
His closer gaze, to recognize the fair :
"All fears," she added, "from thy mind expel ;
Fear not for me, thy life shall be my care ;
By the bright sun in heaven, by heaven itself I swear.

83. "Nay, when thou partest, take me back, my friend,
To my dear prison—(pardon me the phrase ;)
For here in bitter liberty I spend
Whole restless nights and melancholy days ;
And if perchance thou'rt ling'ring here to gaze
Upon our camp, and with ingenious brain
Pry through our plans, great cause hast thou to praise

Thy happy stars ; for I will things explain,
Which else thy utmost skill had fail'd to ascertain."

84. Thus she : but, thoughtful of Armida's snares
He silent stood, considering in his mind ;
"Woman's a false and chatt'ring thing,—she swears
And will and will not, just as sits the wind ;
Simple's the man, and credulous, and blind,
Who trusts a word she says ;" at length he cried,
After long thought, "If thou'rt indeed inclined
To go, so be it ; I will be thy guide ;
Leave we the rest to wait a more convenient tide."

85. And now the gongs and trumpets sound to horse,
And through the host an apt confusion reigns ;
Vafrino leaves her tent, while she perforce
Rejoins her friends, awhile with them remains,
And in gay talk their idlesse entertains
With jocund praises of her new-made knight ;
Then steals off slyly ; mounts her palfrey ; gains
The place prescribed, and with Vafrino light
O'er the wide champaign takes her unregarded flight.

86. When they had reach'd the desert, and in air
Beheld the distant towers of Gaza fade,
Vafrino begg'd the virgin to declare
What secret plot was against Godfrey laid :
She then the whole conspiracy display'd,
The treach'rous web unwinding, fold by fold ;
"Eight warriors are there of the court," she said,
"In this insidious bond of guilt enroll'd,
Of whom the most renown'd is Ormond, base as bold.

87. "These, whether moved by hatred or disdain,
Have thus conspired, and 'tis their shrewd design,
When in pitch'd battle, or to lose or gain
These Asian realms, the two great armies join,
To bear upon their coats the Red-cross sign,
And arm'd like Franks commingle in the fight ;
And as 'tis known the guards of Godfrey shine
In *or* and *argent*, they themselves will dight
In the like foreign vests, emblazoning gold and white.

88. "But all will wear some token on the crest,
Whereby their friends may know them for allies ;
And when both armies lay their spears in rest,
And the war thickens and the tumults rise,
They will your Chief track out, and in the guise

Of guards with amicable zeal crowd round,
To pierce his bosom; if they strike, he dies;
For know, their swords with poison have been ground,
That death may be dealt out in ev'ry separate wound.

89\. "And as their Chieftain learn'd from public fame
That none with surer skill could signify
Your arms and dress, he fix'd on me to frame
Their feign'd array, and forced me to comply.
This is the cause I leave the camp; I fly
Th' imperious biddings which that Asp of Nile
Might further give; his trains of treachery
My heart abhors, nor ever shall such guile
Or mask'd deceit again my virgin heart defile.

90\. "This is the cause, nor this alone,"—and here
She ceased, and, coloring to a rosy red,
Cast down her eyes, nor could Vafrino hear
Well the last words, which much she wish'd unsaid.
Solicitous to know what thoughts could shed
Such deep confusion o'er her cheek, he press'd
The virgin home,—"Of little faith!" he said,
"Why the true causes hide from one whose breast
Is, as thou know'st, of trust? blush not, but speak the rest."

91\. Her bosom heaved with a tumultuous swell,
And from her lips the trembling accents came
Abrupt and prefaced by a sigh: "Farewell
Ill-timed reserve and unavailing shame!
It is in vain—I am no more the same—
In vain conceal'd and close you strive to hide
Love's glowing fires beneath your specious flame!
Due were such scruples ere I stepp'd aside;
But now a wand'ring maid, farewell th' imperfect pride.

92\. "My loss," she added, "on that night of grief,
When my poor country yielded to her foes,
Surpass'd th' appearance; not that then my chief
Misfortune happen'd, but from thence it rose.
My scepter lost, my realms subdued, were woes
Easy to bear, resign'd with little cost;
But with my high estate, my heart's repose
Was also gone; ah me! what folly cross'd
My brain? then sense was wreck'd, and peace forever lost!

93. "Thou know'st, Vafrine, with what a trembling awe,
Seeing such slaughter and foul spoil, I sped
To thy kind lord and mine, when first I saw
Arm'd in my halls the warrior fix his tread;
Thou know'st with what an agony of dread
His knees I grasp'd, and of his conqu'ring glave
Pray'd strong protection: 'Mercy, Prince,' I said,
'I pray not for my life, but save, oh save
My virgin flower unstain'd! 'tis all I come to crave.'

94. "He waited not to hear my finish'd plea,
But took my hand in his, and said, 'Arise!
Fear not, fair maiden! I myself will be
Thy sure defense; cloud not those charming eyes!'
Ah, then I felt, with a divine surprise,
I know not what strange sweetness seize my frame,
Which by degrees, in gratitude's disguise,
Securely creeping through my soul, became,
Ere well I wist, a wound, a sickness, and a flame.

95. "He visited me oft, he saw me grieve,
And with mild accents would my woes allay;
'Thy perfect liberty,' he said, 'receive;
Take back thy treasures, and be cheer'd, I pray.'
Ah, this was cruelty, not kindness! gay
I could not be, when while he drew the dart,
He rudely snatch'd me from myself away;
These he restored to me, the cheaper part
But in restoring play'd the tyrant o'er my heart.

96. "Love's hard to hide; with thee I oft apart
Ask'd of my lord in garden, hall, and grove;
Thou the strong workings of my mind and heart
Perceiving, saidst, 'Erminia, thou'rt in love!'
This I denied—can maids do less? and strove
To dissipate th' idea; but my sighs
Too well sufficed the assertion to disprove;
And while my tongue was mute, perchance my eyes
Shone with th' impassion'd warmth I studied to disguise.

97. "Unhappy silence! had I then but sought
The fitting medicine for my wounds, I ne'er
Had loosed my wishes on a fancy fraught
With no relief, nor fled I know not where.
I left him, hiding in my breast with care
The flame I nursed;—what tongue my pangs can paint,
For death alone I look'd; till with despair

Love in my succor strove, and in th' attaint,
Loosed me from ev'ry tie of feminine restraint.

98. "So that to seek my lord I went, that he
Might cure the ling'ring sickness he had made;
But on my moonbright way, I chanced to be,
By villains, ambush'd in the greenwood shade,
Chased and assaulted; scarce could I evade
Their savage grasp, so hotly they pursued;
To a lone cell at length my palfrey stray'd,
And there I dwelt in genial solitude,
A simple shepherd-girl, a tenant of the wood.

99. "But when that fond desire, which sore dismay
Had for awhile suppress'd, revived again,
Daring the same adventure, on my way
The same misfortune met with me as then;
Nor could I now escape; for in the glen
The lurking freebooters were close at hand;
Thus was I chased and quickly seized,—the men
Were, I soon gather'd, an Egyptian band,
Who straight for Gaza made, swift journeying o'er the sand.

100. "They took me to their Chief, whose ear my prayer
And mournful story so completely gain'd,
That he mine honor did respect, and there
With kind Armida have I since remain'd.
Thus oft have I been harshly entertain'd;
Thus oft have I escaped; ah see, Vafrine,
What scenes I have pass'd through, what ills sustain'd
Yet free, yet captured oft as I have been,
Still my first chains I wear, preserv'd through ev'ry scene.

101. "Ah, let not him who round my soul entwined
The chains from which no power can set me free,
Let him not say, 'Go, vagrant maid, and find
Some other home, thou shalt not stay with me,'—
But kind and dear may my reception be!
'Take back,' Vafrino! to thy master say,
'This trembling dove, and treat her tenderly!'"
Thus spake the Princess; and thus, night and day,
They side by side rode on, and talk'd the time away.

102. The beaten road Vafrino left erewhile,
Seeking a shorter or securer way;
They reach'd at length, what time with farewell smile

The sun hung hov'ring o'er the landscape gray,
Near to the town, a vale of pine and bay ;
Sprinkled with crimson was the green ; and nigh,
Groveling in blood, a lifeless warrior lay
Across the path ; though dead, his Gorgon eye
Yet seem'd to menace death, upstaring on the sky.

103. The fashion of his arms and foreign mien
Spoke him a Pagan ; on Vafrino sped,
And somewhat farther on the encircled green,
As to the right he chanced to turn his head,
Perceived a second : "This," he inly said,
"Must surely be a Christian, by the grain
Of his dark vest ;" he sees the Cross of Red,
Leaps from his steed, the face discovers plain,
And, "O my God !" he cried, "here lies Prince Tancred slain."

104. The pitying Princess had paused to gaze
On the grim form of the Circassian peer,
When that sad voice of anguish and amaze
Came like an arrow on her heart and ear ;
At Tancred's name, she spurr'd like one whom fear
Or wine had render'd mad, her palfrey fleet ;
And when she saw indeed the form so dear,
Pale, and wrapp'd round as with the winding-sheet
Of death, she stepp'd not, no, she darted from her seat.[18]

105. And, with a bursting groan, a stormy shower
Of tears, low bending o'er th' unconscious knight,
"Fortune," she cried, "in what ill-omen'd hour
Bring'st thou me here ? O dire, O fatal sight !
Long wish'd, long sought for, is it in this plight
I find and view thee, oh my love ! laced o'er
With wounds, and all unable to requite
With one kind look the bitter plaints I pour ?
No sooner found again, than lost for evermore !

106. "Ah ! never did I dream that to these eyes
Thou couldst be aught, love, but a pleasing care ;
Would they were dark, no more this blank disguise
Of thy dear face to mark, which ill they dare.
Where is its once expressive smile ? ah where
The mildness beaming from the eye ? the cheek's
Divine carnations, and the brow that bare
Itself so bravely ?—not a feature speaks,—
Gone ! beyond reach, alas, of groans, or tears, or shrieks !

107. "But, though thus pale and dim, thou charm'st me still;
Fair soul! if yet thou light'st this seeming clay,
Yet hear'st my plaints, forgive my daring will
And too rash ardor the fond theft which they
Tempt me to take,—forgive me if I lay
To thine my virgin lips, and one cold kiss
Steal from the dull caresses of decay!
Warmer I look'd for, but twill be some bliss
To seize in death's despite, and die rememb'ring this.

108. "Receive my soul, which flutters to be free,
And thither guide it where thine own is fled!"
Groaning she spoke, and weeping seem'd to be
Apace dissolving with the tears she shed.
Bathed by this quick'ning balm, as from the dead,
The knight revived, and open'd for a space
His languid lips,—dark slumber still o'erspread
His heavy eyes, but as she kiss'd his face,
One blending sigh from him repaid her bless'd embrace.

100. A gleam of hope, at his reviving breath,
Cheer'd the sad maid: "Look up, dear love," she cried,
"On the last melancholy rites of death
Which I with pious tears and sighs provide!
Look on me, Tancred, a funereal bride,
Fain in companionship with thee to take
The long dark path and perish at thy side!
Fly not, fly not so soon, for pity's sake,
'Tis the last boon I ask, the last request I make."

110. Tancred his eyes unclosed, and closed again,
Heavy and dim; and she renew'd her plaint;
"This," said Vafrine, "sooths not the hero's pain,
First cure the wounded, then bewail th' attaint."
He strips him of his arms; Erminia, faint
And trembling, aids him as she can, applies
Her skillful hand, like a ministrant saint,
To search his wounds, and with experienced eyes,
Symptoms of hopeful show, rejoicingly descries.

111. By loss of blood and faintness she perceives
The trance is caused, and by the chill night wind;
But in this lonely wilderness of leaves
Naught save her veil occurs, his wounds to bind:
But Love romantic bandages can find,
And dictate arts of pity strange and sweet,—

For with her radiant tresses, disentwined,
She stanch'd the flowing blood, (divine conceit !)
And swathed the grisly wounds that so acutely beat.—

112. Severing the tresses with his sword ; for ill
Her thin short veil th' occasion could suffice ;
Nor sage nor crocus, dittany nor dill
Found she at hand ; but charms of equal price
She knew, she used, and from his weary eyes
That deadly sleep already shakes away ;
Lightly he lifts them, and with glad surprise
Beholds his servant, and, in strange array,
The maid who o'er him hangs with such benign dismay.

113. "How com'st thou here, Vafrino ?" soft he said,
"And thou, my kind physician ! who art thou ?"
She wept, she blush'd, rejoicing, rosy-red,
She sigh'd, she smiled, she felt she wist not how.
"Thou shalt know all, prince," she replied, "but now
(Thus thy physician bids) be still and rest ;
Health shall return to thy bewilder'd brow,
Prepare the guerdon that shall make me bless'd ;"
And then his head she placed upon her beauteous breast.

114. Vafrino mused how he might best, ere night,
Remove the warrior from the bosky glen,
When lo ! a band of soldiers came in sight,
Whom soon he noted for Lord Tancred's men ;
They on the tower were fighting round him, when
He met the fierce Circassian, blade to blade,
And in appeal of battle dared him ; then
Bade not to follow, they the prince obey'd,
But anxious sought him now, so long the hero stay'd.

115. Numbers beside pursued the search, but these
Alone had the good chance their wish to gain ;
Their arms they join, whereon with perfect ease
To all, the wounded hero they sustain :
"Shall then Argantes," said the knight, "remain,
Brave as he was, the prey of wild birds ? no !
Leave not the hero ; bear him from the plain ;
His gallant relics shall not feed the crow,
Nor want such praise or tomb as Tancred can bestow.

116. "I war not with the pale dumb corse,—he died
Bold as a lion on the hunter's spear ;
Funereal rites 'tis fit that we provide,
The last poor honors that can serve him here."

He said ; his troops construct a simple bier,
And thus in solemn march behind him bear
His slaughter'd foe ; Vafrino in the rear,
His station takes beside th' enamor'd fair,
And tends her o'er the downs with all a page's care.

117. "Not home," said Tancred, "to my wonted tent,
But bear, O bear me to the sacred Town !
That if cut short by human accident,
I there may lay my feverish being down :
Haply a spot of such revered renown
Where died the Lamb of God, may make my way
To heaven more easy ; and 'twill be the crown
Of all my toils, with life's declining ray,
Low at his worship'd shrine my pilgrim vows to pay !"

118. He said, and thither was he borne, and laid
On a soft bed, and in a calm repose
Was soon entranced ; Vafrino for the maid
A near apartment close and secret chose ;
And, leaving her to cheer her amorous woes
With kindling hope's serene perspective, went
Where Godfrey sojourn'd, unforbid by those
Who there kept guard, though then in crowded tent
On the next stroke of war his dubious thoughts were bent.

119. Beside the bed, whence Raymond scarce uprears
His yet enfeebled frame, the Duke was found ;
By a brave garland of his noble peers,
And of his wisest counselors compass'd round.
The Squire his tale begins, and a profound
Regard is mark'd on each beholder's mien ;
None interrupts him : "Sire," he says, "renown'd
Through the wide world ! at thy desire I've been
Amidst th' Egyptian tents, and all their forces seen.

120. "But fancy not that of the mighty host
The countless swarms can be by me ared ;
I saw the hills, and plains, and valleys lost,
E'en as I look'd, beneath their dark'ning tread ;
I saw, where'er they came, where'er they spread,
Rich earth despoil'd of all her grass and grain,
And the flood shrink in its exhausted bed ;
Not Jordan's stream, nor Syria's wide champaign
Can e'er, methinks, suffice, such myriads to sustain.

121. "But of their horse and of their foot by far
The greater part are merely useless shows;
Troops that no signals use nor arts of war,
But at a distance fight with slings and bows;
Yet are there some choice warriors who compose
The Persian host, well mail'd, with sword in hand,
And helmets on their heads; but chiefly those
Illustrious myrmidons my praise demand,
Who guard th' imperial flag, the king's Immortal Band.

122. "Immortal call'd, for when a soldier's lost,
Its number not diminishes; the knight
Next in renown fills up the vacant post,
As though succeeding to his comrade's right;
The Captain, Emireno named, for might
In deeds of arms and wisdom in divan,
Has but few peers; his orders are, despite
Thy utmost phlegm, by all the arts he can,
Into a general fight to force thee or trepan.

123. "Nor can the army its approach retard
Beyond the second day, for 'tis on fire
To act,—look well, Rinaldo, then to guard
Thy head, 'gainst which so many knights conspire.
The most renown'd have whet their swords in ire,
And pledged their honor on the dreadful deed;
While, yet the more to raise incensed desire,
Herself Armida promises in meed
Of him who or by guile or prowess shall succeed.

124. "Chief of the warriers who have sworn thy death
Is Altamore, the king of Samarcand;
Adrastus too, whose realms are by the breath
Of young Aurora at her rising fann'd;
As big and bold a giant as e'er spann'd
A sword in battle; so unlike his kind,
His reins a monstrous elephant command;
And Tisapherne, to whom, of milder mind,
The sov'reign palm of worth and prowess is assign'd."

125. This heard, Rinaldo's soul was all ablaze,
His eyes with gen'rous indignation fill,
He burns to rush amidst his foes, he lays
Hand on his sword, nor stands a moment still.
"This," said Vafrine, "is one impending ill,
But their chief plot, the crowning stroke of all,

Remains to be disclosed ; their utmost skill
In arms, their guile, their hatred, and their gall,
Will be employ'd to work thine own determined fall."

126. He then proceeded, part by part, t' unveil
The latent risk, the meditated fraud,
The poison'd arms, devices, shirts of mail,
The vaunt, the promise, and design'd reward.
Much was inquired, much answer'd ; all applaud
The spy's quick genius and accomplish'd vow :
Silence ensued ; until the chief, unawed
By the near danger, raised his tranquil brow,
And to count Raymond said, "What counsel offerest thou?"

127. "Not as was fix'd," he said, "at rise of sun
To press our foes, but, more to their chagrin,
The tower so strictly to besiege, that none
May at his pleasure or pass out or in ;
Meanwhile refresh our forces, which begin
To need the respite ; strengthen'd thus with rest,
The last great battle we may hope to win ;
But judge thyself at leisure if 'twere best,
Boldly, or here at bay the battle to contest.

128. "But, above all things, of thyself besure
Take every care, as 'tis through thee, they own,
Our armies conquer ; who can else secure
The field, and Europe o'er the East enthrone?
And that the traitors may be clearly known,
Change the devices of thy guardian band ;
So shall the villains for their crime atone,
Caught in the very scheme themselves have plann'd,
And thou be still preserved, our armies to command."

129. "As is thy wont," the pious chief replied,
"Thy kind regard and wisdom dost thou show ;
But what thou leav'st unfix'd, I now decide—
We will march forth against the haughty foe.
Shall armies, recent from the overthrow
Of the proud East, from tower or rampart fight,
When too by such foul guile insulted? No!
Our well-proved swords the traitors shall requite
Both in the open field and all-beholding light!

130. "Neither the rumor of our conquer'd spoils
Shall they sustain ; nor, when in frowns reveal'd,
The victor's aspect, or his arms ; our toils

Are crown'd ; and in their fall our empire's seal'd :
The tower, their last lorn confidence, shall yield,
Or, unrelieved of any, be possess'd,
When the first engine to its walls is wheel'd !"
Here ceased the high-soul'd Chief, for down the west
The glitt'ring stars declined, and call'd them to their rest.

END OF CANTO XIX.

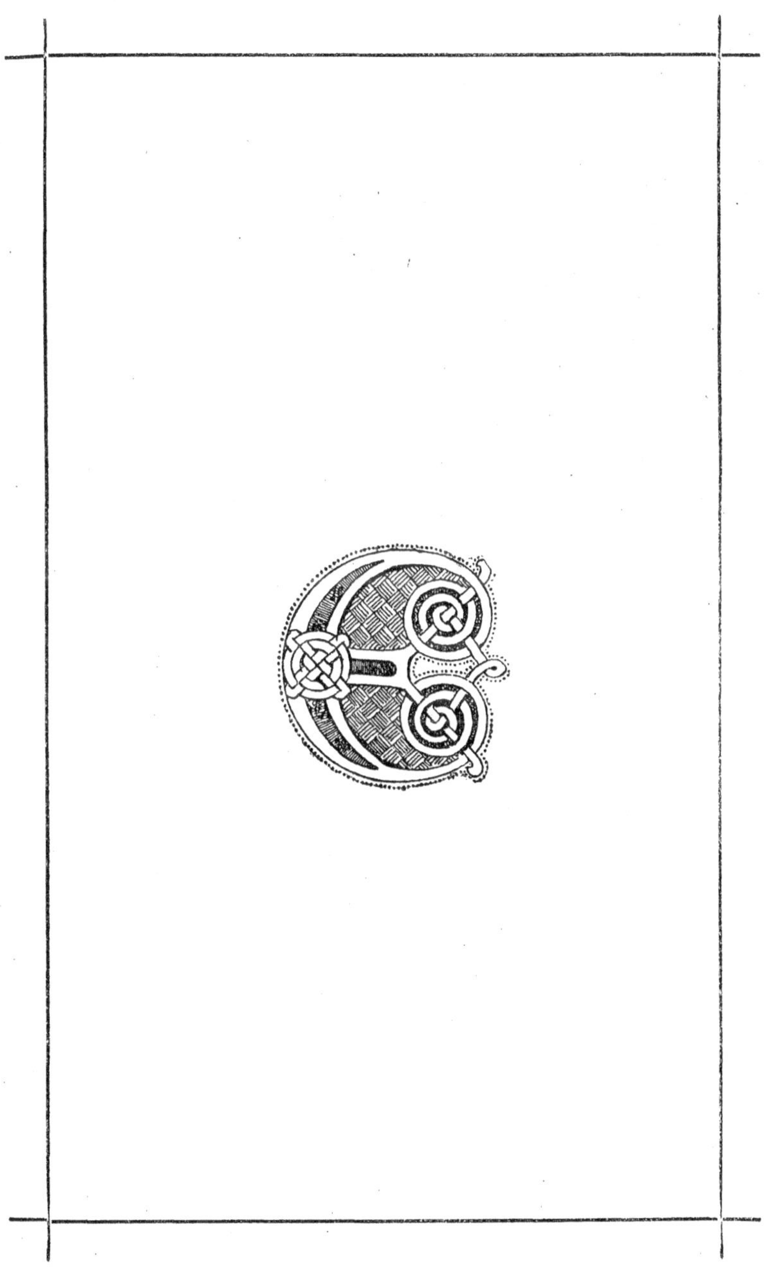

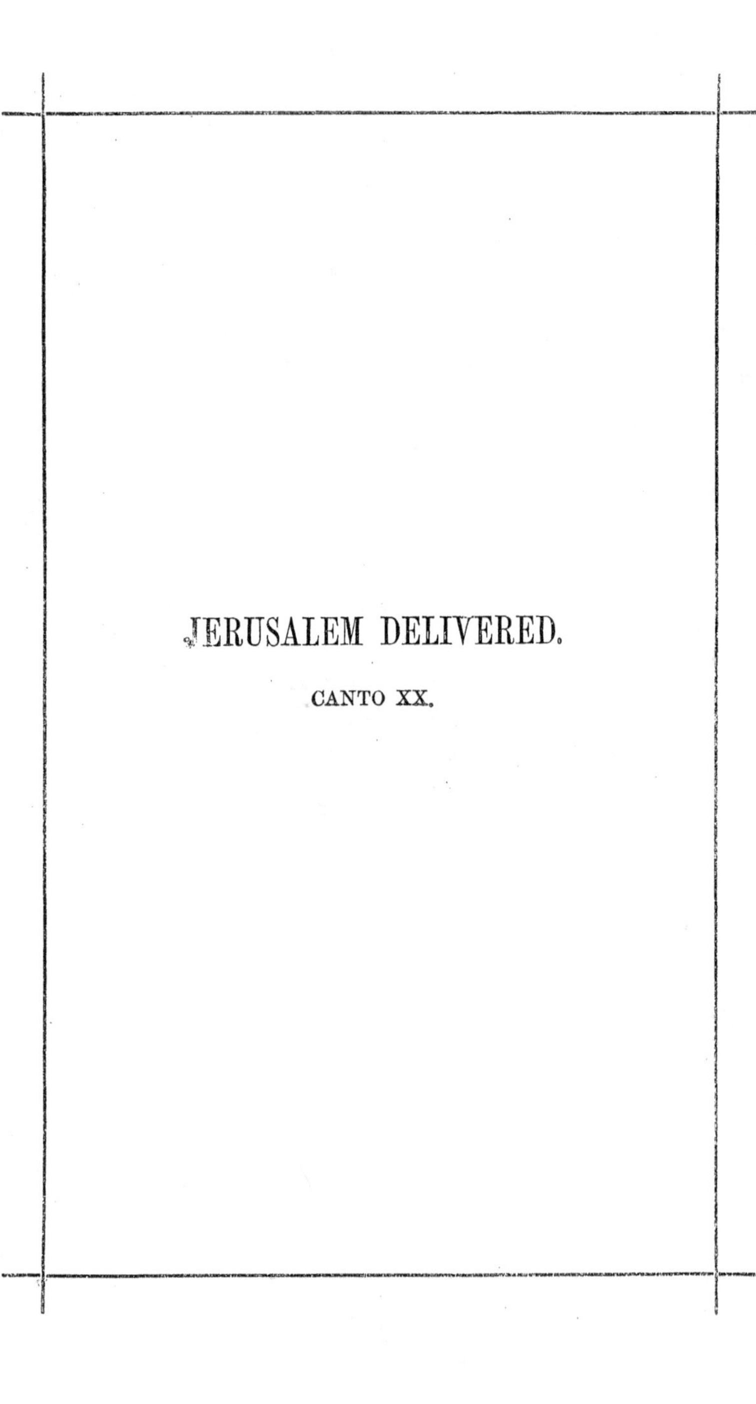

JERUSALEM DELIVERED.

CANTO XX.

ARGUMENT.

THE host arrives. and with the Christian power
Joins in fell battle ; Solyman disdains
To be coop'd up in the blockaded tower,
And sallies out to war upon the plains ;
With him the king in blood his saber stains ;
Both fall by noble hands : the godlike boy
Sooths his forlorn Armida ; daylight wanes,
But the flush'd Croises all their foes destroy,
And to the long-sought shrine proceed with duteous joy.

JERUSALEM DELIVERED.

CANTO XX.

1. THE sun was risen, the dial's circling shade
Had the tenth hour of morn already pass'd,
When, as the Pagans on their tower survey'd
The plains, a gloom th' horizon overcast,
Dark as the cloud which at gray evening fast
Involves the silent world: and now they knew
It was indeed the Egyptian camp, at last
Come to their aid: such clouds of dust upflew,
And shut the heavens, and hills, and valleys from their view.

2. Then from the citadel to heaven they raise
A gen'ral shout, a hoarse discordant cry,
Like that of cranes, when now from wintry Thrace
The must'ring swarms their busy pinions ply,
And through the clouds to a serener sky
In clangor scud before the freezing gale;
The long-wish'd succor lifts their ardor high,
So that already from their marble pale
Prompt is each hand to shoot, each glorying tongue to rail.

3. The Franks, conjecturing whence this sudden glow
Of joy and fury had its impulse, hied
To a commanding station, whence the foe
In all his pomp of numbers was descried;
A gen'rous ardor fires their hearts; they chide
The ling'ring hours, the war-cry they resound;
While the flush'd youth below, on ev'ry side,
With martial murmurs hem the Captain round;
And, "Bid, O bid," they cry, "the tuneful trumpet sound."

4. But till the morrow he denies their prayer,
And wisely tempers their audacious heat;
No flying skirmish will he wage, nor care
For an engagement short of full defeat.
"Anon, brave youths!" he answer'd, "but 'tis meet
That with one day of respite you requite
Your recent labors; rest you, I entreat;
Perhaps this truce may in our foes excite
A rash contempt of us, presumptuous in their might."

5. All stood prepared, and through the long, long night,
Expectant pined for morn's returning ray;
Ne'er did the blue sky show so clear and bright,
As in the dawning of that noted day;
Aurora smiled, and seem'd in her array
Of purple radiance with the sun to vie;
Her amethystine crown she shakes away,
All becomes gold; and, without film, the sky
On great and godlike deeds opes slow its glorious Eye.

6. Soon as he saw the golden morning spring,
Godfrey led forth his marshal'd hosts: behind,
Care of the tower in which the Syrian king
Was coop'd, to Raymond's prowess was assign'd;
Who with his own Provençal knights combined
The num'rous band of Christians late enroll'd
In their deliv'rers' ranks, at Emmaus join'd;
Nor these alone were left to guard the hold,
But a renown'd brigade of Gascons brave and bold.

7. From the Chief's spirits, of his men admired,
The total host on victory presumes:
Heaven sends him grace; wherewith, like one inspired,
A nobler air and grandeur he assumes:
His face the rosy light of youth relumes,
Where imaged honor shines like dews in spring;
Glows his rich hauberk, dance his soldier plumes,
And, as his eye smiles, as his limbs take wing,
He in the sunshine looks like some celestial thing.

8. But far he had not march'd, ere in advance
The whole Egyptian army he descried;
He straight secured a hill which 'twas his chance
To find outspread on his sinister side,
And rear; this seized, upon the champaign, wide
In front, but narrow in the wings, his ranks
He spreads abroad; the foot, well fortified,

He forms his center, and the center flanks
With light-horse wings, composed of Flemings and of Franks.

9. In the left wing, to which the shelving hill,
Held by his guardian chivalry, declined,
He the two Roberts placed, to Baldwin's skill
And wise command the center he assign'd;
Himself the right wing held, where unconfined
The plains stretch'd out upon the beams of noon;
For there th' Egyptian, if he felt inclined,
Might, by th' advancing of his armed moon,
Hope with most sure success t' inclose the whole platoon.

10. Here his own noble Lorrainers he fix'd,
With many a choice and many a well-arm'd knight;
And with his archer-horsemen intermix'd
Footmen well used amid their ranks to fight.
Last, of th' Adventurers, men of noble might,
And the cull'd flower of ev'ry Christian land,
He forms a squadron, station'd to the right
Somewhat apart, and to Rinaldo's hand
Commits the sacred charge of this illustrious band.

11. To whom the Duke: "On thy courageous mind
The final issues of the field depend;
Keep thou thy squadron close conceal'd, behind
These spreading wings that to such length extend;
And when the Egyptian troops draw nigh to blend
In stubborn fight, assail them; give not ground,
But render vain the object they intend;
Which is, if I mistake not, to wheel round,
And turn the wings; be bold, and evermore renown'd!"

12. Then on his steed he like the lightning flew
From horse to foot, from ranging band to band,
Flung up his visor, gave his face to view,—
Lighten his eyes, and waves his armed hand;
He cheers the doubtful; with sublime demand
Confirms the ardent; to the bold recites
The vaunts they made, the wondrous feats they plann'd,
With praise of valor past the brave delights;
And these with views of gold, with honor those incites.

13. At length he paused, where in a gallant line
Are ranged his best and noblest chevaliers;

And from a spot which favors the design,
Begins a speech which fires each soul that hears.
As when the frigid winter melts to tears,
From Alpine peaks, fed with dissolving snows,
The swift, smooth torrent sparkingly careers,
So full, so fluent, as his fancy glows,
From his persuasive lips the sounding period flows.

14. "O my brave knights, of chivalry the flower!
My scourge, my tamers of the Orient! lo,
The final day; behold at length the hour
For which so warmly you were wont to glow!
Not without cause does Heaven its rebels show
Drawn to one center; not without high cause
Guides them to us; is not your ev'ry foe
Brought here, like stags into the lion's paws,
That you may end at once ten thousand mortal wars?

15. "In one, unnumber'd vict'ries will be wrought,
Nor shall the risk nor the fatigue be more;
Take not, O take not then a single thought
On the vast swarms that cloud the landscape o'er;
For, with themselves at discord, they deplore
Their ill conjunction; in their ranks e'en art
Confounds itself; and those who fight will gore
Themselves, or form by far the smaller part,
Thousands will want the room, and thousands more the heart!

16. "Half the vast swarms you view, are naked slaves;
Men void of strength or skill, in helpless plight;
Call'd from the couch or field, from chains or caves,
And dragg'd to battle in their own despite;
E'en now, in terror of the coming fight,
Their drawn swords quiver, shake their shields; I see
The ensigns tremble in their hands! those light
Uncertain sounds are no seal'd signs to me,—
Fear guides their wav'ring march; Death sounds their Lillallié!

17. "That Chief, who, robed in green and purple weed,
Ranges their bands, and seems so fierce to view,
The Moor and Arab in his chains may lead,
But never can resist such knights as you;
What, although wise, though prudent, will he do,
When his disorder'd troops in battle close?
Ill known he is, or only known to few;

Nor well his warriors, none by name he knows;
What can he do, brave souls, when thick the tumult
grows?

18. "But I am Captain of a chosen host,
We fight at once and conquer, side by side;
You serve from choice, and I the knowledge boast
Of each one's country, lineage, lands, and bride.
What noble sword can strike, what javelin glide,
That is to me unknown? yea, at a glance,
As the shaft passes, can I not decide
Whether the same of Ireland were or France,
And whose the sinewy arm that made the bowstring
dance?

19. "'Tis no great thing I ask; let me but find
Each one considerate of his old renown;
Use but your wonted zeal, and keep in mind
Your honor, mine, and His who bore the crown
Of thorns on his pale forehead; go, strike down
His scornful foes, and on their cancel'd creed
Stablish your conquest of the sacred town!
Enough, why argue? in your eyes I read
Victory already won,—the Sepulcher is freed!"

20. At the conclusion of this speech, a tire
Was seen to fall of clear and golden light
Like a descending star or gliding fire
Shook from the blue skirts of a summer night,
Save that 'twas far more beautiful and bright,—
A shower as from the sun's most lucid spring,
Wove to a garland glorious to the sight,
Which round his temples pass'd its golden ring;
And thus, as some divined, mark'd out their future
king.

21. Perchance, if tongue of mortal may aspire
To mortal sight Heaven's secrets to dispread,
A guardian Angel from the blissful choir,
With radiant wings involved his sacred head.
While Godfrey thus his troops exhorting led,
And in these terms provoked their martial pride,
Th' Egyptian Chief was not less active, fed
With equal hopes of victory, to ride
Amid his marshal'd men, and cheer their souls untried

22. He led abroad his sumless squadrons, soon
As his keen eyes discern'd th' advancing Franks;

And lined, in form of an extensive moon,
With foot his center, and with horse his flanks;
Himself the right commands, the left with thanks
The gen'rous Altamore receives; between,
The central foot proud Muleasses ranks;
And in the midst, with anger in her mien,
Shines, like a glorious star, the beauteous Damascene.

23. With Tisaphernes and th' Immortal band,
Frowns on the right the savage King of Ind;
But on the left wing where the plains expand
In scope, for swift maneuvers well design'd,
The Persian kings has Altamore combined,
With those of Libya and the two whose sway
Is o'er the burning sands where scarce a wind
Breaks the hot noon; and there, in grim array,
The slings, and bearded shafts, and twanging cross-
bows play.

24. Thus Emireno ranks his troops; with speed
Gallops from wing to wing, from van to rear;
Speaks by interpreters or not, as need
Requires; with praises mixes threats severe,
Pains with rewards, and with loud chiding, cheer;
To some he shouts; "Why, now, my darlings! why
Your downcast faces? what is there to fear?
What can these do against your thousands? fie!
Our shouts, our very shades will make the cravens fly!"

25. To some; "O yes! with that revengeful face
Come, and like vultures your lost spoils regain!"
To some, sad fancies clear as truth portrays,
And prints th' imagined picture on the brain:
Paints their lamenting country; paints the pain
Of their sad families; the moving pleas
They use; the hands they wring; the robes they
strain;
"Think," he exclaims, "that on her bended knees
Your country speaks through me! ah, think her ac-
cents these!

26. "Guard well my laws; let not my blood descend
To bathe my mosques, or stain their golden spires;
The tombs and ashes of my dead, defend,
Save my chaste maids from their accursed desires.
Sad for their bygone youth, to you my sires
Show each his hoary and unshielded head;
To you my women, mindful of your fires,

Bare their imploring breasts, with tears o'erspread,
Each mother points her babe, each wife her bridal bed!"

27. And to the rest; "Lo, Asia makes you here
The champions of her honor! claims from you
Upon these few base robbers a severe
And bitter vengeance, but most justly due!"
Thus he with various arguments anew
In various tongues each various nation charms
To the near war; but farewell words! adieu
Delay! the stirring trumpet sounds alarms;
Small grows the parting space; they grasp their angry arms.

28. O, 'twas a brave, a grand, and wondrous sight,
Ere front to front the marshal'd hosts combined,
To mark how nobly in their ranks each knight
Burn'd to move on, and for the signal pined!
How the loose flags flew billowing on the wind;
How on ten thousand heads the feathers danced;
How robes, impresses, gems, and arms refined,
Of all rich colors, gold and steel, advanced
Before the flouted Sun, smiled, sparkled, flash'd, and glanced!

29. Like a tall forest of dark pines depress'd
Both armies show, so thick the spears abound;
Drawn are the bows, the lances laid in rest,
Vibrate the darts, the glowing slings whirl round:
Each warring horse is on the wing to bound
Through the snuff'd battle; to the greeting gales
Spreads his broad nostrils, paws the echoing ground,
His lord's raised fury whets and countervails,
Foams, prances, snorts, and neighs, and fire and smoke exhales.

30. Horror itself in that fair scene looks gay,
And joy springs up e'en in the midst of fear;
Nor less the trumpet's organ-tones convey
Both bliss and terror of the gazer's ear.
But the Frank hosts, though less by far, appear
More brisk at heart and eager at the sight;
Their every trumpet with a note more clear
And ardent, sounds its prelude to the fight,
And their coat-armor glows with a diviner light.

31. The Christian trumpets first defiance sound,
The Pagan gongs take up the tuneful gage;

Kneel the rapt Franks, and kiss the sacred ground
With adoration and a holy rage;
Then forward spring to war: the spacious stage
'Twixt the two hosts deceases—disappears
Beneath their rushing charge; they meet—engage—
Shock the four wings; each gallant footman hears
The clang,—they bound abroad, and van with van coheres!

32. What Christian dealt the first auspicious wound?
Who could that guerdon of renown attain?
'Twas thou, Gildippe! thou, who to the ground
Smot'st the stout king of Ormus, great Hircane;
So vast a glory did high Heaven ordain
To woman's hands! brave as he was in show,
She pierced his breast and broke the spear in twain.
Transfix'd he fell, and, falling, heard the foe
Raise a triumphant shout, and praise the glorious blow.

33. Her lance thus snapp'd, she with her manly hand
Drew her good sword and on the Persians flew;
With frequent strokes, of their most serried band
Pierced the thick gloom, and let the sunlight through.
She cut forlorn Zopiro sheer in two,
E'en where th' adorning baldrick clasps the waist;
Then the fell savage grim Alarco slew,
Cleaving the porch of language and of taste;
Who from his charger fell, and spurn'd the sands he graced.

34. A blow fell'd Artaxerxes, and a thrust
Argeo,—the one lay stunn'd, the other slain;
Then, smiting Ismael's wrist, she to the dust
Cast his left hand, which dropp'd the bridle rein;
The sword glanced hissing on the ears and mane
Of his proud-spirited and ardent bay,—
Which, startled by the sound, or stung with pain,
Check'd by no curb, rear'd, turn'd, and plunged away
Through the whole Persian line, in dreadful disarray.

35. All these and numbers more, now lost to song,
She slew or wounded; their disorder'd squares
The Persians close, and charge her in a throng,
Eager to win the precious arms she wears;
But now her faithful lord, who half despairs
For her endanger'd safety, light as wind
Flies to her succor, and his falchion bares;
And the bless'd pair, together thus combined,
In their united swords united vigor find.

36. Arts of defense their gen'rous souls are seen
To use, unpractised and unheard of yet;
He shelters her, she him; and in this keen
Dispute of love, themselves they quite forget;
The ardent heroine, though herself beset,
Beats off the weapons that her lord molest;
He to the spears which her dear person threat,
Is quick to raise his shield, and would be bless'd
No less, if need require, t' oppose his naked breast.

37. Each to the other thus his cares transferr'd,
And each the other's wrongs revenged; his blade
Slew the presumptuous Artabane, whose word
The trembling isle of Böecan obey'd;
And lifeless stretch'd the haughty renegade,
Alvante, who with hand audacious strove
To smite his darling; she the debt repaid;
For at her lord as Arimantes drove,
His brows from eye to eye th' indignant heroine clove.

38. Such deeds they did, but greater was the wrack
Wrought by Prince Altamore; where'er he plied
His fearful sword, or spurr'd to the attack
His haughty steed; he slew or beat aside
Both horse and foot; thrice bless'd was he who died
At the first stroke, nor groan'd beneath the tread
Of his fierce steed; for whom the homicide
Beat down, the cruel creature in his stead
Tore with its gnashing teeth, or proudly trampled dead.

39. By the strong Prince's battle-axe were slain
Brunello sinewy and Ardonio great;
Of that the helm and head he clove in twain,
So that each shoulder dropp'd beneath its weight,
Ere fell the corse; but 'twas Ardonio's fate
Through the quick spleen to be transfix'd, where rise
The nerves whose strings with mirth the heart dilate,
So that (a strange and horrid sight!) he lies
Jocund with mortal pain, and loudly laughing dies.

40. Nor these alone from each delightful tie
Of life and love his murdering weapon tore,
But good Rosmondo and Gentonio, Guy
And Guasco, all lie weltering in their gore.
Who can relate what numbers Altamore
Beat down, what numbers bade the world farewell,
Crush'd by his charger on the sandy floor;
The names of all the slaughter'd who can tell,
How the brave warrior smote, or how th' assaulted fell?

41. There lives not one who with the warrior now
Will break a spear, or meet him face to face ;
Alone Gildippe braves him to his brow,
Nor in the battle to his arm gives place.
Never did Amazon, in stormy Thrace,
When red with blood the swift Thermodon ran,
Brandish her pole-axe or her shield embrace
Dauntless as she, when, issuant from the van,
She rush'd to check the pride of this tremendous man.

42. She smote him where with gold and rich aumaile
Gay on the helm flamed his barbaric crown ;
And, shiv'ring it to atoms, made him veil
His haughty head, and bow benignly down ;
Well judged the monarch that no mean renown
Graced the bold arm that with such reckless might
Enforced its will, and, knitting to a frown
His swarthy brows, rush'd forward to requite
Shame with incensed disdain, and with revenge despite.

43. And in an instant on her basnet served
The gentle Lady with a stroke so sore,
As to deprive her of all sense ; unnerved,
Entranced she sunk,—but her fond lord upbore,
And, were it their good Genius that watch'd o'er
Their forfeit lives, or magnanimity
In him, the check sufficed—he struck no more ;
Like the mild lion, that with gen'rous eye
Upon his prostrate foe just glares, and passes by.

44. Meanwhile Ormondo, to whose impious hands
The purposed treason was consign'd, slipp'd in
With his false mates amid the Christian bands,
Eager to perpetrate th' unfinish'd sin ;
Like midnight wolves, that smoothing their fierce grin
To a meek innocence, assume the guise
Of shepherds' dogs, the wattled sheepfolds win
Through the dusk mist, and there, with sparkling eyes,
Prowl round, their dubious tails upcurl'd betwixt their thighs.

45. Mute they advance, and now with closed ventayle
The bloody Pagan draws to Godfrey's side ;
But when, considerate of Vafrino's tale,
Their forged devices, white and gold, he spied ;
" Lo, the mask'd villains ! lo, my friends," he cried,
" The wretch that creeps with such a stealthy tread

In Frank disguisements near us ! round their guide
See how his ruffians make to me ! " this said,
He on the traitor rush'd, and cloved his helmed head.

46. For the confronted felon, quite amazed,
Nor struck, nor fenced, nor offer'd to be gone ;
But e'en as though the Gorgon on him gazed,
Sate like an ancient warrior froze to stone :
On them all swords were drawn, all darts were thrown,
And to its last inevitable cane
Each quiver emptied was on them alone ;
Thus fell, thus died Ormondo and his train,
To such small pieces cleft, their corpses scarce remain.

47. Godfrey, when once he saw himself imbrued
In Pagan blood, no longer stood at bay,
But quickly flew to where the Persian hew'd
Through the thick squadrons his triumphant way ;
So that his knights now fled in disarray,
Swift as the sands in Libya's drifting waste,
Before the stormy South ; their sore dismay
He check'd with shouts, rebuked their flying haste,
And, staying those that fled, assail'd the Prince who chased.

48. The two stern Chiefs a battle here began,
Such as was never in poetic page
Emblazed, the while on foot good Baldwin ran
With Muleasses elsewhere to engage ;
Nor with less fervor, nor with less wild rage
Mix the bold horsemen on the left, where green
The sloping hills scoop out a spacious stage ;
In person there, his two brave knights between,
Fights the barbaric Chief, high-minded Emirene.

49. With him the Norman Robert joins,—they fight
With equal valor ; but the *Fleming's* mail
The grim Adrastus bores and shatters quite,
And with sharp saber cleaves his barr'd ventayle.
No certain foe has Tisapherne t' assail,
That in close battle can be term'd his peer ;
But on he scours as with the driving gale,
Where most impassive the wedged ranks appear,
And all is hideous death before his wing'd career.

50. Thus fought they long, and still their hope and cheer
In equal balance hung with doubt and dread ;
With shatter'd mails, split shields, the shiver'd spear

And cloven helm, was all the field o'erspread ;
In bosoms gash'd or bowels gored, the red
Revenging sword lies buried deep, or bright
In thousand fragments glitters round the dead ;
Some lie supine, some groveling, and in spite
Seem still the hated earth ferociously to bite.

51. Beside his lord the charger lies outspread ;
The comrade lifeless by his comrade lies :
Foe beside foe ; the living on the dead ;
And on the vanquish'd oft the victor dies :
No silent lull is there, nor formal cries,
But a hoarse, indistinct, unceasing sound,—
Roarings of fury, threats of anger, sighs
Of languid Sorrow, wailing o'er his wound,
And groans and rising shrieks in faint low moanings drown'd.

52. The arms which lately wore so bright an air,
Discolor'd now, and dull, and frightful show ;
The steel has lost its sheen, the gold its glare,
Each sparkling color takes the tint of woe :
Past is the pomp, the glory, and the glow
Of cimeter, and sash, and dancing plume ;
Turban and gem alike are trampled low,
And dust lies thick upon the blood whose bloom
Outvied in dire display the purple of the loom.

53. The Moors, the Ethiops, and the Arabs then,
To the dull discord of the atabal,
Spread out their dusky skirts of moving men,
And on the dexter wing revolving fall ;
Already with their bows and slings they gall
The army from afar, when, like the din
Of earthquake and of thunder, at the call
Of young Rinaldo, his bold knights begin
With shouts their rushing march, and hem th' assailants in.

54. The first he met was Asimire, who led
The Moors of Meröe, an illustrious name ;
Rinaldo smote him where the swarthy head
Towers on the neck, and shore it from the frame ;
And when this taste of vict'ry and of fame
Had whet his angry appetite, the youth
So nobly bore him in the bloody game,
That to relate his deeds would be in sooth
To give mute wonder wing, and wed romance to truth.

55. More deaths than blows he deals, yet momently
His falchion smites ; and as the angry snake
Seems in its single tongue to vibrate three,
With such a fearful swiftness does it shake,
So in dismay these charged barbarians take
The single sword which furiously the knight
Whirls round, for three ; its rapid motions make
The first illusion to the trusting sight,
And awe the portent seals in superstitious fright.

56. Down, down to Tophet, fast the Negro kings
And Ethiopic tyrants bleeding go ;
Each gallant comrade in his footstep springs,
Upon the rest,—with rival zeal they glow :
The Pagan multitudes to earth they mow
With terrible contempt ; and these prepare
No vain defense, but die without a blow ;
A massacre it is, no conflict, where
They yield up here their swords, present their bosoms there.

57. Yet long they stand not to receive their wounds
In noble parts, but scour away—away ;
Fear spurs them on, despair their ranks confounds,
Lost is all art, relax'd their fair array ;
But the flush'd hero still pursues his prey,
Strikes down their standards, breaks their strong crossbows,
Till spent in utter rout their powers decay ;
He then returns, for on defenseless foes
His fiery soul relents, his zeal less fiercely glows.

58. As the strong wind tenfold its rage augments
When hills or sturdy woods its blasts oppose,
But o'er the ample plain at once relents,
And in soft murmurs more serenely blows,—
As on the rock the dashing ocean throws
Its rough, its roaring billows, and boils high,
But in the open main more gently flows,
Rinaldo so, thus unopposed, lays by
Much of his noble rage, and calms his angry eye.

59. Then, on the backs of this defenseless force
Scorning to spend his gen'rous wrath in vain,
He to the infantry directs his course,
Late flank'd by Asimire and Artabane,
Arab and dusky African ; now plain
It stood and naked, for the tribes that well

Might have defensed it, were dispersed or slain;
Crosswise he came, and on their flank, in selle,
With all his men-at-arms in sworded fury fell.

60. He snapp'd their bristling spears, the ranks they form
He clove in twain, and in their pierced array
Plunged, beating down their troops; the windy storm
Whirls the reap'd harvests with less ease away.
On ev'ry side around him does he lay
A bloody pavement, pebbled thick with lance,
Shield, and lopp'd limb; along whose broad highway
The following horse, for Palestine and France,
Uncurb'd, with batt'ring hoofs in gorgeous frenzy prance

61. The Hero came where his forlorn Armide
In warlike pomp stood in her golden car,
Girt by a noble band, who for the meed
Of her sweet smile escort her through the war;
He by his armor known while yet afar,
Was view'd by her with eyes which from desire
And passion trembled like a sparkling star;
He changed but slightly; she, 'twixt love and ire,
From red to deadly pale, from frost to flushing fire.

62. The Knight declined the chariot of the dame,
And like a man that would elsewhere bestow
His thoughts, pass'd on; but her sworn knights for shame
Let not their rival scape without a blow;
One drew his crooked saber, one couch'd low
His lance, his arbalist another bent;
Herself an arrow planted in her blow,
Scorn strung her hand, and nerved her fierce intent,
But love the mood appeased, nor yet the shaft was sent.

63. Love against anger rose, and their dispute
Proved that her flame still glow'd, though hid from view;
Three times her arms she stretch'd abroad to shoot,
Three times took aim, and thrice her aim withdrew;
Disdain at length prevail'd: again the yew
She with an eager and unshrinking arm
Bent, and the bowstring twang'd; the shaft outflew,—
Out flew the shaft, but with the shaft this charm
She the next moment breathed: "God grant it do no harm!"

64. She would have bade the weapon turn again,
And smite the heart whose sternness she resents;
O, well indeed she must have loved him, when
In hate's last pass her soul so soon relents!
But straight again her fondness she repents,
Straight to her stormy heart fresh furies rise;
Thus she the shaft now joys in, now laments,
She will, she will not it should smite, and eyes
With a tumultuous heart the arrow as it flies.

65. Not quite in vain was it discharged; the reed
Smote the young knight's hard coat of mail, too hard
In fact, for female weapons to succeed,—
The steel, instead of piercing it, was jarr'd
Itself to shivers, nor the silver marr'd;
He turn'd away,—she thought in scorn, and ground
Her teeth with anger at his disregard;
Ofttimes she shot, but still no entrance found
Her shafts, and while she shot love dealt her wound on wound.

66. "What! is he then impassive, that he mocks
All hostile force!" she murmurs; "must he mail
His limbs in adamant like that which locks
His haughty spirit in its stubborn scale?
Against his heart nor glancing eyes prevail,
Nor weapon'd night, arm'd proof from top to toe;
While I, alas! at all points foil'd, bewail,
Arm'd or unarm'd, alike or friend or foe,
My thousand arts despised, and droop my pennons low.

67. "Now what new art, what charm shall I essay;
In what new form can I myself present?
Wretch that I am, there is no hope! my day
Of rule is o'er, and all my forces spent!
My knights, where are they? 'tis too evident
All power, all arms are weak to his; in vain
The spear is level'd, and the crossbow bent:"
Thus she repined; for now throughout the plain
She saw her champions pierced, beat down, dispersed, or slain.

68. Alone, she felt defenseless, stood in fear
To be inthrall'd or slain; nor can the aid
Of Dian or Minerva's arms—the spear
Or formidable bow, her heart persuade;
But as the delicate white swan, dismay'd,
O'er which the eagle with fierce pounce impends,

Crouches to earth, and her broad wings display'd
Folds in mute terror,—to the storm she bends;
Just such her motions seem, just such wild looks she sends.

69. But brave Prince Altamore, whose might till now
Had held in check Gildippe, had upheld
The Persian flag when it began to bow,
And by his single arm the Franks repell'd,
When in distress his Goddess he beheld,
Rush'd, or flew rather from the near attack
To her; though honor at the step rebell'd,
Him neither honor nor his host kept back;
So she but rescued be, the world may go to wrack!

70. Round her ill-guarded car he planted spears,
And hew'd an area with his falchion bright;
But meanwhile Godfrey and Rinaldo fierce
With dreadful slaughter put his troops to flight;
The hapless chief beheld their desp'rate plight,
And bore himself far better at the ken
As a fond lover than a warrior knight;
He placed in safety the fair Queen, and then
Return'd untimely back to aid his vanquish'd men.

71. It was too late! those troops, like hunted deer,
Were gone beyond recall; no hope remain'd:
But on the left, the Christians with like fear
Fled from the Infidels, whose swords they stain'd;
One princely Robert scarce the ranks regain'd,
Wounded severely in the breast and face;
And one by grim Adrastus was constrain'd
To yield his sword; an almost equal pace
Both warring hosts thus kept in glory and disgrace.

72. A moment Godfrey takes to reunite
His straggling files, and then without delay
Renews the charge; and thus in stubborn fight
Wings shock with wings in terrible array,
Victor with victor; from their late assay
Tinged comes each soldier to the strife, in sheen
Of spoils from foes torn vauntingly away;
Victory and honor from all parts convene;
And Mars and dubious Fate unsmiling stand between.

73. While thus in furious rivalry of power
The Franks and Pagans stubbornly engage,
The fiery Soldan mounts the lofty tower,

And sees, though far remote, the war they wage ;
As on a theater's illumined stage,
The sad sharp tragedy of human state
He sees,—their hot assaults of grief and rage,
The savage stabs of gladiatorial hate,
And all the thousand turns and accidents of fate.

74. Awhile astonish'd and amazed he stood,
At the first view ; but soon, a sharp desire
To ply his saber in that field of blood
And high achievement, set his soul on fire ;
No dull delay can his revengeful ire
Indulge ; already arm'd in panoply
Of proof, he snatch'd the helmet from his squire ;
And, "Up, pine here no longer !" was his cry ;
"This hour it fits us all to conquer or to die !"

75. Whether it were that providence divine
This furious spirit breathed in him, to close
That day in one bold stroke for Palestine,
His last lorn glories and her own long woes ;
Or that, as Death drew near, the impulse rose,
In pure despite of his declining star,
Boldly to brave him midst a host of foes,
Rapid as rash, he bid the gates unbar,
And in his awful hand bore out unlook'd-for war.

76. He waits not, he, to notice if his knights
Obey the call, but rushes out alone ;
Singly a thousand foes he dares, and slights
Their thousand swords, impassive in his own ;
But by his spirit and audacious tone
Inspired, the rest like bacchanals pursue,
And Aladine himself, who on his throne
Was tim'rous, mean, and base, now reckless grew,
And, less from hope than rage, outrush'd, loud shouting too.

77. Upon the first he met th' atrocious Turk
His dreadful strokes discharged with such disdain;
And sped so swiftly in his murd'rous work,
That dead they fall, ere you perceive them slain ;
Quick from the foremost to the last in train—
Voice after voice—the panic of affright
Speeds with th' alarming news, dispatch'd in vain ;
So that the native Christians on the right,
By the loud tumult scared, at once disperse in flight.

78. But with far less discomfit and dismay
The Gascon chivalry maintain their ground,
Although at unawares their mail'd array
Was charged, as nearest for the falchion found ;
Never did savage vulture, heaven's wing'd hound,
Nor Alpine wolf, the wood's ferocious lord,
With tooth or talon so acutely wound
Wild-fowl or flock, as the mad Soldan's sword,
Strain'd in his angry grasp the Red-cross champions gored.

79. Hungry and ravenous, like a living thing,
It seem'd to crash their limbs and drink their blood ;
With him the Pagans and their hoary king
Struck down and slaughter'd, in their desp'rate mood,
The still-confused besiegers ; but the good
Count Raymond rush'd to where the Soldan slew
His faithful knights ; he fled not, but withstood,
Though well again the red right-hand he knew,
Whose power his anguish'd frame had still such cause to rue.

80. Again he fronts him, smites him, falls again,
Struck as before above his closed ventayle ;
The boist'rous charge if he could ill sustain,
His old age only bear the blame, too frail
To bide such shocks ; this time too, o'er his pale
Mute form a hundred spears and sabers play,
All eager these to guard as those t' assail ;
But the grim Soldan still holds on his way,
Deeming the warrior dead or else an easy prey.

81. Upon the rest he falls, dismembers, maims,
Acts utter wonders on that narrow stage,
Then seeks, by lust allured to loftier aims,
A new arena for his boundless rage.
As one invited by some gentle page
To a brave banquet, from his thrifty board
Hies with delight his hunger to assuage ;
So to a field with ampler victims stored,
Speeds he, on nobler food to flesh his ravenous sword.

82. Down through the shatter'd ramparts he descends
And with all speed to the grand battle goes,
Leaving disdain and fury with his friends,
And doubt and fear amid his scatter'd foes ;
These a dire struggle still maintain, and those
Wax bold, th' unfinish'd vict'ry to complete ;

These yet resist, but their resistance shows
Far fewer signs of triumph than defeat,
And now they quite give way in undisguised retreat.

83. The Gascons slowly face to face give ground,
But the faint Syrians headlong haste away;
Meanwhile the shout of triumph, the known sound
Of arms, and clamor of the wild affray,
Reach'd the near spot where wounded Tancred lay;
Weak as he was, he rose from bed, went out
Upon the roof, and saw with sore dismay
The good Count fell'd, and all his spearmen stout,
Some in forlorn retreat, and some in utter rout.

84. Courage, which never fails the brave, although
The body droops, droops not, but like a charm,
In lieu of blood and spirits strengthens so
His limbs, that inly fortified from harm,
He binds the ample shield upon his arm,
Nor deems the burden grievous; grasps his blade,—
His blade unsheath'd upon the first alarm,
And thus with weapons instantly array'd,
(All that a brave man needs,) no longer there he stay'd.

85. But issuing, loudly to the troops he calls,
"What! do you fly, and leave your lord a prey
To these barbarians? shall their mosques and halls
His arms as trophies of your guilt display?
Go then, return to Gascony, and say,
Say to his son, that from the glorious game
Where his loved father died, you ran away!"
This said, his weak and naked breast became
To thousand vig'rous knights their shelter, and their shame.

86. And with his pond'rous shield which seven bull-hides
Composed, a rough material, underlined
With strong impassive plates of steel besides,
By the pure alchemy of fire refined,
From swords, and shafts, and arms of every kind,
That like a drizzly shower around him play'd,
He guarded the good Raymond, and consign'd
To death such numbers with his brandish'd blade,
That safe the warrior lay as in a silent shade.

87. The brave old Earl, protected thus, respires,
Awakes, and rises in a little space;
While a deep feeling of the insult fires

His heart with anger, and with shame his face ;
He darts his quick bright eyes in every place,
On every side, to spy the man whose might
Had on his crest inflicted such disgrace ;
But not perceiving him, he turns with spite
Upon his following troops, the outrage to requite.

88. Back to revenge alike their Chief's attaint
The flying Gascons the next instant pour ;
And now the late so daring crew turns faint,
And boldness reigns where all was fear before ;
He yields who smote, he slays who late forbore
To smite ; he flies, who lately led the chase ;
Well now did Raymond act the matador,
And with a right good earnestness efface,
By full twice fifty deaths, his own most brief disgrace.

89. While striving thus to clear his shamed renown
Upon the most distinguish'd crests, he spies
Amidst his fighting chivalry, the crown
Of all their strength, and at the Tyrant flies ;
On his helm'd head his battle-axe he plies
With a strong arm ; nor from his strokes refrain'd,
Till with a horrid symphony of sighs
And angry groans the monarch fell, constrain'd,
And, dying, bit the ground o'er which he lately reign'd.

90. Their Chiefs thus absent one, and one destroy'd,
Divided fates the sad survivors sway ;
Some to distraction by despair annoy'd,
Like madd'ning lions, or wild bulls at bay,
A moment fight, then throw their lives away
On the sword's point ; while some bewilder'd run
Back to the tower ; but with their flying prey
The victors enter too, opposed by none,
And raise their loud huzzas,—the last strong tower is won !

91. Won is the tower, and on the lofty stairs,
Or in the very gates the Moslem fall ;
But Raymond in his grasp ascending bears
The Red-cross flag and plants it on the wall
In sight of either host, a sign to all
Of vict'ry, billowing to the charmed wind ;
But this glad token of the country's thrall
The Soldan mark'd not,—his tempestuous mind
Had left th' assaulted tower and tumult far behind.

92. He treads the moist vermilion field, which grows
With blood and carnage momently more red;
So that it seems the Court where Death bestows
His banner'd spoils, and stalks with haughty tread,
Numb'ring his victims; as he turns his head,
He sees a warhorse which without its knight
From the thick press with dangling bridle fled;
On this he lays his ardent hand, leaps light
Into the vacant seat, and spurs it to the fight.

93. Glorious and potent is the aid, but short,
Which to the faint, sad Saracen he gives;
A bright, brief thunderbolt—that, swift as thought,
Unlook'd-for flashes as the cloud it cleaves,
But of its momentary transit leaves
Eternal furrows plow'd in marble stone;
Twice fifty warriors he of life bereaves,
But two in Memory's picturing glass alone
Has Time's admiring hand to weeping Pity shown.

94. O Edward! O Gildippe! your harsh fate
And noble prowess (if my Tuscan rhymes
May be so happy) will I consecrate
To the fond praises of all lands and climes;
That so the world, with all its storied crimes,
Your faith, your love, your virtue may revere,
And cite as models for the best of times;
And that some eyes, to love and feeling dear,
May grace, in solemn verse, your story with a tear.

95. The gen'rous Lady, nobly barb'd and mail'd,
Rush'd where such throngs beneath his saber died;
And with two mighty blows the Turk assail'd,
One clove his buckler, and one plow'd his side;
The ruffian knew her by her vests, and cried:
"Lo, the white harlot! now by bless'd Mahound,
It had for thee been better to have plied
The needle still in England, unrenown'd,
Than thus with sword and slave to flaunt on foreign
ground!"

96. He said; and, fill'd with all a demon's ire,
At the brave dame a sweeping blow address'd,
Which struck—how could it dare?—her bright attire,
Shatter'd her mail, and pierced the beauteous breast
Which Love meant only for a tenderer guest;
She drops the reins, and, fainting with the weight
Of pain, seems sinking to her last long rest;

Poor Edward sees, and if he comes too late
For her defense, alas, 'tis not his fault, but fate!

97. What should he do! within his breast at strife
Were rage and pity, with distracting smart
Urging him, this to aid his drooping wife,
And that to stab the murderer to the heart;
While Love, lamenting Love, with both took part,
Nor would that this or that should plead in vain;
Love taught him modes beyond the reach of art,—
With his left hand would he his dear sustain,
And with the right discharge his vengeance and disdain.

98. But power was wanting to his will; too weak,
Alas, were they, against so strong a foe!
He neither his fair love could aid, nor wreak
On the fell homicide the wrath which woe
Brought to his heart; ere he could strike a blow,
His guardian arm the savage Infidel
Smote off, and, forced thus harshly to forego
His fond embrace, with her he droop'd, he fell,
And falling press'd the form he loved through life so well.

99. As the tall elm to whose sustaining stem
With all her tendrils clings the bridal vine,
If storms uproot or axe to death condemn,
Drags with itself to ground his darling bine,—
Shatt'ring himself the garlands that enshrine
His mossy boughs, and crushing as he lies
Her pleasant grapes to over-early wine,
He seems to mourn his own sad sacrifice
Less than the faithful plant's that round his ruins dies.

100. So falls the knight; and grieves for her alone
Whom Heaven ordains to be forever his;
Fain would they speak, if only to bemoan
Each other's pangs, but death denies them this;
They commune but with sighs, yet still 'tis bliss
To view each other as in times gone by;
Long as they can they gaze, embrace and kiss:
At once their pulses cease, at once they die,
And hand in hand to God their pious spirits fly.

101. Fame, spreading quick her pinions for the flight,
Tells with her thousand tongues the tale to all;
Not from vague rumor only, but a knight
Of special trust Rinaldo learns their fall;

At once love, pity, grief, and duty call
On his resentment for revenge, he flies
To his proud foe ; but here, to whet his gall,
The grim Adrastus crosses him, and cries,
While with his brandish'd blade the hero he defies :—

102. "Ho ! by sure tokens thou the man must be
For whose presented sword I burn and pine ;
All day by title have I called on thee,
And look'd mid thousand shields in vain for thine ;
Now will I pay my vows, now at the shrine
Of the sweet saint for whose regards I die,
Offer thy heart up ; come ! for Palestine,
Our valor, yea, our fury let us try ;
Thou art Armida's foe, her sworn avenger I !"

103. This said, with two tremendous blows he sign'd
His throat and temples gemm'd with gold aumaile ;
The helmet he clove not, (too well refined,)
But to the pommel made the hero veil
His plumes ; ah, then, nor steel nor snaky scale
Helps the huge king ; Rinaldo wounds him so
He needs no further leech ; wail, Indra, wail
For thy gigantic son ! a single blow
Stills his insulting tongue, and lays his proud hopes low.

104. With horror, awe, amazement, and affright,
Cold wax'd the hearts of the surrounding crew ;
E'en Solyman, who saw the wondrous sight,
Changed in his cheer, and inly trembled too :
And pale his ruby cheek, and nerveless grew
His arm, while, prescient of his coming doom,
He knows not what to think or what to do,
A thing in him unusual ; but for whom
Do the stern Fates reverse the issues of their loom ?

105. As when in his brief sleep distressful dreams
Afflict the sick man or the madman's brain,
He strives all eagerly to move, and seems
With more than giant force his limbs to strain,
While not a muscle aids his will ; in vain
Are all the mighty efforts he can use ;
Still as the dead his hands and feet remain ;
He would shout out or scream at what he views ;
But not a shout, or scream, or syllable ensues.

106. So would the Soldan rush the knight to meet,
And musters all his forces for the fight,

But feels not in himself his wonted heat,
Scarce knows himself in his diminish'd might;
What sparks of ardor his desires excite,
A secret terror chills: yet still desire,
Pride, love of glory, anguish, and despite,
And busy mem'ry in his heart conspire,
So that he neither thinks to fly nor to retire.

107. While unresolved he stands, the knight arrives,
It seems to him with an Immortal's pace,
And with a wrath, a grandeur, that deprives
All mortal wrath and grandeur of their grace;
Small while he fights: yet, dying, no disgrace
Stains his long glory; to the last his eye
Glows with the mem'ry of his state and race;
He shunn'd no strokes, he heaved no groan or sigh,
Nor did a single thing but what was great and high.

108. When now the Turk, who in that long crusade
Oft like Antæus fell, to rise again
Each time more fierce and strong, at length had play'd
His final part, and slumber'd with the slain;
Fortune, who fluctuates like th' unstable main,
Hearing the rumor, durst no longer hold
The vict'ry in suspense, but o'er the plain
Stay'd her swift wheel, her errant course controll'd,
And under Godfrey's flag her influences enroll'd.

109. Soon with the rest the kingly squadron flies,
The nerve and flower of all the East, whose name
Was once th' Immortal! mortal now, it lies
Gored with a slaughter fatal to its fame;
But Emireno, seized with gen'rous shame,
Cuts short the standard-bearer's flight, and loud
With indignation sharply makes exclaim:
"Art thou not he whom from a countless crowd
I chose to bear the flag that ne'er in battle bow'd?

110. "Stop! 'twas not given thee thus to bear away
From Saracen and Frank, from sword and spear;
Canst thou then, craven, see thy chief a prey
To the stern foe, and leave him lonely here?
What seek'st thou? safety? change thy mad career,
The road thou takest leads to death! be true
To the borne Crescent, and renounce thy fear;
He fights who wishes here to live; come, woo
Honor with me, thy prince; her path is safety's too!"

111. Blushing the knight obey'd ; with far more stern
And sharp rebuke the others he address'd ;
These threats, these blows, that terror makes to turn,
The chief's sharp saber glittering at his breast ;
And rallying thus his bravest and his best,
Fresh wings he forms, and, as the trumpets sound,
Still with fair hopes ; his heart above the rest
Bold Tisaphernes cheers, who, though hemm'd round,
Fights like a lion yet, nor yields an inch of ground.

112. Wonders that day good Tisaphernes wrought—
The Normans in his wrath he overthrew ;
Scourged the stout Flemings, and, as still he fought,
Young Gernier, Gerard, and De Rosel slew ;
And when by deeds of so divine a hue
He to the measure of eternal fame
His brief existence had prolong'd, he flew
At the sublimest risk of all the game,
Like one to whose concern life laid no further claim.

113. He spied Rinaldo, and though now his shield
Had changed its tincture to a tricolor,
Though the pearl eagle in its sapphire field
With ruby beak and wings was seen to soar,
Known was the proud emblazonry it bore ;
"And lo !" he cried, "the dragon of the fight !
Heaven nerve my arm to do the deed I swore ;
Let but my blade Armida's wrongs requite ;
Thine, good Mahmoud, shall be the trophies of the knight !"

114. Thus pray'd the Persian, but his prayers were vain,
Mahmoud heard not upon his couch of fire ;
But, as a lion, bristling up his mane,
With lashing tail provokes his native ire,
So on the whetstone of his wild desire
His scorn he sharpens, whets his eager zeal,
And, mustering all his strength up for the dire
Assault, coil'd safe behind his shield, his steel
He lifts—and bounds the barb beneath his angry heel.

115. Rinaldo saw him with his saber raised,
And rush'd to meet him in as swift career ;
Far fell the near assailants back, and gazed
On the stern scene, with mingled awe and fear.
Such was the might and fame of either peer,
Such strokes resounded when their weapons cross'd,
That each his own strong cause for grief or cheer,

And the whole host of passions that engross'd
His soul—at once forgot, in breathless wonder lost.

116. That struck alone ; this struck, and wounded, bless'd
With greater strength and arms more sure and sound;
With cloven shield, pierced helm, and shatter'd crest,
The Persian's noble blood distains the ground :
The fair Enchantress sees her champion's wound,
Sees his pierced armor, his half-helmless head,
And, worse, his failing prowess ; gazing round,
She finds the rest dishearten'd, slain, or fled,
And her own safety hang on fortune's slend'rest thread.

117. Late girt by thousand warriors in the strife,
She now stands lonely in her rubied wain ;
Desp'rate of victory as revenge, her life
She holds in hate, she dreads the victor's chain,
And straight, 'twixt terror, fury, and disdain,
Her chariot quitting, on a palfrey near
Springs, and takes instant flight,—her only train
Scorn and unconquer'd love, that in her rear
Hang like two eager hounds behind a hunted deer.

118. So in sharp battle fled alone of yore
Scared Cleopatra, leaving to the blade
Of fortunate Augustus, midst the roar
Of waves and weapons, her fond knight betray'd.
And e'en as he, by tenderness o'ersway'd,
False to himself and to the world he woo'd,
Follow'd her solitary sails display'd,
So the fond Persian would have fain pursued
His pearl of beauty too, but this the foe withstood.

119. To the sad Pagan, when his love was lost,
Day seem'd to darken and the sunshine fled,
And to the knight who thus his wishes cross'd,
He turn'd enraged, and smote his helmed head ;
More lightly falls to fabricate the red
And writhen thunderbolts, at Jove's behest,
Bronte's vast hammer ; well the weapon sped,—
Its pond'rous stroke alighting on his crest,
Made the knight's head bow down benignly to his breast.

120. But soon recovering, in his seat erect
Rinaldo rose, and with his whirling sword
Clove the fine hauberk, 'twixt the ribs direct
Plunged the sharp steel, which in its wrath explored
So deep a passage to the heart it gored,

That far beyond life's citadel it went;
Entering the breast, the Pagan's back it bored,—
The steel drawn forth, supplied a double vent,
Through which the noble soul took straight its wing'd ascent.

121. The conquoror paused to contemplate where next
He should his falchion ply, where render aid,—
His foes in all their movements were perplex'd,
Their colors struck, and scarce a spear display'd.
Here then his terrible career he stay'd,
Curb'd in his courser, to the sheath resign'd
His sword, his martial ecstasy allay'd,
And, calming every passion, call'd to mind
Armida's helpless plight and destinies unkind.

122. Her flight he well observed; mild pity now
Call'd for his courtesy and gracious cheer,
And the remembrance of his parting vow
To stand her firm and faithful chevalier,
Came o'er his mind, with feelings sweet and dear;
So that he follow'd where the dinted ground
Betray'd her goaded palfrey's swift career:
She the meanwhile a dreary glen had found,
Fit place for secret deaths, with cypress compass'd round.

123. Well pleased she was at heart, that chance should guide
Her wand'ring steps to so retired a place;
Here she alighted then, and cast aside
Her bow, her arrows, and their golden case
"There lie," she murmur'd, "in your deep disgrace,
Unhappy arms! that from the war return
With scarce a spot your mistress to aggrace:
There buried lie, there rust amidst the fern,
Since to avenge my wrongs you've shown such small concern!

124. "Ah! midst so many weapons could not one
At least return with hostile crimson blest?
If other hearts to you seem marble, shun,
Spare not your points to pierce a woman's breast;
In this mine own, stripp'd naked for the test,
Achieve your triumphs, and your fame restore;
Tender it is, Heaven knows, to wounds impress'd
By Love's sharp arrows, Love—who evermore
Strikes wheresoe'er he aims, and hurts the sufferer sore.

125. Show yourselves sharp on me and strong; (your past
Degeneracy I pardon;) O poor heart!
Into what straits of fortune art thou cast,
When these alone can peace to thee impart!
But since no other solace to my smart
Remains, none other passport to repose,
Go to! the wounds of this consenting dart
Shall cure the wounds of love,—a few brief throes,
And death shall bring the balm that sooths all earthly woes!

126. "Bless'd, if in dying I bear not with me
This my long plague to pester Hell's foul host;
Hence, Love! come only, dear Disdain, and be
Th' eternal partner of my injured ghost!
Or, rising with it from the Stygian coast,
To the false wretch that did me such despite,
In such a whirlwind of resentment post,
With such grim shapes, that all his dreams by night
May be one ceaseless round of agonized affright!"

127. She ceased; and, fix'd in her intention, drew
The best and sharpest arrow from her case;
Rinaldo reach'd the wood, and caught a view
Of her mad gesture and disorder'd pace;
Saw her last act, and with how wild a grace
She to the fatal stroke her soul address'd;
Already death's pale hue o'erspread her face,
When, just in time her purpose to arrest,
The knight stepp'd in behind, and saved her beauteous breast.

128. Armida turn'd; and saw, to her surprise,
The knight, for unperceived was his advance;
Shrieking, she snatch'd away her angry eyes
From his loved face, and sunk in Passion's trance;
She swoon'd, she sank, like a sweet flower by chance
Snapp'd half in two, that, with its bells abased,
Droops on its stem; he with distracted glance
Upheld her, falling, round her charming waist
Threw his sustaining arm, her clasping zone unbraced;

129. And o'er her snowy breast and face deprived
Of life's warm hues, fond tears of pity shed;—
As by the summer morning's dew revived,
The fading rose resumes its native red,
So she, recovering, raised her drooping head
And cheek, revived by this celestial rain;

Thrice her unclosing eyes sought his, thrice fled
The bitter-sweet enchantment, nor again
Would she look up, but blush'd 'twixt wrath and warm
disdain.

130. And with her languid hand would have repell'd
The nervous arm by which she was sustain'd;
Oft she essay'd, but he the faster held,
The more she strove, the more she was inchain'd;
Yielding herself at length, like one constrain'd,
To that dear bond, for still perchance 'twas dear,
Despite the scorn she show'd, the hate she feign'd.
She sighing thus broke forth, while tear on tear
Gush'd from the downcast eyes she did not, would not
rear.

131. "O! ever, parting and returning, ever
Cruel alike! what dark devices guide
Thy movements now? 'tis strange thou shouldst endeavor
To save the life whose strings thou dost divide.
Thou seek to save me! to what scorn beside
Am I reserved? what modes of misery
Am I to suffer next? no! no! thy pride
And traitorous purpose well we know; but I
Am weak indeed, if e'er I want the power to die.

132. "Thy honors truly must be incomplete,
If unsaluted; there must be display'd,
Chain'd to thy car, or suppliant at thy feet,
A dame, now seized by force, as first betray'd!
This be thy noblest boast: time was, I pray'd
To thee for peace and life, how sweet would fate
Prove to my grief,—but ne'er, false renegade,
Kneel I to thee for it! there's not a state
Which, if it were thy gift, I should not hold in hate!

133. "Of myself, traitor! hope I to unloose,
Some way or other, this most wretched frame
From thy fierce tyranny; and if the noose,
Dagger, and drug, and precipice, and flame
Fail thy chain'd slave, by means as sure my aim,
Thank Heaven, I yet can compass, and defeat
No less thy malice than thy guile; for shame!
Cease thy base flatteries; cease thy false deceit;
How yet he strives with hope my sorrowing soul to
cheat."

134. Thus she laments; and with the floods of tears
Which love and scorn distill from her fair eyes,
A sympathizing part his sorrow bears,
Where some chaste sparks of love and pity rise:
And with a voice sweet as the west wind's sighs,
He to her troubled heart speaks peace: "I crave
Thy grace, Armida! calm thyself," he cries;
"Not to be scorn'd, but crown'd, thy life I save;
No foe, but still, yes still, thy champion, yea, thy slave.

135. "Mark in my eyes, if you my words alone
Distrust, the fervor of my soul: I swear
Again to seat thee on thy father's throne,
And make thy comfort my peculiar care;
And O, would Heaven, auspicious to my prayer,
Chase from thy mind with its celestial flame
Those mists of Pagan darkness which impair
Its inward grace and beauty, not a dame
In the whole East should match thy glory, power, and fame!"

136. Thus does he sooth, thus sue to her; and so
Tempers his suit with tears, his tears with sighs,
That, like a virgin wreath of mountain snow
When zephyr breathes or sunshine warms the skies,
Her haughty scorn, that wore so stern a guise,
And all her cherish'd anger melt away,
And milder wishes in their room arise:
"Behold," she says, "thy handmaid; I obey;
Thy lips my future life, thy will my fortune sway!"

137. This while, th' Egyptian Captain in the strife
Sees his imperial standard fall to ground,
Sees too stout Rimedon deprived of life,
Dispatch'd by Godfrey in a single wound;
And all his men, discomfited around,
Dead, or in flight across the boundless plain;
He in this last sharp act will not be found
Recreant like them, but seeks (nor seeks in vain)
Some noble hand by which he may be nobly slain.

138. Spurring his steed, he against Godfrey rode,
No worthier foe he knew could be descried;
And wheresoe'er he pass'd or came to, show'd
The last brave tokens of despairing pride:
But ere he reach'd his foe, aloud he cried;
"Lo, Chief! I come to spend my final hour
And hopes with thee; but yet it shall be tried

If, overpower'd, I too cannot o'erpower,
And on my conqu'ror fall, as falls a thunder'd tower!"

139. This said, they each at each indignant dash'd;
With lifted swords at once they meet, they smite;
Broken the shield, the vantbrace cleft, and gash'd
Is the left shoulder of the Christian knight:
He, on his part, discharged with matchless might
On the left cheek a blow that prostrate laid
The Pagan chief; and in bewilder'd plight
As to regain the saddle he essay'd,
Through the abdomen thrust, his life-blood bathed the blade.

140. Prince Emirene thus dead, but few remain
Of all that countless host; as he pursued
The vanquish'd, Godfrey saw, and check'd his rein,
How Altamore on foot, in blood imbrued,
With half a sword, and half a helm on, stood,
Breasting a hundred bristling spears, that pour'd
Round the doom'd Prince, whose prowess still they rued;
"Cease, cease," he cried, "Sir Knights! and thou, brave lord,
Yield, ('tis Duke Godfrey speaks,) yield up thy useless sword!"

141. He, who had never till that hour abased
To any act like this his lofty soul,
When now he heard the name which heaven had graced
With such renown from Nubia to the pole,
Yielding his arms, replied; "To thy control
(For thou deserv'st the homage) I my knee
Submit; then midst thy other spoils enroll
The name of Altamoro, who will be
Neither in fame nor wealth a prize unworthy thee.

142. "The gold and gems of kingdoms shall my kind
And faithful lady grant for my release:"
"Heaven has endow'd me with a nobler mind,"
Godfrey replied, "than to desire increase
Of earthly treasure; still retain in peace
All that from Ind or Persia swells thy store,
Bocharian mantle, and Tartarian fleece;
I set no price on life; on Asia's shore
I war in Europe's right, not trade in Asian ore!"

143. This said, he gives him to his guards to tend,
And after those that fled pursues amain ;
These to the rampired camp their lives commend,
Yet thence small respite to their fate obtain ;
Soon is it won ; the trench is choked with slain,
From gay pavilion to pavilion glide
Streams of warm blood, with whose vermilion stain
Each sumptuous trophy of barbaric pride—
Plumes, corslets, turbans, helms, and shields are deeply dyed.

144. Thus conquer'd Godfrey ; and as yet there glow'd
A flush of glory in the fulgent West,
To the freed City, the once loved abode
Of Christ, the pious Chief and armies press'd :
Arm'd as he was, and in his sanguine vest,
With all his knights in solemn cavalcade,
He reach'd the Temple ; there, supremely bless'd,
Hung up his arms, his banner'd spoils display'd,
And at the sacred TOMB his vow'd devotions paid.

END OF THE TWENTIETH AND LAST CANTO.

L'ENVOI.

1. Fare thee well, soul of sweet Romance! farewell,
   Harp of the South! the stirring of whose strings
Has given, by power of their melodious spell,
   Such pleasant speed to Time's else weary wings,
That, rapt in spirit to the Delphic cell,
   Midst its green laurels and prophetic springs,
The tuneful labors of past years now seem
A brief indulgence—an enchanted dream.

2. My pride at noon, my vision of the night,
   My hope at morn, my joy at lonely eve!
Now that thy tones of magical delight
   Are o'er, do I not well to droop, and grieve?
To what new region shall the muse take flight,
   What pictures fashion, what fresh numbers weave,
When all that else had charm'd, must now appear
Tame to the eye, and tuneless to the ear?

3. Much shall I miss thee, when in calm repose
   The Summer moon upon my casement shines;
Much, when the melancholy Autumn strows
   With leaves, my walk beneath th' o'erarching pines;
Nor less when Spring, 'twixt shower and sunshine, throws
   Abroad the sweet breath of her eglantines;
And Winter deepens, with his stormy din,
The quiet charm of the bright hearth within.

4. If with no vulgar aim, no selfish view,
   I sought to give thy foreign chords a tongue,
Let not my hopes all pass like morning dew,
   When on thy cypress bough again thou'rt hung,*

---

* "Tu che ne vai in Pindo,
Ivi pende mia cetra ad un Cipresso,
Salutala in mio nome, e dille poi
Ch' io son dagli anni e da fortuna oppresso."
Rime del Tasso.

But sometimes whisper of me to the few
  I love, the fond, the faithful, and the young;
And those who rev'rence the wrong'd soul that plann'd
Thy world of sound, with archangelic hand.

5. Hear how the strings, dear IDA, sound abroad
  The grief and glory of that matchless mind!
What ardor glows in each seraphic chord;
  How deep a pathos Echo leaves behind!
Yet was he wretched whom all tongues applaud,—
  For peace he panted, for affection pined:
Be thou, while thy mild eyes with pity swim,
More kind to me than AURA was to him:—

6. Else shall I little prize th' indulgent praise,
  Which some may lavish on a task so long;
Else shall I mourn that e'er my early days
  Were given to feeling, solitude, and song;
But thee no light capricious fancy sways,
  To doubt thy truth would be the heavens to wrong;
Peace to thy spirit with the closing spell!
And thou, Hesperian Harp, farewell, farewell!

* * * *

7. Thus went the verse: and thou art now to me,
  All that the cherish'd Muses were of yore,
And, glass'd in other eyes than thine, I see
  Fair visions rise, but dimly traced before.
This peaceful home, this garden, where the bee
  Hums of Hymettus, and these woods, have more
Of stirring music than those old day-dreams
Of airy fame and praised Pierian streams.

8. To him who lives as Wisdom would require,
  As Duty woos, and as the Virtues claim,
Time if it robs the Poet of his lyre,
  Bestows a bliss beyond the wealth of fame,—
Fruits, that refresh the spirit, and inspire
  Th' immortal yearning, and that purer flame,
To quicken which, until they blend with heaven,
The mortal Poet and the Lyre were given.

Froxfield,
4th Month 16th, 1830.

NOTES.

CANTO I. STANZA 5.

(1) *Rival of Godfrey, hear, and hearing, grasp thine arms.*

The memory of the Crusades, a subject always important to the western nations of Europe, was still very lively at the period when Tasso wrote his "Gerusalemme," and a new expedition of that kind was planned by Gregory XIII., who ascended the pontifical chair in 1572. From this stanza, it is evident that the poet thought a new crusade not improbable; and he, perhaps, did not despair of himself gaining laurels in the Holy Land. The mutual jealousy of the Christian princes, however, rendered nugatory the Pontiff's attempts, and Tasso's appeal to the martial spirit of Alphonso served only to exhibit his own zeal.

CANTO I. STANZA 54.

(2) *Roger, of Barneville surnamed, renown*
And ancient story with the noblest class.

The "Ruggier di Balnavilla" of Tasso has been identified by my friend, M. de Gerville, of Valognes, and on unquestionable grounds, with the ancestor of the Russell family in England. Roger, one of the sons of Hugh de Rosel, who came over with the Conqueror, was lord of the two fiefs of Barneville and Rozel, on the western coast of Lower Normandy, and he is celebrated by all those writers on the First Crusade, whose histories are published in the "Gesta Dei per Francos," and whom Tasso is well known to have diligently consulted. From a charter preserved in the "Neustria Pia," it appears that (probably to fit himself out for the expedition to the Holy Land) he sold to the Abbot of St. Stephen's in Caen, his fief at Rosel, near that city,* for £15, by consent of his son Robert, and of his capital lord, Robert, Duke of Normandy; in whose company he went, first to Constantinople, by way of Bulgaria. In the night irruption of Solyman, or Kilidge Arslan, while the Croises were besieging Nice, he was foremost in repelling the attack, "rushing," says Albert of Aix, (p. 267,) "in the midst of the conflict, with lightning-like strokes, and the swiftness of a war-horse, amidst the clash of spears and ringing of swords and helmets." He distinguished himself equally in the ambush before reaching Antioch, (p 225;) again, as one of the standard-bearers, fighting bravely at the bridge of Antioch, (p. 226;) and was the second to scale the tower of that city, when betrayed by Phirouz. But that was the last of his successful exploits upon record. On the first appearance of the advanced guard of the vast Persian army that was marching to reconquer the city,

* There was a third fief of the same name, belonging to the family, in the Isle of Jersey, opposite to the bay of Rozel, in La Manche, and the three hamlets are still existing.

his eager valor led him to sally, with fifteen other knights, from the gates, and he was lured by the flying foe into an ambuscade in a neighboring valley. Observing the great number of his assailants, he sought to regain the city, but was mortally wounded by an arrow, as he crossed the fords of the Pharphar, (p. 248.) Tasso makes him fall by the hand of the Persian Tisaphernes. His head was struck off by the barbaric foe, fixed upon a spear, and borne in triumph to the General Kerboga, the Argantes of Tasso. But the gallant Tancred undertook to revenge the loss of his slain friend; and in his first conflict with the foe, returned to the city with six heads of Infidels whom he had slain, raised aloft on spears, in stern retaliation. The body of De Barneville was borne with weeping and lament to Antioch, and interred in the vestibule of the Church of St. Peter, "the Croises mourning for his loss as one of the bravest of the people; and the Bishop of Puy and the whole clergy of the camp, commending with hymns . nd solemn psalms his soul to Christ, for the love of whom he became an exile and scrupled not to die."—*Albert*, p. 248.

CANTO I. STANZA 55.

(3) *That shield whereon the snake devours a naked child.*

Otho was the first of the family of the Visconti, afterward Dukes of Milan, who have continued the armorial bearing assumed by their ancestor, from his conquest of a Saracen warrior in single combat, viz. *argent*, a serpent wreathed in pale *azure*, crowned *or*, devouring an infant *gules* or *proper*.

CANTO I. STANZA 60.

(4) *A flight well fit some young enthusiast,*
In after days should follow, who would win
The like renown.

The reference in this passage has been wholly mistaken by the commentators who have touched upon it. Paul Beni considered it as some allusoin to Achilles, to whose story it bears no manner of application. The truth is, it was intended as a compliment to Alphonso, who, as we are told by Muratori (Ant. Est., vol. ii, p. 380,) when a youth under twenty, went out one day on the pretence of hunting, passed into the Venetian territories, and thence fled into France, accompanied by five gentlemen. His design, he said, was to see the world, and be present at the wars in that country. Henry II., his cousin-german, made him captain of a hundred men-at-arms, and he was engaged in several conflicts with the Spaniards. His flight took place in May, 1552, and he returned to Ferrara at the end of September, 1554.

CANTO III. STANZA 33.

(5) *Dexterous the darted balls on nimble feet to shun.*

This simile alludes to the game of caroselli, introduced into Italy by the Moors; but I have in vain sought, in a variety of authors, for a particular description of it.

CANTO III. STANZA 37.

(6) *Where the bird argent spreads its plumes for flight.*

An eagle *argent* in a field *azure*, the armorial bearings of the House of Este.

CANTO IV. STANZA 83.

(7) *From her divine lips glides a golden chain,*
That winds to her dear will who most those tears disdain.

The ancients feigned that many chains of gold proceeded from the tongue of Hercules, wherewith the ears of barbaric nations were bound; the fable, says one of the commentators on Tasso, was designed to show the humanizing spirit of eloquence. As illustrative of the subject, it is worthy of remark, that in the Duke of Bedford's collection af engravings is a curious French print after Raphael, entitled, "L'Eloquence," representing the Gallic Hercules surrounded by various figures, to whose ears chains in many directions are represented as passing from his lips.

CANTO XI. STANZA 8.

(8) ——— ———*whose gentle pleas*
Win now thy new successor to unlock
The gracious gates of pardon and of peace.

The poet in these verses pays a passing compliment to the Catholic liberality of Pope Gregory XIII., who, during the jubilee in the summer of 1575, granted a general indulgence to the Roman people. The earnest desire which Tasso had to be a sharer in what he considered as so great a spiritual advantage, is cited by his biographers as one of the principal motives for his visit to Rome at that particular period; and indeed while there, he uniformly spent his mornings in visiting the churches, and in performing those acts of piety which are prescribed for the purpose of receiving a plenary indulgence.

CANTO XII. STANZA 77.

(9) *While hell's pursuing fiends are ever howling nigh!*

This stanza, it may be amusing to mention, was cited by "the self-torturing Sophist," in one of his almost frenzied moods, as an absolute prophecy of his own misfortunes. "'Do you know,' said Rousseau to M. Corancy, suddenly starting from one of those fits of abstraction which this gentleman used to regard as the inevitable prelude to some extravagant proposition, 'do you know why I give Tasso so decided a preference?'—'No, but it is not difficult to conjecture. Tasso, uniting to the most brilliant imagination the good fortune to have lived after Homer and Virgil, has profited of the beauties of both those great poets, and avoided their defects.'—'There is something in that,' said Rousseau; 'but do you know that he has predicted my misfortunes?' 'I made a movement,' says Corancey, 'he stopped me'—'I understand you,' continued he, 'Tasso has come before my time—how could he foretell my misfortunes? I know not how, probably he knew not himself; but, in fine, he has predicted them. Have you remarked that Tasso has this peculiarity, that you cannot take from his work a single stanza, nor from any stanza a single line, nor from any line a single word, without disarranging the whole poem, so precisely and curiously is it put together. Very well; take away the stanza I speak of—the text does not suffer, it remains perfect; the stanza has no connection with those that precede or follow it—it is absolutely useless. We must presume that Tasso wrote it involuntarily, and without comprehending it himself—but there it is,' said he, pointing out the wonderful verse."

CANTO XIV. STANZA 19

(10) *Your blood shall mix, and from that union spring*
A glorious issue, dear to all mankind!

Tasso in these verses makes allusion to the marriage of Francis of Lorraine, Duke of Guise, with Anne of Este. Serassi, however, will have them to be nothing less than a prophecy of the gifted poet, and in the courtly dedication of his work to Maria Beatrice of Este, signifies that they bear reference to her marriage with the Archduke Ferdinand of Austria! "The commentators of our poet," he pompously observes, "deserve to be pardoned, if none of them has understood and explained this most important passage; since, in their times, the prediction had not yet been accomplished. But it is my happy fortune to be the first to explain it to the world, and, at the same time, to congratulate your royal highness and Italy, on the felicity which is predicted to both in your glorious descendants. And, in truth, if the prophecy of the poet has been already fulfill'd in that part of it which seemed the most remote and difficult, there is no reason to doubt that its accomplishment will be complete."

CANTO XIV. STANZA 42.

(11) *Her gloomy Dives and Afrits to compel.*

In deference to critical opinion, I have altered all other allusions to the Mahometan Mythology.

CANTO XIV. STANZA 74.

(12) *Mirth overpowers the man, he laughs, and laughing dies.*

Pomponius Mela speaks of such a fountain as existing in the Fortunate Islands:—Una singulari duorum fontium ingenio maximé insignis: alterum qui gustavere, risu solvuntur in mortem.—Lib. iii. cap. 10.

CANTO XV. STANZA 15.

(13) *Not distant, trees o'er waving trees appear*
To clothe a hill embrowning all the deep
That bathes its base.

Mount Cæsius.

CANTO XV. STANZA 32.

(14) *These shall suffice to make thy memory long*
In history's page endure or some divinest song.

Tasso having been proved above to be a *vates* in both senses of the word, I will indulge the fancy of supposing that he here makes alllusion to "the Voyage of Columbus" of my friend Mr. Rogers, the chastest and most tasteful of all modern poets, whose writings, often as I read them, seem always fraught with new graces, and a yet more classical charm. From the beautiful fragments which he has given us on this interesting subject, the happy selection of his imagery, which is always highly poetical, and his perfect familiarity with all that the Spanish chroniclers relate of the adventure, it is easy to perceive with how finished a poem he might have enriched the world, had he put forth all the powers of his mind, and filled up the outline which he has so well designed. Imperfect as this is, it resembles in value some of those free and spirited sketches from the pencils of the great masters of painting, which are to be met with in the portfolios of their most passionate admirers.

CANTO XVI. STANZA 15.

(15) *Now, now, while 'tis youth, pluck the roses of love!*

As it is possible the change of measure here introduced may meet with some objectors, I affix a translation of the song in the stanza of Spenser, although it is somewhat perilous to attempt it after him. Vide his Description of the Bower of Bliss, in the "Faery Queen," canto xii., stanzas 74 and 75.

"Ah see," she sang, "the bashful blushing rose
Spread through green leaves its bosom to the light;
Half bud, half blossom yet, through dews it glows,
And charms the more, the more it shuns the sight!
Ah see how boldly soon it courts the bright
And burning sun; how soon it droops and fades;
Nor seems the same rich blossom of delight
Desired so much in songs and serenades,
By thousand amorous youths and thousand blooming maids!

"So passes, in the transit of a day,
Of mortal life the verdure and the bloom,
Nor will the sunshine of a second May
The leaf re-open, or the flower relume;
Gather the rose then in its rathe perfume
And morning beauty, ere the skies above
O'ercast the landscape with funereal gloom;
While, loved and loving, none the bliss reprove,
Now, while it yet is youth, pluck, pluck the rose of love!"

CANTO XVI. STANZA 35.

(16) *Meanwhile Armida, by the regal gate*
Starts to behold her savage keeper dead.

As Tasso makes no previous allusion to this guard of the palace, the passage may seem to need some explanation. The truth is, there was introduced into the first edition of the poem, at the close of the 15th Canto, a combat between this warder and the knights, which the author's good taste probably led him afterwards to omit. This allusion he seems either to have overlooked, or to have purposely left the incident of the conflict to the imagination of the reader.

CANTO XVIII. STANZA 30.

(17) *A rude Silenus oft the days of old*
Have seen unclose, and yield some Goddess fair.

Già nel' aprir d'un rustico Sileno,
Meraviglie vedea l'antica etade;
Ma quel gran Mirto da l'aperto seno,
Imagini mostrò piu belle e rade.

I confess myself indebted to Dr. Black for the correct rendering of this obscure passage, which has much perplexed all the former translators of Tasso In his appendix to the Poet's Life, vol. i, p. 336, he has devoted some pages to its illustration, and not unhappily ridicules the versions hitherto given to it.

The real explanation is to be found in a passage of Plato, of whose writings Tasso was always an ardent admirer. Toward the end of the "Symposium," Alcibiades says, that just as rough cases in the forms of Satyrs and Sileni are covers to protect admirably sculptured or carved Statues of Divinities, so the language and metaphors used by Socrates are often so coarse as to lead ordinary hearers to think he is an ignorant and unpolished man; whereas, if you look beneath the outward form of his expressions, and dive into the real, though veiled meaning of his discourse, you will find them to contain the most precious truths of human and divine things. We learn from this, that it was a frequent custom with the Greeks to inclose their most admirable statues in images of Sileni, for the purpose of preserving them, and partly perhaps to set off by contrast the wonderful grace of the included divinity.

CANTO XIX. STANZA 104.

(18) ———*She stepp'd not, no, she darted from her seat!*

There is a tradition that Tasso had never been able to express the velocity with which Erminia descends from her palfrey in this interesting scene, until one day, while walking with some friend on the bank of the Tiber, he saw a young man, who was advancing at full gallop, fall from his horse. Whereupon he is said to have immediately burst forth with the admirable line:

Non scese, nò, precipitò da sella :

The spirit of which I flatter myself I have preserved, as well as the genius of our language and of the Alexandrine will admit.

CANTO XX. STANZA 144.

(19) *And at the sacred Tomb his vow'd devotions paid.*

I cannot close the pages of this enchanting poem, without expressing my admiration of the character of Godfrey as it is delineated by Tasso. Tancred and Rinaldo are doubtless the general favorites, but Godfrey is recommended to my fancy as the perfect model of a patriotic general. He always appears to us in the most amiable light, no less by his private deeds than by his public actions. He is uniformly dignified, virtuous, generous, and humane. To the general wish of his Barons he yields gracefully, as a ruler ought; but he is firm in high emergencies, in repressing disaffection and the pride of hostile embassies. His uniform devotion never reduces him to a tame level with the "pious Eneas" of Virgil:—he is like a lion in the battle: when all his knights seem to decline the combat with Argantes, he is ready himself to meet him as a private soldier; as a private soldier he fights in the first assault on Jerusalem, beats back Solyman in his midnight slaughter of the camp, defies him on the battlements, which he is the third to scale, kills Emireno, the Egyptain leader, and in the universal slaughter that ensues, sets the crowning charm upon his heroic character, by saving from the fury of his knights the death-devoted Prince of Samarcand. In a word, he always speaks and acts exactly as he ought, "nor," like the dying Solyman, "does a single thing but what is great and high." It is a fresh source of pleasure in the contemplation of his character, that Tasso's representation of his virtues has all the truth of history. Mr. Mills observes that in him "the gentlest manners were united to the firmest spirit; the amiableness of virtue to its commanding gravity. He was alike distinguished for political courage and for personal bravery. His lofty mind was capable of the grandest enterprises. His deportment was moral; his piety was fervent. He regretted the stern necessity which drew him from the immediate service of God; but when in arms, he was a hero; and his martial zeal in the cause of Heaven was always directed by prudence, and tempered by philanthropy." * In proof

* History of the Crusades, vol. i, pp. 83, 84.

of his unfeigned piety, it should never be forgotten that while, under the mask of religion, his brother Baldwin gratified his worldly ambition, Bohemond his pride, and Raymond his avarice, the Duke of Lorraine, faithful to his first simple wish of becoming the defender and advocate of the holy sepulcher, and pressed as he was by the voice of all the Croises, refused to wear a diadem in the city where his Saviour had worn a crown of thorns.* His tomb was watered not only by the tears of his friends, but was honored by the lamentations of many of the Moslems, whose affection his virtues had conciliated. The church of the holy sepulcher received his ashes, and to the present day his tomb may be seen, bearing the following brief inscription:

HIC JACET INCLYTUS DUX GODEFRIDUS DE BULION, QUI TOTAM ISTAM TERRAM ACQUISIVIT CULTUI CHRISTIANO; CUJUS ANIMA REGNET CUM CHRISTO. AMEN.

There too are seen the spurs of the hero, and that long and formidable sword, which in his hands, on the bridge of Antioch, clove in twain a gigantic Saracen from the helmet to the waist.

Turning for a moment from the Champion to the Poet of the Cross, I cannot refrain from observing that in no point is Tasso's superiority to Virgil more observable than in the skill with which he portrays his characters, and the individuality and interest with which he supports them to the close. My preference of Tasso to Virgil will perhaps be deemed quixotic by some; but in the teeth of Boileau and of Addison. I will not scruple to maintain that the "Gerusalemme" of Tasso is both in action and in plan a far more successful production as an epic poem than the Eneid of Virgil, admirable as this unquestionably is in the polished elegance of its phrase, and the music and mechanism of its numbers. This, however, is a question not to be discussed in the short compass of a note; and I will end the present passing comment on his merits by the following graceful sonnet, with which I have been honored from the elegant pen of the Archdeacon Wrangham, than which I could scarcely desire a more appropriate conclusion:

INSCRIPTION FOR A BUST OF TASSO.

From the Italian of Matthias.

Here in these groves, of every Muse the haunt,
By Life's rough tempests shatter'd and oppress'd,
Torquato from his toils aspired to rest,
And in their sheltering bowers, lone habitant,
Has found safe refuge. Here their magic choir
Still the sweet Sirens hold, and by the side
Of echoing streams, the swan in stately pride
Nests mid the strings of the melodious lyre.
Then, Stranger, whether from the icy Pole,
Buoyant of heart, or where the blazing noon
Scorches swart Afric's race, thou sojourn'st here,
To this bright marble bow thy reverent soul,
And o'er the bust of sweet Sorrento's son,
Strew pious flowers and shed the holy tear.

* History of the Crusades, vol. i, p. 266.

THE END.

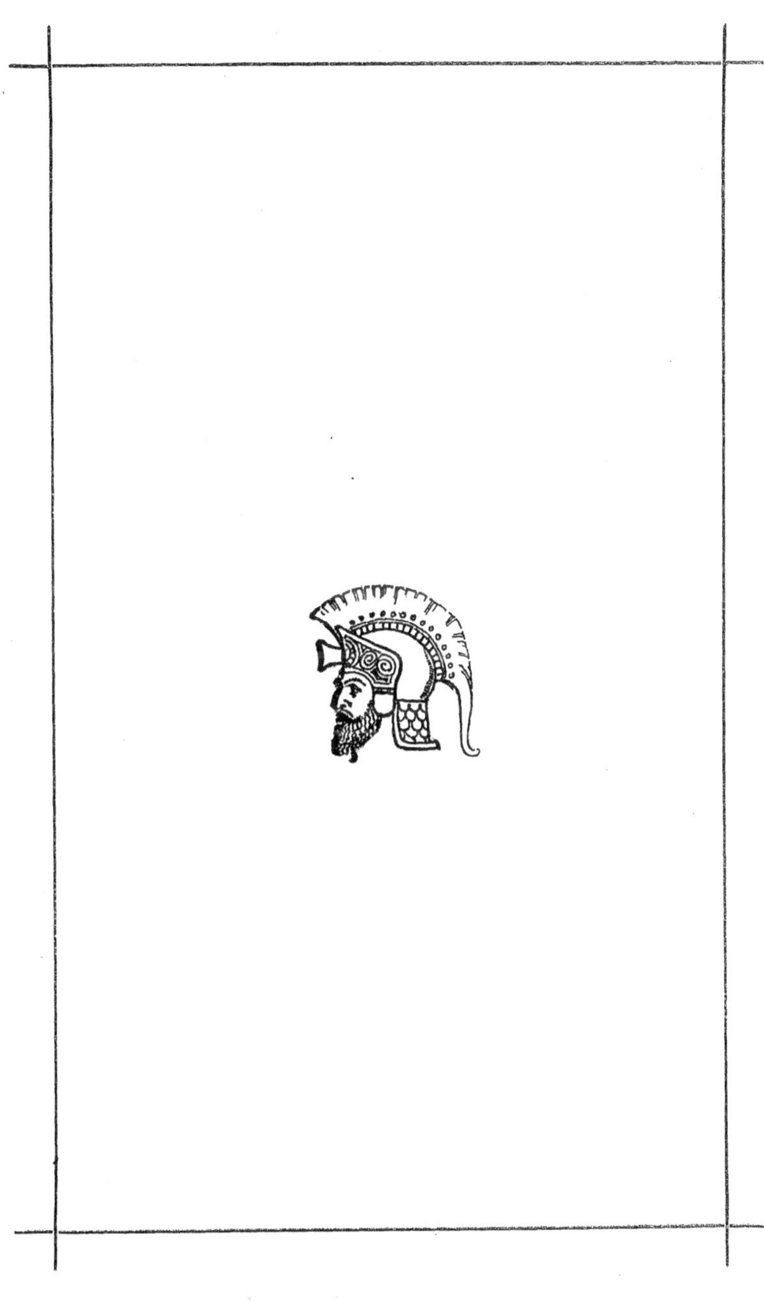

www.ingramcontent.com/pod-product-compliance
Lightning Source LLC
LaVergne TN
LVHW021321110826
845150LV00003B/641

* 9 7 8 1 4 2 5 5 5 6 8 5 3 *